Regions and Regionalism in History

3

NORTH-EAST ENGLAND
IN THE LATER MIDDLE AGES

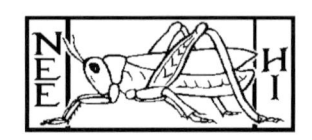

Regions and Regionalism in History

ISSN 1742–8254

This series, published in association with the AHRB Centre for North-East England History (NEEHI), aims to reflect and encourage the increasing academic and popular interest in regions and regionalism in historical perspective. It also seeks to explore the complex historical antecedents of regionalism as it appears in a wide range of international contexts.

Series Editor
Dr Peter Rushton, School of Health, Natural and Social Sciences, University of Sunderland

Editorial Board
Dr Richard C. Allen, University of Newcastle
Dr Barry Doyle, University of Teesside
Bill Lancaster, University of Northumbria
Bill Purdue, Open University
Professor David Rollason, University of Durham
Dr Peter Rushton, University of Sunderland

Proposals for future volumes may be sent to the following address:

AHRB CENTRE FOR NORTH-EAST ENGLAND HISTORY
Department of History
43 North Bailey
Durham
DH1 3EX
UK

Already Published

Volume I: *The Durham Liber Vitae and its Context*, edited by David Rollason, A. J. Piper, Margaret Harvey and Lynda Rollason, 2004

Volume II: *Captain Cook: Explorations and Reassessments*, edited by Glyndwr Williams, 2004

NORTH-EAST ENGLAND
IN THE LATER MIDDLE AGES

Edited by
Christian D. Liddy
Richard H. Britnell

THE BOYDELL PRESS

© Contributors 2005

All Rights Reserved. Except as permitted under current legislation
no part of this work may be photocopied, stored in a retrieval system,
published, performed in public, adapted, broadcast,
transmitted, recorded or reproduced in any form or by any means,
without the prior permission of the copyright owner

First published 2005
The Boydell Press, Woodbridge

ISBN 1 84383 127 9

The Boydell Press is an imprint of Boydell & Brewer Ltd
PO Box 9, Woodbridge, Suffolk IP12 3DF, UK
and of Boydell & Brewer Inc.
668 Mt Hope Avenue, Rochester, NY 14620, USA
website: www.boydellandbrewer.com

A CIP catalogue record of this publication is available
from the British Library

Library of Congress Cataloging-in-Publication data
North-east England in the later Middle Ages / edited by Christian D. Liddy, R.H. Britnell.
   p. cm. – (Regions and regionalism in history, ISSN 1742–8254)
   Includes index.
   "This volume arose from a conference held at Trevelyan College in Durham in June 2002. The conference was organised under the auspices of the AHRB Research Centre for North-East England History" – T.p. verso.
   Summary: "The medieval development of the distinct region of north-east England explored through close examination of landscape, religion and history" – Provided by publisher.
   ISBN 1–84383–127–9 (acid-free paper)
   1. England, North East – History. 2. Great Britain – History – Medieval period, 1066–1485. 3. Archaeology, Medieval – England, North East.
I. Liddy, Christian D. (Christian Drummond), 1973–   II. Britnell, R. H.
III. Title. IV. Series.
   DA670.N8N55 2005
   942.803–dc22   2005002726

This publication is printed on acid-free paper

Typeset by Pru Harrison, Hacheston, Suffolk
Printed in Great Britain by
Cromwell Press, Trowbridge, Wiltshire

Contents

List of Illustrations		vii
Contributors		ix
Preface		xi
Abbreviations		xii
	Introduction: A.J. POLLARD	1
1	St Cuthbert and the Border, *c*.1080–*c*.1300 RICHARD LOMAS	13
2	John Hardyng, Northumbrian Identity and the Scots ALASTAIR J. MACDONALD	29
3	Remembering the Legal Past: Anglo-Scottish Border Law and Practice in the Later Middle Ages CYNTHIA J. NEVILLE	43
4	Scaling the Ladder: The Rise and Rise of the Grays of Heaton, *c*.1296–*c*.1415 ANDY KING	57
5	Land, Legend and Gentility in the Palatinate of Durham: The Pollards of Pollard Hall CHRISTIAN D. LIDDY	75
6	Local Law Courts in Late Medieval Durham PETER L. LARSON	97
7	The Free Court of the Priors of Durham CONSTANCE M. FRASER	111
8	Church Discipline in Late Medieval Durham City: The Prior as Archdeacon MARGARET HARVEY	119
9	Economy and Society in North-Eastern Market Towns: Darlington and Northallerton in the Later Middle Ages CHRISTINE M. NEWMAN	127
10	Newcastle Trade and Durham Priory, 1460–1520 MIRANDA THRELFALL-HOLMES	141

11	The Size and Shape of Durham's Monastic Community, 1274–1539 A.J. PIPER	153
12	Peasants, Landlords and Production between the Tyne and the Tees, 1349–1450 BEN DODDS	173
13	Wastes, the Margins and the Abandonment of Land: The Bishop of Durham's Estate, 1350–1480 SIMON J. HARRIS	197
14	Framing Medieval Landscapes: Region and Place in County Durham BRIAN ROBERTS, HELEN DUNSFORD and SIMON J. HARRIS	221

Index   239

List of Illustrations

Maps

1.1	St Cuthbert's Estate: North Durham	14
1.2	St Cuthbert's Estate: Berwickshire and Roxburghshire	20
5.1	Township of Pollards Lands, Co. Durham	85
13.1	Parishes, Locations and Physiographic Regions, Co. Durham	200
13.2	Reconstructed Limits of Waste (*c.*1625) and Grants of Waste, Co. Durham	204
13.3	Episcopal Estates and Ward Boundaries, Co. Durham	206
13.4	Steward Shield Meadow, Co. Durham	208
14.1	Commons and Wastes, Co. Durham	223
14.2	County Durham Terrains	225
14.3	Commons and Wastes and Moorland Farms, Co. Durham	227
14.4	Hallowell Moss and Steward Shield Meadow, Co. Durham: Summary Diagrams	230
14.5	Commons and Wastes and Village Forms, Co. Durham	233

Plate

13.1	Relict Fields at Bishopley and Bollihope in Weardale, Co. Durham	202

Figures

5.1	The Pollards of Pollard Hall	79
5.2	Pollard family arms produced for the 1584–5 Yorkshire heraldic visitation	87
11.1	Minimum number of Durham monks, 1274–1540	154
12.1	Estimated arable output from Durham Priory parishes between Tyne and Tees	174
12.2	Decennial average percentage of vills recorded as 'waste' or 'not sown' in the Durham Priory bursars' accounts	180
12.3	Durham grain price data collected by Lord Beveridge's International Committee on Wages and Prices	183
12.4	Total grain tithe receipts from Billingham	185
12.5	Total grain tithe receipts from Cowpen Bewley (Billingham parish)	185
12.6	Total grain tithe receipts from Newton Bewley (Billingham parish)	186
12.7	Total grain tithe receipts from Wolviston (Billingham parish)	186

12.8	Estimated total sown acreage on Pittington demesne, 1376–1399	188
12.9	Number of breeding ewes at Saltholme, near Billingham	192
13.1	Structure of coroners' accounts	211

Tables

12.1	Total sown acreages on the almoner's manors, 1340–54	176
12.2	Decennial standard deviation of output indices, 1350–1449	195
13.1	Comparison of acreages in the Hatfield Survey	205
13.2	Coroners' accounts for Darlington ward	213
13.3	Coroners' accounts for Easington ward	214
13.4	Coroners' accounts for Stockton ward	215
13.5	Coroners' accounts for Chester ward	216

Contributors

Ben Dodds	University of Durham
Helen Dunsford	University of Northumbria
Constance M. Fraser	University of Newcastle upon Tyne (Emeritus)
Simon J. Harris	University of York
Margaret Harvey	University of Durham (Emeritus)
Andy King	University of Durham
Peter L. Larson	Kenyon College, Ohio
Christian D. Liddy	University of Durham
Richard Lomas	University of Durham (Emeritus)
Alastair J. Macdonald	University of Aberdeen
Cynthia J. Neville	Dalhousie University
Christine M. Newman	University of Durham
A.J. Piper	University of Durham
A.J. Pollard	University of Teesside
B.K. Roberts	University of Durham (Emeritus)
Miranda Threlfall-Holmes	University of Durham

Preface

This volume arose from a conference held at Trevelyan College in Durham in June 2002. The conference was organised under the auspices of the AHRB Research Centre for North-East England History and brought together many of the leading scholars in the field, the fruits of whose recent research is published here. Several people have helped to transform a series of conference papers into publishable essays, and we would like to single out the important contributions of Helen Dunsford of the University of Northumbria and Ben Dodds of the University of Durham. We would also like to express our gratitude to Margaret McAllister, who administered the conference, and to David Rollason, who, in his capacity as the director of the Centre for North-East England History, has done much to foster a collaborative model of research which we hope is evident in the essays that follow.

Christian D. Liddy
Richard Britnell

Abbreviations

AA	*Archaeologia Aeliana*
AgHR	*Agricultural History Review*
BB	*Boldon Buke: A Survey of the Possessions of the See of Durham*, ed. W. Greenwell (Surtees Society 25, 1852)
BIHR	*Bulletin of the Institute of Historical Research*
BJRL	*Bulletin of the John Rylands Library*
BL	British Library
CCR	*Calendar of Close Rolls*
CChR	*Calendar of Charter Rolls*
CDS	*Calendar of Documents Relating to Scotland*, ed. J. Bain et al. (5 vols., Edinburgh, 1881–8)
CFR	*Calendar of Fine Rolls*
CIM	*Calendar of Inquisitions Miscellaneous*
CIPM	*Calendar of Inquisitions Post Mortem*
CP	G.E. Cokayne, *The Complete Peerage of England, Scotland, Ireland, Great Britain and the United Kingdom*, ed. V. Gibbs (12 vols., London, 1910–59)
CPR	*Calendar of Patent Rolls*
DAR	*Durham Account Rolls*, ed. J.T. Fowler (3 vols., Surtees Society 99–103, 1898–1900)
DCM	Dean and Chapter Muniments (Durham)
DRO	Durham Record Office
DUL	Durham University Library, Archives and Special Collections
EcHR	*Economic History Review*
EHR	*English Historical Review*
Foedera (1739–45)	*Foedera, Conventiones, Literae, Et . . . Acta Publica*, ed. T. Rymer (10 vols., The Hague, 1739–45)
Foedera (1816–69)	*Foedera, Conventiones, Litterae . . . Et Acta Publica*, ed. T. Rymer (4 vols., London, 1816–69)
FPD	*Feodarium Prioratus Dunelmensis: A Survey of the Estates of the Prior and Convent of Durham compiled in the Fifteenth Century*, ed. W. Greenwell (Surtees Society 58, 1872)
HPD	*Halmota Prioratus Dunelmensis: Containing Extracts from the Halmote Court or Manor Rolls of the Prior and Convent of Durham*, ed. W.H.D. Longstaffe and J. Booth (Surtees Society 82, 1886)
HS	*Bishop Hatfield's Survey: A Record of the Possessions of the See of Durham*, ed. W. Greenwell (Surtees Society 32, 1856)

IPM	Inquisition post mortem
IR	*Innes Review*
JBS	*Journal of British Studies*
JHG	*Journal of Historical Geography*
JMH	*Journal of Medieval History*
JTH	*Journal of Transport History*
MH	*Midland History*
NH	*Northern History*
N&Q	*Notes and Queries*
NRO	Northumberland Record Office (Gosforth)
NYCRO	North Yorkshire County Record Office
P&P	*Past and Present*
PRO	The National Archives: Public Record Office
Rot. Parl.	*Rotuli Parliamentorum* (6 vols., London, 1783)
Rot. Scot.	*Rotuli Scotiae in Turri Londinensi et in Domo Capitulari Westmonasteriensi Asservati*, ed. D. MacPherson et al. (2 vols., London, 1814–19)
RPD	*Registrum Palatinum Dunelmense: The Register of Richard de Kellawe, Lord Palatine and Bishop of Durham, 1311–1316*, ed. T.D. Hardy (4 vols., Rolls Series, London, 1873–8)
Scriptores Tres	*Historiae Dunelmensis Scriptores Tres, Gaufridus de Coldingham, Robertus de Graystanes, et Willielmus de Chambre*, ed. J. Raine (Surtees Society 9, 1839)
SHR	*Scottish Historical Review*
SR	*The Statutes of the Realm* (11 vols., 1810–28)
TRHS	*Transactions of the Royal Historical Society*
VCH Durham	*The Victoria History of the County of Durham*, ed. W. Page (3 vols., London, 1905–28)
VCH North Riding	*The Victoria History of the County of York: North Riding*, ed. W. Page (2 vols., London, 1914–25)
VCH York	*The Victoria History of the County of York*, ed. W. Page (3 vols., London, 1907–25)

Introduction

A.J. POLLARD

> The North East is different. The people of the region share a history and culture which is unique.

So began a manifesto of the Constitutional Convention, the campaign for regional devolution in the north east, in 2000. That campaign has been successful to the degree that a referendum is to be held in 2004 as to whether these same people really want a regional assembly with barely more power than the London Assembly. There already is a regional government office, a regional development agency, a regional museums, libraries and archives council, a regional arts body, a regional Tourist Board (the only one I think to use the word 'Northumbria') and even a 'Unis4Ne', a consortium of the five English universities in the region acting together to promote its development. Regionalism is all the rage.

Underlying the rhetoric deployed by those campaigning for greater regional autonomy (and thereby bringing to the plethora of regional quangos some degree of democratic answerability) lies an assumption that the north east has a deeply rooted historical identity, and that it is this deep root that makes it the most 'natural' of the English regions. The idea that the north east has a distinctive history is the most frequently stated justification for regional government. Peter Hetherington opened a piece in *The Guardian* on 16 June 2003 entitled 'Geordies look to saint for inspiration' with the words, 'with a distinctive history, culture and musical heritage, it is a region set apart from the rest of England'. Hetherington proceeded to quote amply from an unreferenced article by John Tomaney in which St Cuthbert was invoked as a symbol of the region's political and cultural identity and a long proud period of self-determination going back to the Middle Ages was asserted.[1] Peter Scott, vice-chancellor of Kingston University, singing from a slightly different hymn sheet for *The Guardian* on 2 April 2002, declared more cautiously that, 'regions are difficult to define . . . The north east can claim coherence based on mish-mash memories of the age of Bede, its boundaries established by the ambitions of Northumbrian warrior kings, and when the industrial revolution was engineered on the banks of the Tyne.'

This is a brilliant passage. It correctly identifies the mish-mash that is memory. It demonstrates, perhaps inadvertently, how unreliable memories are, for the boundaries

---

[1] The article is probably J. Tomaney, 'In search of English Regionalism: The Case of the North East', *Scottish Affairs* 28 (1999), 62–82.

of the kingdom of Northumbria were forever changing. It pinpoints accurately that the 'North East' is a modern creation, deriving from nineteenth-century industrialisation. And it draws our attention to the fact that many people see the campaign for a regional assembly as no more than a campaign for engineering the subjection of the further reaches of the two counties of Durham and Northumberland to a Novocastrian yoke.

Precisely whether the two historic north-eastern counties of England formed a region historically is the guiding light of the AHRB Research Centre for North-East England History. Through its different projects, it is setting out to test the current assumptions as to whether there has been something discernible as a regional identity over the longue durée. There is, of course, rather a long gap between the ages of Bede and Armstrong. It was to some extent to attempt to fill part of this vacuum that the AHRB Centre sponsored a conference at Durham on 28–30 June 2002 on 'North-East England in the Later Middle Ages' initiated and organised by Richard Britnell and Ben Dodds, of which the essays in this volume are some of the proceedings. Regional identity was not the specific theme; contributors were invited to present papers on their research in progress. One consequence was, and is, that the topics are source-determined; and perhaps inevitably, in most, the sources upon which they draw are the records of the bishop and priory of Durham, especially the priory, which continue to provide a rich seam. There is therefore a heavy slant towards the county palatine and the community of St Cuthbert: Northumberland is not proportionately represented in these pages. Moreover, though the *later* Middle Ages strictly speaking cover the whole period since the Norman Conquest (assuming that this label covers the long period 400–1500), the majority of the essays in the volume are concerned with the very last phase of the medieval North East, marked by the beginning of the Three Hundred Years' War with Scotland. Yet all touch, if only tangentially in some cases, on the broader questions surrounding the quest for regional identity. This introduction, unapologetically deploying a broad brush, seeks to relate what the authors reply to the question, 'was there a north-east region in the later Middle Ages?' To endeavour to answer what is probably the unanswerable, it is necessary first to consider the use of the notion of the north east by historians, before exploring (in a cursory way) concepts of regionality and how they apply to our knowledge of the north-eastern parts.

One should start, where else, with Dick Lomas's *North-East England in the Middle Ages*, which is a history, from the Norman Conquest to the sixteenth century, of the pre-1974 counties of Durham and Northumberland 'considered as a single region'. As Dr Lomas acknowledges, he owed something to Norman McCord's *North East England: An Economic and Social History*, but he also owed much to the common assumption, which we all have shared, that Durham and Northumberland are the north east. He is in good company. Michael Thompson, two decades ago, shaped the first volume of his Cambridge Social History on 'Regions and Counties'. He commissioned David Rowe to write about the same 'North East', while not finding it necessary to have similar chapters on East Anglia or the South West. Everyone knew what the north east was and that it was more significant than other regions. A little earlier, in 1967, Graham Turner commented, perhaps excessively, in his travelogue, *The North Country*, that on crossing the Tees (going northwards) one virtually entered another country. He pictured a dying industrial north east in the counties of Durham and Northumberland surrounded by a no-man's land (or was it *cordon sanitaire*?) of countryside. It was nevertheless the same region as McCord's, based on and shaped by the Great Northern Coalfield.[2]

We should note, however, that it was always the Great *Northern* Coalfield (and we now have the great *North* Run). When was the term 'the north east' coined? Rob Colls, in a thought-provoking contribution to a celebratory collection entitled *Geordies*, has suggested that the region first found its identity in the last decades of the nineteenth century, when, in response to the modernising and centralising juggernaut, people started to talk about 'Northumbria' and its glorious past. As a result, as he puts it, 'in carefully constructed textual and actual encounters, the North East was reborn as a terrestrial unity'. And he argues that there has been a continuous discourse since then about this reborn terrestrial unity (does he mean territorial?) as it has boomed, slumped and revived until, I suppose, we arrive at the current hoped-for glorious resurgence.[3] The north east has become a discourse. As for the actual phrase, as opposed to the idea, Bill Lancaster has recently come up with the suggestion that it was invented in 1929 when a body calling itself the North-East Coast Shipbuilders Association was formed to lobby successfully for special regional status. And then, on the other hand, rejecting all of this, Richard Lewis has proposed that the north east did not really enter public consciousness until the introduction of a system of regional television companies in the 1950s, and even then, the ITV company took the name Tyne-Tees because it was aware of Teesside sensitivity.[4] We could debate whether the thing existed before it was named, the signified before the signifier, which would be even more postmodern; but, there are strong arguments for supposing that the 'north east' is a modern invention, a phenomenon of recent times.

But yet, but yet. Colls saw a region reborn, *reborn* in the image of 'Northumbria'. Was there an older region, a region upon which, as it were, the modern north east was overlain? For this, it is high time to consider what we mean by a 'region'. At its simplest, from the Latin and Roman usage, it is a unit of localised devolved rule, which, if one thinks about it in the contemporary context, is rather neat. There is a region because there is devolved government within bounds laid down by the state. On this level, one could say, obviously, that there was something approaching a region in the Middle Ages in the shape of the county palatine of Durham. But there is more to it than this, for regional *identity* comes from within. Here, to cut through a very complex issue, there are, it seems to me, two essential approaches: the physical and the cultural.[5]

---

[2] R. Lomas, *North-East England in the Middle Ages* (Edinburgh, 1992); N. McCord, *North East England: An Economic and Social History* (London, 1979), and, idem, 'The Regional Identity of North-East England in the nineteenth and early twentieth centuries', in *Issues of Regional Identity*, ed. E. Royle (Manchester, 1998), pp. 102–17; D.J. Rowe, 'The north-east', in *The Cambridge Social History of Britain, 1750–1950, I: Regions and Communities*, ed. F.M.L. Thompson (Cambridge, 1990), pp. 415–70; G. Turner, *The North Country* (London, 1967), pp. 299–300. For my own earlier discussion of the idea of a region in the north east in the fifteenth century, see A.J. Pollard, *North-Eastern England during the Wars of the Roses: Lay Society, War and Politics, 1450–1500* (Oxford, 1990), pp. 9–27.

[3] R. Colls and B. Lancaster, 'Born-again Geordies', in *Geordies: the Roots of Regionalism*, eds. R. Colls and B. Lancaster (Edinburgh, 1992), pp. 3–8.

[4] These comments have been made in conversation.

[5] Similar work is being undertaken by Diana Newton for the early modern period, which adopts this approach to the question of regional elites in her study of 'North-Eastern Elites, 1569–1625' for the AHRB Research Centre for North-East England History.

Historians who have grappled with the question of regional history have tended to found their concept of regions on real space, on physical space as delineated by geology, geography and landscape. In geographical circles the critical features often deployed are land forms and land uses, the physical features and the human uses. Thus, Norman McCord's north east is founded on the geology which created the Great Northern Coalfield. It is literally underlain by geo-physical formation. And, on this base, a dynamic economy was created, particular social structures developed and a distinctive culture was formed. It also happened to focus on Newcastle-upon-Tyne, the north east being, some might think, essentially another name for greater Newcastle ('Geordies look to saint for inspiration'). The region has a cultural identity and a cultural awareness, but it derives ultimately from its fixed geographical and economic base.

This approach has been taken to its most sophisticated level by Charles Phythian-Adams, who has proposed that England should be subdivided into fourteen cultural provinces, of which one is the north east. These cultural provinces are in most cases based on river basins (rivers forming the heartlands), such as Yorkshire and the Ouse. The cultural identity of these provinces flows as it were from their physical existence, or as he has put it in a private communication, 'identities arise from real circumstances and are therefore incomprehensible without reference to those circumstances . . . Social space (or cultural identity) is tethered, however distantly, in real space, to the realities of the relevant region of origin.'[6] To which one might add the stress that identities are complex and multiple. A region is not cut off from the centre; there is no iron curtain (or *cordon sanitaire*) between it and its neighbours; patterns of association within and outside vary according to status and occupation. But ultimately its existence is determined by the physical landscape.

This approach is exemplified in the essay by Brian Roberts, Helen Dunsford and Simon Harris, reporting some of the findings of a research project on the medieval landscapes of County Durham. They identify two broad landscape zones: one to the north-west of the Barnard Castle – Bishop Auckland – Durham – Chester-le-Street – Gateshead line, which was predominantly upland wood/pasture land with scattered farms, and the other to the south and east characterised by lowland open field arable agriculture and nucleated settlements. These they describe as two distinct regions, the landscape shaping different economies and, by implication, social and cultural relationships. And this is only County Durham. A similar exercise in Northumberland could well reveal an equivalent division. Following this procedure we have not one region, but several. And even if we compromise and call them sub-regions, from the perspective of landscape and topography, the contrast remains.

If we shift the focus from landscape to the economy, however, a different pattern appears. Miranda Threlfall-Holmes, in her discussion of 'Newcastle Trade and Durham Priory' after 1460, suggests, from the evidence of the priory's purchases of provisions, that towards the end of the Middle Ages Newcastle emerged as the commercial centre for its immediate region. The priory employed an extensive network of agents to purchase its supplies. During the fifteenth century they became more localised and focused on Newcastle, suggesting that in an era of retrenchment

---

[6] C. Phythian-Adams, 'Introduction: An Agenda for English Local History', in *Societies, Culture and Kinship, 1580–1850: Cultural Provinces in English Local History*, ed. C. Phythian-Adams (Leicester, 1993), pp. 1–23, figures 1.1 and 1.2.

the regional economy was the principal beneficiary. Besides being at the lowest bridging point at the head of the navigable waters of the Tyne, Newcastle also lay on the extension of the line of market towns positioned where the two landscape and agricultural zones met. It was ideally placed to be the commercial focus for both northern Durham and southern Northumberland. But whether its emerging role as a regional commercial centre extended beyond the Coquet or into the Tees Lowlands is more difficult to determine.

In Phythian-Adams's scheme, only four rivers are borders: two being the Tees and the Tweed. His north east is essentially a two-river basin region, the limits determined by two other river basins. Yet all regional boundaries are porous. In the case of the historic counties of Northumberland and Durham both the Pennines to the west and the North Sea to the east are only superficially barriers. The North Sea, in particular, was itself at the centre of a maritime region and close by the shore provided a principal highway, perhaps *the* principal highway, north and south from Aberdeen to London, upon which Newcastle was an important stop.

The porousness of boundaries is revealed in different ways by Christine Newman, Dick Lomas and Cynthia Neville. Newman's comparative study of the two episcopal market towns of Darlington and Northallerton stresses that both lay, at strategic places, on the main north and south highway by land. Both, during the economic recession of the later Middle Ages, came to depend more on passing trade. Darlington, in particular, which had been a commercial centre with international links in the late thirteenth and early fourteenth centuries (links no doubt maintained through the port of Yarm at the head of the navigable waters of the Tees), contracted to a sub-regional market town. The comparison between Darlington and Northallerton is also a reminder that the interests of the bishop of Durham, or the priory for that matter, did not end at the River Tees. While an attempt to incorporate the liberty of Allertonshire into the palatinate in 1448 was abortive,[7] the liberty was a significant extension of the bishop of Durham's seigniorial authority south of the river, while many of its churches were appropriated to the priory.

The Tees valley, albeit that the river was a significant ecclesiastical and civil boundary, was as much an economic, social and political focus as it was a border. There are many examples of how the Tees was easily crossed. Wool from Northern Yorkshire was exported through Newcastle; the people of several parishes in Northallertonshire took their wills to Durham for probate; the fifteenth-century lords of Richmondshire recruited retainers in south Durham. In fact, to ease communication between what he hoped would remain the interests of the favoured junior branch of his family, Ralph Neville, earl of Westmorland left a bequest in 1425 for the building of a bridge across the Tees at Winston (not, I think fulfilled, any more than Raby passed to the cadet line). Archaeologists have identified a medieval Tees pottery ware, which is found widely distributed north and south of the river. But perhaps the best indicator of the centrality of the Tees in the local landscape is the choice of Oxen-le-Fields, just north of the river crossing at Croft, as the place for the rendezvous of the Richmondshire, Cleveland and south Durham hosts at the start of the Pilgrimage of Grace in 1536.[8]

---

[7] Pollard, *North-Eastern England*, p. 252.
[8] See A.J. Pollard, ' "All Maks and Manders": The Local History of the Tees Valley in the later Middle Ages', *Cleveland History* 65 (1994), 13–27. For an alternative view, see R.B. Dobson, 'Cathedral

The same to some extent applies to the Tweed, even though the river was an international boundary. The extension of the patrimony of St Cuthbert south of the Tees was never as significant as it was north of the Tweed. Dick Lomas focuses, in his essay on 'St Cuthbert and the Border', upon the large triangle of land running inland from the coast either side of the Tweed which was held by the bishop and the priory between them. The estates south of the Tweed, which would later become known as Norhamshire and Islandshire, had been acquired before the Conquest by the Community of St Cuthbert. When, after the Conquest, the trusteeship of St Cuthbert separated into the bishopric (or palatinate) of Durham and Durham Cathedral Priory, both institutions came to have significant interests immediately to the south of the Anglo-Scottish border. The priory, thanks to the particularities of Scottish politics, then extended its influence north of the Tweed into Scotland, marked by the grant and establishment of the priory cell of Coldingham in the first decade of the twelfth century. Thereafter, for almost two hundred years, the Tweed, in its lowest reaches, flowed through the middle of an economic, social and cultural district that happened to be divided by an international boundary. As Lomas points out, tenurial arrangements and agricultural practice were the same on Scottish and English sides; Berwick itself, before the outbreak of the Three Hundred Years' War, was one of the most important Scottish ports, drawing on both a Scottish and English hinterland; and the inhabitants shared an affiliation with St Cuthbert. Anglo-Scottish hostilities after 1296 disrupted this; even so, in the mid-fourteenth century, when the English held south-eastern Scotland, it looked for a while as though the old days would return. It was the war, a specific historical phenomenon, which determined that the border would become a barrier and that the Tweed would cease to be a local focus and become a more distinct boundary.

The manner in which the international border hardened after the outbreak of the war is highlighted in Cynthia Neville's essay on Anglo-Scottish border law and practice. She reminds us that, even in the long peace of the thirteenth century, there was a border between two kingdoms. This was particularly relevant for the inhabitants in that different legal systems operated on either side of that line. A perennial and immediate problem was how to resolve disputes and deal with cases involving subjects of different kings. Before the outbreak of war a system of local law, with its own codification, was adopted, whereby six Scots and six English would adjudicate according to the custom of the March. The 'Law of the March' was in effect devolved by the two kings. This was unacceptable to Edward I, who insisted that all law, throughout his kingdom, should be his law. After 1296, this in his view included Scotland. Thus, an attempt was made to suppress the 'Law of the March'. But the attempt failed, along with the failure of the kings of England to impose their authority on Scotland. The 'Law of the March' survived in a modified form in the Marcher law exercised from the mid-fourteenth century by the wardens of the Marches, who continued to call upon mixed juries to determine cases. Here we see the enforcement of a boundary, regional as well as international, being resisted by its inhabitants. The borderers, Scottish and English, wished to administer their own law to compensate for the fact

Chapters and Cathedral Cities', *NH* 19 (1983), 17, and C. Phythian-Adams, 'Frontier Valleys', in *The English Rural Landscape*, ed. J. Thirsk (Oxford, 2000), pp. 244–8, 250 and esp. 262, where it is stressed that English frontier valleys such as the Tees, 'unambiguously defined in physical terms', were 'enduring in their informal function' and 'continued to separate cultural blocs'.

that they lived under different monarchs. It was the king of England who insisted on determining a rigid boundary. The only solution Edward I and his immediate successors would accept was the imposition of English common law on both sides. Resistance, English as well as Scottish, was successful. The borderers themselves were able to achieve a compromise which reflected their real needs. Here, in the March, one can witness the friction that was generated on the edge of regions determined not by landscape or by the economy, but by the exercise of central authority and the division between kingdoms.

Away from the border, however, English kings seemed more willing to allow different legal forms. Peter Larson, in his essay on the 'Local Law Courts in Late Medieval Durham', lays bare the unusual overlap in the palatinate between what was the conventionally separate business of manorial and hundred courts elsewhere in the kingdom of England. In Durham, on both priory and episcopal estates, there was but one local law court, the halmote, for which records are voluminous after 1300 and which dealt with all matters tenurial, the regulation of behaviour, minor misdemeanours, debts and even matters of personal status, for all persons, free and unfree, within the locality. There was, he concludes, a unique local system of law particular to the palatine. Constance Fraser explores another aspect of this in 'The Free Court of the Priors of Durham', whose records, unlike those of the halmote, are relatively scant. Her examination of the free court of the priors between 1302 and 1426, established under the terms of the agreement with Bishop le Poore in 1229 known as *le convenit*, shows how in the early fourteenth century this court was a thriving alternative resort for the priory's free tenants. But it ceased to operate in the fifteenth century, by which time, it would seem, the halmotes had supplanted it.

These courts reveal, just as the Marcher courts do, the existence of local peculiarities, but they do not establish a regional difference. For one, they are restricted to the estates of the bishop and priory of Durham which were heavily concentrated in the lowland zone of the south east of the county. As Larson stresses, few records of courts in secular hands have survived, and it is not clear whether the structure of halmote courts was adopted in them. It could have been estate specific. It is also not known whether such a legal system extended into the upland zone of the palatinate to the north and west, or into other liberties. There is a possibility, therefore, that this was but one in a patchwork of local court structures within the palatinate itself, and certainly within the two historic counties as a whole.

One says the two historic counties, but strictly speaking there was but one royal county, the county of Northumberland stretching from the Tees to the Tweed. Durham was, technically, the largest and most significant of several liberties within the county. This is made explicit in disputes from time to time over the precise limits of the palatinate, especially in the vexed matter as to whether the lordship of Barnard Castle lay within its bounds. The late medieval lords, the Beauchamps until 1449, owed their title to royal grant (after the confiscation from the Balliols), not to the bishop. Thereafter, they were careful to maintain this legal nicety. Thus, in 1400, shortly before his death, Thomas Beauchamp, earl of Warwick, conveyed to his son and heir, Richard, the lordship, which, the conveyance specified, lay within the wapentake of Sadberge which is in the body of the county of Northumberland.[9] Other

---

[9] PRO, E 40/658. I owe this reference to Melanie Devine.

instances arose, in respect of Barnard Castle but also Hart, in the possession of the Cliffords. Always the legal point at issue was whether the property lay in the county palatine, in which case superior lordship lay with the bishop, or within the county of Northumberland, in which case it lay with the king. This may seem a highly legalistic point, but it offers the explanation as to why there was no parliamentary representation for Durham; it was subsumed in that of Northumberland. In so far as Durham could enjoy a voice in parliament it was through its bishop, the prior of Durham Priory and their proctors, or, presumably, friends who sat for Northumberland, another county or an amenable borough. Looked at from the narrow point of view of royal administration, there was a region: it was the county of Northumberland.

The diocesan boundary marched with the county boundary of Northumberland. Here was another unifying administrative feature; spiritual as distinct from secular. In 'Church Discipline in Late Medieval Durham City' Margaret Harvey explores a specific aspect of this diocesan structure, namely the priory's right to exercise archidiaconal jurisdiction over all its appropriated churches in Durham and Northumberland. The court met in Durham, usually in St Oswald's Church, every three weeks on Thursdays, dealing with the usual matters concerning personal behaviour. This court thus brought people from the whole diocese to Durham. But whether it and other administrative and legal procedures generated a regional identity is another matter.

The alternative, and generally less fully explored, approach to discovering regions in the past is through the study of mentalities, that is, how people perceived their own identity. This, one might say in contradistinction from the dominant 'physical space' model, is a 'cultural space' paradigm. Putting it another way, a region can only exist when it is conscious of being a region. The daunting challenge for the late medievalist is finding the evidence to reveal how people imagined their multi-layered identities in the later Middle Ages; daunting, but perhaps not impossible, and certainly worth the attempt. There are two aspects upon which one might concentrate here, both given prominence by advocates of a regional assembly in the twenty-first century: St Cuthbert and Northumbria.

The palatinate of Durham was a unique liberty, partly by virtue of its delegated powers and partly by virtue of the fact that it was ecclesiastical and thus not heritable. It included North Durham, comprising Norhamshire and Islandshire, but also Bedlingtonshire, as well as the land 'between Tyne and Tees'. Its status was closely linked to the heritage of St Cuthbert, to whom of course the cathedral was dedicated, and within which the shrine of his miraculously composed body lay. The liberty was St Cuthbert's liberty. Thus, in the course of the long-running dispute as to where the lordship of Barnard Castle lay, a contrite Robert Rhodes, lay steward of the priory, conceded in 1461 that he had wrongly given testimony in 1439. He admitted to Bishop Booth that he had done great hurt to the liberty and title of the Church of St Cuthbert by stating to an enquiry then that Barnard Castle stood outside the palatinate.[10] Entering the Saint's liberty, as Bishop Booth did in 1457, was an important ritual. Christian Liddy quotes Bishop Cosin's vivid description of his reception on horseback in the middle of the Tees in 1661 with the presentation, 'in the usual ceremony', of the Conyers falchion. Similarly when the bishop entered his palace at Bishop Auckland he was presented with another falchion by the head of the Pollard

---

[10] Pollard, *North-Eastern England*, pp. 148–9.

family. A mythology grew up in the sixteenth century concerning the origins of these ceremonies in the slaying of a serpent and a wild boar respectively, but initially (and the presentation of the Pollard falchion can be traced back to the early fifteenth century) the ceremony was a more prosaic, symbolic acknowledgement of the bishop's temporal authority on behalf of all his tenants.

The notion of the people living within the county palatine of Durham (and, by extension, the land they occupied) being under St Cuthbert's special protection has Anglo-Saxon origins. Originally, one supposes, in the threatening days of Danish invasion and settlement, it had particular force. But the concept of the 'Haliwerfolc', the people of the saint, had continuing resonance in the later Middle Ages. It was to them that King John granted a charter of liberties in 1208. In 1433, when a faction challenged Langley's palatine authority in the name of 'Goddes Kyrk and Seint Cuthbert of Duresme', the notion of the 'Haliwerfolc' was still germane.[11] It is not surprising, therefore, that whenever the people of the saint were threatened by the Scots in the later Middle Ages his banner was ceremonially carried on the field of battle, more usually than not with the desired effect. This protection extended, of course, to North Durham, and throughout the diocese.

Preservation of the memory of St Cuthbert and the responsibility to ensure that he still worked for those under his protection lay with the community of the priory. As Alan Piper shows in his essay, 'The Size and Shape of Durham's Monastic Community', the priory was a resilient house, surviving the shocks of the loss of Coldingham, the catastrophe of the first pestilence in 1349 when fifty-two monks died, and its own internal crises, with minimal disturbance. The complement of monks, notionally one hundred (thirty at Coldingham) in 1238, fluctuated between sixty-four and eighty-three in the two centuries between the Black Death and the Dissolution. Admissions were carefully managed to match stretched resources. To keep the numbers up, a lower standard of living was accepted. There was no apparent shortage of suitable applicants. It was, it seems, like the modern university nearby, an admitting rather than recruiting institution. This itself suggests that a desire to serve St Cuthbert continued to retain a significant appeal.

The community did its best to promote its saint, encouraging visitors (and a valuable income stream) to his shrine. It maintained a long historical tradition celebrating his life and its existence, where necessary embellishing the relationship between him, themselves and his people. And it kept alive, in the *Liber Vitae*, the book of remembrance used since the ninth century, the awareness of how the saint continued to work, in answer to the monks' prayers, for the good of the souls of the departed named therein. Sustaining the memory of St Cuthbert as a continually living presence was a significant element in the creation of a special identity and a shared history for the people of the saint. But who the people of the saint were is harder to pin down. In many ways, they went beyond the confines of Durham and its diocese. The charters by successive Scottish kings bestowing Coldingham on Durham Priory in the early twelfth century (which may or may not have been forged by the monks) reveal, as Dick Lomas points out, that the community maintained the belief that St Cuthbert's patrimony, and thus his people, extended into south-east Scotland. Many of those listed in the *Liber Vitae* for special prayers came from well beyond the two counties of

---

[11] R.L. Storey, *Thomas Langley and the Bishopric of Durham, 1406–1437* (London, 1961), pp. 125–6.

Northumberland and Durham. Yet, nevertheless, Durham was the focal point, and it was to Durham that pilgrims, specially devoted to the saint, came.

That there was something substantial to the attachment to St Cuthbert as a specific focus of identity is indicated also by the fact that it was contested. This is made apparent by the determination of the Minster establishment at York to deny it, or rather to assert its superiority over it, articulated, for instance, in the metrical history available to all visitors as a kind of cathedral guide, which claimed the cultural leadership of the whole of northern England and south-west Scotland. It is also revealed in the programme of stained glass in York Minster, which championed St Cuthbert as a kind of tributary saint. This claim was put into practice in the assertion by the archbishop of his right to administer the diocese of Durham during a vacancy, a claim vigorously countered, if usually in vain, by the cathedral priory of Durham in the superior name of St Cuthbert.[12]

It would seem, therefore, that one can discern something approaching a regional identity around the notion of St Cuthbert's folk. It was not an identity deriving from the landscape, or tethered to the reality of the physical setting. It was cultivated. It arose out of a set of specific religious and historical circumstances. It need not have been focused on a bend in the River Wear. It could have had its home anywhere: indeed, had the body of St Cuthbert finally come to rest at Ripon, it could have been centred there.

Northumbria is a far more diffuse concept. The idea of Northumbria, Robert Colls argues, was reborn in the nineteenth century. The principal difficulty lies in the fact that the Latin for Northumberland was *Northumbria*, for the inhabitants of Northumberland, *Northumbrenses*, and for the earl of Northumberland, *comes Northumbrae* (or *Northanhumbrorum*). Walsingham, several times in his works when dealing with the history of the far north, refers to the *Northumbrenses* or *in partibus Northumbrorum*.[13] The matter needs further exploration both in the context of Walsingham's writings and other parallel usages. What one would really like to know is whether Walsingham used the word *Northumbria* merely as a Latin form of Northumberland, just as today the adjective commonly used for persons or things pertaining to the county is 'Northumbrian'; whether he had in mind the whole royal county of Northumberland or the part north of the Tyne/Derwent; or whether he had some sense of the ancient kingdom which stretched from north of the Humber into southern Scotland before it was dismembered in the late ninth century. Sir Thomas Gray, the author of the *Scalacronica*, Andy King has pointed out, saw himself and his neighbours in the far north of the county as men of the March and not men of either Northumbria or Northumberland.[14]

The issue is addressed directly in Alastair Macdonald's essay, 'John Hardyng, Northumbrian Identity and the Scots', which focuses on the mentalities revealed in

---

[12] M.L. Holford, 'Locality, Culture and Identity in Late Medieval Yorkshire, *c*.1270–*c*.1540' (unpublished D.Phil. thesis, University of York, 2001), pp. 120–36. I am grateful to Dr Holford for allowing me to cite from his work. For one incident in the long-running dispute over archidiaconal jurisdiction, see R.L. Storey, 'The North of England', in *Fifteenth-Century England, 1399–1509*, ed. S.B. Chrimes et al. (Manchester, 1972), pp. 140–1.

[13] *CP*, IX, 701; Thomas Walsingham, *Chronicon Angliae*, ed. E.M. Thompson (Rolls Series, London, 1874), pp. 109, 202, 239.

[14] A. King, 'Englishmen, Scots and Marchers: National and Local Identities in Thomas Gray's *Scalachronica*', *NH* 36 (2000), 223–5.

Hardyng's mid-fifteenth-century chronicle. Macdonald detects a heartfelt hatred for the Scots in Hardyng's work, an attitude in marked contrast to that found in Gray's earlier chronicle. The Scots were not a respected enemy; there were few cross-border sympathies. Hardyng's view of the world presented in the chronicle, shaped in the service of the Percy family in his youth before 1403, and the Umfravilles thereafter, is militaristic, intensely loyal to the crown and focused on the north. He draws a clear distinction between the north and the south, but where, in his mind, the line lay is harder to detect. His focus is on the eastern side, and, in so far as it is oriented on the deeds of the Percies and Umfravilles, concentrates on the borders and Northumberland. His lack of interest in the Nevilles, upon which Macdonald remarks, leads to neglect not only of the West March but also of the palatinate. He is at pains to demonstrate that these 'northerners', good fighting men, are loyal to the crown. Indeed, Macdonald suggests, perhaps he protests too much. It may be, as is argued below, that Hardyng was aware of the potential conflict between local and national loyalties. But perhaps also we should bear in mind that when the author completed his second version of the chronicle, in about 1463, there was a very pressing political reason to emphasise that the Percy family and their followers in Northumberland were fundamentally loyal to the crown and could be won back to Edward IV if he adopted, as had earlier kings, an aggressive policy towards the Scots.[15] Perhaps, too, we see reflected in the old man's attitude to Scotland the agenda of his first lord, the first earl of Northumberland, who had been set on retaining his position north of the border. The problem is not just determining how reliable Hardyng is, but additionally of judging how typical he was of opinion in the north-eastern counties at the time. One suspects that a follower of the Nevilles of Middleham would have had a different view.

Not surprisingly one finds multiple, overlapping and conflicting associations, loyalties, and identities at play in the historic counties of Northumberland and Durham in the later Middle Ages. Moreover, while there is much that was distinguishing and differencing in aspects of the economy, society, political institutions and culture, there was also much that was similar to elsewhere in England. In 'Peasants, Landlords and Production between the Tyne and the Tees' Ben Dodds, through his systematic and ground-breaking analysis of the tithal income of the priory, drawn from the lowland arable parishes it held, confirms an economic pattern in the century following the Black Death that one would expect: early recovery, subsequent contraction in the face of repeated epidemics, abandonment of some arable to pasture, and renewed crisis after 1430. This is a pattern familiar to lowland arable zones in England, with the added, and well-documented, twist of the northern agrarian crisis of the 1430s. It is at one with the Roberts, Dunsford, Harris typology of the landscape. Simon Harris himself, in his essay, 'Wastes, the Margins and the Abandonment of Land', proposes a pattern of development that might well have implications for England as a whole. The evidence he amasses for the episcopal estates in Durham suggests that we should not assume that, because rents fell, land was being abandoned and reverting to waste. Not only was there conversion to pasture, in both highland and lowland zones, but also a pronounced reluctance of tenants to pay rents. While one

---

15 Pollard, *North-Eastern England*, pp. 225–30.

might have expected the more recently cleared and marginal land to be most seriously affected, the evidence indicates a more complex pattern.

In other ways, too, these studies reveal that eastern England north of the Tees was little different from other parts of the kingdom. Margaret Harvey's archidiaconal court books show the same issues – concerning adultery, marriage, mortuaries or failure to observe the Sabbath – as would be found in most places in the kingdom. Only it seems in the more disturbed district of the border itself, as Anthony Goodman has shown, did spiritual discipline break down.[16] In 'Scaling the Ladder', an account of the remarkable history of four generations of the Grays of Heaton, a family who stand out for their military service to the crown from Bannockburn to Agincourt, Andy King reveals a rising gentry family typical of England in the fourteenth century, differentiated perhaps only by their greater willingness than some to put chivalric ideas into practice. The family's military service was largely on the Scottish border, but it did not exclude fighting in France. Christian Liddy, focusing lower down the social scale, unearths the history of a family, the estimable 'Pollards of Pollard Hall', who established themselves as lesser gentry in the neighbourhood of Bishop Auckland by episcopal service. Through piecemeal accumulation of small parcels they built up an estate, which, by the sixteenth century, enabled them to support manorial pretensions. What is unusual is not that this was possible in County Durham, but that it is a common process not so easily revealed anywhere in the kingdom.

A late medieval regional identity for the north east seems to remain a will-o'-the wisp. If there were nevertheless a north-east region of England in the later Middle Ages it would be in some obvious respects, physically and culturally, different from the region of the twenty-first century. Whereas the modern region is dominated by and takes its lead from Newcastle, *then* it would have taken its lead from Durham. This is not just the coincidental impression given by a collection of essays drawing largely on the records of Durham's two great ecclesiastical institutions. One cannot be sure either that people would have had the same territorial unity in mind in defining their 'north east'; it could have been either more extensive, or more concentrated. Then as now, north Northumberland was semi-detached and the Tees valley, albeit now dominated by the remnants of nineteenth-century industrialisation, then, as now, looked two ways, northwards as well as southwards. While the younger generation of Middlesbrough people tend to think of themselves as north easterners, the older generation know that they are from Yorkshire.[17] The region in history, like Aristotle's womb and Cuthbert's remains, wanders. But perhaps any effort to demonstrate the deep-rooted region in the north east is futile. For it is but a cultural construct of the past by the present, driven now by a contemporary political discourse. If, because of current preoccupations, we choose to look for something we call a region in the north-eastern parts of the realm, we may well find it, for history, as the monks of Durham knew well, is often but the moulding of the past to fit contemporary needs. But empirical historians will be relieved to know that the findings of the essays that follow, securely based on evidence drawn from the sources, mainly regional, have not been predetermined by such a search.

---

[16] A. Goodman, 'Religion and Warfare in the Anglo-Scottish Marches', in *Medieval Frontier Societies*, ed. R. Bartlett and A. MacKay (Oxford, 1989).

[17] I owe this information to Barbara Fennell and Carmen Llamas from their research on Teesside English.

1

St Cuthbert and the Border, *c*.1080–*c*.1300

RICHARD LOMAS

The liquidation of the Cuthbertian interest in Scotland in the fourteenth and fifteenth centuries has been analysed in great detail by several historians,[1] and the severe diminution of the value of the properties on the English side of the border in the same period has also been the subject of recent scrutiny.[2] This essay addresses two questions relating to the evolution of the landed and spiritual interest of St Cuthbert in the border region up to 1300. The first concerns the nature of the properties and rights St Cuthbert possessed in north Northumberland and southern Scotland *c*.1300 and the extent of their potential income yield. The second is to consider why the success evident in 1300 was in fact much less than was originally hoped and striven for in the late eleventh and early twelfth centuries. In dealing with these matters, it is important to recognise that, as a result of the foundation of the Benedictine chapter of Durham Cathedral in 1083, the trusteeship of St Cuthbert bifurcated into two institutions: one headed by the bishop of Durham; the other, the cathedral priory of Durham. Although the monks attempted with considerable success to appropriate the role and to present themselves as the sole guardian, to exclude the bishop of Durham would be to distort and falsify the picture.

On the eve of the Three Hundred Years' War between England and Scotland, which began on 26 March 1296, St Cuthbert, in the form of his trustees, was the major force (and in many parts the controlling force) in a triangle of territory that bestrode the border. The hypotenuse of this triangle was a thirty-mile stretch of coastline from Pease Bay in the north to Budle Bay in the south and its apex was at Cornhill on Tweed, fifteen miles up river from Berwick. It covered roughly 170 square miles, slightly more than half of them lying north of the border. It is worth noting, however, that the border only became fully significant after 1300: for the men of the late eleventh century St Cuthbert's property on either side of the Tweed had a unity that the post-1300 world was not prepared to allow.

Of the two Durham parties, the bishop had the more restricted interest, in that it

---

[1] R.B. Dobson, 'The last English Monks on Scottish Soil', *SHR* 46 (1967), 1–25; A.L. Brown, 'The Priory of Coldingham in the late Fourteenth Century', *IR* 23 (1972), 91–101; N. Macdougall, 'The Struggle for Coldingham Priory, 1472–1488', *IR* 23 (1972), 102–14; M. Dilworth, 'Coldingham Priory and the Reformation', *IR* 23 (1972), 115–37.
[2] R. Lomas, 'The Impact of Border Warfare: The Scots and South Tweedside, *c*.1290-*c*.1520', *SHR* 75 (1996), 143–67.

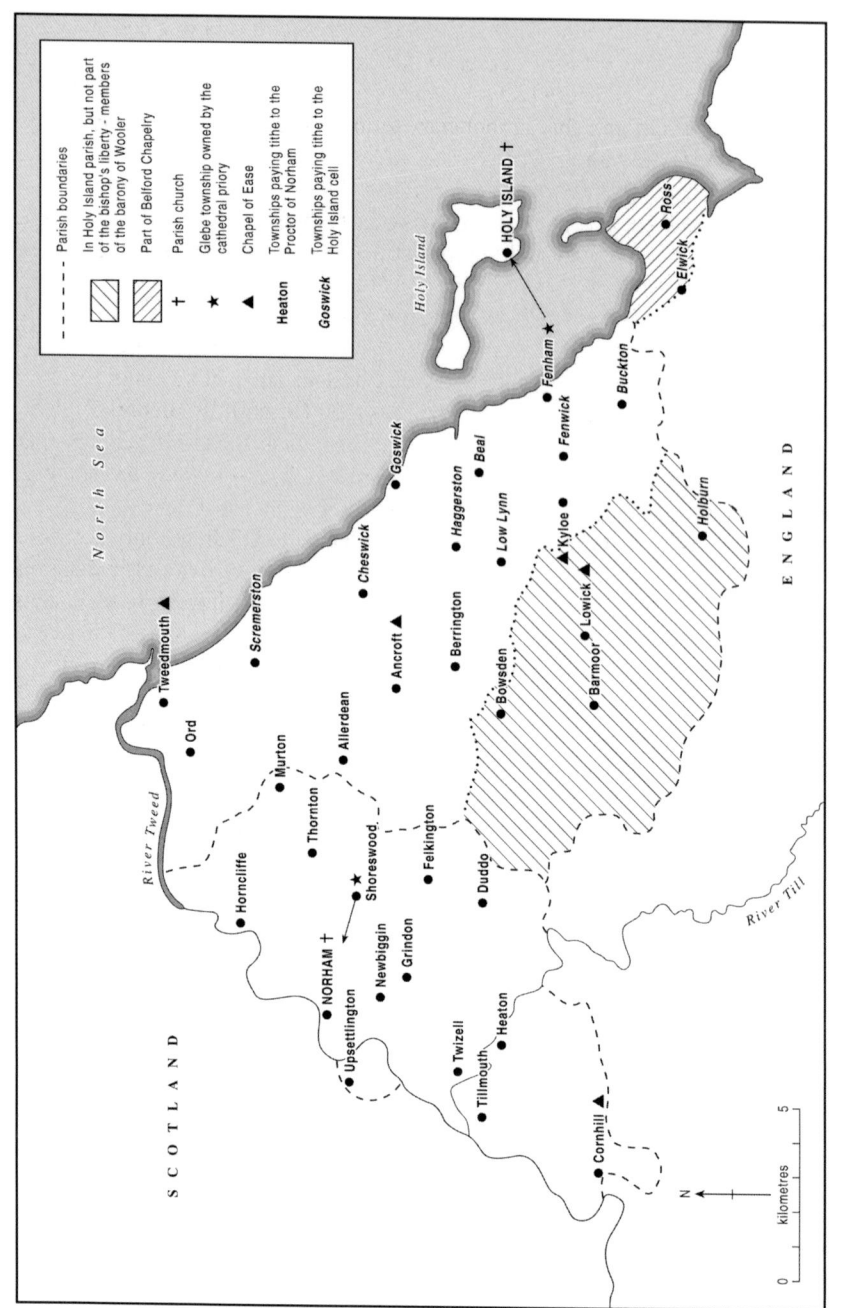

Map 1.1 St Cuthbert's Estate: North Durham

was entirely confined to England, with one small exception.[3] This was the township of Upsettlington in Berwickshire and thus in Scotland, an unexplained anomaly that serves as a reminder of the artificiality of the border. As will become apparent, the episcopal estate was less valuable in monetary terms, absolutely and comparatively, than that belonging to the cathedral priory. It comprised diocesan jurisdiction over the parishes of Norham and Holy Island on the English side of the border and the secular lordship of most, but not all, of the same areas, which for secular purposes were classed as 'shires'. Their social and tenurial structures, as described in the survey carried out after the death of Bishop Philip of Poitou in 1208,[4] display the partial 'Normanisation' which David Roffe has suggested was characteristic of the country as a whole.[5] Of the twenty-nine townships mentioned, five (Norham, Horncliffe and Grindon in Norhamshire, and Fenwick and Buckton in Islandshire) were held in demesne. Horncliffe had been acquired in exchange for Cornhill by Bishop Hugh du Puiset as part of his wide-ranging reordering of the episcopal estate.[6] When this deal was struck is not certain, but it must have been before 1183–4, since the entry in Boldon Book clearly portrays it as a demesne township.[7]

The remaining twenty-three townships were in tenancy. Of these, only six were feudal. The largest comprised Ancroft and Allerdean (in Islandshire) and Felkington (in Norhamshire), held by the service of one knight. By 1208 it had become divided into two halves. It was not created at one stroke, however, but developed over a period of about ten years. Its origin was the grant c.1122 by Bishop Ranulf Flambard to Papedy, the man whom he had installed as his sheriff of Norham, of the township of Ancroft for the service of half a knight. This act was almost certainly contemporary with, and connected to, the building of the castle (and possibly the founding of the borough) at Norham, begun by Flambard at the instigation of Henry I. Papedy's fee was considerably enlarged: Flambard added to it the neighbouring township of Allerdean; and after Flambard's death in 1128, but before 1135, Papedy acquired the township of Felkington, which was adjacent to both Ancroft and Allerdean. As a consequence, the service was increased to one knight.[8] Presumably it was intended that this enlarged fee, comprising three contiguous townships, should form a compact block of land strategically situated at the centre of the episcopal estate. In addition to Papedy's, there were three other feudal fees at Heaton, Tillmouth and Ross, each held by the service of half a knight.

The remaining townships appear not to have been disturbed by the incoming Norman regime. The survival of pre-Conquest tenures is unequivocally evident in a further seven townships. Kyloe, Berrington and Low Lynn constituted a thanage, whose holder owed a rent of £6 and certain services. This was probably a typical thanage in that surviving evidence suggests that in this region such tenements normally comprised three or four townships.[9] In addition, Goswick, Thornton, half of

---

3 See map 1.1.
4 H.C. Maxwell-Lyte, *Liber Feodorum* (3 vols., London, 1920–3), I, 26–8.
5 D. Roffe, *Domesday: The Inquest and the Book* (Oxford, 2000), pp. 42–3.
6 G.V. Scammell, *Hugh du Puiset, Bishop of Durham* (Cambridge, 1956), pp. 183–241, esp. p. 205.
7 *BB*, p. 42.
8 *Durham Episcopal Charters, 1071–1152*, ed. H.S. Offler (Surtees Society 179, 1968), pp. 92–3.
9 For example, Halton, Clarewood and Great Whittington: *A History of Northumberland* (15 vols., Newcastle-upon-Tyne, 1893–1940), X, 389.

Beal and one and a half carucates in Buckton were classed as drengages. They too owed money rents and services, including ploughing and carting. Of the remaining townships, three, Cheswick, Tweedmouth and Upsettlington, were socages. The other eight and a half townships – Cornhill, Newbiggin, Grindon, Twizell, Duddo, Scremerston, Haggerston, Ord and half of Beal – were described as free tenements. These and the socage tenants owed money rents only.

Because of an almost complete lack of documentary evidence, it is impossible to put an accurate figure on the value of this estate to the bishop. The only indication is to be found in the surviving parts of a stray minister's account for 1261–2 printed and discussed by R.B. Pugh.[10] This shows that the demesne farms at Norham, Horncliffe and Fenwick were still substantially in hand and subject to direct exploitation, but the missing parts of the account deny us the knowledge of how much they earned. The income that is recorded amounted to £204 6s. 0d., made up of £102 10s. 1d. assized rents, £21 9s. 3d. from the disposal of surplus land and services, and £80 6s. 8d. from the leases of ten mills and a payment by the men of Kyloe to be free of suit of mill. However, it seems unlikely that this was all, since total expenses came to £366 13s. 9d. (of which £195 4s. 1½d. was accounted for by four cash liveries to Durham). This was only £19 5s. 4¾d. more than income, which, since there is no mention of arrears, suggests that total income may not have been far short of £350. The estate was run by a management team headed by the constable of Norham assisted by a clerk and four bailiffs.

In contrast to the bishop's estate, that of the cathedral priory was dual, one part located in Scotland, the other in England. The two estates were broadly similar in having ecclesiastical and secular components, although the balance differed considerably and the income deriving from them was split between the mother house at Durham and local cells. The latter were staffed for limited periods by Durham monks, the length of whose stay was determined by their prior, in whose power it was to recall them to Durham, or move them to another cell.

The estate on the south side of the Tweed comprised the parishes of Norham and Holy Island.[11] The former was coincident with Norhamshire, but the latter did not fully coincide with Islandshire in that it included the townships of Lowick, Barmoor, Bowsden and Holburn, which for secular purposes were members of the barony of Wooler, not of the episcopal estate. As a result, these four townships were always in the county of Northumberland, whereas the remainder of the two shires/parishes were part of Durham until 1844. There were two further anomalies. The township of Ross was within the bishop's secular jurisdiction, but ecclesiastically it was a member of the chapelry of Belford in the parish of Bamburgh.[12] The case of its neighbour, Elwick, was even more curious. It too was in the chapelry of Belford, but for secular purposes it was divided, its southern half belonging to the crown while its northern half pertained to the bishop.[13] Consequently, until 1844 it was half in Durham, half in Northumberland.

As was the case in many extensive northern parishes, the inconvenience arising

---

[10] R.B. Pugh, 'Ministers' Accounts for Norhamshire and Islandshire, 1261–62', *NH* 11 (1976), 17–26.
[11] See map 1.1.
[12] *History of Northumberland*, I, 404.
[13] Ibid., I, 408.

from distance from the parish church was partially overcome by the creation of chapels of ease to cater for most of the spiritual needs of the people without undermining or diminishing the rights and income of the parish church and its rector. Such chapels were created in both parishes. In Norham, there was only one, at Cornhill, which served the three townships to the west of the River Till. In Holy Island, a more extensive parish, where the parish church was located on the island and thus cut off from the mainland by the tide twice every twenty-four hours, four were provided for the benefit of the mainland townships. They were at Tweedmouth, Ancroft, Kyloe and Lowick, each one serving four or five townships. When these divisions were instituted is not known, although it was certainly before 1145, when they were included in Pope Eugenius III's confirmation of the priory's possessions,[14] a fact supported by the earliest parts of the fabric of the church of St Anne at Ancroft.[15] That the ecclesiastical chapelry of Lowick was exactly that part of Islandshire that the bishop had lost to the barony of Wooler may indicate that the chapelries predated the barony, which, it is suggested, was created in the very first years of the twelfth century. As to who was responsible for the formation of these chapelries, there can be little doubt that it was the prior of Durham, possibly Turgot.

The division of the priory estate favoured the mother house.[16] To Durham went the income from the township of Shoreswood, which was the glebe of Norham parish. It was a typical Northumbrian township with a core community of fifteen bondmen and six cottars. In addition, by the late thirteenth century, the priory had acquired several small but not very valuable properties in Norham, Cornhill, Elwick, Bowsden and Murton. The bulk of the income destined for Durham, however, was derived from the tithes and altarage of all fourteen townships of the parish of Norham (including Upsettlington) and nine of the twenty townships of Holy Island parish. Managerial responsibility for these sources of income devolved upon an officer known as the proctor of Norham. In the 1290s this office appears to have been discharged by one of the parish clergy, but by 1314 it had been transferred to one of the monks stationed on Holy Island.

The endowment of the cell located on Holy Island next to the parish church was similar in composition to that managed by the proctor. The core of its secular element was the western part of Holy Island and the township of Fenham, located on the mainland opposite the island. Like Shoreswood, it was the parish glebe and it too was a community of bondmen and cottars, although their numbers are not recorded. Like the proctor, the cell had acquired properties in the course of the twelfth and thirteenth centuries, but on a much larger scale: rents, from some places substantial in amount, were drawn from twelve townships within the parish and from Norham.[17] But, as with the proctor, the major part of the cell's income was derived from the tithes and altarage of eleven townships in the parish, including Holy Island. Responsibility for

---

[14] W. Holtzmann, *Papsturkunden in England* (3 vols., Berlin, 1935–52), II, 206.
[15] J. Grundy et al., *The Buildings of England: Northumberland* (2nd edn., London, 1992), p. 146.
[16] The details in this and the subsequent three paragraphs are derived from DCM, Bursar's Account Rolls, Proctor of Norham's Accounts and Holy Island Cell Accounts.
[17] J. Raine, *The History and Antiquities of North Durham* (London, 1852): Raine was able to identify most, but not all, of these acquisitions. They are calendared on pp. 77–9, and are printed in the appendix, nos. DCLXXII–DCXCIII.

the management of this estate rested on the prior of the cell, who was required to present his accounts for audit at Durham once a year.

What income were these properties capable of generating? For those allocated to the mother house, accurate figures can be produced with reasonable confidence, thanks to the survival of many of the account rolls of the bursar, to whom the proctor sent his surplus or profit. These point to a pre-war gross annual income potential of around £420. A little over three-quarters of this sum derived from the garb tithes, which were not collected but leased to local men. Rents from Shoreswood and the handful of small properties elsewhere were expected to yield a mere £12 10s. The balance was made up of income from lesser tithes and altarage. Out of this revenue, the proctor had to finance landlord's repairs and to pay the stipends of the vicar of Norham and his staff and the chaplain of Cornhill. This level of income was sharply reduced by the fighting in 1297 and 1298, but after a brief period of recovery income levels very close to those before 1296 were maintained until after the battle of Bannockburn, which initiated a rapid decline in the priory's fortunes in this border area.

Because there are no extant records of the cell's finances prior to 1326, that is, when the war and the economic crisis of the second decade of the century had permanently and significantly changed conditions, we cannot be anything like as certain about the income of the Holy Island cell. The best indication is provided by the status of 1328, which records what should have been received as well as what came in. This indicates that the pre-war income of the cell was at least £278. Of this sum, £50 derived from secular rents, two-fifths of which came from Fenham. Ecclesiastical sources, however, produced £228, £160 from great tithes and £68 from lesser tithes and altarage.

In total, therefore, the potential annual gross yield to the priory of Durham from its two churches on the south bank of the Tweed was in the region of £700, that is, around twice the sum the bishop could expect from his portion of the estate.

The priory's estate on the north side of the Tweed was larger, more diverse and more complex.[18] Moreover, its secular and ecclesiastical components were less discrepant, and it was to the cell located at Coldingham, not to the mother house, that the lion's share of the income was assigned. The secular component comprised all or parts of twenty-two townships. Thirteen of these can be classed as being in demesne, twelve of them agricultural communities and one the fishing village, Eyemouth. Between them, the demesne farms of the agricultural townships (Coldingham, Swinewood, Old Cambus, Renton, East Reston, West Reston, Upper Ayton, Nether Ayton and Auchencrow, which constituted Coldinghamshire, and Fishwick, Swinton and Edrom in Berwickshire) had 3,562 acres of arable land and 135 acres of meadow. They were occupied by 180 bondmen, seventy-one cottars, 105 tenants called variously bovaters and *firmarii*, and thirty-five free tenants. In addition, there were nine townships, belonging in whole or in part to the cell that were held on feudal or freehold terms by members of the local armigerous class. In all respects, including terminology, there were no significant differences between landed society in Berwickshire and that in Northumberland.[19] These secular properties were matched by an

---

[18] See map 1.2.
[19] 'Rentale Antiquum de Redditibus, Tenementis etc. in Scocia', in *The Priory of Coldingham*, ed. J.

ecclesiastical estate that was almost as extensive. It comprised eight parishes (Coldingham, Berwick, Earlston, Ednam, Edrom, Lamberton, Fishwick and Swinton) and six parochial chapels (Ayton and Prenderguest in Coldingham, and Blackadder, East Nisbet, Kelloe and Kimmerghame in Edrom).[20]

Thanks to the *Taxatio* of 1291 and the *Rentale* of 1298 a reasonably accurate estimate of the annual value of the Scottish properties can be calculated. In total it amounted to between £710 and £720, around £460 from the churches and around £260 from the secular properties. Just under £150, being the entire income from the churches of Ednam and Earlston and half of the income of the church of Edrom, was sent to the bursar of the priory at Durham. The remainder of the ecclesiastical income and all that from secular sources, amounting in total to nearly £570, was assigned to the monks at the Coldingham cell. The fact that Coldingham's income was over twice that of the cell at Holy Island suggests that the complement of monks the priory stationed in Scotland was considerably larger than that in Northumberland. It also meant that Coldingham, although a dependent cell, was wealthier than any of the other independent monastic houses in Lothian, the nearest, both geographically and financially, being Kelso with an annual value of £315.[21]

When the values of the priory's Northumberland and Scottish estates are added together the total comes to over £1,400. It is, of course, unlikely that this sum was ever realised in any one year, and it has to be remembered that various local expenses had to be borne. Nevertheless, the crude total gives a broad indication of the extent of the priory's spiritual responsibilities and economic interest in the Tweed hinterland and of the contribution of its properties to its overall revenue.

How did this situation in the border region arise and was it the one that was hoped for and intended by St Cuthbert's trustees? Basically, the answer is that it was the product of the restructuring of the upper stratum of border society in the two generations after 1080. Those principally responsible were four kings, William II (1087–1100) and Henry I (1100–35) of England, and Edgar (1097–1107) and David I of Scotland (1124–53), the latter as king from 1124, but before that as earl under his brother, Alexander I (1107–24). Two bishops of Durham, William of St Calais (1081–96) and Ranulf Flambard (1099–1128), and the prior of Durham, Turgot (1087–1107), also had an input, but their influence was essentially modifying rather than fundamental: as will become clear, bishops and priors might propose, but it was kings who disposed. And it is most important to be aware from the outset that, although the situation towards the end of the thirteenth century suggests that St Cuthbert's trustees had been hugely successful in creating valuable assets, they in fact suffered reverses and many of their hopes and ambitions remained unrealised.

For the bishops, the most significant developments were entirely negative, leaving them with an attenuated diocese, the geography of which was to endure until 1882, when it was divided into the present dioceses of Durham and Newcastle. The process

---

Raine (Surtees Society 12, 1841), appendix, pp. lxxxv–civ. It is evident that this survey was compiled in the aftermath of the battle of Falkirk in 1298.

[20] 'Taxa et Decimae Ecclesiarum et Decanatuum ac Monasteriorum Diversorum in Scocia', in *Coldingham*, appendix, pp. cviii–cxvii. This is part of the valuation of the Scottish church carried out on the orders of Pope Nicholas IV in 1291: I.B. Cowan, *The Parishes of Medieval Scotland* (Edinburgh, 1967), pp. 5–204.

[21] 'Taxa et Decimae Ecclesiarum', pp. cxv–cxvi.

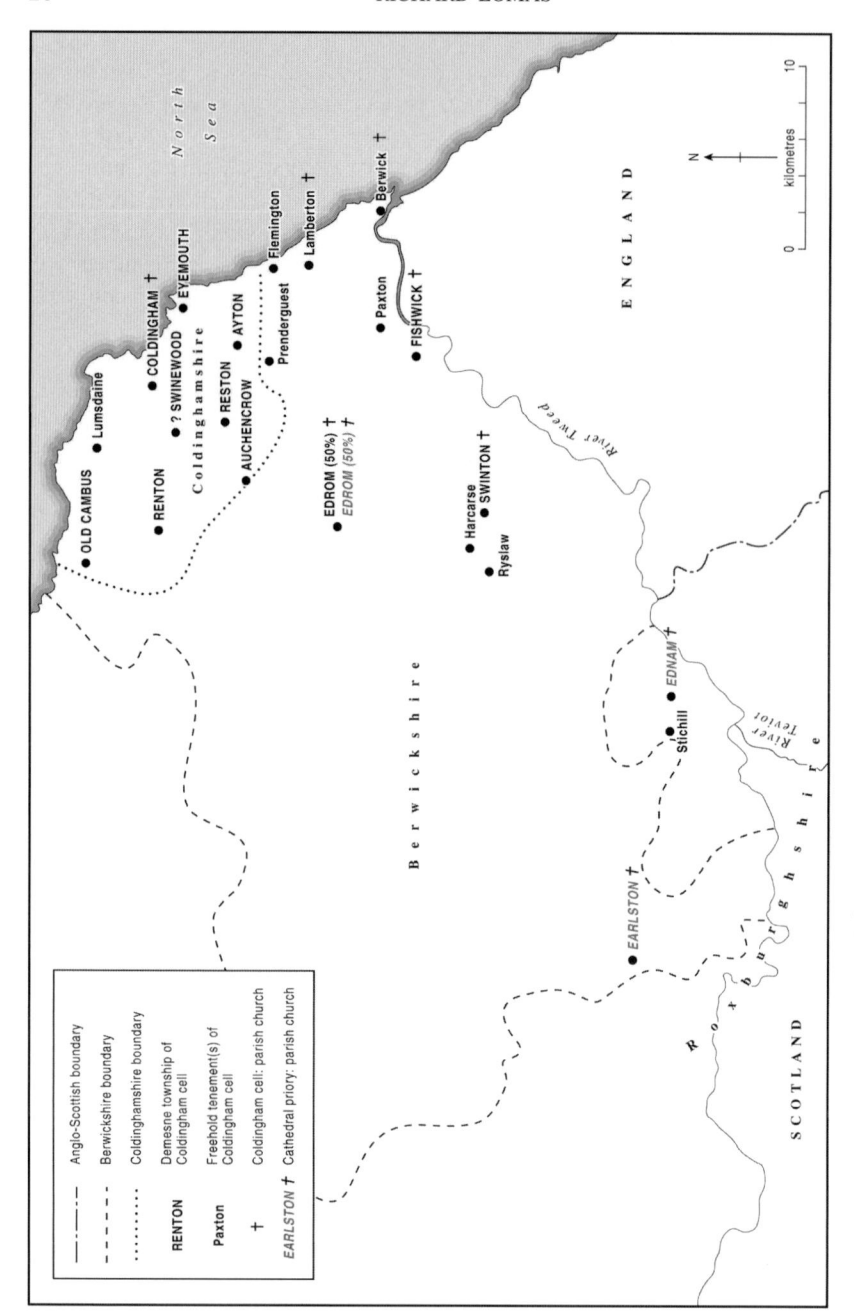

Map 1.2 St Cuthbert's Estate: Berwickshire and Roxburghshire

began with the loss of Hexhamshire in 1071 and 1080, which henceforth was a member of the diocese of York and, for secular purposes, governed until 1572 by the archbishop's officers.[22] Some compensation was achieved, albeit briefly, in 1092 following William II's annexation of Cumbria, when the king gave ecclesiastical jurisdiction over the region to the bishop of Durham. But this gain did not outlast the opening years of Ranulf Flambard's pontificate. Following his escape from the Tower and desertion to Duke Robert of Normandy, ecclesiastical control of Cumbria was transferred to the archdeacon of Richmond, in effect making it part of the diocese of York. Hope of recovery was not wholly unrealistic, since the transfer could be reversed. What ended that hope, however, was the creation of the diocese of Carlisle in 1133.

The bishop also lost any hope of reviving Durham's claims to jurisdiction north of the border in Teviotdale. Although perhaps more pious than realistic, it was based upon the knowledge of Lindisfarne's earlier extensive interests in that area before the kingdoms of England and Scotland had come into being. It is almost certain that Durham's jurisdiction in Teviotdale was terminated during Flambard's exile in 1100 and 1101, but what ensured that the loss was permanent was the creation (or recreation) of the diocese of Glasgow by Earl David sometime between 1109 and 1114. Similarly, the other Scottish border diocese, St Andrews, vacant after the death of Flothad in 1093, was reinvigorated after 1107 by Turgot and his reforming successors.[23] Thereafter, both Scottish bishoprics can be observed marching *pari passu* with Durham, both in the development of diocesan organisation and in the determination of their incumbents to assert their diocesan rights.[24] Together, these ensured that Dunelmian ecclesiastical imperialism ceased to be tenable.

If the bishop's hopes and aspirations north of the border were never likely to be realised, his rights in Norhamshire and Islandshire should have been incontrovertible. Yet even here he suffered loss. The townships of Lowick, Barmoor, Bowsden and Holburn continued to be within the parish of Holy Island as the chapelry of Lowick, but although there is no concrete evidence, it is most likely that the loss occurred in 1100 or 1101 when Ranulf Flambard was in disgrace. It was probably then that the barony of Wooler, to which the townships henceforth belonged, was created for Robert de Muschamp.[25] When mapped, it becomes clear that Muschamp's barony was constructed with a strategic purpose in mind. It formed a compact block of land sweeping in an unbroken arc from the summit of the Cheviot to the sea at Budle Bay.[26] Had the four townships not been included, the barony would have lacked its necessary monolithic structure. Muschamp chose to locate his castle at Wooler, where the roads to and from Scotland diverged and converged, one of which, known as the Devil's Causeway, ran to and from Tweedmouth through Lowick. The bishop almost lost the township of Ross, but it was regained through the intervention of

---

[22] *History of Northumberland*, III, 121.
[23] N.F. Shead, 'The Origins of the Medieval Diocese of Glasgow', *SHR* 48 (1969), 220–5; M. Ash, 'The Diocese of St Andrews under its "Norman" Bishops', *SHR* 55 (1976), 105–26.
[24] Ash, 'Diocese of St Andrews'; N.F. Shead, 'The Administration of the Diocese of Glasgow in the Twelfth and Thirteenth Centuries', *SHR* 55 (1976), 127–50.
[25] W.P. Hedley, *Northumberland Families* (2 vols., Newcastle-upon-Tyne, 1968), I, 37.
[26] R. Lomas, *County of Conflict: Northumberland from Conquest to Civil War* (East Linton, 1996), p. 23.

Queen Matilda, although the recovery was little more than nominal in that the Muschamps continued in possession as feudal tenants.[27]

The cathedral priory had rather better fortune than did the bishop. From William of St Calais, it obtained as part of its foundation endowment the churches of Norham and Holy Island, its title to which was never challenged. Thereafter, although it made some gains, these were less than its aspirations, and it did suffer losses. These may be said to have begun, before the Benedictine chapter was created, with the failure in 1074 to re-establish a Cuthbertian presence at Melrose. The cause of this failure was the problem of allegiance, Malcolm III insisting that the English monks who wished to revive monastic life at St Cuthbert's birthplace could do so only on condition of swearing fealty to him as king of Scots, a condition which they found unacceptable.[28]

Harder to bear was the loss of Hexham and Tynemouth, both of which should have become priory cells. The failure to hang on to Tynemouth was the result of Bishop William of St Calais's quarrel with the then earl of Northumberland, Robert de Mowbray, in the 1080s. The upshot was that Mowbray seized Tynemouth from the Durham monks and handed it over to a rival Benedictine house at St Albans in Hertfordshire, which thereafter was its distant cell at the mouth of the Tyne.[29] The loss of Hexham in 1080, it may be argued with some justification, was an act of betrayal on the part of its priest, Eilaf, who was also the treasurer of the pre-Conquest Community of St Cuthbert. The loss became irrevocable in 1114, when Archbishop Thurstan of York founded an Augustinian canonry there.[30]

The priory also failed to hold on to the parish of Carham, which comprised seven townships immediately to the east of Norham on the south bank of the Tweed. The church was gifted to the monks by Henry I's queen, Matilda, and with it the priory secured control of parochial life and income along the south side of the Tweed frontier, that is, from the mouth of the river to Reddenburn, the point where the border leaves the river and moves south up to the summit of the Cheviot. This acquisition was partially matched on the north side of the river by the priory's ownership of the churches of Berwick, Fishwick and Swinton. But Carham proved to be a temporary acquisition. Not long after Matilda's death in 1118, Henry I repossessed the church and gave it, together with its neighbours, Kirknewton and Ilderton, to Walter Espec, lord of Helmsley in the North Riding of Yorkshire, for whom he created the barony of Carham.[31] Like Wooler, this barony had an obvious strategic purpose in that it provided a strong presence on the Tweed. Significantly, Espec chose not to site his castle at the ancient estate centre at Carham, but to erect it on a much more obviously defensible spot, a precipitous ridge overlooking the river, which acquired the name Wark as the result of this construction. This development coincided almost exactly with Flambard's building of his castle on a similar riparian eminence seven miles downstream at Norham.

For the priory, the loss was compounded by Espec's decision to give his three parishes to the Augustinian canonry he had founded in 1121 at Kirkham, close to Helmsley, the *caput* of his Yorkshire honour. His intention was that the canons should

---

[27] *History of Northumberland*, XI, 12.
[28] A.A.M. Duncan, *Scotland: The Making of the Kingdom* (Edinburgh, 1975), p. 123.
[29] *History of Northumberland*, VIII, 44–8.
[30] Ibid., III, 121–7.
[31] Ibid., XI, 12–13, 117, and XIV, 256.

create a cell at Carham, which would be in effect a mission station from which they would more effectively serve the three parishes. It was about this time that Henry I gave the immensely wealthy church of Bamburgh to Nostell, another Augustinian house in Yorkshire, with the same intention, although, there, a series of events conspired to prevent its implementation until the late 1220s.[32] Nevertheless, the moves by the king and his vassal threatened Cuthbertian pre-eminence at the heart of the saint's territory by establishing a highly popular rival monastic organisation with greater scope and flexibility in the business of parochial management.[33]

The only gain that the priory managed to hang on to was the parish of Branxton, which, as a single township parish, was among the smallest and poorest in the diocese. The origins of Branxton as an independent parish are obscure, and were perhaps dubious. At the end of the twelfth century the church was gifted to the monks of Durham by Richard son of Gilbert. Durham's right to ownership was challenged by the Augustinian priory of Kirkham, which put forward the claim that Branxton was not an independent parish but a chapel of Kirknewton. The case was adjudicated in Durham's favour in the time of Innocent III, but there may have been enough substance in Kirkham's case to ensure that, although Durham got its way, it had to agree to pay Kirkham an annual pension of 4s. in perpetuity. The parish was appropriated in 1258.[34]

The priory's real gains were in Scotland rather than Northumberland, but it is worth repeating that, although substantial, they were far less than the monks had hoped for. The extent of these hopes is revealed in the charters allegedly issued by Duncan II and Edgar in the 1090s, that is, before either of them obtained the throne of Scotland. Whether these documents are genuine or spurious is arguably irrelevant in this context.[35] Except in the narrowest sense, the outcome of the debate about their authenticity is immaterial, since both documents exist and make significant statements. What they describe is, I believe, what the monks of Durham wished to acquire and what the two pretenders to the Scottish throne were prepared to offer in an attempt to secure St Cuthbert's backing. In other words, they were the counters in the diplomatic game. And Durham's bids were neither fantastical nor unrealistic, in that estates the documents purported to grant had belonged to, or been closely associated with, St Cuthbert and the monastery at Lindisfarne during the saint's lifetime.

The charter of Duncan II listed the possessions of the ancient monastery at Tyningham (Tyningham, Auldhame, Scougall, Broxmouth, Hedderwick and Knowes), with which St Cuthbert had been associated.[36] Edgar's grant related to the properties of the monastery at or near Coldingham associated with St Ebba.[37] It comprised Coldingham and twenty-seven places in what is now Berwickshire. Both monasteries had been satellites of Lindisfarne. Nothing more was heard of the Tyningham grant, partly because of the brevity of Duncan II's reign (he was king for

---

[32] Ibid., I, 73–83.
[33] For the promotion of the Augustinian order in the reign of Henry I, see D. Nicholl, *Thurstan, Archbishop of York 1114–1140* (York, 1964), pp. 127–39.
[34] *History of Northumberland*, XI, 96–8.
[35] *Early Scottish Charters prior to 1153*, ed. A.C. Lawrie (Glasgow, 1905); A.A.M. Duncan, 'The Earliest Scottish Charters', *SHR* 38 (1958), 103–35; J. Donnelly, 'The Earliest Scottish Charters?', *SHR* 68 (1989), 1–22; A.A.M. Duncan, 'Yes, the Earliest Scottish Charters', *SHR* 78 (1999), 1–38.
[36] *Early Scottish Charters*, pp. 10, 240.
[37] Ibid., pp. 12–13, 246–9.

only a few months in 1094), but also because the ownership of the properties concerned had been transferred to the see of St Andrews, probably by the Scottish crown when it annexed Lothian in the early eleventh century.[38] Duncan's grant was possible because at that time the see was vacant. Once it was again *sede plena* after 1107, Tyningham and its pendicles reverted to episcopal control.

Edgar, however, reigned for ten years and was therefore unable to avoid keeping his promise, particularly as he had been put on the throne with English support. But once he was securely on the throne, he was in a position to diminish his generosity. Instead of the twenty-eight places of his earlier grant, he gave the monks Coldingham and its ten pendicles, to which he added Swinton, Paxton and Fishwick.[39] Shortly afterwards (possibly in 1105), with Edgar's approval, Thor Longus granted Ednam, which he had restored from dereliction, to the monks.[40]

Thus, substantial though this estate was, it was clearly nothing like what the monks had schemed for. They did add to these original properties during the twelfth and thirteenth centuries by means of gift, purchase and foreclosure. Their most outstanding increment was Edrom, which Earl Gospatric II granted to them *c*.1130.[41] There is insufficient scope here for a full analysis of their numerous but less spectacular gains.[42] The example of Old Cambus will serve to illustrate their activities.[43] The monks acquired the lordship in 1198 in exchange for Lumsdaine. Subsequently, they gradually gained more direct control by inducing four of the freehold tenants to make over their land to them.[44] By 1298, Old Cambus was one of the priory's demesne townships. The monks of Coldingham also engaged in colonisation of the waste: within the township of Coldingham a satellite settlement called 'Schatteby' was created, comprising twenty-four tofts, which were worth £1 10s. 9d. a year when fully tenanted.[45] But these various gains and developments were relatively modest compensation for Edgar's failure to honour his original generosity. Had he done so, Durham would have recreated the hegemony which the monks believed that their predecessors at Lindisfarne had enjoyed. It is easy to dismiss their ambition as unrealistic, but they had knowledge of their past and an unquestioning commitment to what they perceived as the rights of the saint who was their *raison d'être*.

The monks were marginally more successful on the ecclesiastical front, although here, too, they failed to gain or to hold on to everything to which they aspired. Possessed of the churches of Coldingham, Ednam, Swinton and Fishwick from before 1107, a generation later (probably in the early 1130s), the monks acquired Edrom from Earl Gospatric II and St Mary's, Berwick from David I, the latter being the king's compensation to them for giving up Melrose or, perhaps more accurately, their claim to it.[46] Fifty years later, in 1171, the arbitration of their dispute with Kelso

---

[38] Ash, 'Diocese of St Andrews', 109.
[39] *Early Scottish Charters*, pp. 16–17, 253–5, and 17–18, 256–9.
[40] Ibid., pp. 19, 259–60.
[41] Ibid., pp. 90, 355–6.
[42] Raine, *North Durham*, appendix, nos. I–CCCLXVII. These documents record grants of property and rights to Coldingham issued in the twelfth and thirteenth centuries by Scottish kings, nobles and bishops.
[43] See map 1.2.
[44] Raine, *North Durham*, appendix, nos. CLXXVI–CXCI.
[45] 'Rentale Antiquum', p. xcvii.
[46] Raine, *North Durham*, appendix, nos. CXI, XVIII; Cowan, *Parishes of Medieval Scotland*, pp. 60, 17.

secured their possession of Earlston (then a chapel of their parish of Edrom but later acquiring parochial status), and gave them the church of St Laurence, Berwick, in exchange for the church of Gordon.[47] However, in 1193 and 1204 they lost the chapels of Nenthorn and Newton in Ednam parish to successive bishops of St Andrews, Roger de Beaumont and William Malvoisin, as the price of freedom from episcopal procurations for their churches in the diocese.[48] This matter was part of a prolonged struggle between the monks and their ordinary about the rights of him and his officers over them and their churches within his diocese. In this, as in other respects, the Durham monks gained far less than they had anticipated, and with justified optimism, at the beginning of the twelfth century.[49] It is also worth noting that about this time, Durham lost control of the church of Smailholm, which was originally a dependency of Earlston, and although it was granted the church of Old Cambus by Roger de Beaumont, its tithes were immediately assigned to the monks serving on the Inner Farne and so in effect lost to Coldingham.[50]

A further question to be addressed concerns when and why the cells at Coldingham and Holy Island were created. One fact seems clear enough: they were not contemporary with the churches to which they were attached at a later date. Here, Alan Piper's examination of the fabric of the monastic church on Holy Island is significant in that it revealed the absence of the normal entry point between the church and the claustral range.[51] Moreover, at the time of its foundation, the cathedral priory comprised twenty-three monks, and it is unlikely that the number increased so rapidly for it to have been possible for either Coldingham or Holy Island to have been assigned the canonical complement of twelve monks and a prior at an early date.

At the same time, possession without presence, personal and physical, would have been to risk loss. Hence the presence of one (at least) member of the Durham community in the border region from an unknown date until at least the mid-1120s. Apart from his name, Edward, there is little information about him or his activities. But what there is suggests that he was in effect the cathedral priory's agent in the border area, charged with building its churches and thereby creating essential statements of ownership. It is, therefore, likely that he was responsible for initiating and overseeing the building of the first churches at Coldingham and Holy Island.[52]

As regards the former, there is reliable documentary evidence that the church of St Mary was completed, or was sufficiently advanced, to be dedicated before the year 1107, for it was in this year that King Edgar, who was present, gifted Swinton to the monks of Durham.[53] At Holy Island, however, the only conclusive evidence for the date of construction is architectural. But this does suggest that the church there – the substantial ruins of which show it to have been a miniature version of the new cathedral then rising at Durham – was in course of construction at about the same time. This

---

[47] Raine, *North Durham*, appendix, no. DCXLIII; Cowan, *Parishes of Medieval Scotland*, pp. 57, 17.
[48] Raine, *North Durham*, appendix, nos. CCCCLXII, CCCCLXXIII.
[49] F. Barlow, *Durham Jurisdictional Peculiars* (Oxford, 1950), p. 138.
[50] Cowan, *Parishes of Medieval Scotland*, pp. 184, 5.
[51] A.J. Piper, 'The First Generation of Durham Monks and the Cult of St Cuthbert', in *St Cuthbert, His Cult and His Community to AD 1200*, ed. G. Bonner et al. (Woodbridge, 1989), p. 444.
[52] A.J. Piper, 'The Early Lists and Obits of the Durham Monks', in *Symeon of Durham, Historian of Durham and the North*, ed. D. Rollason (Stamford, 1998), p. 166; *Reginaldi Monachi Dunelmensis Libellus*, ed. J. Raine (Surtees Society 1, 1835), pp. 44–7.
[53] *Early Scottish Charters*, p. 17.

may have been more than coincidence or the result of current architectural fashion. It is now argued that the location, in the centre of the nave towards the crossing of this new church, of a cenotaph on the spot where the coffin of St Cuthbert had lain in the original church of St Peter, demonstrates that the new church was built around the holy spot with the deliberate intention of demonstrating the high status of the saint and acting as a magnet to pilgrims.[54] The same consideration appears not to have been at work in the case of Coldingham, where the new church was some distance from the earlier monastery associated with St Ebba. This may have been a deliberate move on the part of the Durham monks to hinder a possible counter attraction to St Cuthbert. Such a precaution appears to have been justified by the number of charters granting land to Coldingham which include St Ebba among the dedicatees.[55]

It is, therefore, certain that the priory placed its mark upon both its estates at the outset. And, once in being, the two churches must have been staffed, probably with a handful of monks. But when these arrangements were replaced by fully developed cells cannot be pinpointed. Again, the evidence for Coldingham is the more certain. In the late summer of 1139, David I's son, Henry, earl of Northumberland, issued a charter in favour of 'the church of St Mary and St Cuthbert of Coldingham and the monks serving there'.[56] Previous charters recording grants used phrases such as 'to God and St Cuthbert and his monks'. Added support for this date is that by 1151 there was a prior of Coldingham, Herbert.[57] It is reasonable to think, therefore, that in or close to 1139 the priory established a fully developed monastic community at Coldingham.

Was this development coincident with, or did it precede, a similar move at Holy Island? Such pointers as there are indicate that the Holy Island cell may have been brought into being somewhat later than that at Coldingham. The earliest evidence of a monastic community there comes from the early 1170s, and it coincides, so far as the interpretation of the architectural evidence allows, with the remodelling of the chancel in which the short, tri-apsidal original was replaced by a longer, square-ended version capable of accommodating a larger number of bodies.[58] The earliest known prior of Holy Island, Ralph, dates from *c.*1217.[59]

It would seem, therefore, that the creation of cells in the form in which they appeared towards the end of the thirteenth century took place a generation or more after the acquisition of the properties and the building of the churches. And it is reasonable to think that it would not have been until that time that the priory had sufficient monks to support such enterprises. Yet there may have been more urgent reasons for this development. One factor may have been the need to be able to exercise closer control, particularly as the twenty years after 1136 were uncertain ones for the region. Another was that David I, like his mentor, Henry I, favoured the newer monastic orders and actively promoted their introduction into the Scottish border

---

[54] J. Blair, 'The Early Churches at Lindisfarne', *AA*, 5th ser. 19 (1991), 47–53.
[55] For example, Raine, *North Durham*, appendix, nos. CXCIV, CXCVI, CXCVIII relating to Auchencrow, and nos. CCXIII, CCXIV, CCXV, CCXVII relating to Ayton.
[56] Ibid., appendix, no. CIII.
[57] *Coldingham*, preface, p. xvi.
[58] E. Cambridge, 'The Medieval Priory', in D. O'Sullivan and R. Young, *Lindisfarne: Holy Island* (London, 1995), p. 70.
[59] Raine, *North Durham*, p. 79.

region during the first half of his reign. In 1128, he transferred the Tironensians he had earlier settled at Selkirk to Kelso, uncomfortably close to Coldingham; and in the following decade he founded the Cistercian house at Melrose (1136) and the Augustinian canonry at Jedburgh (1138). To have a monastic cell at Coldingham that could rival, and indeed surpass, all of these new houses may have seemed a sensible means of defending St Cuthbert's interests. And this may explain why the cell at Coldingham was so much bigger than that at Holy Island and why it was decided to rebuild its church on a much larger scale early in the thirteenth century.[60]

The founding of the cells at Coldingham and Holy Island was the one major development to take place after the acquisition of the estates in the late eleventh and early twelfth centuries and it follows, of course, that the administrative arrangements, whereby the management of property and the receipt of income was divided between the mother house and the dependent cells, were not created until those cells had been established. What arrangements obtained before that time for the supervision of what were large and complex estates that yielded very substantial incomes is not known. Nor do we know when and why the decisions were made to adopt the precise arrangements that become visible at the end of the thirteenth century, although for practical reasons it cannot have been long after the cells were created. The stationing of members of the community on the estates may have been seen as a convenient and attractive solution to the problem of estate management, although it did mean that the central funds of the priory would be depleted in order to finance the needs of groups of brethren living away from home.

Thus far, this essay has been concerned to describe the situation existing around the year 1300 and to look back to determine its origins rather than examine its subsequent development. Yet it is only by examining conditions at the end of the fourteenth century that the full importance of these border estates can be gauged. In doing so, we have the invaluable evidence provided by that most competent of priors, John Wessington (1416–46), who in 1420 set down a description and an explanation of the fall in income from the priory's ecclesiastical sources of revenue since the 1290s.[61] The reasons he gave were four in number. The last two applied generally: many landlords had converted land to pasture and so deprived the priory of the valuable grain tithe; and many farms were deserted as the result of plague. The first two, however, were specific to the border. One was that no income had been received from the Scottish estates for sixty-eight years, because the Scots would not allow its export. The other was that the war between England and Scotland had adversely affected church revenues, especially those in Northumberland.

Wessington's figures (which relate only to the priory's main estate managed by the bursar, and do not include any from properties assigned to the minor obedientiaries) are worth closer scrutiny. Those for 1293 show that in that year the Scottish churches answering to the bursar were valued at £149, while Norham and Holy Island were worth, respectively, £260 and £158. In total, the ecclesiastical element of the cross-border estate yielded £567. Income from ten other churches – Ellingham (Northumberland), Jarrow, Pittington, Merrington, Hesleden, Heighington, Aycliffe, and Billingham (Durham), and Northallerton and Eastrington (Yorkshire) – was

---

[60] G.A.C. Binnie, *The Churches and Graveyards of Berwickshire* (Berwick upon Tweed, 1995), p. 89.
[61] *Scriptores Tres*, appendix, pp. ccxl–ccl.

reckoned to be £894. Consequently, of the grand total of £1,461, the border churches contributed thirty-nine per cent. The figures for 1392 tell a very different story. The Scottish churches yielded nothing and the income from Norham and Holy Island came to only £23. In contrast, the aggregate income from the other ten churches was £414. Thus, of the grand total of £437, the border's contribution was a mere five per cent.

Looked at another way, income from the other churches had fallen by fifty-four per cent, but that from the border region had gone down by no less than ninety-six per cent. Excursions into the realm of counter-factual history may be beguiling but are also dangerous. Nonetheless, it is worth considering what the 1392 situation might have been had there been no Anglo-Scottish war and had the border churches produced forty-six per cent of their 1293 income. The yield would have been £68 from Scotland, £120 from Norham and £73 from Holy Island, a total of £261. This would have raised the bursar's spiritual income to £675, or thirty-five per cent more than it in fact received. These figures, actual and imaginary, underline the pre-1300 importance of the cross-border estate to the economy of St Cuthbert's principal trustee and the sore loss it suffered as the result of Anglo-Scottish conflict in the fourteenth and fifteenth centuries.

2

John Hardyng, Northumbrian Identity and the Scots[1]

ALASTAIR J. MACDONALD

In life, John Hardyng was clearly a slippery individual. By his own account he was a spy; he was also a forger; and he appears to have been a thief as well.[2] It is not surprising, then, that his textual legacy as a chronicler is also far from straightforward. Hardyng's *Chronicle* exists in two versions. The second, shorter one on which Hardyng seems still to have been working when he died, probably in 1464, is relatively well known, although no modern edition of the text has been published.[3] The longer first version is known to exist in only one manuscript, probably the presentation copy for Henry VI, which was delivered to the king in 1457.[4] Much of the scholarly attention paid to the two versions of Hardyng's *Chronicle* has focused on its literary importance. This interest is not based on the quality of the author's poetry (the work is largely in verse, in rhyme royal stanzas). Judgements on Hardyng's literary abilities are, indeed, overwhelmingly negative. It has been argued that his work is of no literary merit, his verse an exercise in 'doggerel stupidity'.[5] Much of the interest in Hardyng from a literary perspective centres instead on the sources on which he drew, such as Geoffrey of Monmouth and Chaucer, and on his influence upon other writers. There has also been detailed examination of Hardyng's role in developing the Arthurian tradition in England, specifically his influence on Malory's *Le Morte Darthur*.

---

[1] I am grateful to the University of Durham and the Northern European Historical Research Network (NEHRN) for allowing me the opportunity to give a paper in 2001 featuring some of the material presented here, and to David Ditchburn for his comments on a draft.

[2] For the theory that Hardyng stole documents from Henry V's treasury archives, see *Edward I and the Throne of Scotland 1290–1296: An Edition of the Record Sources for the Great Cause*, ed. E.L.G. Stones and G.G. Simpson (2 vols., Oxford, 1978), II, 386–7. The known facts about Hardyng's life have been described in a number of places: C.L. Kingsford, 'The First Version of Hardyng's Chronicle', *EHR* 27 (1912), 462–82; A. Gransden, *Historical Writing in England II: c.1307 to the Early Sixteenth Century* (London, 1982), pp. 274–7; E.D. Kennedy, 'Chronicles and other Historical Writing', in *A Manual of the Writings in Middle English VIII*, ed. A.E. Hartnung (New Haven, 1989), pp. 2645–7; F. Riddy, 'John Hardyng's Chronicle and the Wars of the Roses', in *Arthurian Literature XII*, ed. J.P. Carley and F. Riddy (Cambridge, 1993), pp. 91–108. For Hardyng's forgeries see A. Hiatt, 'The Forgeries of John Hardyng: The evidence of Oxford, Bodleian MS Ashmole 789', *N&Q* 244 (1999), 7–12.

[3] The most recent edition is *The Chronicle of John Hardyng*, ed. H. Ellis (London, 1812).

[4] BL, MS Lansdowne 204; A.S.G. Edwards, 'The Manuscripts and Texts of the Second Version of John Hardyng's *Chronicle*', in *England in the Fifteenth Century*, ed. D. Williams (Woodbridge, 1987), p. 75.

[5] *English Verse between Chaucer and Surrey*, ed. E.P. Hammond (Durham, North Carolina, 1927), p. 233; E.D. Kennedy, 'John Hardyng and the Holy Grail', in *Arthurian Literature VIII*, ed. R. Barber (Cambridge, 1989), p. 186.

Hardyng has even been identified as a direct source for Shakespeare and the inspiration behind the depiction of Hotspur in *Henry IV Part 1*.[6]

From a historical perspective, there are challenges as well as opportunities in using Hardyng as a source. It has to be accepted initially that the *Chronicle* is innately untrustworthy. It was composed to justify the English claim to suzerainty over Scotland, and historical accuracy was not allowed to get in the way of this goal. Hardyng's intention in composing his chronicle seems to have been to provide historical context and validation for his own forgeries, which purported to record submissions of Scottish kings to their English counterparts and related materials. Eighteen such forgeries have been identified and they were delivered to successive English governments in batches between 1422 and 1463.[7] Hardyng makes it clear in the *Chronicle* that he felt he had never been rewarded adequately for his efforts in providing these documents. Having been sent on a mission to Scotland to gather his 'evidences' (and gain practical information for a future English invasion), he claims to have been promised the manor of Geddington in Northamptonshire by Henry V before he was frustrated in this ambition by the king's untimely death. Unrewarded for his efforts – Hardyng stated that he had suffered a mysterious incurable wound on his mission to Scotland and had spent 450 marks on acquiring documents – the *Chronicle* was designed to secure material rewards from Henry VI (in the case of the first version) and Edward IV for his labours.[8] Certainly, details of the relationship between England and Scotland cannot be relied upon in Hardyng's historical work: he invented to suit his case and slanted his treatment of real events to show that the Scots could be conquered easily if a renewed English royal campaign were to be launched.

The chronicler also shows himself to be unreliable well beyond this sphere. It has long been recognised that the two versions of the *Chronicle* offer radically varying accounts of English political history in Hardyng's own lifetime. The first version, composed for Henry VI, is suitably sympathetic to the Lancastrian ruler, while the second was composed for the new Yorkist line and supports its claim to the throne.[9] Hardyng's integrity as an accurate recorder of the past is entirely compromised by a comparison of the two versions. As well as his propensity to lie and distort, he was also muddled and forgetful, particularly when composing the second version, when age (he was in his eighties) began to tell.[10] The amount of original material he included was in any case limited; the suggestion that little historical usefulness attaches to the

---

[6] F. Riddy, 'Glastonbury, Joseph of Arimathea and the Grail', in *The Archaeology and History of Glastonbury Abbey: Essays in Honour of the Ninetieth Birthday of C.A. Raleigh Radford*, ed. L. Abrams and J.P. Carley (Woodbridge, 1991), pp. 317–31; A.S.G. Edwards, 'Hardyng's Chronicle and Troilus and Criseyde', *N&Q* 229 (1984), 156; E.D. Kennedy, 'Malory's Use of Hardyng's Chronicle', *N&Q* 214 (1969), 167–70; R.H. Wilson, 'More Borrowings by Malory from Hardyng's "Chronicle" ', *N&Q* 215 (1970), 208–10; P.J.C. Field, 'Malory's Minor Sources', *N&Q* 224 (1979), 107–10; Kennedy, 'John Hardyng and the Holy Grail', pp. 199–204; F. Riddy, 'Reading for England: Arthurian Literature and National Consciousness', *Bibliographical Bulletin of the International Arthurian Society* 43 (1991), 314–32; T. McCarthy, 'Malory and his Sources', in *A Companion to Malory*, ed. E. Archibald and A.S.G. Edwards (Cambridge, 1996), pp. 75–95; G. West, 'Hardyng's *Chronicle* and Shakespeare's Hotspur', *Shakespeare Quarterly* 41 (1990), 348–51.

[7] Hiatt, 'Forgeries of John Hardyng', 7.

[8] BL, MS Lansdowne 204, fols. 3r–4r; Kingsford, 'First Version', 463–5.

[9] Kingsford, 'First Version', 462, 479–80; Riddy, 'Hardyng's Chronicle and the Wars of the Roses', pp. 94–104.

[10] Riddy, 'Hardyng's Chronicle and the Wars of the Roses', p. 96; Riddy, 'Glastonbury', p. 318.

Chronicle is hardly surprising.[11] This verdict seems to hold true even where we might expect Hardyng to have been well informed. He is regarded as only being a minor source, for instance, for the reign of Henry IV; and his assertion (in only the second version of the chronicle) that the Percies opposed the deposition of Richard II in 1399 is vastly unreliable.[12]

Despite these limitations, there are ways in which Hardyng's *Chronicle* can still offer something to the historian, especially the under-utilised and lengthier first version.[13] There remains value, for instance, in Hardyng's account of events in his own lifetime, especially where there is a northern connection. Having entered the household of Sir Henry Percy at the age of twelve in 1390, Hardyng was in the service of another very active Northumbrian figure, Sir Robert Umfraville, from 1403 until 1436.[14] With this type of connection, Hardyng was well placed to provide information (which must of course be treated with caution) on border affairs not found elsewhere. One example of this is his account of the Otterburn campaign in 1388, much lengthier in the unpublished earlier version. Hardyng confirms that the battle of Otterburn was fought on 5 August. One plank of an already weak case seeking to date the battle *c*.19 August is the possibility that Hardyng (in the printed version) and others mistakenly mentioned St Oswald's Day (5 August) when they meant St Oswin's Day (20 August); the Lansdowne text has 'Of August so the fifte day'.[15] The first version of the chronicle also provides powerful supporting evidence that there was an actual encounter at Newcastle-upon-Tyne between the invading Scots and defensive forces prior to the battle, as found in Froissart's account and the ballad tradition.[16] No mention is made in Hardyng's accounts of the earl of Douglas carrying off a Percy standard – but this is the sort of detail that might have been jettisoned as not entirely favourable to his hero. Certainly, the overall impression of Otterburn as a triumph for Sir Henry Percy 'Hotspur' in which his capture arose from a combination of muddle and Scottish sneakiness is not safe to accept at face value. On the other hand, the emphasis in both chronicle versions on the role of George Dunbar, earl of March, in the battle and its aftermath is a useful counterpoint to the personalisation of

---

[11] Edwards, 'Manuscripts and Texts', p. 75; Riddy, 'Glastonbury', p. 319; L.D. Duls, *Richard II in the Early Chronicles* (The Hague, 1975), p. 220.

[12] J.L. Kirby, *Henry IV of England* (London, 1970), pp. 6, 80; J.M.W. Bean, 'Henry IV and the Percies', *History* 44 (1959), 216–17. There is support, though, for Hardyng's allegation that the future Henry IV made an oath in 1399 not to seize the throne: *Chronicles of the Revolution, 1397–1400*, ed. and trans. C. Given-Wilson (Manchester, 1993), p. 40.

[13] Extracts from the first version have been published, notably by Kingsford (C.L. Kingsford, 'Extracts from the First Version of Hardyng's Chronicle', *EHR* 27 (1912), 740–53), who also sought to highlight some other material he considered useful (Kingsford, 'First Version', 469–82).

[14] Kingsford, 'First Version', 462–3.

[15] BL, MS Lansdowne 204, fo. 198v. For proponents of the rival datings, see A. Grant, 'The Otterburn War from the Scottish Point of View', and C. Tyson, 'The Battle of Otterburn: When and Where was it Fought?', in *War and Border Societies in the Middle Ages*, ed. A. Goodman and A. Tuck (London, 1992), pp. 62 n. 86 and 72–4 respectively. Even in very recent works a later date is still sometimes preferred: A. Rose, *Kings in the North: The House of Percy in British History* (London, 2002), p. 337.

[16] BL, MS Lansdowne 204, fo. 198r; *Oeuvres de Froissart*, ed. Kervyn de Lettenhove (25 vols., Brussels, 1867–77), XII, 210–11; BL, Cotton MS Cleopatra CIV, fols. 64v–65r (printed in J. Reed, 'The Ballad and the Source: Some Literary Reflections on *The Battle of Otterburn*', in *War and Border Societies*, ed. Goodman and Tuck, pp. 115–16).

the encounter as primarily a Douglas/Percy affair. Dunbar's prominent involvement fits well with other contemporary evidence.[17]

On the whole, however, reconstruction of events is not the area in which the greatest historical value of Hardyng's *Chronicle* can be found. The very topics to which the chronicler might bring new material – Anglo-Scottish relations and the activities of northern lords – are the subjects about which he was most partial. More productive as an area of enquiry might be the mentalities that Hardyng's work reveals, and it is to this topic that the remainder of the essay will be addressed. In this regard, we might even be able to turn some of Hardyng's flaws to our advantage, because the issues he felt moved to distort and misrepresent were presumably of importance to him.

One source of much comment in the two versions of Hardyng's *Chronicle* is war. The writer, as we have seen, was a military man for much of his life, engaging even in the dark arts of espionage, possibly on a number of occasions.[18] With his track record of military service on the borders, but also in the French wars of Henry V, we have a rarity among chronicle writers, someone well placed to give a sense of the nature of war and of the mentalities and attitudes of warriors, in his own time. One element of the contemporary military mindset was the bundle of ideas we term 'chivalry'. Seeking this concept in Hardyng's work, we certainly find that his chronicle is suffused with enthusiasm for war, a predilection central to the chivalric ethos. Key chivalric virtues, meanwhile, make an appearance in Hardyng's writing. These seem most obvious in the chronicler's lengthy account at the end of the Lansdowne text of the qualities of his lord of long standing, Sir Robert Umfraville.[19] Hardyng's vision of the ideal knight is presented, brave and wise in war, generous and loyal to his followers, a lover of justice and protector of the common good. Of these virtues, it is perhaps loyalty that emerges most strongly from Hardyng's account, and this is a trait the chronicler himself demonstrates in devoting so much space, in the first version in particular, to praise of Umfraville. Hardyng reaches sentimental heights in his remembrance of this chivalric paragon: 'My herte with hym shalbe bothe day and nyght.'[20]

To a practical military figure, traits such as courage and loyalty had an obvious functional value. We might expect less enthusiasm, from one who had deep personal experience of war, for what are regarded as the trappings rather than the core virtues of chivalry. It has recently been noted, for instance, that Sir Thomas Gray of Heaton, a fourteenth-century chronicler who, like Hardyng, had military experience on the Anglo-Scottish border, had little time for the frivolity of the conventional tournament.[21] Hardyng does not share this prejudice. He mentions tournaments with approval where they reflect the glory of English kings or cast a flattering light on his favoured protagonists.[22] Still, such occasions are by no means the chronicler's main

---

[17] BL, MS Lansdowne 204, fo. 198r–v; *Chronicle of John Hardyng*, pp. 342–3; A.J. Macdonald, *Border Bloodshed: Scotland and England at War, 1369–1403* (East Linton, 2000), pp. 104–9.

[18] For the possibility of Hardyng making other spying expeditions to Scotland after his lengthy trip there between 1418 and 1421, see Kingsford, 'First Version', 463–5.

[19] BL, MS Lansdowne 204, fols. 220r–221v; printed in Kingsford, 'Extracts', 746–8.

[20] BL, MS Lansdowne 204, fo. 220v.

[21] A. King, 'A Helm with a Crest of Gold: The Order of Chivalry in Thomas Gray's *Scalacronica*', in *Fourteenth Century England I*, ed. N. Saul (Woodbridge, 2000), p. 26.

[22] BL, MS Lansdowne 204, fols. 176r–v, 213v.

concern and seem to bear little relevance to the realities of war in the north. Similar trends in Hardyng's work appear evident with regard to courtly love. This finds a place in, for instance, the Arthurian section of the chronicle. When dealing with warfare in his own time, however, courtly love has little importance. At the same time, it is not treated with the ironic disdain recently imputed to Sir Thomas Gray.[23]

Above all, Hardyng comes over as a realist in his attitude towards warfare. One indication of this is in the material he provided to facilitate an English conquest of Scotland. He went to the trouble of providing maps, itineraries and practical information on how Scotland might be 'hostayed and distroyed': information was provided on the strength of towns and castles, on river crossings, forage for horses and harbours suitable for supporting fleets.[24] Hardyng's pragmatic view of warfare is evident in other sections of the chronicle. He makes the suggestion that disturbers of the peace should be shipped overseas and used as soldiers in France, a technique that the English crown had already found useful.[25] Hardyng also delights in the artifices and stratagems of war. Descriptions are offered, for instance, of the use of fire-ships by Sir Robert Umfraville on seaborne raids against the Scots. Methods of taking castles are also commended, even when the castle was Edinburgh and the captor the Scottish king, Robert I. This exploit is treated as a positive exemplar for the youthful student of war. Hardyng is fascinated by the guerilla tactics adopted by Scottish leaders at this time, in particular Robert I. He provides vivid descriptions of the effectiveness of the Scottish way of war.[26]

War is, of course, a nasty business and Hardyng does not flinch from this fact. He is certainly an advocate of war cruel and sharp. The chronicler gives, for instance, a graphic description of the Scottish campaign of Edward Balliol and Edward III in 1335: he describes the burning of buildings and crops, and the killing of anyone who came into the path of the invaders.[27] Atrocities in the *Chronicle* are often recounted with deadpan indifference. Edward I's massacre of the citizens of Berwick in 1296 is justified by, among other things, the abusive songs directed by the Scots at the English king. Usually, however, no excuse is needed for the violence intrinsic to war. Even the Scots are not condemned for their periodic devastations of northern England. War is about destruction, and no lament for its prevalence is offered.[28] War is also a process of material enrichment and in this sphere Hardyng's approach is again that of a military realist. Among the reasons offered for praise of Sir Robert Umfraville is his acquisition of prisoners and booty on raids in Scotland. We are told that Umfraville earned the sobriquet 'Robyne Mendmarket', an indication that in

---

[23] L.D. Benson, *Malory's Morte Darthur* (Cambridge, Mass., 1976), p. 160; King, 'Helm with a Crest of Gold', pp. 28–30.

[24] BL, MS Lansdowne 204, fols. 223r–226r; *Chronicle of John Hardyng*, pp. 414–20. Hardyng has recently been described as producing a 'grotesque tour guide' on how to conquer Scotland: D. Wallace, *Cambridge History of Medieval English Literature* (Cambridge, 1999), p. 280. Reproductions of Hardyng's maps can be found in P.D.A. Harvey, *Medieval Maps* (London, 1991), p. 70 (part of the Lansdowne map), and *Facsimiles of the National Manuscripts of Scotland* (3 vols., London, 1867–71), II, plates LXVIII–LXX.

[25] Kingsford, 'First Version', 473; M. Prestwich, *Armies and Warfare in the Middle Ages: The English Experience* (London, 1996), p. 126.

[26] BL, MS Lansdowne 204, fols. 208r–v, 180v, 177r–v.

[27] BL, MS Lansdowne 204, fo. 189r.

[28] BL, MS Lansdowne 204, fols. 171v, 179v, 181r.

Hardyng's view at least wider economic benefits could accrue from the spoils of successful campaigns.[29]

Perhaps the old, hard-bitten soldier's approach to war is best captured in his account of the battle of Baugé (1421) in the first version of his *Chronicle*. Hardyng describes an English force under the duke of Clarence advancing impetuously to defeat at the hands of a larger Franco-Scottish army.[30] His interest in Baugé, and the reason that he seems to have a well-informed account, is due to the presence there of prominent northerners, in particular, Sir Gilbert Umfraville, nephew of Hardyng's own long-term lord. In the chronicler's account Clarence is depicted as being rash in insisting on an immediate advance against the enemy with a limited number of troops. Hardyng the military pragmatist is critical of this decision, and the battle-hardened northerners present in the English force attempt to advocate a more cautious approach. Yet when Clarence accuses them of fearing to engage the enemy their honour is threatened, and so they all advance together to defeat. Hardyng makes it clear that the advance is military folly – but with the core chivalric value of honour at stake, he also accepts that the northerners had to accompany Clarence to their death. The folly of Umfraville and his fellows is acceptable because they acted to preserve their honour. The final twist to the tale offered by Hardyng is that the English were lured to defeat by superior enemy espionage. Clarence met his death 'By counsayll of Andrewe fals Lumbarde/That was his spy bytrayed hym thiderwarde'.[31] War is a serious business to Hardyng; but while he was acutely aware of (and indeed seems to have relished) the grim reality of conflict, he was able to reconcile this side of war with some of the trademark elements of the common chivalric code of the warrior classes.

Linked to Hardyng's approach to war is his attitude towards his favoured enemy, the Scots. In some ways this is a very straightforward topic to consider. He displays a heartfelt hatred of them, one obvious manifestation of which is expressed in terms of the human failings of the Scots: they are full of treachery and deceit. The chronicler goes further than this, however, in linking them to the demonic imagery of Pluto, king of Hell. The sea must mourn, because its fate is to touch the Scottish shore.[32] Back in the real world, Hardyng took an earthy joy in the price that Archibald, fourth earl of Douglas, was forced to pay for his capture at the battle of Shrewsbury in 1403: 'He loste one of his stones for his raunson.'[33] Hardyng is not alone, of course, as a northerner holding hostile attitudes to the Scots. A similar intensity of feeling can be found in other writings emanating from the north of England, by the likes of Laurence Minot and the Lanercost chronicler in the fourteenth century. In the sixteenth century, in regions safe from the reach of Scottish raiding, there were still anti-Scottish poetical

---

[29] *Chronicle of John Hardyng*, pp. 366–7.
[30] BL, MS Lansdowne 204, fo. 214r–v. There is a shorter account of the battle in *Chronicle of John Hardyng*, pp. 384–5, and a prose version of this in *English Historical Documents IV, 1327–1485*, ed. A.R. Myers (London, 1969), p. 230.
[31] BL, MS Lansdowne 204, fo. 214r.
[32] *Chronicle of John Hardyng*, pp. 419–20; C. Peterson, 'John Harding and Geoffrey of Monmouth: Two Unrecorded Poems and a Manuscript', *N&Q* 225 (1980), 202–4.
[33] *Chronicle of John Hardyng*, p. 381. Hardyng is referring to Douglas losing a testicle in this encounter: cf. Walter Bower, *Scotichronicon VIII*, ed. D.E.R. Watt (Aberdeen, 1987), pp. 58–9. He shows little sympathy, especially since Hardyng, in Henry Percy's service, fought on the same side as Douglas at Shrewsbury.

traditions. It has recently been suggested that even in the civil wars of the seventeenth century loyalties in northern England were partly shaped by continued animosity to the traditional enemy, the Scots.[34]

Not all northern writing, though, expressed hatred towards the Scots. In his chronicle Sir Thomas Gray of Heaton evinced no particular hostility towards the Scottish enemy. Indeed, there is even a hint of respect for the Scots explicable by cross-border ties stretching back to the pre-war period and a shared set of martial and aristocratic values.[35] An attempt to find echoes of this sort of tolerance will make only meagre progress in an examination of Hardyng's writing. There is evidence of admiration for particular Scottish figures based on appreciation of their skills in war. This is the case for William Wallace, Robert I, Sir James Douglas and even David II, who fought 'full lyke he was a man' before being captured at Neville's Cross in 1346.[36] In the end, though, there is more than a hint of unsavoury pleasure displayed in the *Chronicle* at the grizzly execution of Wallace and the foul death by leprosy of Robert I.[37] George Dunbar, earl of March is also briefly praised for 'manfully' guarding the captive Henry Percy from Scots who sought to avenge the death of James, earl of Douglas in the battle of Otterburn. Yet the moral being drawn seems to reflect more on the viciousness (and cowardice) of the murderous Scots who tried to kill Percy than the admirable qualities of his guardian.[38] Whenever Hardyng dwells on the nature of Scots in general his verdicts are condemnatory.

From the evidence of his writing it is ultimately easy to agree with the verdict that Hardyng genuinely hated the Scots.[39] At the same time, he had an abiding interest in them. His maps and itineraries, as well as comments in the *Chronicle*, clearly show that he had carefully acquired information relating to Scotland. His accurate observation on the Scottish coinage, which Hardyng typically presents as providing further proof of subservience to England, has attracted comment. He also suggested that Scottish kings were set 'brechelesse' on the Scone inauguration stone, another antiquarian observation.[40] For the time, Hardyng had an advanced grasp of the geography of Scotland, and he also knew something about its people. To the chronicler, there was no doubt that Scotland was a land divided between the wild inhabitants of the highlands and the more docile lowlanders. He could also conceive of the Isles as a separate entity from the Scottish kingdom proper.[41] None of this interest in Scotland detracts from the hostility at the heart of Hardyng's conception of the Scots. The evidence of the chronicler's anti-Scottish sentiments points to a hardening of attitudes in the hundred years since Gray's *Scalacronica* was written. Equally, Hardyng's

---

34 J. Barnie, *War in Medieval English Society: Social Values in the Hundred Years War, 1337–99* (Ithaca, N.Y., 1974), pp. 49–52; D.A. Lawton, '*Scottish Field*: Alliterative Verse and Stanley Encomium in the Percy Folio', *Leeds Studies in English*, new ser. 10 (1978), 42–57; T. Thornton, ' "The Enemy or Stranger, that shall Invade their Countrey": Identity and Community in the English North', in *War: Identities in Conflict*, ed. B. Taithe and T. Thornton (Stroud, 1998), pp. 57–70.
35 A. King, 'Englishmen, Scots and Marchers: National and Local Identities in Thomas Gray's *Scalacronica*', *NH* 36 (2000), 219–20.
36 *Chronicle of John Hardyng*, p. 328.
37 BL, MS Lansdowne 204, fols. 175r, 177v, 186r.
38 BL, MS Lansdowne 204, fo. 198v.
39 Gransden, *Historical Writing II*, p. 287.
40 A. Gransden, 'Antiquarian Studies in Fifteenth-Century England' in idem, *Legends, Traditions and History in Medieval England* (London, 1992), p. 323; *Chronicle of John Hardyng*, p. 87.
41 BL, MS Lansdowne 204, fols. 188v, 189r.

Chronicle strongly suggests that we should not unquestioningly accept that the inhabitants of the fifteenth-century Anglo-Scottish borderlands readily developed cross-national sympathies based on cultural similarities.

Alongside his hatred of the Scots, Hardyng had a very firm idea of the relationship which ought to exist between the Scottish and English crowns. Such was his keen interest in this regard that the chronicler has been regularly depicted as obsessive about the topic.[42] The rationale of his writing was, of course, to provide proof that the Scots were historically and of right subject to the English crown. In tiresome detail Hardyng listed real and (mostly) imagined submissions of kings of Scots to their English counterparts. He also reiterated and altered the *Brut* origin legend to counter the Scots' own version of the British past, promulgated with increasing vigour in the course of the fourteenth century.[43] This historical battle was a serious matter to Hardyng. Scota, supposed daughter of Pharoah, whom the Scots claimed as the progenitor of their nation, was presented as a bastard by the chronicler. This was far from an aimless effort to further denigrate the Scots: it was central to Hardyng's purpose to refute the Scottish version of history in every way that he could. Perhaps more gratuitous was his dismissal of Perth, or St Johnston: 'Seynt Jonstoun hight I wote nought for whose sake/For Seynt John thare dyd never yit slepe ne wake'.[44] Even at the seemingly trivial level of the naming of a town, the Scots were to be accorded no divine blessing. One exception to this in the *Chronicle* comes in the person of St Margaret, who is, to Hardyng, a rightly venerated queen of Scots. Tellingly, though, St Margaret had been a devotee of St Cuthbert and a benefactress of Durham.[45]

The logical practical outcome of Hardyng's image of the historical relationship between the two realms was the subjection of Scotland to England, and the chronicler was forcefully insistent that this should and would come to pass. His commitment to this vision is such that his military realism seems to be abandoned when advocating strategy towards the Scots. The chronicler's initial estimate was that three years of military action would suffice to restrain the Scottish 'rebellion'. In the first version's itinerary for the conquest of Scotland an even more optimistic one year is suggested.[46] Such optimism is sustained by two techniques. One is simply to ignore the logistical problems facing the prospective invader. So Hardyng does not mention Pease Dean, a major topographical challenge for an invading army, and one that was surely familiar to him, in advocating a straightforward advance between Berwick and Dunbar.[47] The other technique is to discuss problems without addressing them. Just prior to his estimate of one year for the conquest of Scotland the chronicler discusses in detail the

---

[42] Kennedy, 'John Hardyng and the Holy Grail', p. 188; Kennedy, 'Chronicles and other Historical Writing', p. 2646; V.J. Scattergood, *Politics and Poetry in the Fifteenth Century* (London, 1971), p. 39.

[43] Kennedy, 'John Hardyng and the Holy Grail', pp. 191–203; Riddy, 'Reading for England'; D. Broun, *The Irish Identity of the Kingdom of the Scots* (Woodbridge, 1999); S. Boardman, 'Late Medieval Scotland and the Matter of Britain', in *Scottish History: The Power of the Past*, ed. E.J. Cowan and R.J. Finlay (Edinburgh, 2002), pp. 47–72.

[44] *Chronicle of John Hardyng*, p. 86; BL, MS Lansdowne 204, fo. 172v.

[45] *Chronicle of John Hardyng*, pp. 239–40, 300; BL, MS Lansdowne 204, fo. 174v; D. Matthew, 'Durham and the Anglo-Norman World', and G.W.S. Barrow, 'The Kings of Scotland and Durham', in *Anglo-Norman Durham, 1093–1193*, ed. D. Rollason (Woodbridge, 1994), pp. 9 and 313–14 respectively.

[46] BL, MS Lansdowne 204, fols. 2v, 225v.

[47] BL, MS Lansdowne 204, fo. 223v.

difficulties of assailing Dumbarton Castle. Such is the strength of its site that, even if the walls were knocked down, the only way to force a garrison to surrender would be through hunger.[48]

This fits well with Hardyng's purpose of attempting to encourage an aggressive policy against the Scots in the hope that he would gain suitable rewards for his labours. But the first version of the *Chronicle* was presented to Henry VI in 1457. There was no prospect of launching either a one- or three-year attempt to subdue the Scots in the light of the state of English crown finances, deep political divisions and recent comprehensive defeat in foreign war at the hands of France. The invocation to embark on a huge venture of foreign war and conquest was to a royal establishment wracked by crisis.[49] Hardyng's own chronicle in any case showed the difficulties of attempting to subjugate the Scots, particularly in his thorough illustration of the helplessness of the English military when faced with the unorthodox methods of war employed by Robert I.[50] Naivety and wishful thinking mark Hardyng's approach to the Scots as much as pragmatism informs his attitude to war. Edward I, he writes, would have been able to conquer Scotland if only he had treated the Scots as he had treated the Welsh, keeping all Scotsmen locked out of their own towns and castles between sunset and sunrise every day. There is no hint that the chronicler considered the difficult logistics that this policy would have entailed, or the differences between Wales and Scotland.[51] Even in the slanted version of the past provided by Hardyng, so evident is it that war with the Scots provided no easy answers to the Anglo-Scottish relationship that on occasion he declares that cessation of hostilities was beneficial for both sides.[52] Hardyng's strategic vision for dealing with the Scots, namely vigorous war leading to conquest, was hopelessly unrealistic. This much is unwittingly suggested by aspects of his own historical treatment of Anglo-Scottish relations, and by his detailed plans for the vanquishing of his enemies.[53]

Relations with the Scots is not the only sphere where there are evident tensions and contradictions in the historical work of John Hardyng. Similar difficulties occur in approaching the subject of the regional and national identities suggested in the *Chronicle*. One important question in this context is the tricky issue of John Hardyng's own regional origins. It has usually been assumed that he was of gentry stock from Northumberland and he has been credited with producing the 'Northumbrian version' of English history in his written work.[54] There is plenty of support for these viewpoints. Hardyng certainly produced material heavily partisan towards the north east of England and its people (notably certain aristocratic families active there). By his own account, he was recruited into the service of Sir Henry Percy at an early age. As proof of local roots we must balance against this evidence, however, the knowledge that the

---

[48] BL, MS Lansdowne 204, fo. 225r.
[49] R.A. Griffiths, *The Reign of King Henry VI* (2nd edn., Stroud, 1998), ch. 24.
[50] BL, MS Lansdowne 204, fols. 175v, 177r, 180v, 182v.
[51] BL, MS Lansdowne 204, fo. 167v.
[52] BL, MS Lansdowne 204, fols. 183r, 214v.
[53] Cf. in this context Hardyng's vastly ambitious suggestion that all of Scotland south of the Forth could be wasted without royal intervention by the two wardens launching co-ordinated invasions designed to meet up in Glasgow after ten days: BL, MS Lansdowne 204, fols. 225v–226r.
[54] A.J. Pollard, *North-Eastern England during the Wars of the Roses: Lay Society, War and Politics, 1450–1500* (Oxford, 1990), pp. 17, 207; Riddy, 'Hardyng's Chronicle and the Wars of the Roses', p. 96.

Percies were perfectly capable of recruiting retainers from well beyond Northumberland and the fact that Hardyng is a thoroughly unreliable witness. The chronicler's exact origin may well remain a mystery. We can, though, on linguistic grounds alone, suggest that the *Chronicle* was written by a northerner.[55] We should be fairly confident also that Hardyng did serve for much of his life in the Percy and Umfraville affinities successively; it is unlikely that he would have created an entirely false life to present before his intended royal patrons. His loyalty to the Percies and Umfravilles, meanwhile, seems genuine enough, especially as the recipients of his strongest praise were dead and could do him few further favours. He is also a well-informed source on northern affairs throughout the years he claims to have been in the service of these great north-eastern families. We cannot rely on the details of Hardyng's autobiographical comments, but there is surely enough evidence to be confident with their general thrust; and whatever his precise place of origin he seems to present an emotive and heartfelt attachment to beloved families and a particular location.

In trying to work out precisely to which region Hardyng expresses loyalty we must again be careful. The vocabulary the chronicler uses is varied. He clearly has an image of a territory which can be labelled the 'North'; and his vision explicitly encompasses a differentiation between this entity and the 'South'. For instance, Edward III fought in France with the aid of 'many a worthy knyght bothe of South and North'.[56] Hardyng also uses the term 'marchers' quite freely, and, while such labels are not precisely defined, there is a sense of east-coast affinity in the *Chronicle*. On occasion 'west marchers' are specified; when they are not, it is obvious that the writer's centre of gravity is located east of the Pennines.[57] This north-eastern bias is obvious in the individuals and families that Hardyng eulogises and in those that he chooses to treat with brevity. The Nevilles, so prominent on the West March, receive little detailed treatment; and when Ralph Neville, earl of Westmorland, and others took vigorous action to combat Archbishop Scrope's rebellion in 1405 they did so not of their own initiative but at the prompting of the easterner, Sir Robert Umfraville.[58] The overtly condemnatory attitude to Andrew de Harclay, earl of Carlisle, in the second version of the chronicle may in part reflect a lack of sympathy for a western figure, as well as showing revulsion at his role in the demise of Thomas of Lancaster.[59] Hardyng's eastern interests and enthusiasms are also evident in occasional details. He is at pains to mention the lavish Christmas entertainments of Edward I at Newcastle in 1292, an event hardly central to the broad sweep of his narrative; and he is happy to equate the pre-Arthurian castle of Ebranke with the familiar Bamburgh.[60]

If we can confidently assert that the regional identity expressed by Hardyng's historical work is a north-eastern one, we can be even more certain that this identity has military prowess at its core. Individuals from the chronicler's favoured families are singled out for their military exploits. In his discussion of late thirteenth- and early fourteenth-century Anglo-Scottish relations, the martial skills and administrative and

---

[55] C.J. Grindley, 'An early paper copy of Hardyng's *Chronicle*', *N&Q* 242 (1997), 24–6.
[56] BL, MS Lansdowne 204, fols. 202r, 203v; *Chronicle of John Hardyng*, p. 324.
[57] BL, MS Lansdowne 204, fols. 177r, 179v.
[58] BL, MS Lansdowne 204, fo. 206v.
[59] *Chronicle of John Hardyng*, pp. 311–12; BL, MS Lansdowne 204, fo. 181v.
[60] BL, MS Lansdowne 204, fo. 169v; Field, 'Malory's Minor Sources', 108.

military prominence of Gilbert Umfraville, earl of Angus, and his son, Robert, are mentioned at every opportunity. Hardyng's lord, the Sir Robert Umfraville active a century later, is praised for his knightly qualities in exhaustive detail.[61] It is not just the prominent aristocrats who are guardians of the north east's reputation in this regard. Credit is given to the great lords for victory over the Scots at Neville's Cross in 1346, but also to 'sherefes with the shyres/With gentylls hole and all the yomanry'.[62] It is 'all the floure of northerne chyvalry' that sends James I of Scotland fleeing from before the walls of Roxburgh in 1436; and in the aftermath of the failed Scottish assaults on Roxburgh and Berwick two decades earlier south-eastern Scotland was terrorised by forces gathered from Northumberland and Durham, with no outside help required.[63]

Martial prowess, especially against the Scots, is, then, a key component of the local identity articulated in Hardyng's *Chronicle*. It has long been accepted that the 'North' was far from being an homogenous unit and that identities, like social and economic patterns, varied greatly in different parts of the region.[64] In the value he attaches to bravery against the Scots, moreover, Hardyng was also expressing a fairly widespread northern sentiment, which can be seen in counties such as Cheshire and Yorkshire that had only experienced Scottish inroads by land in the early fourteenth century if at all.[65] Echoes of Hardyngesque pride in military activity are evident in the depositions submitted during the Scrope-Grosvenor armorial dispute, where northern nobility and gentry detailed their experience in arms. It is also clear in the proud family tradition, maintained as late as 1567, that a member of the Swinburnes of Edlingham died bearing the standard of Richard III at Bosworth in 1485.[66] The fifth earl of Northumberland's ownership of a manuscript of Hardyng's *Chronicle* may suggest approval of the celebration of war to be found in its pages.[67] Yet if the chronicler's sentiments fit with those of a wider community of northerners, his militant attitude to war and the Scots is much more extreme than most. At their most forceful, Hardyng's views on the value of military prowess perhaps reflect attitudes among the particular sub-group of northern society to which he belonged, career soldiers regularly engaged in combating the Scots. When the chronicler lauds 'marchers', it is invariably those who fight on the Marches against the Scots. Hardyng would surely have accepted happily into his community of warriors the twelve Gascons, 'cunnyng and able men of werre', who were defending Berwick in 1457.[68]

---

61 BL, MS Lansdowne 204, fols. 172r, 173r, 174r–v, 175v, 177v, 180r, 220r–222v; *Chronicle of John Hardyng*, pp. 301–3, 307. For the Umfraville family, see W.P. Hedley, *Northumberland Families* (2 vols., Newcastle-upon-Tyne, 1968), II, 208–15.
62 BL, MS Lansdowne 204, fols. 191v–192r. In the second version a less explicit and detailed 'all the North' is given due credit: *Chronicle of John Hardyng*, p. 328.
63 BL, MS Lansdowne 204, fo. 219v; *Chronicle of John Hardyng*, p. 382.
64 B.W. Beckinsale, 'The Characteristics of the Tudor North', *NH* 4 (1969), 79–80; Pollard, *North-Eastern England*, pp. 9–14; R.B. Dobson, 'Politics and the Church in the Fifteenth-Century North', in *The North in the Age of Richard III*, ed. A.J. Pollard (Stroud, 1996), pp. 1–3.
65 J.W. Kirby, 'A Northern Knightly Family in the Waning Middle Ages', *NH* 31 (1995), 90, 96; Thornton, 'Enemy or Stranger', p. 63.
66 *The Controversy between Sir Richard Scrope and Sir Robert Grosvenor in the Court of Chivalry*, ed. N.H. Nicolas (2 vols., London, 1832), passim.; Hedley, *Northumberland Families*, I, 115.
67 Gransden, *Historical Writing II*, p. 279.
68 PRO, E 404/71/1/59.

If martial ability was absolutely central to Hardyng's particular conception of northern identity, another important component was loyalty to the English crown. This is implicit in much of the detail on staunch northern resistance to the Scots throughout the chronicle, but is made most explicit in the ringing statement: 'doute it not, the North parte bee your trewe legemen'.[69] Instances when the north was not filled with true liegemen of the English crown had to be addressed by the chronicler, but his treatment of these occasions tends to temper evident disloyalty with assertions of the faithful behaviour of the king's true lieges. So we find that the early fourteenth-century Northumbrian rebel, Sir Gilbert de Middleton, is an accursed knight, and his rising is opposed by the wider community. Archbishop Scrope's rebellion in 1405 is not so roundly condemned, but the focus is still on the faithful Marchers who, according to Hardyng, were vital in suppressing the rising.[70] A linked conceit is that the loyalty of the North is vital to the English crown. This is a region that demands careful royal attention, and such concern will be repaid profitably with loyalty and military success. These sorts of sentiments are central to Hardyng's agenda of inspiring renewed thoughts of conquest in Scotland and gaining rewards for himself. Clearly, we cannot assume that northerners were particularly loyal to the crown in the fifteenth century; this is a component of northern identity that Hardyng is at pains to emphasise, rather than one which necessarily existed.

The issue of loyalty to the crown raises the topic of the nature of national allegiances found in Hardyng's work. In this sphere also the chronicler expounds strong beliefs. From the evidence of the *Chronicle*, Hardyng feels himself to be at once an Englishman and a borderer. This is certainly possible. Recent historical study has suggested that the imperatives of defence against the Scots could be a factor tending towards integration of the locality into the wider national unit and that the border defensive system did not work against the development of ties of loyalty to the crown.[71] Hardyng's version of Englishness is, not surprisingly, very militaristic in tone. Kings who are praised by the writer are those who showed themselves willing to fight to uphold their rights, in Scotland but also further afield. Edward I, for instance, is lauded for fierce defence of his rights and for military successes in the conquest of Wales.[72] The version of the Grail Quest presented by Hardyng in the Arthurian section of the work is not inspired by religiosity or mysticism, but serves to show the ancient use in an English context of the red cross of the warrior St George.[73] There is also a strongly imperial slant to Hardyng's attitude to his country. Obviously the English crown should rightfully rule Scotland (and indeed Wales and Ireland), but the chronicler goes much further than this. In the second version he asserts the English right to France, Castile and even Jerusalem. As with the approach to Scotland, English rights to this ambitious list of possessions can be backed up, if need be, by

---

[69] *Chronicle of John Hardyng*, p. 380.
[70] BL, MS Lansdowne 204, fols. 180r, 206v–207r. For the rebellions, see A.E. Middleton, *Sir Gilbert de Middleton* (Newcastle-upon-Tyne, 1918), and P. McNiven, 'The Betrayal of Archbishop Scrope', *BJRL* 54 (1971–2), 173–213.
[71] F. Musgrove, *The North of England: A History from Roman Times to the Present* (Oxford, 1990), pp. 121–2; A. Goodman, 'The Defence of Northumberland: A Preliminary Survey', in *Armies, Chivalry and Warfare in Medieval Britain and France*, ed. M. Strickland (Stamford, 1998), pp. 167–9, 172.
[72] BL, MS Lansdowne 204, fo. 168r.
[73] Riddy, 'Glastonbury', pp. 330–1.

falsification of the past.[74] Joseph of Arimathea's arrival in England, meanwhile, demonstrates divine approval for a blessed land; and the kings of that land can, in one manuscript, trace their holy lineage back to Adam.[75]

The identity expressed in Hardyng's *Chronicle* is, then, muscular in the extreme. He is a militant northerner who desires above all else the subjection of the Scots, and expresses strong loyalty to an English crown which should throw its weight behind this enterprise. The writer's overlapping local and national identities do not mesh seamlessly, however, and we can perceive unresolved tensions between the two foci of loyalty. Hardyng's very use of terminology can demonstrate difficulties. Describing Edward Balliol's invasion of Scotland in 1332 the chronicler notes that Edward III would not let Englishmen go on the expedition which thus consisted of only 'soudyours and marchers'.[76] This suggestion that Marchers (and soldiers) should be differentiated from Englishmen is a rare instance. More serious questions are raised by Hardyng's dealings with evidence of northern disloyalty, even open rebellion. We have seen that his tendency is to downplay the seriousness of such incidents and instead to assert the fidelity of the Marchers. When this proves more than usually difficult, for instance when the widespread adherence of men of Tynedale to Robert I is noted, the authorial voice is awkwardly silent.[77] Sir Gilbert de Middleton's behaviour, meanwhile, is an aberration. Hardyng's writing conveys a sense of protesting too much about northern loyalty. A telling contrast can be made here with Sir Thomas Gray's fourteenth-century chronicle. Dealing with the same incident, he noted that all of Northumberland joined Middleton in his rebellion.[78] There is no need for a whitewash. Could this reflect a writer more at ease in his identity as both a northerner and an Englishman, and one who had much less reason to feel that the affairs of the north (he was active in the reign of Edward III) had been neglected by the royal administration of his time?[79]

Given the family's sequence of rebellions against the crown, it is regarding the Percies that some of the more obvious tensions and contradictions in Hardyng's work occur. Dealing with the 1403 Percy rebellion in the first version there is, by this author's normal standards, an unfamiliar lack of strong judgement. Henry VI, to whom the work was intended, no doubt did not want to hear that the rebels who came closest to ending his grandfather's hold on power were fighting in a just cause.[80] For Yorkist patrons this was no longer a problem, and the second version treats the reader to an extended and fanciful justification of the Percies' activities and a condemnation of Henry IV.[81] Here the illusion of complementary loyalties begins to slip. There is scarcely any doubt that the old man writing his chronicle, like the youth who fought

---

74 *Chronicle of John Hardyng*, pp. 20–1; A. Goodman and D. Morgan, 'The Yorkist Claim to the Throne of Castile', *JMH* 11 (1985), 64–5.
75 Riddy, 'Glastonbury'; Riddy, 'Hardyng's Chronicle and the Wars of the Roses', p. 103.
76 BL, MS Lansdowne 204, fo. 187r.
77 *Chronicle of John Hardyng*, p. 308.
78 *Scalacronica, by Sir Thomas Gray of Heton, Knight*, ed. J. Stevenson (Edinburgh, 1836), pp. 144–5.
79 For the ease with which Gray was able to reconcile a Northumbrian identity alongside an English one, see King, 'Englishmen, Scots and Marchers'.
80 BL, MS Lansdowne 204, fo. 206r.
81 *Chronicle of John Hardyng*, pp. 349–54. For the Percy rebellion, see Bean, 'Henry IV and the Percies', and P. McNiven, 'The Scottish Policy of the Percies and the Rebellion of 1403', *BJRL* 62 (1979–80), 498–530.

for the Percies at Shrewsbury, knew where his loyalties ultimately lay when ties of locality and lordship clashed with allegiance to the crown. Similarly, what are we to make of the famous assertion that the Percies 'have the hertes of the people by North'?[82] Unstinting devotion to the house of Percy in the early years of the fifteenth century could hardly live alongside loyalty to the crown. Those who are said to have shouted 'Henry Percy Kyng' at Shrewsbury (John Hardyng among them?) were unable to resolve their problem by making the royal line and the Percies one and the same.[83]

Despite Hardyng's strident insistence on northern loyalty, a close reading of the writer's chronicle suggests that problems of potentially conflicting local and national identities are not resolved. Undoubtedly, loyalty to the crown emerges as an important trait. But it seems to be a very conditional loyalty. It is based on the crown vigorously asserting its rights in Scotland (first and foremost) and elsewhere through war, and on the crown taking an active role of leadership in the region to channel northern prowess and pride. As Hardyng wrote, a divided and distracted English crown became less and less likely to present itself as a suitable focus for the energies of the martial community of north-eastern England. Careful attention to Hardyng's *Chronicle* seems to betray some of the problems caused by this set of circumstances; and it perhaps suggests that in the fifteenth century, no matter how much a writer like Hardyng might protest, local particularism in the north east was growing at the expense of national loyalty.[84]

---

[82] *Chronicle of John Hardyng*, p. 380. The comment is directly followed in the text by the statement that those of the north are true lieges of the crown also.

[83] 'Annales Ricardi Secundi et Henrici Quarti', in *Johannis de Trokelowe et Anon Chronica et Annales*, ed. H.T. Riley (Rolls Series, London, 1866), p. 368.

[84] A process which has been depicted as increasing during the Wars of the Roses: A. Goodman, *The Wars of the Roses: Military Activity and English Society, 1452–97* (London, 1981), pp. 225–6.

3

Remembering the Legal Past: Anglo-Scottish Border Law and Practice in the Later Middle Ages[1]

CYNTHIA J. NEVILLE

In October 1371 Henry Percy, warden of the East March, wrote to the chancellor of England requesting the arrest and detention of Sir Hugh Dacre until the latter should find surety for the sum of £100 that Percy had paid to the Scottish earl of Douglas 'to maintain the truce'.[2] In his letter Percy noted that Dacre had been condemned by 'a solemn assize of English and Scotsmen', and that his unwillingness to pay the sum posed a threat to the current truce. In the end, Percy secured a judgment permitting him to levy £100 from Dacre's estates in Lincolnshire in repayment for the monies he had disbursed.[3] The importance of this document lies not so much in its tenor – for by 1371 the Percies were already practised at petitioning the crown for the expenses they incurred as wardens – but rather in the information it provides about the existence of tribunals in the northern border lands and the means by which cross-border disputes were settled. The letter is, above all, valuable because it is one of a relatively small body of extant records relating to the workings of these courts, and of the unique resort, in the fourteenth century, to juries drawn from the English and Scottish allegiances. The use of mixed juries and, more generally, the existence of legal customs that called for the testimony of special juries, form the subject of this essay. It explores the use of these juries in the north and the jurors' appeal to custom in the thirteenth and fourteenth centuries; it argues, moreover, that these men laid claim to a 'custom' that, ironically, was itself constantly in a process of change. The essay is also firmly based on the premise that the political concerns of the English crown profoundly influenced the northerners' perceptions about border law and border custom.

For most of the thirteenth century relations between England and Scotland were cordial. There were occasional quarrels, especially with respect to the boundary between the realms. But for the most part these disputes were merely the stuff of diplomatic discussion, and the marriage in 1251 of King Alexander III with Margaret, the daughter of the English ruler Henry III, inaugurated 'a long period of peace and very good relations between the kingdoms'.[4] That harmony came to an abrupt end in

---

[1] I would like to acknowledge the financial support of the Social Sciences and Humanities Research Council of Canada in the research undertaken for this essay.
[2] PRO, SC 1/40/188.
[3] *CCR, 1369–74*, p. 338.
[4] A. Young, 'Noble Families and Political Factions in the Reign of Alexander III', in *Scotland in the*

the last decade of the century, when Edward I began a long (and ultimately fruitless) attempt to conquer Scotland. Open war erupted in 1296 and, although a treaty of 1328 eventually acknowledged the sovereignty of the smaller kingdom, hostility between the realms endured until the end of the Middle Ages, and well beyond. Among the myriad consequences of war was the elaboration of a body of law designed to deal with border-related disputes, and more particularly with offences involving subjects who were in the allegiance of two warring kings. The medieval history of border law in the frontier lands has been a difficult one for scholars to reconstruct because, unlike the common law in England, its administration generated no single or uniform body of record materials. There can be little doubt, however, that border laws and customs were shaped against the backdrop of several competing, and seldom complementary, forces. Chief among these were the efforts of the English king, Edward I, to impose procedural and substantive legal uniformity over the northernmost reaches of his kingdom and, from the 1290s, simultaneously to impose English rule over Scotland.

Recourse to panels of jurors drawn from different kingdoms was not a regular feature of English common law. The first statutory references to mixed juries occur in the 1350s, although one study has noted that these acts merely made official a practice already well established in local and royal courts, notably in cases that involved disputes between English and foreign merchants.[5] This observation is especially pertinent in the context of northern England, where by 1350 the mixed jury already enjoyed a long history. In the spring of 1245 the prior of Carham in Northumberland initiated a suit against the Scottish lord, Bernard de Howden, over some lands that each claimed as his own.[6] Although a treaty sealed between England and Scotland in 1237 had formalised an already ancient boundary between the realms along the line of the Rivers Solway and Tweed,[7] the precise course of the border line remained of pressing concern to lords whose territories lay close to, or appeared to straddle, it.[8] In 1245 the litigants sought to clarify the location of the 'true and ancient marches' between the realms, but it is clear that the matter involved more than a mere squabble over the boundaries between two relatively minor estates. Professor Barrow has convincingly argued that Henry III and Alexander II were both experienced enough as rulers to know that the March lands represented much more than a vaguely defined region 'where the English and Scottish kingdoms as it were shaded off into each other'.[9] Underlying the controversy of 1245, in fact, were fundamental questions about which of the kings ought to exercise lawful jurisdiction in the determination of border-related disputes. Anxious to claim cognisance of such matters, in October 1245 the English crown assigned the sheriff of Northumberland, Hugh de Bolbec, to oversee the settlement of the dispute. Given the nature of the enquiry, it was entirely

---

Reign of Alexander III, 1249–1286, ed. N. Reid (Edinburgh, 1990), p. 17; K.J. Stringer, 'Scottish Foundations', in *Uniting the Kingdom? The Making of British History*, ed. A. Grant and K.J. Stringer (New York, 1995), pp. 85–7.

[5] M. Constable, *The Law of the Other: The Mixed Jury and Changing Concepts of Citizenship, Law, and Knowledge* (Chicago, 1993), p. 96.

[6] *CCR, 1204–24*, p. 496, misdated here to 1222.

[7] *Anglo-Scottish Relations 1174–1328: Some Selected Documents*, ed. E.L.G. Stones (Oxford, 1965), pp. 38–53.

[8] G.W.S. Barrow, 'The Anglo-Scottish Border', in idem, *The Kingdom of the Scots* (London, 1973), pp. 139–61.

[9] Ibid., p. 140.

appropriate that he should have assembled a mixed jury of English and Scottish knights to participate in the deliberations. Six men from each of the realms duly met near Carham at Reddenburn, a traditional meeting place along the River Tweed. According to Bolbec, divided opinions about the location of the disputed estates quickly generated bitter quarrelling among the jurors. The Scots, he reported, 'entirely disagreed with . . . and contradicted' their English fellows, and no consensus could be achieved. The following year a second attempt to revisit the competing claims of Carham Priory and Bernard de Howden proved equally problematic: although a panel of twelve English jurors provided a detailed statement about the boundaries that divided one property from the other, the dispute remained unresolved.[10]

By 1246, however, the quarrel between two relatively minor landholders had developed into a much larger question concerning the customs that governed the adjudication of cases arising in the Marches of either realm. In 1248 the grievance of another Scottish border lord provided fresh impetus for a renewed attempt to settle competing jurisdictional claims, and moved Alexander II to complain that 'the laws and customs of the marches of the kingdoms hitherto used in the time of their predecessors, kings of England and Scotland, were now less well observed'.[11] The matter at issue this time was the unlawful appeal of larceny and the wrongful treatment of the suspect, the Scotsman Nicholas de Soules. Alexander's ire did not represent mere posturing. At stake here was the Scottish crown's legal right to take cognisance of cases of felony in a Marcher region that had only recently been ceded formally by treaty to Scotland, but which customary practice had also long designated as the appropriate venue for the resolution of cross-border disputes.[12] On this occasion, Henry III acknowledged the strength of King Alexander's recollection of March custom when he ordered six of his northern knights to travel to the banks of the River Tweed, there to assemble with an equal number of Scottish recognitors 'for the purpose of correcting offences against the said march laws and customs'. This time there was unanimous agreement among the jurors that Soules had been unlawfully treated in that he had been summoned to England to appear before English common law justices alone. According to all twelve seniors 'no one residing in England who commits an offence in Scotland, or residing in Scotland who commits an offence in England, ought to be impleaded other than at the march'. While questions arising from the precise location of the boundary line between the realms would continue to trouble relations between the kings for many years still to come, as early as 1248 there was agreement that, in matters of felony at least, the border lands were the proper venue for the adjudication of disputes and, more important, that such cases fell clearly within the purview of ancient customs and procedures peculiar to the Marches.

Alexander II appears to have followed up this victory – and victory it surely was for the smaller kingdom – with a request for a further meeting of Scottish and English representatives. The intention this time was nothing less than a formal codification of the procedures that had been the subject of such scrutiny in the cases involving

---

[10] PRO, C 47/22/12 (4).
[11] PRO, C 145/3 (15), transcribed in *CDS*, I, 559–60, with an English translation in *CIM*, I, no. 71.
[12] C.J. Neville, 'Scottish Influences on the Medieval Laws of the Anglo-Scottish Marches', *SHR* 81 (2002), 164–5.

Howden and Soules. A large panel of twenty-four jurors, twelve from each kingdom, assembled anew in the spring of 1249; some brought with them experience of serving as recognitors in the disputes of the preceding years.[13] Here they achieved the formulation of a code of law that, in systematic fashion, purported to recall ancient usage in the March lands of either realm in the matter of cross-border disputes.[14] The antiquity of the practices that the jurors identified in 1249 as customary, once a matter of some dispute, has now been widely accepted.[15] Of particular significance was the place that the laws accorded to local knights drawn from either side of the border, and despite its many later medieval elaborations the mixed jury remained a crucial feature of March law and its application. Henry III was certainly prepared to recognise its central role. Within months of the meeting in 1249 he issued a writ to the sheriff of Cumberland ordering him to observe local custom in the settlement of Soules's grievance, in order 'that no further complaint of failure in justice be heard'.[16]

The Scottish king's ambition to extract from the English crown formal recognition of a distinct body of March law occurred at an important period in the development of Scottish identity vis-à-vis its larger and more powerful neighbour to the south. Like other European rulers of his day Alexander II found extremely seductive the arguments of civilian scholars that defined sovereign authority above all as the power and the right to make and to change law. In the mid-thirteenth century Alexander was expending considerable energy to establish his jurisdiction over a 'kingdom of the Scots' still in a vital stage of its political and territorial formation. The elaboration of the customs which comprised the laws of the March and formal recognition of the customary practices and procedures of the border lands as a valid system of law served several important purposes. In one sense they were merely one facet of a growing awareness 'that to allow the king's subjects to be treated under the law of another kingdom would be in prejudice of royal authority and national identity'.[17] The formal redaction of border laws was also a conscious articulation of beliefs then current in Europe and the British Isles about the potency of written legal texts and a manifestation of the Scottish kingdom's claim to membership of the 'international fraternity of jurisprudence'.[18] Finally, the code drafted in 1249 neatly distinguished the customs and practices of the frontier region from those of the nascent common law

---

[13] These included the English knights Roger Fitz Ralph, Robert Malenfant, Robert de Ulster and William de Skemerston. The names of the Scottish jurors in 1245 and 1246 are not known, but Ralph de Bonkill, Robert de Bernham and Robert de Durham had represented Scotland in 1248. The sheriffs of Northumberland and Berwick had also been present at the earlier proceedings. See W.W. Scott, 'The March Laws Reconsidered', in *Medieval Scotland: Crown, Lordship and Communities*, ed. A. Grant and K.J. Stringer (Edinburgh, 1993), pp. 115–20.

[14] The most recent edition of the code is found in G. Neilson, 'The March Laws', ed. T.I. Rae, *Stair Society Miscellany I* (Stair Society, 1971), pp. 11–77.

[15] Ibid., pp. 12, 24; Barrow, 'The Anglo-Scottish Border', pp. 139–61. See also H. Summerson, 'The Early Development of the Laws of the Anglo-Scottish Marches', in *Legal History in the Making: Proceedings of the Ninth British Legal History Conference, Glasgow, 1989*, ed. W.M. Gordon and T.D. Fergus (London, 1991), pp. 29–31.

[16] *CCR, 1245–51*, p. 345.

[17] H.L. MacQueen, '*Regiam Majestatem*, Scots Law, and National Identity', *SHR* 74 (1995), 10.

[18] M.T. Clanchy, *From Memory to Written Record: England 1066–1307* (2nd edn., Oxford, 1993), p. 26. See also H. Pryce, 'The Context and Purpose of the Earliest Welsh Lawbooks', *Cambrian Medieval Celtic Studies* 39 (2000), 48; A.A.M. Duncan, *Scotland: The Making of the Kingdom* (Edinburgh, 1975), p. 541.

in Scotland, itself in a period of considerable development under Alexander II.[19] In 1249 Henry III himself offered tacit acceptance of an interpretation of the border lands as a distinct territory boasting its own customs and procedures. His recognition of the jurors' findings, however, later proved a bitter pill for his son and successor, Edward I, to swallow.

In the north, the expertise of panels of Englishmen and Scotsmen was consulted on a regular basis in the years after 1249. A border tribunal was convened in the middle years of the 1260s, when a judicial duel settled a grievance involving a tenant of the abbot of Jedburgh.[20] An English inquest of 1272 reiterated clearly the custom governing fugitive bondsmen that had been articulated in 1249.[21] A decade and a half later, the bishop of Durham complained that the Scots were encroaching into episcopal territories in Norhamshire. Scottish intransigence eventually led to a diplomatic debacle, but Edward I was nevertheless prepared to submit the matter to the arbitration of local recognitors drawn from both realms.[22] In similar fashion the revival of the old disagreement between the English priory of Carham and the Scotsman Bernard de Howden was assigned once again to the deliberations of a mixed jury.[23]

In spite of the diplomatic tensions generated by these disputes, the notion remained strong among the inhabitants of the border region that the proper venue for making enquiry into the matter of the border line and for dealing with a host of other border-related grievances was the Marches of the kingdom, and the appropriate expertise that of local men drawn from both realms. Occasionally there were complaints about long delays in obtaining justice,[24] but such grumblings were hardly exclusive to the frontier region, nor did unhappy litigants suggest that other tribunals and other legal procedures ought to govern the settlement of their disputes. Thus, a letter of Antony Bek bishop of Durham, dated March 1287, reveals that parties involved in cross-border disputes continued to convene at traditional border sites.[25] Even a complex suit involving Richard Knout, sheriff of Northumberland, who was charged with unlawfully distraining men of Scotland, was tackled initially in the Marches, and removed to Edinburgh only after the Guardians of Scotland entered the fray.[26] But there were no calls from the borderers themselves for the abolition of what was obviously tried and true custom, and in 1301 it was according to the regulations

---

[19] H.L. MacQueen, 'Expectations of the Law in Twelfth- and Thirteenth-Century Scotland', *Tijdschrift voor Rechtsgeschiedenis* 70 (2002), 286–90; W.D.H. Sellar, 'The Common Law of Scotland and the Common Law of England', in *The British Isles 1100–1300: Comparisons, Contrasts and Connections*, ed. R.R. Davies (Edinburgh, 1988), pp. 86–7; Duncan, *Making of the Kingdom*, pp. 539–41.

[20] *Rotuli Scaccarii Regum Scotorum: The Exchequer Rolls of Scotland*, ed. J. Stuart et al. (23 vols., Edinburgh, 1878–1908), I, 29. This and the cases cited immediately below are discussed in C.J. Neville, *Violence, Custom and Law: The Anglo-Scottish Border Lands in the Later Middle Ages* (Edinburgh, 1998), p. 8.

[21] PRO, C 66/90, m. 1, calendared in *CPR, 1266–72*, p. 658.

[22] PRO, SC 1/13/155; C 47/22/9 (15); SC 1/13/86; SC 1/20/148; *Foedera* (1739–45), I, ii, 160, 177; PRO, SC 1/20/154; SC 1/20/157. The dispute, however, remained unresolved in 1279.

[23] PRO, SC 8/332/15973; *CPR, 1281–92*, p. 211; PRO, C 47/22/9 (16); C 47/22/1 (3); *Rot. Parl.*, I, 47. This dispute, too, remained unresolved several years after the death of Alexander III in 1286.

[24] PRO, SC 1/7/84; SC 8/277/13807.

[25] PRO, SC 1/29/185.

[26] *CPR, 1281–92*, pp. 269, 292; PRO, C 47/22/1 (20, 21), SC 1/30/84. Most of these documents are transcribed in full in *Documents Illustrative of the History of Scotland 1286–1306*, ed. J. Stevenson (2 vols., Edinburgh, 1870), I, 35, 125–8.

peculiar to the frontier region that royal officials dealt with a band of 'notorious thieves' apprehended in Roxburgh forest.[27]

As early as the opening years of Edward I's reign, however, there is evidence of concern on the young king's part about the autonomy that his father had accorded the borderers in the settlement of their disputes, and of a wish to limit, and even to reverse, the encroachment of border legal customs on royal prerogatives. Alexander II and his successor, Alexander III, were not alone in their conviction that the authority to make law was the hallmark of a sovereign prince and that kingdoms owed a great deal of their sense of identity to the existence of distinct laws.[28] Perhaps more than any of his predecessors on the English throne Edward I, too, was animated by the allure of such ideas. For Edward, the existence of a body of law within England independent of – and in competition with – the common law represented a threat to the integrity of his sovereign powers. Already in the early 1270s the sheriff of Cumberland reported that in parts of the Marches of his county he was unable to prosecute men who colluded with the Scots in *plusiurs larcins, roberies et homicides* because the latter refused to acknowledge his jurisdiction over such offences.[29] By the end of that same decade Edward was warning the sheriff of Northumberland that the customs governing the treatment of felons who fled to Scotland must not threaten royal interests in the region.[30]

The death of King Alexander III in 1286 provided Edward I with the opportunity to address more directly the implications of his father's recognition of the special status of border law. When the Scottish king's only heir, his granddaughter Margaret, perished on a journey from Norway the Scots were thrown into confusion. The events of 1291 and 1292, which culminated in Edward's selection of John Balliol as king, are well known and need not be rehearsed here. Of real importance, however, were the advantages that the deliberations in the Great Cause presented to a king already preoccupied with the independence of his northern subjects and already inclined to view the flourishing of a distinct body of custom and law as inimical to his interests. In 1291 Edward took care to secure possession of a substantial collection of documents pertaining to earlier thirteenth-century border cases, including a copy of the codification of 1249.[31] The following year, moreover, he appears to have instructed royal justices about to embark on the northern circuit to pay particularly close attention to March-related cases the adjudication of which might represent a challenge to the authority of the common law. At sessions of the eyre convened in Carlisle the justices duly bullied local jurors into admitting that practices and procedures peculiar to border legal practice had been abolished by Edward I.[32] Likewise, at sessions held in Newcastle-upon-Tyne the justices lectured several panels of jurors about the king's status as 'lord superior of the king of Scots'.[33] Local men did not acquiesce to royal

---

[27] PRO, C 47/22/3 (63, 106).
[28] MacQueen, '*Regiam Majestatem*', 2; more generally, see S. Reynolds, *Kingdoms and Communities in Western Europe, 900–1300* (Oxford, 1984), pp. 250–3; Stringer, 'Scottish Foundations', pp. 91–2.
[29] PRO, SC 1/7 (4).
[30] PRO, SC 1/13 (156, 162).
[31] *Acts of the Parliaments of Scotland*, ed. T. Thomson and C. Innes (12 vols. in 13, Edinburgh, 1814–75), I, 109–10, 112, 114.
[32] PRO, JUST 1/137, m. 13.
[33] PRO, JUST 1/653, m. 27. The deliberations of justices and jurors at the sessions are reviewed in some detail in Neville, *Violence, Custom and Law*, pp. 10–11.

pressure without strong and vociferous objection, but, by the time the eyre justices had completed their work in the north, border laws and customs had been roundly condemned.

In the period between Edward I's triumphant march around a newly conquered Scotland in 1296 and the mid-fourteenth century the English crown came very near to accomplishing the near-total suppression of the distinct body of custom and usage that had long governed the settlement of cross-border disputes in the north. The conflict that Edward initiated in 1296 may have ended formally in 1328 with the sealing of the treaty of Edinburgh-Northampton,[34] but hostilities between England and Scotland continued with little respite until the end of the sixteenth century. Periods of open conflict, it is true, were suspended by long and frequent truces, but the accord that in the thirteenth century had permitted the flourishing of March law was never recovered. The development of the system of border law, then, cannot be separated from the background of mutual hostility against which it occurred. Attempts to deal with cross-border incidents were always undertaken in the light of current political and diplomatic concerns. At times, it was advantageous for the English crown to promote a spirit of cooperation with the enemy by encouraging the strict maintenance of the truce. Thus, in the spring of 1300 Edward I ordered the sheriffs of Lanark and Perth to observe a recent agreement concerning the release of Scottish prisoners held to ransom.[35] On other occasions, the depredations committed by Scottish offenders in the northern border shires were skilfully manipulated to further the objectives of the war. The questionable activities of Malise Earl of Strathearn in 1297, for example, provided Edward with the opportunity to forge a close link with this important Scottish magnate and later to turn him into a valuable agent of English policy within his considerable Perthshire territories.[36]

For several years after the conquest of 1296 the question of punishment for offences done by Englishmen against the Scots became to all intents and purposes a dead letter, and the crown was quite prepared to ignore cases of felony in which the injured party was a Scotsman. This was especially true of the decade immediately after 1296, that is, the last years of Edward I's reign. In the autumn of 1300, for example, the king readily pardoned two English subjects who confessed to the homicide of a Scotsman.[37] Similarly, Scottish plaintiffs found it extremely difficult to secure redress for, or resolution of, the harms they suffered at English hands. When the abbot of Jedburgh, for example, petitioned the crown for compensation after losing £100 worth of animals to a band of English thugs, he received neither satisfaction nor even an answer.[38] Edward's intention to suppress altogether the customs and practices of the March lands could not have been more evident to the borderers. His actions spoke clearly of the determination, so evident in the last years of his life, to bring his rebellious Scottish subjects to heel. Such aggression was wholly consistent

---

[34] *Anglo-Scottish Relations*, p. 339.
[35] PRO, C 47/22/5 (60), C 47/22/7 (6).
[36] C.J. Neville, 'The Political Allegiance of the Earls of Strathearn in the War of Independence', *SHR* 65 (1986), 138–43.
[37] PRO, C 81/22, no. 2162 A-E; *CPR, 1292–1301*, p. 576. The case is reviewed in Neville, *Violence, Custom and Law*, pp. 15–16.
[38] PRO, SC 8/117/4432.

with his treatment of the smaller realm as a 'kingdom in abeyance';[39] so, too, did it recall in unmistakable fashion his abolition in 1277 of Irish laws as 'detestable to God' and, in 1284, his suppression of Welsh customs that he considered inimical to 'God and justice'.[40] On his deathbed in 1307 Edward I is said to have sworn his most faithful noblemen to the obligation of carrying his bones against the enemy Scots until the last one of them had been routed.[41] Historians have long seen in the story an invention of the active imagination of the chronicler Froissart, but it speaks in telling fashion of the frustration that, even on his deathbed, the king felt at his ultimate failure to crush his foe.

Edward's demise signalled a turning point in the history of border law. The further development of the procedures and customs that governed the adjudication of cross-border offences remained fraught with difficulty in subsequent years, but it is also true that the English crown never again demonstrated Edward I's ruthlessness in attempting to exterminate border legal custom. The kings of England remained throughout the fourteenth and fifteenth centuries unhappily aware of the existence of a distinct body of law on their northern frontier and of the challenge that it represented to their sovereign authority. For many years, moreover, they refused to address the question of border law directly, and chose instead to concentrate their efforts on securing truces with the Scots intended to minimise tensions between the realms, and to delegate responsibility for maintaining the armistice to the wardens of the Marches. Just how the latter were supposed to do so in the absence of legal precedent they left unclear. Thus, the text of the truce of 1323 included the rather vague clause that 'in all things touching the law of the march, let the law be observed in all matters, as it was between the realms in times of peace',[42] and commissions appointing conservators merely directed that they 'punish' breaches of the truce without specifying the procedure for so doing.[43] Edward III's earliest pronouncements in respect of border legal custom were similarly ambivalent. Although he was prepared to see the treaty of peace of 1328 include specific provision for the use of March law in the settlement of cross-border disputes, he took care nonetheless to reserve the adjudication of contentious matters to his own royal council.[44] The resumption of open war with the Scots in 1333, moreover, enabled Edward III to adopt a more aggressive stance in the matter of March law and, although truces were sealed in 1335 and 1340, neither made any mention of border legal procedure, nor did the king appoint conservators.[45] For a generation and more thereafter the texts of Anglo-Scottish truces explicitly linked peace and security on the northern frontier, but the English crown nevertheless

---

[39] R. Nicholson, *Scotland: The Later Middle Ages* (Edinburgh, 1974), p. 51.
[40] R.R. Davies, *Domination and Conquest: The Experience of Ireland, Scotland and Wales, 1100–1300* (Cambridge, 1990), pp. 114–15, and idem, *Conquest, Coexistence and Change: Wales 1063–1415* (Oxford, 1987), p. 367; L.B. Smith, 'The Statute of Wales, 1284', *Welsh History Review* 10 (1980), 151–2; D. Walker, *Medieval Wales* (Cambridge, 1990), pp. 143–4.
[41] *Sir John Froissart's Chronicles of England, France, Spain . . . and the Adjoining Countries*, ed. and trans. T. Johnes (London, 1839), 38; M. Prestwich, *Edward I* (London, 1988), p. 557.
[42] PRO, C 47/22/13 (4), printed in *Foedera* (1739–45), II, ii, 74. See also the conditions proposed by representatives of the two realms for the truce in PRO, C 47/22/13 (3). The texts of truces sealed in 1317 and 1319 are, unfortunately, lost, but for references to these agreements, see *Foedera* (1739–45), II, ii, 108–9, and *The Chronicle of Lanercost 1272–1346*, ed. and trans. H. Maxwell (Glasgow, 1913), p. 228.
[43] *Foedera* (1739–45), II, ii, 65.
[44] PRO, C 7/12, m. 5, printed in *Anglo-Scottish Relations*, pp. 338–9.
[45] *Rot. Scot.*, I, 335; *Foedera* (1739–45), II, iv, 83–4.

remained firm in its insistence that the punishment of truce breakers must be undertaken according to the laws and customs of England.[46] As had been the case in the time of Edward I, the crown's recognition of the distinctive nature of border legal procedures would have undermined Edward III's territorial claims, secured in the course of a bitter war, to the lowland regions of Scotland. It would simultaneously have represented tacit acknowledgement of the Scottish crown's jurisdiction over the Marches, and it is worth recalling here that it was not until after the middle of the century that Edward formally abandoned his claims to southern Scotland and withdrew his support for the puppet-king Edward Balliol.[47] Political considerations, then, dictated that English rulers continue to reject the existence of a distinct border law.

And yet the 'ancient laws and customs of the marches' survived both the vagaries of war and the English crown's attempts at suppression. That they did so even in the face of official hostility on the part of the Edwardian government reflected the determination of the northerners themselves to preserve a body of law that was uniquely suited to the conditions of life in the frontier region. As noted above, the jurors assembled in 1292 in Carlisle and Newcastle submitted only reluctantly to the intimidation of royal justices. They recited in clear and unambiguous fashion some of the provisions of the agreement of 1249 and tried to insist that these customs had been observed 'of ancient times'.[48] Despite Edward I's abolition of the laws and customs of the Marches local record sources provide clear indications that the borderers continued to apply customs peculiar to the frontier region in the resolution of cross-border offences. Such evidence bears witness to the reluctance of plaintiffs and defendants alike to bow under the pressure of the royal will. At sessions of gaol delivery held in Newcastle in 1309, for example, jurors dutifully applied common law principles in convicting a thief, but took advantage of the presence of a Scottish baron to restate once again the 'custom of the said march'.[49] The following year an inquest concerning revenues pertaining to a ferry service over the River Tweed heard testimony from a mixed jury of English and Scottish recognitors.[50] Sir Andrew de Harclay, sheriff of Cumberland, and his brother John apparently continued the practice of exchanging fugitives with the Scots at a customary meeting place on the Solway Firth,[51] and Harclay's sensitivity to the peculiarities of border custom may well have added to Edward II's anger at his sheriff's actions in the border counties in the years leading up to his disgrace in the winter of 1323.[52] Despite Edward III's firm refusal to permit his wardens and conservators to apply March law, there are indications that the borderers nevertheless continued quietly to have recourse to its provisions. Thus, in 1335 the earl of Atholl demanded – and was apparently allowed – the

---

46 Neville, *Violence, Custom and Law*, pp. 29–39.
47 J. Campbell, 'England, Scotland and the Hundred Years War', in *Europe in the Late Middle Ages*, ed. J.R. Hale et al. (London, 1965), p. 201.
48 PRO, JUST 1/137, m. 13.
49 PRO, JUST 3/53/2, mm. 4/1d–4/2; Neville, *Violence, Custom and Law*, pp. 17–18.
50 PRO, C 81/293 (15737).
51 PRO, C 47/22/10 (35).
52 Harclay's fall from grace is chronicled in *The Brut or The Chronicles of England*, ed. F.W.D. Brie (2 vols., Early English Text Society, 1906–8), I, 227, and *Chronicle of Lanercost*, pp. 241–5. It is discussed in J.G. Bellamy, *The Law of Treason in England in the Later Middle Ages* (Cambridge, 1970), pp. 52–3, and J. Mason, 'Sir Andrew de Harcla, Earl of Carlisle', *Transactions of the Cumberland and Westmorland Antiquarian and Archaeological Society*, new ser. 29 (1929), 114–35.

opportunity to defend himself against charges of treason 'on the march'.[53] In 1344 an English merchant who had lost a valuable cargo to Scottish pirates successfully claimed that, 'when an offence is committed on the march between England and Scotland it must be determined before justices in the said marches, that is, before six men of England and six of Scotland, and not elsewhere'.[54]

The resilience of border custom despite royal injunctions against its application can hardly have escaped the notice of a ruler as vigilant as Edward III. This was especially the case when, as occurred in the last example cited above, litigants were prepared to challenge crown opinion in venues as close to the centre of royal government as the exchequer, or when the northerners themselves directly petitioned the king for the revival of border legal custom, as they did in 1343.[55] Edward II and his son appear, rather, to have been willing to turn a blind eye to occasional infringements of their ban on the use of customs peculiar to the March lands; the former in large part because difficulties at home kept him preoccupied with matters other than the Scottish conflict, the latter because simultaneous war against Scotland and France dictated a policy of frequent truce making in order to ensure the security of his northern front. In requiring that the texts of formal agreements remain deliberately vague on procedural and especially jurisdictional matters, both rulers for a time at least successfully maintained the illusion that border law and custom survived only in notional form and only thanks to their magnanimity. Such a fiction permitted them to sustain the long-standing claim of English sovereignty over Scottish border territories and to perpetuate the position articulated by Edward I that distinct laws and customs had no place in the legal and political landscape of the English north.

Edward III might have preserved this façade had a series of circumstances not intervened to direct his energies and attention elsewhere. One was the readiness – sometimes overt but more often than not tacit – of royal agents themselves in the frontier region, in their capacity as wardens of the Marches or conservators of the truce, to apply the unique laws and customs of the border lands to the resolution of particularly intractable cases. Another was the shift in the conduct of the English war in the French theatre after 1346.

In 1323 Andrew de Harclay, warden of the West March, was convicted of the treasonable offence of adhering to the king's enemies in part because he effected a truce with Robert I by which he presumed to acknowledge the sovereign authority of the Scots king.[56] The example that Edward II made of him accomplished its purpose, and thereafter his successors in the office of warden were careful to ensure that their actions in negotiating with the Scots did not exceed the limits of their commissions. But like Harclay, many of the crown's wardens shared the belief of the northerners that cross-border disputes were most appropriately settled according to traditional customs and practices, in traditional March tribunals. Thus, in 1323 Anthony de Lucy, warden of the West March, convened a court 'where all those who wished to make plaint from one side or the other' appeared,[57] and within months of the

---

[53] *Roberti de Avesbury De Gestis Mirabilibus Regis Edwardii Tertii*, ed. E.M. Thompson (Rolls Series, London, 1889), p. 302.
[54] PRO, E 13/71, mm. 41, 41d.
[55] PRO, SC 1/42 (19).
[56] See the source cited above at n. 51.
[57] PRO, SC 1/35 (165).

commencement of the truce of that year Scottish officials were once again delivering captured felons and fugitives to him.[58]

By the mid-1340s the combined pressure of local opinion and wardenial practice appears to have convinced the crown that it was no longer feasible to maintain the fiction that the laws and customs of the March had become defunct. Edward III's ambitions to dominate lowland Scotland had been steadily eroded by the determination of Scottish patriots and protracted war had exerted a heavy toll on the material lives of the northerners. Assize sessions had apparently been suspended for some years because border lords were too busy defending the region to attend them, and the justices themselves feared to travel to the northern parts. Indeed, in 1347 Edward himself ordered the indefinite cancellation of further sessions owing to the dangerous state of local conditions.[59] The capture of the Scottish king, David II, at the battle of Neville's Cross in 1346 and the intensification of war against France that same year together effected a change in royal policy. David remained a prisoner in England until 1357. In the intervening years the crown, in consultation with its wardens and conservators, began to consider how these officials might be employed in future as a permanent feature of the legal administration of the north, and how border law might be made to complement the existing machinery of the common law. The delicate matter of English sovereignty which was so closely tied to the question of jurisdiction in the March lands, need not – could not – be abandoned altogether, but in the mid-fourteenth century, with Edward's military involvement in France showing no sign of abating, it was no longer as pressing a concern as it had once been. So long as the crown officially maintained its claim to overlordship of Scotland – which it did for the rest of the medieval period – there was room for some flexibility in acknowledging the borderers' fierce loyalty to March custom in the adjudication of border offences. The treaty in which the terms of David II's release and ransom were set out, therefore, marked another watershed in the history of border law, for it incorporated the foundations of a system of rules and regulations that was to endure into the early modern period.[60] 'True and perpetual peace' between England and Scotland was not achieved until the reign of King Henry VII. But from the time of Edward III March custom played a valuable role in preventing cross-border disputes and breaches of the truce from escalating into open warfare. It became once again part of the legal and political fabric of royal administration in the north.

One of the great ironies in the long history of later medieval border law was the enduring strength of the notion that its provisions perpetuated ancient and revered custom. Respect for the alleged antiquity of specific bodies of law was hardly unique to the inhabitants of the March lands. Such beliefs characterised legal thinking throughout Europe and found an especially receptive audience among the Celtic peoples of the British Isles. By the 1350s, however, many of the 'customs' peculiar to the northern Marches had already long been forgotten. The procedures and practices of border law certainly included vestiges of the 'ancient usage and custom' that had been familiar to northerners of the mid-thirteenth century, but they had been altered

---

[58] *Foedera* (1739–45), II, ii, 100.
[59] PRO, C 46/F7, no. 20; *Rot. Scot.*, I, 695.
[60] C.J. Neville, 'Keeping the Peace on the Northern Marches in the Later Middle Ages', *EHR* 109 (1994), 7.

substantially and irrevocably by time, under the influence of English common law, and perhaps most important, as a consequence of war. Although trial by battle, for example, remained a highly popular method of proof in the border tribunals throughout the later medieval period, the *handwarsil* (wager of battle), described in the code of 1249,[61] had long fallen into desuetude. So, too, had the fine known as *manbote*, similar to the wergeld of Anglo-Saxon England.[62] The officials who presided over days of March were no longer the sheriffs of the border shires, but local noblemen, acting under commissions as conservators of the truce. The peace between the kingdoms, which had once made it possible for plaintiffs to distrain suspects on either side of the border line (the *inborch* and *utborch* of 1249),[63] had been irretrievably destroyed. From 1367, this responsibility, as well as that for making restitution, fell to the wardens within their respective kingdoms.[64] Developments in the common law further eroded the appropriateness of ancient March customs in the resolution of later medieval border problems. Competition between conservators of the truce on the one hand and justices of assize and of the peace on the other for cognisance of border-related offences became apparent as early as the 1360s and bedevilled relations between the crown's judicial agents in the north throughout the fourteenth and fifteenth centuries.[65] The increasing sophistication of legal thought that was so prominent a feature of the fourteenth century in England touched even the distinct tribunals of the March lands when in 1373 'men learned in the law', that is, the Roman civilian tradition, were instructed henceforth to join the conservators who acted as justices in the adjudication of cross-border offences,[66] and, in 1397, when provision was first made for written bills of complaint.[67]

An inquest of 1359 nevertheless makes it clear that, in some respects, past practice had not altered altogether. It revealed that border tribunals had met at Billymire and Wardlaw, where questions concerning the unlawful ransoming of two Scotsmen were adjudicated on two separate occasions by mixed juries of 'good and law worthy' Englishmen and Scotsmen.[68] The function of the special jury, moreover, recalled that of an earlier age, for its members swore on oath to the veracity of the plaintiff's claims, and the latter was still required to find guarantors to prosecute his suit. Trial by combat remained a method of proof in many border disputes, especially those involving treason.[69] But increasingly, the courts convened by the wardens became the chief venue for the adjudication of cross-border disputes and the punishment of offenders. Here, borderers recalled 'ancient usage and custom' as they had done in the thirteenth century, but custom now newly adapted to wartime conditions. Indeed,

---

[61] Neilson, 'The March Laws', p. 20.
[62] Ibid., p. 21.
[63] Ibid., p. 18.
[64] Neville, 'Keeping the Peace on the Northern Marches', 14–15.
[65] Neville, *Violence, Custom and Law*, pp. 57–61, 84–7, 114–15, 174–6; Summerson, 'Early Development', pp. 37–8.
[66] *Foedera* (1739–45), III, ii, 6.
[67] Ibid., III, iv, 136–7.
[68] PRO, C 145/178 (23), m. 2. Membrane 1 records a royal commission to Thomas de Gray and John de Coupland to make enquiry into the suit of Simon Chandy, burgess of Berwick, sued in connection with the case. The commission was issued in response to a petition by Simon, for which see PRO, SC 8/209/10443.
[69] Neville, 'Keeping the Peace on the Northern Marches', 14–15.

when in 1386 the English crown ordered restitution in the matter of unlawfully taken ransoms, 'according to the courts of arms and the customs of the said marches',[70] it made explicit the extent to which the laws of war had infiltrated and reshaped old traditions. In essence the crown had sanctioned a whole new body of March 'custom', a 'custom' only a couple of generations old. But the new practices were quickly adopted and accepted by the communities of the northern border lands. Indentures sealed in 1398 and again in 1429 set out an elaborate system for the exchange of grievances and for the payment of compensation, and these practices endured well into the sixteenth century.[71] An indenture of peace sealed at Durham in 1449 (often, although mistakenly, referred to as the 'second great code of border laws')[72] gave expression to the myriad changes that had altered procedural and substantial practices, yet both the English and the Scottish crowns undertook to observe these 'firmly and inviolably, as was done in ancient times according to custom'.[73]

Given the vigour with which rulers from Edward I's time onwards promoted the fiction that the kings of England exercised superiority over the smaller realm of Scotland, it is also rather ironic that from the mid-fourteenth century the legal procedures and especially the terminology of the border courts should have borrowed as heavily as they did from Scottish law.[74] In such varied matters as pledges, sureties, distraint, liability, and injury the laws of the March resembled much more closely the substance of the Scottish tradition than they did English common law. The terms that northern litigants used to describe actions of debt, detinue, distraint, and assythment (amercement), and a host of others, the northerners owed to the language of Scots law, a reflection not merely of the suitability of the Scots English tongue to the business of their unique courts, but also of the enduring appeal of concepts and notions which had long disappeared from England under the growing authority of the common law and the practices of its lawmen.

Edward I came close to achieving sovereign authority over the Scots kingdom and its Marches in 1296, and closer still in the years thereafter to abolishing altogether the laws and customs according to which the borderers had long resolved their disputes. It is apparent, however, that for most of the period between 1296 and 1357 the attitude of the crown contrasted sharply with that of its northern subjects. Compelled to labour under the shadow of a ferocious enemy the inhabitants of the border lands sought and found in the re-imagining of their legal past a way of obviating the difficult conditions of ongoing hostilities. Ultimately, the notion of a body of law peculiar to the frontier regions and responsive to its unusual requirements triumphed in the collective memory of the northerners and emerged fundamentally unscathed from the experience of war. It was not until the seventeenth century, when the northern counties finally ceased to be border shires, that March custom eventually withered away. And then, it was not royal interference, but rather obsolescence, that finally brought about the suppression of the 'ancient usage and custom' of the Marches.

---

[70] *Rot. Scot.*, II, 76; Summerson, 'Early Development', p. 38.
[71] *Foedera* (1739–45), III, iv, 150–1, 152–3 (1398); PRO, E 39/92/39, *Foedera* (1739–45), IV, iv, 148-9 (1429).
[72] See, for example, G.B. Douglas, *A History of the Border Counties* (Edinburgh, 1889), p. 230.
[73] *Leges Marchiarum or Border Laws*, ed. W. Nicolson (London, 1705), p. 58.
[74] This argument is developed at length in Neville, 'Scottish Influences', 161–85.

4

Scaling the Ladder: The Rise and Rise of the Grays of Heaton, c.1296–c.1415[1]

ANDY KING

In May 1297 William Wallace got his career as a Scottish patriot off to a good start by killing William de Heselrigg, the English sheriff of Lanark. One of the English casualties of this skirmish was Heselrigg's fellow Northumbrian, Thomas Gray, stripped and left for dead on the field. Fortunately, he had fallen between two burning houses, put to the flames by Wallace and his men, and the heat kept him alive through the night; in the morning, he was found by English forces, subsequently making a full recovery.[2] We know all of this, because some sixty years later, in October 1355, his son, Thomas, was ambushed and captured by the Scots. To while away the hours as he was held prisoner in Edinburgh Castle, Thomas decided to write a book of 'the chronicles of Great Britain, and the deeds of the English'. He was greatly aided in the planning of this endeavour by the classical prophetess, the Sybil, who came to him in a dream one night. Along with some supervisory guidance on its structure and source materials, she suggested a title for his work: the *Scalacronica*.[3] This was partly a witty allusion to Ranulf Higden's *Polychronicon*, one of its main sources; but the title was also a punning reference to Gray's own surname, of the sort common in medieval heraldry, for the Old French word *gree* means 'step, stair', equivalent to the Latin *scala* of the chronicle's title (which might be translated into modern English as the 'Scaling-Ladder Chronicle'). Certainly, the symbol of a ladder was used as a Gray family badge in the fifteenth century.[4] However, *gree* had the additional meaning of 'degree, station (in life)'; and in this context, a ladder is a not inappropriate symbol for the Gray family during the fourteenth century. In just four generations, the Grays rose from comparative obscurity on the Anglo-Scottish border to national prominence, with marriage links to the highest echelons of the English nobility, and a title in

---

[1] I would like to thank the members of the Medieval North-East Seminar Group at Durham for valuable comments on this paper, and Anne Curry, Andrew Ayton and Claire Etty for kindly supplying or checking various MS references. I would also like to thank Miss Etty for detailed comment.
[2] *Scalacronica, by Sir Thomas Gray of Heton, Knight*, ed. J. Stevenson (Edinburgh, 1836), pp. 123–4. A new edition and translation of the *Scalacronica* is being prepared by the current author.
[3] Ibid., pp. 2–4.
[4] See *Anglo-Norman Dictionary*, ed. W. Rothwell et al. (London, 1992), *sub verbo*. The ladder badge decorates the sumptuous tomb of Sir Ralph Gray at Chillingham, of c.1450; D. Heslop and B. Harbottle, 'Chillingham Church, Northumberland: The South Chapel and the Grey Tomb', *AA*, 5th ser. 27 (1999), 131. See also C.H. Hunter Blair, 'A Medieval Armorial Signet Ring', *AA*, 4th ser. 12 (1935), 277–9. It is, of course, possible that the ladder badge was inspired by the title of the chronicle.

English-occupied Normandy.[5] Fourteenth-century England boasts many examples of upward social mobility, such as the de la Poles, the Chaucers, the Scropes, and more pertinently (as we shall see), the Percies and the Nevilles; but the social climbing of the Grays was spectacular by any standards. So what provided the rungs for the social ladder they so successfully scaled?

Until 1296 the Grays were a family whose interests straddled the Scottish border. Thomas Gray the elder was probably the son of Thomas Hugtoun, a younger son of Sir John Gray. John held the manor of Heaton in Norhamshire, and had served across the Scottish side of the border as mayor of Berwick in 1253. And so like many cross-border families — such as the Umfraville earls of Angus, the Dunbar earls of March, the Comyns, and the Bruces — the Grays faced a thorny conflict of loyalties and interests in 1296, a conflict which was to split the family.[6] Nevertheless, Thomas Gray nailed his colours firmly to the English mast from the start, serving the crown under arms throughout his adult life, an impressive record of military service which was to set the pattern for his son and grandson after him. Just a month after his ordeal at Lanark, Gray took out letters of protection for service in the retinue of the earl Warenne, along with his fellow Northumbrian, Robert de Raymes. He served with Warenne again in 1298; and the following January he was serving in the garrison of Berwick with Robert fitz Roger, lord of Warkworth. In August 1301 he was employed in Selkirk forest with Hugh de Audley; in September 1302, he was with Patrick Dunbar, earl of March, and probably fought alongside him the following February, when the English were defeated at the night-time battle at Roslin (of which the *Scalacronica* has a fairly detailed account). In May 1303, serving with Audley again, he was captured in a Scottish night-time attack, whilst quartered comfortably — if somewhat rashly — in Melrose Abbey, in advance of the main army. However, he must have been released fairly quickly, for he served at the siege of Stirling Castle in the following spring, with Henry de Beaumont.[7] Robert Bruce's rebellion ensured continuing employment for Gray, and he was under arms throughout the Scottish wars of Edward II's unhappy reign.[8] He served as constable of the castle of Cupar, Fife;[9] and he was at Bannockburn in June 1314, where he was captured in a skirmish the day before the main battle, after a battlefield row with Henry de Beaumont. Nevertheless, his relationship with Beaumont must have been repaired by March 1317,

---

[5] The descent of the family is outlined in *A History of Northumberland* (15 vols., Newcastle-upon-Tyne, 1893–1940), XIV, facing p. 328.

[6] A. King, 'Englishmen, Scots and Marchers: National and Local Identities in Thomas Gray's *Scalacronica*', *NH* 36 (2000), 218–19. The dilemmas facing cross-border landholders in the Scottish Marches are discussed in idem, 'War, Politics and Landed Society in Northumberland, c.1296–c.1408' (unpublished Ph.D. thesis, University of Durham, 2001), pp. 1–32.

[7] *Rot. Scot.*, I, 47, 52; *Scotland in 1298: Documents Relating to the Campaign of Edward the First in that Year, and especially to the Battle of Falkirk*, ed. H. Gough (Paisley, 1888), p. 44; *CDS*, V, nos. 272, 2198; *Scalacronica*, pp. 126–7. For a fuller account of the careers of the first Thomas Gray and his son, the author of the *Scalacronica*, see A. King, 'Sir Thomas Gray's *Scalacronica*: A Medieval Chronicle and its Historical and Literary Context' (unpublished M.A. thesis, University of Durham, 1998), pp. 9–30.

[8] Gray took out letters of protection for service against the Scots in July 1306, October 1308, January and June 1310, October 1311 (serving with Henry de Beaumont), March 1312, October 1318 (with John de Mowbray), and July 1319, as well as fighting at Bannockburn, Lintalee and the siege of Norham: *CDS*, V, nos. 2621, 2744, 2756, 2921, 2932, 3180; *Rot. Scot.*, I, 58; *Calendar of Chancery Warrants, 1244–1326* (London, 1927), p. 438.

[9] *Scalacronica*, pp. 138–9.

when he accompanied him on the earl of Arundel's ineffectual incursion into Jedwood forest. Here they were ambushed by James Douglas at Lintalee, and Gray lost a horse named 'Arselli', for which he received compensation of twenty marks.[10] In October 1318 he was serving with John de Mowbray.[11] He went on to serve as constable of Norham Castle, on the banks of the Tweed, for Louis de Beaumont, bishop of Durham, the brother of Henry; he endured two lengthy sieges there, until the truce of 1323 brought a temporary halt to hostilities.[12] And Gray continued to serve into the 1330s, when the Scottish wars were re-ignited by Edward Balliol and his Disinherited followers.[13]

Gray's son, the chronicler, may have had his first taste of war with the Disinherited, on their expedition to Scotland in August 1332, which culminated in an overwhelming victory at Dupplin Moor. This was a private expedition, and there are no records to indicate who served amongst the forces of the Disinherited. However, the *Scalacronica* provides a particularly vivid account of the battle and the events leading up to it, which reads very much like an eyewitness report;[14] given the elder Gray's connections with Henry de Beaumont and David of Strathbogie, both of whom were prominent amongst the Disinherited, it is not unlikely that the younger Gray was with them on the expedition. He presumably served in Scotland alongside his father in the 1330s. Certainly, he served in Flanders, for in June 1338 Thomas Gray *le fitz* received letters of protection to accompany William de Montague (newly created earl of Salisbury) across the sea, in the service of the king; whilst there, he was recompensed for losing a horse valued at £20.[15] In 1340 he was back on the Marches, where he helped to defeat an incursion by the earls of March and Sutherland.[16] In 1345, he replaced Robert de Manners in his father's erstwhile office as constable of Norham.[17] In the same year, he took out letters of protection for the proposed expedition to Sluys, though this came to little in the event.[18] He fought at Neville's Cross, October 1346, where he captured two prominent Scots, and was among the twelve northerners who received personal letters from Edward III, thanking them for their good service.[19] And in 1355, of course, he was captured in pursuit of a Scottish raiding party, across the border at Nesbit. This by no means put an end to his military career, however, for

---

[10] Ibid., p. 143 (the *Scalacronica*'s account of Lintalee omits to mention the presence of either Gray or Beaumont); London, Society of Antiquaries, MS 120, fo. 52v; C. McNamee, *The Wars of the Bruces: Scotland, England and Ireland 1306–28* (East Linton, 1997), pp. 149–51.

[11] *CDS*, V, no. 3180. Neither of them could have envisaged that some sixty-six years later, Mowbray's great-granddaughter would marry Gray's grandson.

[12] *Scalacronica*, pp. 145–7.

[13] *CDS*, V, no. 3525; and see p. 63 below. The 'Disinherited' were a bellicose faction of English magnates who had lost lands formerly held in Scotland.

[14] *Scalacronica*, pp. 159–60.

[15] *Foedera* (1816–69), II, ii, 1048; *The Wardrobe Book of William de Norwell, 12 July 1338 to 27 May 1340*, ed. M. Lyon et al. (Brussels, 1983), p. 311. The Thomas Gray who was serving with Montague at the siege of Dunbar Castle in January 1338 was presumably the younger Gray rather than his father: PRO, E 101/35/3, m. 2d. (I owe this reference to the kindness of Andrew Ayton).

[16] *Scalacronica*, p. 299 (Leland's abstract); PRO, E 101/22/40 (calendared in *CDS*, V, no. 809); A. King, ' "Pur Salvation du Roiaume": Military Service and Obligation in Fourteenth-Century Northumberland', *Fourteenth Century England II*, ed. Chris Given-Wilson (Woodbridge, 2002), p. 25.

[17] 'Durham Records: Calendar of the Cursitor's Records: Chancery Enrolments', in *The Thirty-First Annual Report of the Deputy Keeper of the Public Records* (1870), pp. 133, 146, 147.

[18] PRO, C 76/20, mm. 8, 13 (I have Andrew Ayton to thank for this reference); *RPD*, IV, 312.

[19] *Rot. Scot.*, I, 675, 678.

he fought on Edward III's French expedition of 1359–60, garnering ample material for his chronicle the while.[20]

The military career of the third Sir Thomas Gray, born c.1359,[21] is rather more difficult to trace, as the defence of the Marches had been sub-contracted out to the wardens of the Marches by the middle of the century; but he served in the retinue of the earl of Northumberland, probably during Richard II's lacklustre Scottish expedition of 1385, and fought at Otterburn in 1388. Around April 1395, he was appointed constable of Norham Castle like his father and grandfather before him, and was on active service there in August 1400, shortly before his death, when he was sent reinforcements of fifty men-at-arms and 100 archers, to defend the castle during Henry IV's equally ineffective Scottish expedition.[22] He was also willing to engage in warfare against the Scots on his own account: in July 1386, he was prominent amongst a list of northern gentry ordered to observe the truce with Scotland; and on another occasion, he and Sir William Swinburne wrote to the Percy retainer, John de Middleham, inviting him to bring the earl of Northumberland's men on a quick *chevauchée* across the border.[23] His son and heir, the fourth Thomas Gray (born November 1384),[24] had a somewhat less impressive record, though he was serving as constable of Berwick under the earl of Northumberland in February 1405, just before the latter's rebellion; and he contracted to serve on Henry V's French expedition of 1415, with twenty-three men-at-arms and forty-eight archers – an obligation he was unable to fulfil due to the loss of his head.[25] However, the martial career of his younger brother, John, more than made up for this, as we shall see.

The Grays thus had a record of continuous military service to the crown throughout the fourteenth century (albeit their service as constables of the bishop of Durham's castle of Norham was only indirectly service to the crown), and this record goes a long way to explaining their rising social status. On a basic level, continuous military service brought the Grays into contact with many of the nobility, providing ample opportunity to acquire noble patronage. Over the course of his career, the first Thomas served with Earl Warenne, Robert fitz Roger, Hugh de Audley, the earl of

---

[20] *Foedera* (1816–69), III, i, 443.
[21] He was recorded as aged ten at his father's death in 1369: 'Durham Records: Cursitor's Records: Inquisitions Post Mortem', in *The Forty-Fifth Annual Report of the Deputy Keeper of the Public Records* (1884), pp. 201–2. His career is outlined in *The History of Parliament: The House of Commons, 1386–1421*, ed. J.S. Roskell et al. (4 vols., Stroud, 1992), III, 222–5.
[22] BL, Cotton Roll XIII.8 (and see A. Tuck, 'The Percies and the Community of Northumberland in the Later Fourteenth Century', in *War and Border Societies in the Middle Ages*, ed. A. Tuck and A. Goodman (London, 1992), p. 194 n. 41); *The Chronicle of John Hardyng*, ed. H. Ellis (London, 1812), p. 342; *Oeuvres de Froissart*, ed. Kervyn de Lettenhove (25 vols., Brussels, 1867–77), XIII, 210, 227; 'Durham Records: Calendar of the Cursitor's Records: Chancery Enrolments', in *The Thirty-Third Annual Report of the Deputy Keeper of the Public Records* (1872), pp. 62, 65; *Proceedings and Ordinances of the Privy Council of England*, ed. N.H. Nicolas (7 vols., London,1834–7), I, 125.
[23] NRO, ZSW, 1/104, printed by J.A. Tuck, 'Richard II and the Border Magnates', *NH* 3 (1968), 31; A. King, ' "They have the Hertes of the People by North": Northumberland, the Percies and Henry IV, 1399–1408', in *Henry IV: The Establishment of the Regime, 1399–1406*, ed. G. Dodd and D. Biggs (Woodbridge, 2003), p. 149. For Middleham's service to the earl, see King, ' "They have the Hertes of the People by North" ', pp. 147, 150, 152.
[24] J.C. Hodgson, 'Proofs of Age of Heirs of Estates in Northumberland', *AA*, 2nd ser., 22 (1900), 119 (note, however, that according to the inquests *post mortem* on his father, in 1401, Thomas must have been born in 1382–3: *CIPM*, XVIII, nos. 433–4).
[25] *CDS*, V, no. 932; PRO, E 404/31/356, E 101/45/5, m. 5 (my thanks to Anne Curry for the MS references).

March, Henry de Beaumont, the earl of Arundel, John de Mowbray and Henry Percy; and it was the Frenchman, Henry de Beaumont, who was to prove the most useful of these contacts. Beaumont had entered the service of Edward I in 1297, becoming a knight of the royal household at about the same time as Thomas Gray began his career in arms. He was related to Eleanor of Castile, Edward I's first wife; and his sister, Isabella, was the widow of John de Vesci, who had been one of Edward's closest associates.[26] As Vesci's widow, Isabella held part of the extensive Vesci barony of Alnwick as her dower, and the Beaumonts seem to have harboured ambitions to extend their influence within Northumberland, for, in November 1304, Isabella was appointed custodian of Bamburgh Castle. It is, therefore, hardly surprising that her brother, Henry, should have employed a Northumbrian knight such as Gray. Gray served in his retinue at the siege of Stirling Castle in the previous spring; the *Scalacronica* has a dramatic account of how, during the siege, he rescued Beaumont, who had been hooked by a Scottish engine and almost pulled across the walls. But as he dragged his lord to safety, Gray himself was hit in the head by a bolt from a springald. Not surprisingly, it was assumed that he had been killed, and so he enjoyed the unusual experience of attending his own funeral, reviving just as he was about to be buried.[27] Purely personal factors could have a profound influence on a knight's career in the service of his lord; for example, the rapid advancement of Sir Robert Holland in the service of Earl Thomas of Lancaster seems to have been largely due to the simple fact that the earl liked and trusted him.[28] Similarly, Gray now seems to have enjoyed the confidence of Henry de Beaumont, and it is not unreasonable to suppose that this stemmed at least in part from gratitude for Gray's prompt action at Stirling. A mark of this confidence was his appointment as an attorney, along with Henry himself, for Isabella de Vesci, in an inquiry taken at Perth in May 1305, concerning her rights in the barony of Crail, in Scotland.[29] More importantly, however, this connection was eventually to bring him the office of constable of Norham Castle. In September 1317 Henry and his brother Louis, bishop-elect of Durham, were kidnapped and held to ransom by the Northumbrian royal household knight, Gilbert de Middleton. This left Bishop Louis in urgent need of reliable supporters amongst the local gentry; and one of his brother's most trusted followers would have been an obvious starting point.

The Beaumonts did not, however, manage to retain the favour of Edward II throughout his reign. 1323 saw the outbreak of peace with Scotland, if only in the form of a thirteen-year truce. However, as earl of Buchan, by right of his wife, Henry de Beaumont stood to lose a great deal as the truce abrogated English claims to Scottish lands. So angered was he by this that he stormed out of a royal council meeting in May 1323. He was threatened with imprisonment, and Thomas Gray stood as mainpernor for him, along with prominent northern 'hawks' such as Henry Percy and Ralph de Neville, and William Ridel (a Norhamshire knight, and one of Gray's neighbours).[30] In September Gray witnessed Gilbert Aton's confirmation of Antony Bek's

---

[26] M. Prestwich, 'Isabella de Vescy and the Custody of Bamburgh Castle', *BIHR* 44 (1971), 148–9.
[27] *Scalacronica*, p. 127.
[28] J.R. Maddicott, 'Thomas of Lancaster and Sir Robert Holland: A Study in Noble Patronage', *EHR* 86 (1971), 449–72.
[29] *CDS*, II, no. 1670.
[30] *CCR, 1318–23*, p. 717; McNamee, *Wars of the Bruces*, pp. 236–7; N. Fryde, *The Tyranny and Fall of*

grant of Alnwick to Henry Percy, in the company of such prominent Disinherited lords as Robert de Umfraville and, of course, Percy himself.[31] Clearly, Gray's interests and associations now aligned him with this northern faction, which favoured the resumption of war with Scotland, suggesting that Gray himself considered that the war had been beneficial for him, and would continue so to be. However, his chief patron, Henry de Beaumont, was disgraced; nor was his brother, Louis, in much higher favour, lambasted by the king for his 'default, negligence and laziness' in defending his bishopric in a heavily sarcastic letter of February 1323.[32] The Beaumonts were, therefore, no longer in a position to further Gray's interests. As the constable of a strategically vital castle, aligned with the court party – albeit one whose patron was now in disgrace – Gray was sought out by the Despensers, who were anxious to ensure that such castles were kept in the hands of their own supporters. As the Despensers had secured a stranglehold on royal patronage after the battle of Boroughbridge, it is hardly surprising that, by June 1325, Gray had chosen to become a lifetime retainer of the younger Hugh; he was paid a fee of 200 marks from the king's chamber, at Hugh's instigation, 'who wished above all else that the said Sir Thomas should remain with him for the term of his life'.[33] Despite Hugh's enthusiasm, Gray clearly regarded his link with the Despensers as a marriage of convenience, and maintained his links with the Disinherited, witnessing a licence from Henry Percy for Alnwick Abbey to receive lands from Robert Soppeth, in October 1325. Certainly, if the disparaging comments of the *Scalacronica* reflect the elder Gray's opinions, he had no very high regard for his new patrons.[34] Sir John de Felton, another Northumbrian retainer of the Despensers, was an active supporter of his patrons, defending Caerphilly Castle in their interest after Edward's regime had collapsed;[35] by contrast, there is no evidence to suggest that Gray did anything whatsoever to prevent their fall from power.

Nevertheless, no matter how lukewarm his support for the Despensers, Gray could hardly have been considered entirely trustworthy by the new Mortimer regime; and when the Scots tried to take Norham Castle by stealth, on the very day of Edward III's coronation (1 February, 1327), it was Robert de Manners, described as *custos castri*,

---

Edward II 1321–6 (Cambridge, 1979), p. 159. Ridel appears with Gray as a witness to various deeds of Bishop Kellawe: *RPD*, II, 1170–1, 1178, 1179–80. The *Scalacronica* makes no reference to Beaumont's fall from favour, despite the elder Gray's personal involvement as a mainpernor for him.

[31] *The Percy Chartulary*, ed. M.T. Martin (Surtees Society 117, 1909), p. 232.

[32] *CCR, 1318–23*, p. 697.

[33] ...*qe desirast sur toute rien qe le dit monsire Thomas demorast ouesque liu a terme de vie*: Society of Antiquaries, MS 122, fo. 29; N. Saul, 'The Despensers and the Downfall of Edward II', *EHR* 99 (1984), 28–9. The chamber account refers to Gray specifically as the constable of Norham (interestingly, Gray is described as the king's constable, and not the bishop's; it would appear that Edward had tired of Louis de Beaumont's 'default, negligence and laziness', and taken Norham into royal control; Edward's not altogether happy relations with Bishop Beaumont are discussed by H. Schwyzer, 'Northern Bishops and the Anglo-Scottish War in the Reign of Edward II', in *Thirteenth Century England VII*, ed. M. Prestwich et al. (Woodbridge, 1999), pp. 252–4).

[34] *Scalacronica*, p. 150; G. Tate, *The History of the Borough, Castle and Barony of Alnwick* (2 vols., Alnwick, 1868–9), II, p. xviii. Saul's description of Gray as an 'important Despenser accomplice' ('Downfall of Edward II', 29) thus rather overstates the case.

[35] Saul, 'Downfall of Edward II', 7, 29–30; *History of Northumberland*, VII, 113; Fryde, *Tyranny and Fall*, pp. 184–5, 191. The *Scalacronica* makes no mention of Felton's defence of Caerphilly, claiming that although Despenser hoped to find help and support in Wales, this *touz ly faillerent* ('completely failed him'): *Scalacronica*, p. 151.

who beat them off.[36] Gray had obviously been removed from the post. Yet Mortimer does seem to have been anxious to buy his support. The previous December, the sheriff of York had been ordered to pay the arrears of Gray's pension of 6d. a day. The following February, within a month of the deposition, Gray's pension was confirmed by the new king and three weeks later converted to an annuity of £20, which more than doubled its value.[37] Given the threat from Scotland, Mortimer could hardly afford to alienate any of the Marcher gentry; and his efforts seem to have conciliated Gray, who did not apparently resent his dismissal. Indeed, the *Scalacronica* singles out Manners for praise, for his successful defence of Norham in 1328.[38] In fact, Gray's Despenser connections seem to have done no lasting harm to his prospects. He established new links with David of Strathbogie, the disinherited earl of Atholl, witnessing a quit-claim in favour of the earl's steward in June 1333, and receiving from him a five-year grant of Mitford Castle (or what was left of it after Gilbert de Middleton had used it as his base). Similarly, he witnessed Henry Percy's grant of the manor of Newburn to Ralph de Neville in 1332.[39]

As well as adding to Thomas Gray's social stature, these various associations with the nobility provided him with valuable patronage. He owed his constableship of Norham to his links with the Beaumonts; he was appointed constable of Somerton Castle in Lincolnshire in June 1322, apparently in association with Henry de Beaumont; and he served as Percy's deputy when the latter was appointed warden of Berwick, after the town was recaptured from the Scots in 1333.[40] Perhaps more significantly, these same links with the nobility brought Gray into contact with the king, as when he attended the coronation of Edward II, in February 1308, presumably in the retinue of Henry de Beaumont.[41] Just as Robert Holland's links with Thomas of Lancaster brought him advancement in royal service, so Gray's association with Beaumont opened up an avenue to royal patronage; thus, in 1306, in the aftermath of the collapse of Edward's settlement of Scotland, he was able to petition the king for various lands of Walter de Bickerton of Kincraig (Fife) and of Alexander Fraser, son of Andrew Fraser – though even if these petitions were actually granted, the deteriorating situation in Scotland would have rendered them of little practical worth.[42] But the exigencies of war brought Gray into personal contact with the king on his own account; in October 1306, he was employed to take some money to the royal

---

[36] *Chronicon de Lanercost*, ed. J. Stevenson (Edinburgh, 1839), pp. 258–9. This is confirmed by a deed of November 1328 concerning the manor of Murton near Norham witnessed by Robert Manners, *tunc constabulario castri de Norham*, printed in *History of Northumberland*, II, 238 n. 94.

[37] *CCR, 1323–7*, p. 627; *CPR, 1327–30*, pp. 15, 30; Fryde, *Tyranny and Fall*, p. 195. For the pension, see below at n. 45.

[38] *Scalacronica*, p. 155. Gray was himself another of the witnesses to the deed concerning Murton, along with Manners.

[39] *CPR, 1338–40*, p. 213; *CIPM*, VII, no. 677; *CPR, 1330–4*, p. 261. Almost certainly, the grant of Mitford was a lease, to finance Strathbogie's part in the 1332 expedition of the Disinherited.

[40] *CFR, 1319–27*, p. 133; *CIM, 1307–49*, no. 939; *Lanercost*, p. 275; *The Anonimalle Chronicle 1333–81*, ed. V.H. Galbraith (Manchester, 1927), p. 1 (derived from the same source as *Lanercost*); *Rot. Scot.*, I, 256.

[41] *Scalacronica*, p. 138.

[42] Maddicott, 'Thomas of Lancaster', 465–6; *Documents and Records Illustrating the History of Scotland, Preserved in the Treasury*, ed. F. Palgrave (London, 1837), pp. 303–4, 313; M. Prestwich, 'Colonial Scotland: The English in Scotland under Edward I', in *Scotland and England 1286–1815*, ed. R.A. Mason (Edinburgh, 1986), pp. 10–11.

household at Lanercost, where Edward was lying 'gravely ill'; and it was probably on this occasion that the king promised him land at 'Ughtrotherestrother'.[43] The accession of Edward II brought Gray into closer contact with the court, for Beaumont was a favourite of the new king. In October 1307 Gray was able to obtain a grant of free warren for Henry de Ilderton of Northumberland; and in December he stood as mainpernor for Christiana de Seton, who had been detained in Sixhills convent, Lincolnshire, by reason of her husband's adherence to the Scots.[44] After his release from captivity, following his capture at Bannockburn, he received ten marks as a gift from the king 'in aid of his maintenance'; he was subsequently granted a pension of 6d. a day (in February 1320), to be paid by the sheriff of York.[45] And Gray's standing as a mainpernor for Henry de Beaumont, when the latter was disgraced in 1323, is itself an indication of the extent to which he was being drawn into contact with the court.

Gray's son, the chronicler, was rather less assiduous in cultivating links with the nobility for the simple reason that he could afford to be. Although he held a considerable estate of the Percy barony of Alnwick,[46] his links with the Percy family were not close. He twice served as a warden of the March with Henry Percy, father of the first earl (in 1361 and 1368), and was a member of various crown commissions; and in January 1357, shortly after his release from captivity in Scotland, he witnessed a licence granted by Percy at Warkworth, for Robert de Hilton to build himself a mill-pond.[47] Yet this hardly constitutes evidence that he was a Percy client, as Gray had similar dealings with many other Northumbrians of considerably lower social standing. Clearly, the patronage of the Percy family was not a prerequisite for a successful military career in the East March in the mid-fourteenth century. Gray did serve with William de Montague, earl of Salisbury, in Flanders, along with John de Coupland, a figure who was later to dominate Marcher society and with whom Gray was to be closely associated. Montague had been granted the castle of Wark on Tweed in 1329 by the king, but there were rival claimants; and his recruitment of locals such as Gray and Coupland may have been an attempt to buy local support for his lordship. If so, he was evidently not very successful, for Montague was one of those whose elevation to the nobility was criticised in the *Scalacronica* as a waste of crown resources. As Gray went on to relate how, in 1340, Montague and the earl of Suffolk were captured through their own carelessness (*par lour noun avisement de un fole chevauche furent suppris devaunt Lile et prisoneris*), he seems to have been less than impressed by the *parvenu* earl with whom he served, and it is tempting to speculate that they had some sort of falling-out.[48] Anyway, since he was able to obtain

---

[43] *CDS*, V, no. 510; *Documents and Records*, p. 313. Despite the elder Gray's service in Scotland at the time, the *Scalacronica* still manages erroneously to record Edward as present in Dunfermline in 1306: *Scalacronica*, p. 132.

[44] *CChR, 1300–26*, p. 107; *CCR, 1307–13*, p. 14; *CDS*, III, no. 27.

[45] *CPR, 1317–21*, p. 28; *CCR, 1323–7*, p. 202; *History of Northumberland*, X, 346; PRO, E 403/178, m. 5. It has to be said that Gray experienced considerable difficulty in getting the sheriff of York to actually pay up: *CCR, 1318–23*, p. 452; *CCR, 1323–7*, pp. 202, 480.

[46] The manors of Doddington, Weetwood, Hawkhill, Ewart and Howick, amounting to two knights' fees: *CIPM*, XII, no. 242, pp. 228–9).

[47] *CPR, 1348–50*, pp. 317, 452; *CPR, 1361–4*, pp. 65, 291–2; *Rot. Scot.*, I, 857, 914; *Percy Chartulary*, p. 346.

[48] *Scalacronica*, pp. 167, 170. The grant of Wark to Montague (and the subsequent legal challenge) is discussed in *History of Northumberland*, XI, 39–41.

employment in royal service on his own account, following his services at the battle of Neville's Cross, Gray simply did not need the patronage of a good lord to further his career.

The estate that Gray inherited on his father's death in 1344 was by no means inconsiderable, and after the crushing defeat suffered by the Scots at Neville's Cross in 1346, the threat of Scottish raiding was greatly reduced (though not entirely removed, as he was to discover in 1355). Furthermore, with the outbreak of the French war in 1337, Edward devoted his energies to France, and encouraged his nobility to do so as well, including the northern magnates, many of whom spent much of their time in France, especially after Neville's Cross. The result was that the defence and administration of the Marches was left increasingly in the hands of the Marcher gentry.[49] In these conditions, fighting men such as Gray, and his fellow Northumbrians, the Herons, the Manners, and – especially – John de Coupland, were able to gain plentiful royal patronage so as to help build up their social standing. Their military exploits also earned them an *entrée* to royal service of a more peaceful nature. Thus, Thomas Gray received a letter of thanks from a grateful Edward III for his efforts at the battle of Neville's Cross, and was summoned to Westminster in the following January, along with fifteen other northern magnates (including all those – except the archbishop of York – who received letters of thanks for their services at Neville's Cross), to discuss the defence of the realm and Edward Balliol's proposed expedition to Scotland. A year later, in April 1348, he received his first appointment to a crown commission, to inquire into violations of the truce.[50] Others followed: in May 1349 he was appointed a commissioner to inquire into the seizure of an English ship by Scottish pirates off Holy Island; in July 1352 he was appointed to a royal commission of oyer and terminer to inquire into an assault on Thomas Hatfield, bishop of Durham, when the latter had been travelling to Berwick for negotiations concerning the release of David II; and in the following February, Gray was appointed to a similar commission to deal with an assault and maiming perpetrated in Benwell, near Newcastle-upon-Tyne. He had also acted as a justice in the bishop's court at Durham in January 1352. Nor did such duties interfere with his continuing military career; in June 1355, less than six months before he was captured fighting against the Scots, he was appointed to a commission to investigate the abduction and robbery of Isabel de Eslington at North Gosforth.[51] Other royal patronage followed: for example, after Gray's capture in October 1355, he was granted a royal licence to export 100 sacks of wool directly from Berwick (saving him the expense of carting them to Newcastle), by way of a contribution towards his ransom.[52] In October 1357 he was entrusted with the custody of the Scot, John Gray, one of the hostages for the ransom of King David. In February 1359 he was appointed to inquire into various misdoings of his fellow Northumbrian, Sir John de Clifford, the constable of Berwick. In October 1361 he

---

[49] For example, when the Scots attacked Berwick in 1355 (shortly after they ambushed Thomas Gray), its keeper, William, Lord Greystoke, was in France with Edward III, having left the town in the charge of the Northumbrian squire, Robert de Ogle: *Rot. Parl.*, III, 11.
[50] *Foedera* (1816–69), III, i, 91–2; *Rot. Scot.*, I, 679, 713–14.
[51] *Rot. Scot.*, I, 713–14; *CPR, 1348–50*, pp. 317, 452; R.W. Hodgson, 'Deeds Respecting the Manor of Offerton', *AA*, 1st ser. 2 (1832), 276; *CPR, 1350–4*, pp. 339, 446; *CPR, 1354–8*, p. 291.
[52] *Rot. Scot.*, I, 798.

gained a rather more substantial office, appointed warden of the March, along with Henry Percy, Ralph de Neville, Richard Tempest and John de Coupland.[53]

The most important facet of royal patronage in furthering the rise of the Gray family, however, was the granting of land. The English Grays, descended from a collateral branch of the family, undoubtedly owed their landed wealth to their record of continuous and loyal military service to the English crown. The first Thomas Gray may already have held some property in England at the start of his military career in 1297, for he regularly took the trouble of obtaining letters of protection, which would have been of little use to a landless man.[54] This would also help to account for his undivided loyalty to the English crown. Nevertheless, it was his record of military service that enabled him to recover the most substantial of the Gray family's English holdings, the manor of Heaton, Norhamshire, which would become the family *caput*. It had been seized by the grasping hands of Bishop Antony Bek as a forfeit of war, when Thomas's uncle, Sir Robert Gray, died in Scotland a rebel against Edward I, leaving a son, John, who was also deemed a rebel. When Bek died in March 1311, Edward II took immediate advantage of the resulting vacancy in the bishopric to reward his yeoman, Walter de Wodeham, with an hereditary grant of Heaton. On Wodeham's death, shortly thereafter, the escheator north of the Trent attempted to take the manor into the king's hand, in accordance with the resumption of recent royal grants imposed on Edward by the Lords Ordainer. By then, however, Richard Kellawe had been installed as the new bishop. Naturally, he objected strenuously to this infringement of his franchise, and he therefore allowed Thomas Gray to take seisin of the manor, who claimed right *par descente deritage*, formally quitclaiming it to him in October 1312.[55] Undoubtedly, it was largely political circumstance that occasioned Gray's recovery of Heaton, for Bishop Kellawe was primarily concerned to re-establish his bishopric's rights over the manor, and Edward would not have been unhappy to see the Ordainers circumvented. However, it was Gray's service to the crown, and doubtless also his association with the court favourite Henry de Beaumont – itself a result of his military service – that made Gray acceptable to the king, and ensured that he was able to profit from the disinheritance of his cousin John, and to recover his family's lands. And it was his continuing record of military service, along with that of his son, which ensured that they were able to fend off the persistent attempts of Walter de Wodeham's heirs to regain their lost estate.[56]

As a retainer of Henry de Beaumont, Gray was able to benefit from the forfeitures of those who had supported the rebellion of Gilbert de Middleton. Gray petitioned for, and in May 1319, received, an hereditary grant of lands in Howick, near Alnwick,

---

[53] *CDS*, III, no. 434; *CIM, 1348–77*, no. 343; *Rot. Scot.*, I, 857; J.A. Tuck, 'Northumbrian Society in the Fourteenth Century', *NH* 6 (1971), 37. John Gray was probably a relative, from the Scottish branch of the family.

[54] A. Ayton, *Knights and Warhorses: Military Service and the English Aristocracy under Edward III* (2nd edn., Woodbridge, 1999), pp. 162–3.

[55] *CFR, 1307–19*, p. 243; *CPR, 1307–13*, p. 337; *RPD*, I, 77–8, II, 1170–1; *Northumberland Petitions: Ancient Petitions Relating to Northumberland*, ed. C.M. Fraser (Surtees Society 176, 1961), pp. 23–4. The Juliana de Gray mentioned in these documents was presumably Robert's wife; for the probable relationship between Robert and Thomas Gray, see King, 'Englishmen, Scots and Marchers', 218–19.

[56] As late as 1354 Reynold son of Simon de Wodeham (presumably the grandson of Walter) quitclaimed all his rights in the manor of Heaton, suggesting that Gray's acquisition of Heaton was still being contested some forty years afterwards: *CCR, 1354–60*, p. 97.

forfeited by John Mautalent, an adherent of Walter de Selby, one of Middleton's most prominent allies.[57] This highlights the fact that while the disastrous decade after Bannockburn, when Scottish raiding was at its height, undoubtedly brought ruin to many whose lands lay in the Marches, this in itself created a supply of land for those who earned the favour of the king. This is well demonstrated by the fate of William de Beanley. He had served in the garrison of Berwick and, after its fall, had petitioned the king for relief from the rent of twelve marks he now owed to the king, following the forfeiture of Patrick Earl of March. He had also lost his horse and had been despoiled of all his goods and chattels by the Scots. Evidently, the petition fell on deaf ears, as, by 1320, he was reduced to selling off land to the former household knight, Sir John de Lilleburn. After this, he went over to the Scots, and his lands in Howick were forfeited into the king's hand; and in March 1326, Edward granted these lands to Gray for life. Thus, Beanley's loss was Gray's gain; and this windfall fell into his lap as a result of his access to the king's favour – a commodity which Beanley had been signally unable to obtain.[58] Further grants of a similar nature followed under Edward III, including the hereditary grant of a messuage in Berwick in June 1334; and another hereditary grant, the following January, of land in Nesbit, Northumberland, which had escheated to Edward II by the rebellion of John de Trollope.[59]

Gray's son, the chronicler, also benefited from the forfeitures of his fellow Northumbrians. In March 1344, 'in consideration of his good service beyond the seas as well as within', he was granted the custody of the manor of Middlemast Middleton in Coquetdale, worth ten marks *per annum*, in the king's hand because the rightful heir, William Middleton, had gone over to the Scots at the end of Edward II's reign. Within a month, the same manor had been re-granted to Gray in fee.[60] In May he was granted joint custody (with his brother-in-law, John de Eure) of Calverton Darras in Northumberland, forfeited by Robert Darreyns for debts incurred whilst he was sheriff; and in August 1345 he was granted a burgage and dovecote in Newcastle forfeited by a felon.[61] He was also granted free warren in various of his demesnes and a licence to make a park in May of that year.[62] The fact that these grants came at the same time that Gray was being recruited for the abortive expedition to Sluys surely indicates that they were intended not only to reward past service, but in earnest of that to come. Gray also managed to acquire a great deal more land by other means; exactly when and how he did so is not clear, but he certainly left a considerably larger estate than he himself inherited. The standing which this land and office brought him in Northumbrian society is demonstrated by the position of Gray's name at the head of a

---

57 *CIM, 1307–49*, nos. 366, 375; *CDS*, III, nos. 610, 635; *CPR, 1317–21*, pp. 333–4; A.E. Middleton, *Sir Gilbert de Middleton* (Newcastle-upon-Tyne, 1918), p. 93. The lands were valued at £7 10s. in time of peace, with the reversion of a further £6 worth of land, held by Mautalent's mother in dower.
58 *CPR, 1324–7*, p. 254; *CDS*, III, no. 881; *Northumberland Petitions*, pp. 165–6; H.H.E. Craster, 'Woodman Charters', *AA*, 3rd ser. 5 (1909), 48.
59 *Rot. Scot.*, I, 270; *CPR, 1334–8*, p. 62; *History of Northumberland*, XIV, 138–40. The messuage in Berwick had been forfeited by one Ralph de More, for unspecified reasons.
60 *CPR, 1343–5*, pp. 220, 252, 275; *CDS*, III, no. 1431; *CFR, 1337–47*, pp. 364–5; *CIM, 1307–49*, no. 1893; Middleton, *Gilbert de Middleton*, pp. 94–5. This grant has been assigned to Thomas Gray of Horton (*History of Northumberland*, XIV, 300); however, the grantee is refered to as *le fitz*, and as Horton died at a fair age in 1347, leaving a son called David as his heir, this identification seems unlikely.
61 *CFR, 1337–47*, p. 381; *CPR, 1343–5*, p. 537.
62 *CChR, 1341–1417*, p. 38.

list of nineteen (mostly) prominent Northumbrians who put their seals on a petition to Edward III of June 1346, on behalf of 'the whole community of the knights and sergeants of the county of Northumberland'.[63] It was probably this same Thomas Gray who chose to mark out in stone his family's increasing status by building the castle at Heaton. Unfortunately, virtually nothing remains of it, and there are no documentary references before 1415, when a survey of the castles and fortalices of Northumberland listed Heaton Castle as owned by Thomas Gray (Thomas's grandson). However, a sketch from the reign of Elizabeth shows it to have been a courtyard castle very much in the mould of Ford and Chillingham, which were licensed in 1338 and 1344 respectively; and it seems reasonable to suppose that Heaton was roughly contemporary with them.[64]

The rising status of the Grays can also be charted in their marriages. The first Thomas Gray married Agnes de Bayles, a woman of obscure family, albeit an armigerous one.[65] He was able to obtain better marriages for his children. He married his daughters to John de Eure, William de Felton, William Heron, and the Yorkshireman, Gerard Salvayn, all of them eldest sons of prominent knightly families; of these, Eure and Salvayn were minors in royal custody, and Gray owed their marriages to royal favour.[66] His eldest son, Thomas, was married to Margaret, the daughter of William de Presfen, a Northumbrian squire with a distinguished military record, including the capture of the earl of Moray in a border skirmish in 1335.[67] The children of Thomas and Margaret were able to acquire far better marital prizes. Their daughter, Elizabeth, married Philip, Lord Darcy; but their son, the third Thomas Gray, trumped that in c.1384, with his marriage to Joan, the sister of Thomas de Mowbray, recently created earl of Nottingham. The Grays owned no lands south of the Tees, and, at the time of the marriage, the earl of Nottingham had no interests in the far north; a marriage of such eminence, propelling Thomas into the social circles of the titled nobility, suggests that his family had achieved a national standing, in just three generations.

By the beginning of Richard II's reign, when the third Thomas Gray came of age, the Anglo-Scottish Marches were once again under threat from Scotland, pushing them towards the top of the crown's agenda, while the status of the Gray family was now so well-established that the third Thomas was actively sought after as a retainer by both the nobility and the crown. He received considerable royal patronage, being retained by Richard II in October 1389 at a fee of £50 a year and serving on numerous commissions. Shortly before, he had been appointed steward of the bishopric of Durham by the newly installed Bishop Walter Skirlaw. From 1397 he was a royal justice of the peace, and he served as knight of the shire for Northumberland in 1397 and 1399.[68] His standing in northern society was such that when Ralph, Lord Lumley, built his castle at Lumley in the 1390s, Gray's arms were chosen to adorn the main

---

[63] PRO, C 49/7/20 (2); King, 'War, Politics and Landed Society', pp. 242–3, 262.
[64] C. Bates, 'The Border Holds of Northumberland', *AA*, 2nd ser. 14 (1891), 14, 329; *CPR, 1338–40*, p. 114; *CPR, 1343–5*, p. 191.
[65] The *Scalacronica* describes how its author's arms were quartered with his mother's device (*signe*): *Scalacronica*, p. 1.
[66] PRO, CP 40/411, m. 218 (I would like to thank Claire Etty for kindly checking this reference); *Northumberland Petitions*, pp. 10–11.
[67] *Scalacronica*, p. 166; *Foedera* (1816–69), II, ii, 923.
[68] For details of his career, see *House of Commons*, III, 222–5.

gate, in the illustrious company of those of the earl of Northumberland, Ralph, Lord Neville, Ralph, Lord Lumley, William, Lord Hylton, and the king.[69] He was evidently on good terms with the Percies, for his son was born in 'le Midyllgathouse' of Alnwick Castle in November 1384.[70] He also remained close to his brother-in-law, serving as Mowbray's deputy when the latter was appointed warden of the East March in March 1389.[71] In October 1398, when Mowbray (recently created duke of Norfolk) went into exile following the dramatic accusation of treason levelled against him by Henry Bolingbroke, Gray was the first named of the nine-strong council licenced by the king to look after his interests in his absence – though in the event, this could not have made much demand on his time, for Mowbray died of plague in the following September, in Venice.[72] Mowbray's death did not, however, leave Gray without patrons amongst the higher nobility; in September 1398, just before Mowbray left the country, Thomas was enfeoffed with the border castle and lordship of Wark on Tweed by Ralph de Neville, Earl of Westmorland. This was probably part of the settlement accompanying the marriage of his eldest son, Thomas, to Ralph's daughter, Alice.[73] The Nevilles were, of course, the main allies of the house of Lancaster, and it is this connection which explains Gray's ability to accommodate himself to Henry Bolingbroke's coup, joining with him as soon as he landed in England, despite the fact that Bolingbroke was in large part responsible for Mowbray's ruin. In fact, Gray accommodated himself to the new regime so well that, following his election to the extraordinary parliament of September 1399 (as a knight of the shire for Northumberland), he was one of the two representatives of the knightly estate chosen to witness Richard II's renunciation of his throne.[74] Unfortunately, the Scots took advantage of his absence to sack Wark Castle and ransom his family, but this only served to underline his importance in the defence of the Marches. Naturally, he retained Henry IV's favour, expressed in an increased annuity of 100 marks; and at his premature death in November 1400, the future looked bright for his sixteen-year-old heir, Thomas.[75] However, just fifteen years later, Thomas was to put all his family's achievements in jeopardy by indulging in a wildly unrealistic and incompetent conspiracy against Henry V.

The *Gesta Henrici Quinti* described the fourth Thomas Gray as 'a knight famous and noble if only he had not been dishonoured by this stain of treason'.[76] He had initially enjoyed the good lordship of his father-in-law, the earl of Westmorland, who retained him for life in August 1404, purchasing for him the office of constable of

---

[69] A. Emery, *Greater Medieval Houses of England and Wales, 1300–1500, I: Northern England* (Cambridge, 1996), pp. 117–18.
[70] Hodgson, 'Proofs of Age of Heirs', 119; and see n. 24 above.
[71] *Rot. Scot.*, II, 96. It may be that Mowbray's links with Gray were a factor in Mowbray's appointment as warden in the first place, as he was one of the few magnates who had any connections to the Northumbrian gentry.
[72] *CPR, 1396–9*, p. 422.
[73] *CPR, 1396–9*, p. 410; *House of Commons*, III, 224.
[74] *CPR, 1399–1401*, p. 287; *Chronicles of the Revolution, 1397–1400*, ed. and trans. C. Given-Wilson (Manchester, 1993), pp. 163–5, 169, 185. The other knight was the stalwart Lancastrian, Sir Thomas Erpingham. This Neville connection was missed by King, ' "They have the Hertes of the People by North" ', p. 144.
[75] For Thomas's age, cf. n. 24 above.
[76] 'Militem famosum et nobilem si non eum hec prodicionis macula violasset': *Gesta Henrici Quinti*, ed. and transl. F. Taylor and J.S. Roskell (Oxford, 1975), p. 19.

Bamburgh Castle from the king.[77] However, he also associated himself with the earl of Northumberland, whom he was serving as constable of Berwick;[78] and by February 1405, such an association was neither compatible with a Neville connection nor, indeed, very wise. There is nothing to suggest that Gray actually joined Percy's rebellion of May 1405, but even so, he appears to have lost his father-in-law's favour, and the constableship of Bamburgh, which passed to Richard Arundel in May 1408.[79] He continued to receive crown office, being appointed to commissions of the peace in November 1405, February 1407 and May 1410, and serving as sheriff of Northumberland in November 1408; that October, he was also granted an annuity of £40 by the prince of Wales.[80] His annuity, though, soon dried up, and he seems to have faced considerable financial difficulties, perhaps related to the increasingly unsettled condition of the Marches at this time. And so while his younger brother, John, basked in the affluent glow of royal favour (as we shall see), Thomas faced outlawry for a debt of £2 to a London spur-maker.[81] He may also have resented the fact that he did not succeed his father as constable of Norham Castle, for, on the latter's death in 1400, the king had secured the appointment of the long-serving Lancastrian retainer, William de Carnaby.[82]

Nevertheless, Thomas retained sufficient of his 'fame and nobility' to enable him to marry his son, the imaginatively named Thomas (who was then only eight years old), to Isabel, the daughter of Richard of York, earl of Cambridge, in 1412. The marriage hinged around Gray's purchase of the lordship of Wark in Tynedale from the childless Edward, duke of York, Richard's elder brother, for the knockdown price of £500, payable in six annual instalments of £83 6s. 8d. As the lordship was reckoned to be worth over 200 marks *per annum* in time of peace, this was a veritable bargain, at perhaps half the customary market rate.[83] Unfortunately, however, it was a bargain apparently beyond Gray's means, and he was left in considerable financial difficulties, with little in the way of royal patronage or good lordship to compensate. In the circumstances, it is not perhaps altogether surprising that he allowed himself to be dragged into the deluded plotting of the earl of Cambridge; indeed, he himself attributed his ruin to 'poverty [and] covetousness'.[84] Yet despite his condemnation and execution for treason, the family emerged unharmed from this escapade, and his son went on to inherit an undiminished estate. This was in sharp contrast to the fate of the Scropes of Masham. Although Henry, Lord Scrope, was somewhat peripheral to Cambridge's plotting, and certainly less culpable than Gray, his entanglement led to the forfeiture of most of the family lands, which were held in fee simple. Though Scrope's heirs were eventually able to recover some (though by no means all) of these lands, they were never able to recover their former prominence, and their role in

---

[77] 'Private Indentures for Life Service in Peace and War, 1278–1476', ed. M. Jones and S. Walker, *Camden Miscellany XXXII* (Camden Society, 5th ser. 3, 1994), no. 100; *CPR, 1401–5*, p. 412.
[78] *CDS*, V, nos. 930, 932.
[79] *CPR, 1405–8*, p. 453.
[80] *CPR, 1405–8*, p. 495; *CPR, 1408–13*, p. 484; T.B. Pugh, *Henry V and the Southampton Plot of 1415* (Gloucester, 1988), p. 103.
[81] In fact, the outlawry was pardoned: *CPR, 1408–13*, p. 124 (November 1409).
[82] King, ' "They have the Hertes of the People by North" ', p. 143.
[83] Pugh, *Southampton Plot*, p. 104.
[84] Ibid., p. 161.

Yorkshire political society was severely curtailed.[85] Why did the Grays not meet a similar fate?

At the time the Southampton plot was uncovered, Henry V had already set in motion the restoration of the Percies.[86] In large part, the defence of the Anglo-Scottish Marches and the settling of cross-border disputes under March law had depended on the experience, contacts and resources of the Percy family. The problems caused by their removal, following the rebellions of 1403 and 1405, might not have been insuperable were it not for the hawkish Scottish policy espoused by Henry IV, a policy which he had neither the resources nor the inclination actually to effect. The result was an outbreak of uncontrollable cross-border raiding, accompanied by a spiralling level of internal feuding within Northumberland.[87] Henry V, determined to pursue his ambitions in France without any distraction from the Scots, hoped that the rehabilitation of the Percies would secure some measure of much-needed stability in the Marches.[88] And the same factors meant that, on the eve of his expedition to France, he was hardly in a position to further destabilise the East March by attainting one of its most important knightly families. Consequently, on 8 August, just six days after Thomas Gray was beheaded, all of his lands and properties were placed in the keeping of his brother, John, without any charge to the exchequer, during the minority of Thomas's son and heir, Thomas.[89]

As the Lancastrians lost interest in Scottish affairs, and lacked the money and inclination to maintain the March warden system at its accustomed levels, so the opportunities for advancement declined; and it is symptomatic of this that after fighting a judicial duel on the Scottish borders in June 1404,[90] John Gray went on to make his fortune fighting in Wales and France, rather than on the Scottish Marches as his forebears had done – and as his unfortunate elder brother had signally failed to do. As a king's knight, John was a recipient of Henry V's favour, having been granted an annuity of twenty marks by him as prince of Wales in 1408, for service against Owain Glyn Dwr, and another of forty marks, for good service to the king (Henry IV) and the prince of Wales in August 1409. In December 1412 he had been granted a half share in a forfeited merchant ship and cargo, valued at £135. The following September, shortly after Henry's accession to the throne, the two annuities had been amalgamated as a lifetime annuity of £40; and a couple of months later, he was granted the £110 which the alien priory of Lancaster was obliged to pay to the exchequer during the war with France.[91] The fact that John was on hand at Portchester with a retinue of nineteen men-at-arms and sixty archers,[92] ready to sail with the king to France, can only have

---

[85] Ibid., pp. 119–20, 131.
[86] Henry Percy, Hotspur's son, was allowed to petition for his restoration at the Westminster parliament of November 1414: *Rot. Parl.*, IV, 37; G.L. Harriss, 'The King and his Magnates', in *Henry V: The Practice of Kingship*, ed. G.L. Harriss (2nd edn., Stroud, 1993), p. 37.
[87] King, ' "They have the Hertes of the People by North" ', pp. 153–7.
[88] Harriss, 'The King and his Magnates', pp. 37–9.
[89] *CPR, 1413–16*, pp. 349, 359.
[90] *CPR, 1401–5*, p. 410.
[91] *CPR, 1408–13*, pp. 101, 460; *CPR, 1413–16*, pp. 100, 130. For thumbnail sketches of John Gray's career, see *CP*, VI, 136–7; Pugh, *Southampton Plot*, p. 104.
[92] PRO, E 101/45/5, m. 2d. (thanks to Anne Curry for this reference). The 'Agincourt Roll' records John Gray as serving on the campaign with a larger retinue of thirty-five men-at-arms and ninety-six archers: H. Nicolas, *History of the Battle of Agincourt* (3rd edn., London, 1833), pp. 346–7. In a personal

served to remind the king of the Gray family's exemplary record of military service, and of the advantages to the crown of allowing their landed wealth to remain intact. John went on to prove the point, with an illustrious – if somewhat brief – career in France, where he was granted the county of Tancarville, and was elected as a knight of the garter (after October 1419), before being killed at the ignominious English defeat at Baugé, in Anjou, in March 1421. As a result, although the young Thomas died in his minority, his younger brother and heir, Ralph, came into an undiminished patrimony; and even now, Ralph's continuing affluence is ostentatiously displayed by the splendid monument which his son had built for him in Chillingham Church, as 'a statement . . . of the family's importance'.[93]

It has long been recognised by modern historians that during the fourteenth century the Scottish wars created conditions that encouraged the rapid promotion of northern magnate families such as the Percies and the Nevilles;[94] but as the successful careers of successive generations of the Grays demonstrate, the same conditions applied equally further down the social scale, enabling many northern gentry families to make their political and landed fortunes. Certainly, no other Northumbrian gentry family managed to advance itself on quite the same scale; but there were some whose advancement was almost as impressive, such as the Ogles, who rose from comparative obscurity to the ranks of the parliamentary peerage in just over a century-and-a-half after 1296. Individuals such as John de Coupland and John de Strivelyn also did very nicely for themselves, while, in the West March, Andrew de Harclay's rise was even more spectacular – at least until, like Coupland, Fortune's Wheel brought him low, and he came to a grievous end.[95] Crucially, Northumbrian gentry families such as the Grays were able to make profitable military careers without ever having to leave home; even in prison in Edinburgh Castle in 1355–6, Thomas Gray was nearer to his family *caput* at Heaton than he would have been when attending to his judicial duties at Durham. And this also enabled them to combine military service to the crown with the administrative service which brought them influence within the county. The Grays also provide a nice illustration of the relatively low level of risk attendant on a military career in the fourteenth century. Four successive generations of Grays spent their adult lives under arms. Thomas Gray fought at Bannockburn in 1314; his son fought at Neville's Cross, 1346, and possibly Dupplin Moor, 1332; his grandson fought at Otterburn, 1388; his great-grandson, John Gray, fought at Agincourt, 1415; yet the only one of them to have been killed in action was John, killed at Baugé in 1421. The first Thomas Gray survived being shot in the head by a bolt from a springald, and was twice captured by the Scots, at Melrose Abbey in 1303 and at Bannockburn; his son was also captured, in 1355; and his grandson's family was held to ransom when Wark Castle was sacked by the Scots in 1399. Yet none of this seems to have had any significant impact on the family's wealth and prosperity, or to have hindered in the least its continued scaling of the social ladder. Indeed, of

---

correspondence Professor Curry has suggested that John might have recruited some of the men from his brother's retinue after the latter's execution.
[93] Heslop and Harbottle, 'Chillingham Church', 126.
[94] J.A. Tuck, 'The Emergence of a Northern Nobility, 1250–1400', *NH* 22 (1986), 1–17.
[95] For the Ogles, see *CP*, X, 21–31; for Coupland and Strivelyn, see King, 'War, Politics and Landed Society', passim; for Harclay, see H.R.T. Summerson, *Medieval Carlisle* (2 vols., Cumberland and Westmorland Antiquarian and Archaeological Society, extra ser. 25, 1993), I, 231–56.

these four generations of Grays, just as many died on the block, executed for treason against the English crown, as died on the battlefield, in the service of the same crown.[96]

Nevertheless, it was the risk of failure in the male line that came closest to finishing the Grays. According to John Fordun (writing a couple of decades after the event), when the second Thomas Gray was captured at Nesbit in 1355, his son and heir, Thomas, was captured with him. According to Andrew Wyntoun (writing c.1420), Thomas knighted his son, William, just before the battle. However, William was dead by Michaelmas 1362, and the younger Thomas must have died by 1366/7, when John Gray appears as the eldest son in an enfeoffment to use set up by that time; and John died early too, for when his father died in late 1369 his heir was the ten-year-old Thomas, named after John in the chain of remainders in the enfeoffment to use of 1366/7.[97] Clearly, the young Thomas was named after an elder brother who had presumably already died by the time of his birth c.1359; and he was the only one of at least four sons to outlive his father. This Thomas was to die comparatively young in 1401; if he had not survived his first decade, then the Gray estates would have been split up between his sisters, Agnes and Margaret.

Writing about the English soldiers who made their fortunes fighting in France, Thomas Gray, the author of the *Scalacronica*, commented, 'these Englishmen had established themselves on their own account in many parts of the kingdom of France after this war. These were men who were gathered, as unknown youths, from different regions of England, many beginning as archers, and then becoming knights, and some of them captains.'[98] Clearly, Gray was well aware of the social advances that war could bring; and little wonder, for his own family benefited from them more than most.

---

[96] The relative risks of military service on the Scottish Marches are examined in A. King, ' "According to the Custom Used in French and Scottish Wars": Prisoners and Casualties on the Scottish Marches in the Fourteenth Century', *JMH* 28 (2002), 263–90.

[97] Johannes de Fordun, *Chronica Gentis Scotorum*, ed. W.F. Skene (Edinburgh, 1871), p. 372; *The Original Chronicle of Andrew of Wyntoun*, ed. F.J. Amours (6 vols., Scottish Text Society, 1903–14), VI, 206–7; PRO, CP 40/411, m. 218; 'Durham Records: Calendar of the Cursitor's Records: Chancery Enrolments', in *The Thirty-Second Annual Report of the Deputy Keeper of the Public Records* (1871), pp. 279–80; *Forty-Fifth Annual Report*, pp. 201–2.

[98] *Scalacronica*, p. 181.

5

Land, Legend and Gentility in the Palatinate of Durham: The Pollards of Pollard Hall[1]

CHRISTIAN D. LIDDY

On 22 August 1661 the new bishop of Durham, John Cosin, wrote to William Sancroft, later archbishop of Canterbury, relating details of the warm greeting he had received on his arrival into the bishopric from the south:

> The confluence and alacritie both of the gentry, clergie, and other people was very greate; and at my first entrance through the river of Tease there was scarce any water to be seene for the multitude of horse and men that filled it, when the sword that killed the dragon was delivered to me with all the formality of trumpets and gunshots and acclamations that might be made.[2]

That the reception given to Cosin in the middle of the River Tees made a favourable impression upon the bishop and his entourage is confirmed by another letter written to William Sancroft a day later by Miles Stapleton, the bishop's secretary, informing him of the 'petty triumph' which he had witnessed on Cosin's approach to the bishopric, during which, 'when my Lord came, the usual ceremony of delivering a great drawne faulchion was performed'.[3] This would not be the last time that Bishop Cosin would encounter such a sword or a legend associated with it. In 1662, a year after his triumphant entry into the bishopric of Durham, Cosin undertook a survey of the episcopal estate. Among a list of the customs and services due from Bishop Auckland, where the bishop had a major residence, it was noted that:

> the freeholders in Bongate at Bishop Auckland are to present a fauchion to the Bishop at his first coming thither, called Pollard's fauchion, wherewith as that tradition goeth, he slew of old a venomous creature that did much hurt to man and beast in these parts, for by this present they hold their lands.[4]

The sword presented to Bishop Cosin on his crossing of the River Tees in 1661 was

---

[1] I am grateful to Helen Dunsford for help with the production of the map and to Philippa Hoskin for allowing me to see, prior to publication, the results of her research on the thirteenth-century Durham episcopal acta.
[2] *The Correspondence of John Cosin, D.D.*, ed. G. Ormsby (2 vols., Surtees Society 52, 55, 1868–70), II, 21.
[3] R. Surtees, *The History and Antiquities of the County Palatine of Durham* (4 vols., London, 1816), III, 406.
[4] DUL, Sharp MS 167, p. 2.

a falchion, a type of broad curved sword rather like a machete, which belonged to the Conyers family of Sockburn, a manor on the most southerly tip of the county palatine of Durham. Five years later, in the summer of 1666, the palatinate was the subject of a heraldic visitation by William Dugdale, Norroy King of Arms. Dugdale was shown the falchion at Sockburn, which so impressed him that he sketched the sword, complete with measurements, making a note that, 'by which Faucheon the family of Coniers anciently Lords of this place did hold this lordship, by the service of Meeting the Bishop at his entrance into the Bishoprick in the middle of the River Teyse, and presenting the same to him'.[5] Dugdale duly made a drawing of the knightly effigy in Sockburn Church, which he ascribed to one Sir John Conyers, who, '(as the tradition is) . . . finding a serpent in the ground west of this Church . . . slew him'.[6]

In the late nineteenth century the Conyers falchion excited a lively local antiquarian disagreement over the precise date of the sword, which Dugdale drew in 1666 and which is currently on display in Durham Cathedral treasury.[7] More recently, while there has been continuing local curiosity in the legend surrounding the sword,[8] the Conyers falchion has attracted a great deal of scholarly interest, most notably from a distinguished historian of medieval literacy exploring the use of physical objects to symbolise the transfer and tenure of land.[9] Writing in the late sixteenth century William Camden described Sockburn as the residence of the Conyers, an 'ancient and Noble familie' of the palatinate of Durham.[10] Thanks to the recent book by William Aird on Anglo-Norman Durham, much is now known about the early history of the Conyers: they were granted the manor of Sockburn with other neighbouring estates north and south of the Tees during the episcopate of Ranulf Flambard (1099–1128) and were among a small group of families who formed the baronial elite of the palatinate in the twelfth century known as the *barones et fideles Sancti Cuthberti*.[11] The Conyers of Sockburn, it would seem, had much in common with the Venables of Kinderton, an ancient baronial family in the palatinate of Chester, one of whose ancestors was remembered in the second half of the sixteenth century for having slain a dragon which had terrorised the people of Middleton and for which act of valour the Venables had been granted the local lordship.[12] By the early modern period, the

---

[5] *Durham Monuments*, ed. C.H. Hunter Blair (Newcastle-upon-Tyne Record Series 5, 1925), p. 64. See also J. Cherry, 'Symbolism and Survival: Medieval Horns of Tenure', *The Antiquaries Journal* 69 (1989), 112, plate xvii.

[6] *Durham Monuments*, p. 58.

[7] C.C. Hodges, 'The Conyers Falchion', *AA*, new ser. 15 (1892), 214–17. For a response, see the letter of Baron de Cosson in *Proceedings of the Society of Antiquaries of Newcastle-upon-Tyne*, new ser. 5 (1891–3), 42–3, 253.

[8] J. Wall, 'The Conyers Falchion', *Durham Archaeological Journal* 2 (1986), 77–83.

[9] R.E. Oakeshott, *The Archaeology of Weapons* (London, 1960), pp. 235–7; *Age of Chivalry: Art in Plantagenet England 1200–1400*, ed. J. Alexander and P. Binski (London, 1987), p. 259; Cherry, 'Medieval Horns of Tenure', 111–18. The most important recent work on the Conyers falchion is by M.T. Clanchy, *From Memory to Written Record: England 1066–1307* (2nd edn., Oxford, 1993), pp. 35–43.

[10] W. Camden, *Britannia* (London, 1590), p. 602, translated by P. Holland in W. Camden, *Britain* (London, 1610), p. 737.

[11] W.M. Aird, *St Cuthbert and the Normans: The Church of Durham, 1071–1153* (Woodbridge, 1998), ch. 5, esp. pp. 211–12.

[12] T. Thornton, *Cheshire and the Tudor State, 1480–1560* (Woodbridge, 2000), p. 53.

medieval ancestors of the Conyers, like those of the barons of Cheshire, enjoyed 'semi-mythical status'.[13]

In comparison, the Pollards of Pollard Hall, Bishop Auckland, who also held a falchion and around whom a similar legend developed, have received scant attention. The only work on the family and the sword is antiquarian, consisting largely of a few pages in William Hutchinson's three-volume *The History and Antiquities of the County Palatine of Durham*, which was first published in the late eighteenth century.[14] There are several reasons for this scholarly neglect, which can only in part be explained by the fact that the Pollard falchion, unlike the Conyers sword, has not survived to the present day. The main explanation must be sought in the historiography of the county palatine of Durham. Historians working on the palatinate have found it hard to escape the shadow of G.T. Lapsley's history of the late medieval liberty published in 1900, whose sub-title, *A Study in Constitutional History*, provides a good indication of its range of subject matter, namely the development of the institutions of palatine government, such as the courts, the council and the representative assembly.[15] Since the publication of Lapsley's seminal study, there has been considerable interest in the extent of the palatinate's juridical and administrative independence, particularly in the late thirteenth and early fourteenth centuries, which Lapsley saw as the decisive period in the liberty's gradual decline.[16] The result is that rather less is known about the landowners – particularly the lesser landowners – whose lives interacted with the institutions of the palatinate. This essay is an attempt to explore another, much neglected, aspect of the history of Durham, namely the process of gentrification within the late medieval palatinate. The Pollards are an interesting and important family because, measured by the indicators of gentility most commonly used by historians of the late medieval English gentry – wealth, title, officeholding, military service, or the size, nature and distribution of estates – they were conspicuously different from the Conyers of Sockburn. The Pollards occupied a position at the lower end of the social and economic hierarchy of gentry society. It was not until the second half of the sixteenth century that they held their own manor, the possession of which Christine Carpenter has taken as the 'basic definition' of gentility in the later Middle Ages, since manorial lordship brought with it lordship over men and resources.[17] Indeed, the story of the Pollards and their falchion has more than local significance since they are precisely the kind of sub-manorial gentry family often ignored in gentry studies which have tended to focus upon the better documented greater gentry, the leading figures in county society and politics.[18]

So who were the Pollards? Why did they have a falchion, and what was its significance to the family? The Pollards were minor landowners in Bishop Auckland from

---

[13] Ibid., p. 53.
[14] W. Hutchinson, *The History and Antiquities of the County Palatine of Durham* (3 vols., London, 1785–94), III, 350–1.
[15] G.T. Lapsley, *The County Palatine of Durham: A Study in Constitutional History* (London, 1900).
[16] C.M. Fraser, 'Edward I of England and the Regalian Franchise of Durham', *Speculum* 31 (1956), 329–42; idem, 'Prerogative and the Bishops of Durham, 1267–1376', *EHR* 74 (1959), 467–76; J. Scammell, 'The Origin and Limitations of the Liberty of Durham', *EHR* 81 (1966), 449–73; and J.W. Alexander, 'The English Palatinates under Edward I', *JBS* 22 (1983), 1–20. See also C.M. Fraser's biography, *A History of Antony Bek, Bishop of Durham, 1283–1311* (Oxford, 1957).
[17] C. Carpenter, 'Gentry and Community', *JBS* 33 (1994), 353.
[18] On this point, see ibid., 344–5 n. 15.

the early thirteenth century who seem to have owed their landed position in Durham, in the first instance, to their employment in episcopal service.[19] In one of the versions of Boldon Book, the episcopal land survey originally compiled in around 1183–4, there is an extremely brief statement recording that *Pollardus tenet x acras et dimidiam* in the vill of North Auckland, as Bishop Auckland was then known.[20] The date of this entry is difficult to establish precisely since, although the survey was produced in the early 1180s, the original text is no longer extant. Instead, there are four versions of the survey, each of which shows evidence of later amendment and alteration in light of the changing circumstances upon the bishop's estate. The Pollard entry is only found in the version of Boldon Book copied in the late fourteenth century and it would appear, on the basis of H.S. Offler's close textual analysis of the different texts of Boldon Book, that this alteration was probably made not long after about 1220.[21] Interestingly, there is no information within the document regarding either the service or rent which the bishop expected Pollard to owe for the ten and a half acres he held of the bishop, perhaps an indication that he received this smallholding free of rent and service in return for his employment on the bishop's behalf.[22] This inference is supported by references to the same individual, again known simply as 'Pollard', acting as a witness to several charters issued by one of the favoured domestic household servants of Bishops Hugh du Puiset (1153–95) and Philip of Poitou (1197–1208). Although undated, internal evidence suggests that the charters to Durham Priory, one of which concerned land in Bishop Auckland, are from the episcopate of Richard Marsh (1217–26).[23]

Episcopal charter witness lists reveal that, a generation later, his son, William Pollard, was a member of the household of Bishop Walter de Kirkham (1249–60), witnessing five of Kirkham's *acta* relating to original grants or confirmations of grants of land and property rights in various locations within the palatinate.[24] Although a date is assigned to only one of the charters – concerning property in the vill of Stanhope in the western extremity of the county palatine –[25] the five charters provide enough evidence to place him with some confidence within the bishop's household. William Pollard also seems to have been in receipt of a land grant from Bishop Kirkham, for a 1273 charter of Kirkham's successor, Robert de Stichill (1260–74), to 'our beloved and faithful clerk', Thomas de Levesham, granted Levesham fourteen acres of land in Wolsingham, which was described as once held

---

[19] See figure 5.1 for the Pollard pedigree so far as it is known.
[20] *BB*, p. 24. Pollard seems to have been 'a nickname from ME *pollard* "close cropped, beardless, bald" ': V. Watts, *A Dictionary of County Durham Place-Names* (English Place-Name Society Popular Series 3, 2002), p. 96.
[21] H.S. Offler, 'Re-reading Boldon Book', in idem, *North of the Tees: Studies in Medieval British History*, ed. A.J. Piper and A.I. Doyle (Aldershot, 1996), ch.12, esp. pp. 25–6. The Pollard entry is to be found in PRO, SC 12/21/28, p. 209.
[22] For a possible comparison, see the Wolsingham entry in which it is recorded that one 'William de Gisburn holds 30 acres, and renders 10s., but he is quit of this so long as he is in the Bishop's service': *BB*, p. 63.
[23] DCM, 2.12.Spec.15 and 1.11.Spec.39. The grants were made by Monk the cook and among the witnesses were Richard the chaplain, Walter the chaplain and Robert the reeve, presumably also members of the bishop's household. It would appear from a later document (DCM, 3.9.Spec.31) that Pollard's real name was John.
[24] DCM, Misc. Ch. 6109, 3.2.Pont.7a (3.2.Pont.7b is another original of the same document), 3.2.Pont.9b, 4.3.Pont.1a (4.3.Pont.1b is the same document), and BL, Egerton Charter 520.
[25] DCM, Misc. Ch. 6109 is dated 12 July 1259.

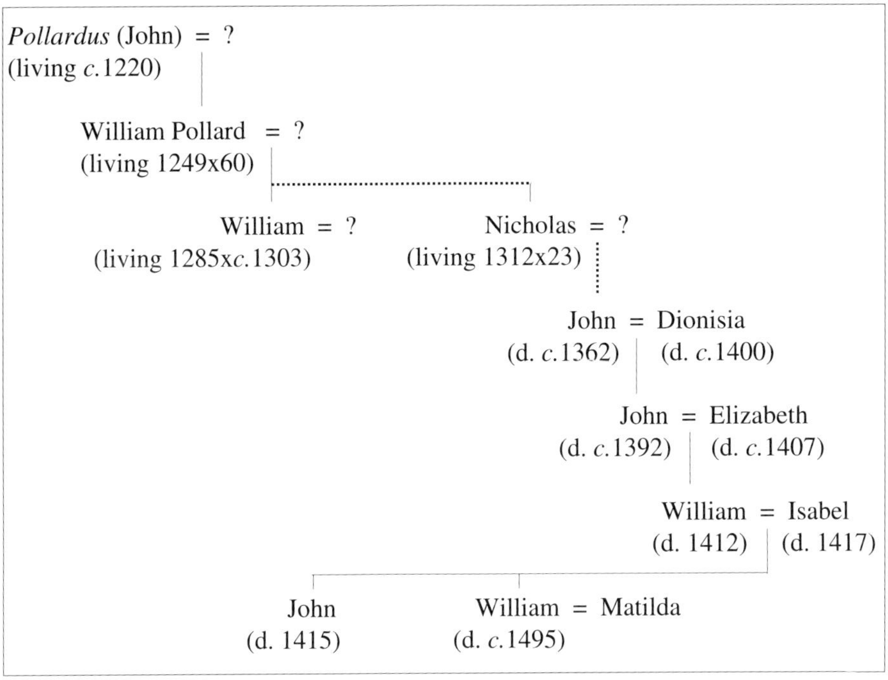

```
Pollardus (John) = ?
(living c.1220)
    |
    William Pollard = ?
    (living 1249x60)
         |------------------------------|
         William = ?                    Nicholas = ?
         (living 1285xc.1303)           (living 1312x23)
                                             |
                                        John = Dionisia
                                        (d. c.1362)  (d. c.1400)
                                             |
                                        John = Elizabeth
                                        (d. c.1392)  (d. c.1407)
                                             |
                                        William = Isabel
                                        (d. 1412)  (d. 1417)
                              |----------------------|
                              John              William = Matilda
                              (d. 1415)         (d. c.1495)
```

Fig. 5.1 The Pollards of Pollard Hall

by William Pollard of the bishop (*de nobis aliquando tenuit*).[26] Although William Pollard's precise status in the household is uncertain, the fact that his name does appear towards the end of the witness lists of all five charters may be a significant indication of his relatively minor status. As for his role in the household, the evidence is again not wholly clear, but he was neither a clerical member of Walter de Kirkham's household, nor important enough to have been included among the names of the members of the 'extended' episcopal household comprising the bishop's most powerful lay tenants within the palatinate such as Sir Marmaduke Fitz Geoffrey and Sir William Basset.[27] Perhaps William Pollard's role was within the bishop's domestic circle as one of the numerous *ministri*, but this can only be speculation.

Charter witness lists continue to provide the best evidence of the family's activities and interests in the late thirteenth and early fourteenth centuries. Although not especially numerous, they all suggest that the Pollards were consolidating and extending their position in and around Bishop Auckland. For example, another William, son of the aforementioned William Pollard, was a witness to an indenture sealed in 1285 granting a ten-year lease of pasture within the parish of Auckland St Andrew on the north side of the River Wear between the vill of Willington and Sir Roger Bernard's estate of Helmington Hall.[28] This William Pollard also witnessed seven *acta* of

---

[26] DCM, Misc. Ch. 6466. This document is an *inspeximus* by Richard Claxton, prior of Durham, of the charter of Robert de Stichill.
[27] For the composition of the bishop of Durham's household in the slightly earlier period, see the introduction to *English Episcopal Acta 24: Durham 1153–1195*, ed. M.G. Snape (Oxford, 2002), pp. xxxix–li.
[28] DRO, D/Gr 57. For Bernard's estate, see *HS*, p. 16.

Bishop Bek dating from January 1292 to November 1300, such frequency suggesting perhaps that he too was part of the episcopal household. Some local families did continue to work as household members across episcopates, and the recent work of Constance Fraser and Margaret Harvey has disclosed the names of several clerical dynasties who served the bishop and/or prior of Durham.[29] While there are no known Pollards in the households of either Robert de Stichill or Robert de Insula, the Pollards would appear to be a lay example of a service family. While four of the seven *acta* concerned land in the parish of Auckland St Andrew, the other three related to grants of land much further afield, in the western parish of Stanhope and the eastern parish of Kelloe.[30] William Pollard appeared regularly as one of the first names on the witness lists, after the clerks and knights, alongside Walter de Bermeton, who is definitely known to have been an episcopal servant: Walter was rewarded 'for his homage and service' around 1294 with a large grant of 127 acres of wasteland in Witton-le-Wear, Escomb and Stanhope, to which Pollard was one of the witnesses.[31] William was dead by 1303, murdered at Brusselton in the parish of Auckland St Helen by a group of Richmondshire knights including Thomas de Richmond and Conan de Ask, who were imprisoned in the gaol of Durham Castle and subsequently pardoned by Edward I for their offence in return for agreeing to serve with the king in Scotland.[32]

A Nicholas Pollard, perhaps a brother,[33] seems to have been a fairly important landowner in the vicinity of Bishop Auckland in the early fourteenth century. For example, in September 1321 he witnessed the creation by Bishop Louis de Beaumont of a moorland farm in Coundon, the neighbouring territory, and two years later, in November 1323, he was, along with the steward of Durham, the bailiff of Bishop Auckland and a prominent local knight, among the witnesses to a gift of land in Bishop Auckland.[34] Indeed, between September 1312 and November 1314 Nicholas Pollard appeared as a regular witness to episcopal grants of land, especially waste, in the adjoining parishes of Auckland St Andrew and Auckland St Helen.[35]

By the mid-fourteenth century the Pollards were part of what Peter Fleming has described as the 'parish gentry',[36] minor landed figures, who served in lesser administrative offices within the shire, whose pattern of landholding was very localised, and whose social and political horizons were bounded by their parishes, which, in the case of the Pollards, was the parish of Auckland St Andrew. In early 1343, when it was decided 'by the common counsel and unanimous consent of the entire community' of the palatinate of Durham to secure a truce with the Scots, Richard de Bury, bishop of Durham, appointed a series of commissions to collect a general tax

---

[29] For the Rakets, see *Durham Quarter Sessions Rolls 1471–1625*, ed. C.M. Fraser (Surtees Society 199, 1987–8), pp. 20–1, 346. For other clerical families such as the Elvets, Berehalghs and Tangs, see the forthcoming study of the Church in Durham by Dr Margaret Harvey.

[30] *Records of Antony Bek, Bishop and Patriarch, 1283–1311*, ed. C.M. Fraser (Surtees Society 162, 1947), pp. 32, 42–4, 53–5, 78–80.

[31] Ibid., p. 43.

[32] *CFR, 1301–7*, pp. 137, 148, 153, 165, 171; DCM, 3.9.Spec.31. The cause of the attack is not known.

[33] The aforementioned William Pollard 'died without an heir of his body': DCM, 3.9.Spec.31.

[34] DRO, D/St/D7/1–2.

[35] *RPD*, II, 1168–9, 1200–2, 1207, 1231–2, 1243–4, 1248–50, 1263–5.

[36] P.W. Fleming, 'Charity, Faith and the Gentry of Kent 1422–1529', in *Property and Politics: Essays in Later Medieval English History*, ed. A.J. Pollard (Stroud, 1984), p. 36.

throughout the liberty between the Tyne and the Tees.[37] Among the seven members of the commission for the ward of Darlington, of which the parish of Auckland St Andrew was a part, was John Pollard, the head of the family at this time. Similarly, it would appear that John was an estate official on the episcopal lands around Bishop Auckland: in October 1360 an inquisition was held before the bishop's steward in the halmote court meeting at Bishop Auckland concerning the obligation of the tenants of the neighbouring communities of Bondgate, Escomb and Newton Cap to render a customary rent in kind known as *multura*, in which John Pollard was named as the bishop's representative.[38] Further evidence of the small world in which the Pollards operated in this period is provided by the charter dated at Bishop Auckland which John Pollard witnessed in May 1347 confirming the grant of a single burgage in the vill of Bishop Auckland. Pollard's name was second on the witness list after John de Thropton, an estate official on the bishop's manor of Auckland in the 1330s and then, a decade later, a coroner and member of Bishop Bury's council.[39] Among the other witnesses were two clerical members of the bishop's household, William the clerk and Simon de Schapp, to whom, in the exchequer year 1349–50, the bailiff of the manor of Auckland rendered account for the construction of 'a stone wall newly built around Auckland Park'.[40]

The Pollards' lands were confined to the parish of Auckland St Andrew. More precisely, it is evident from the inquisitions held in 1362 upon John Pollard's death and in 1400 upon the death of John's widow, Dionisia, that, with the single exception of a forty-acre holding of arable and meadow in Binchester, the Pollards' lands lay entirely in Bishop Auckland, Coundon and Coundon Moor. The estate included seventeen burgages in Bishop Auckland and amounted to a total of over 250 'Durham acres', that is, around 375 statute acres.[41] In fact, neither was John's estate especially large nor does it appear that his income was particularly substantial. It is very difficult to determine the level of personal wealth of members of the Durham gentry in the late medieval period because of the paucity of the source material. Durham's exemption from royal taxation means that there are no easily accessible statistics about the distribution of landed wealth in the palatinate, which have been used so profitably by historians studying other counties.[42] Furthermore, while Durham had its own system of taxation, separate from that which operated from Westminster, there is no reference to its existence after 1348.[43] Instead, the valuations of property recorded in the inquisitions *post mortem* held on the death of the

---

[37] *RPD*, IV, 273–7. For the significance of this tax-granting assembly, see Lapsley, *County Palatine*, ch. 4, esp. pp. 119–20.

[38] PRO, DURH 3/12, fo. 258v.

[39] DRO, D/Gr 176; *HS*, p. 207; and *RPD*, IV, 349. See also the 1344 charter of Richard de Bury, dated at his manor of Auckland, concerning the grant of land in the vill of Bishop Auckland, to which John Pollard was one of the witnesses: *RPD*, III, 367.

[40] *HS*, p. 214.

[41] PRO, DURH 3/2, fols. 68v and 129r–v. Although this IPM of Dionisia does not provide the acreages of the land she held at the time of her death, her grandson's IPM is more revealing: PRO, DURH 3/2, fols. 282r–283r. It is important to note that these acreages, like those in other episcopal records of the period, were given in 'Durham acres', each of which was equivalent to 1½ statute acres: B.K. Roberts, *The Green Villages of County Durham* (Durham County Library Local History Publication 12, 1977), p. 7.

[42] See, most notably, S. Payling, *Political Society in Lancastrian England: The Greater Gentry of Nottinghamshire* (Oxford, 1991), ch. 1.

[43] Lapsley, *County Palatine*, pp. 119–20.

bishop's tenants-in-chief can help to gauge approximate income levels. Palatine status meant that the bishop of Durham rather than the king was the 'universal landlord' within the liberty, since 'no land was held of the king and all land was held, mediately or immediately, of the Bishop'.[44] The IPMs are a problematic source since, for a variety of reasons, they generally undervalued property,[45] but they do at least provide a picture of the relative if not absolute distribution of landed wealth among Durham's lay landowners, and a regular series of abstracts of IPMs from the palatinate is extant from the beginning of Thomas Hatfield's pontificate in 1345. The IPMs of John Pollard and his wife indicate that the family's net income from land and urban property was just over £9 *per annum*,[46] although it is clear that it was supplemented by other potentially profitable sources of revenue. In 1353 and again in 1357, for example, John Pollard secured three-year leases of the farm of the borough of Bishop Auckland, which included the profits from market tolls, the borough's mills and the perquisites of the borough court.[47]

The real difficulty lies in establishing when and how the Pollards were able to build up their estates by the mid-fourteenth century, because unfortunately there are no extant charters showing how their land was acquired. Clues do exist, however. The Pollard estate, upon John's death, consisted of fifteen separate parcels of land, the largest recorded of which was eighty acres, suggesting that it was obtained piecemeal. Moreover, the IPM of John Pollard reveals that by 1362 the family held four pieces of assarted waste, that is, land recently drawn into cultivation through the clearing of wood and moorland. The most concerted phase of the colonisation of the waste in the county palatine took place in the second half of the thirteenth and early fourteenth centuries, most notably during the pontificate of Antony Bek, when the bishop oversaw the intensive reclamation of the waste on a number of his episcopal manors, such as Bishop Auckland, through grants of wasteland to his episcopal servants as a reward for service.[48] Three of the seven episcopal *acta* witnessed by William Pollard in the 1290s concerned grants of wasteland in the vicinity of Bishop Auckland. Although there is no documentary evidence of the Pollards receiving episcopal grants of waste, there can be little doubt that the Pollards, through their small-scale, piecemeal waste enclosure, were participating in the colonising movement taking place at this time in the parish of Auckland St Andrew.[49]

Before the Black Death and the dramatic socio-economic changes which followed in its wake, the Pollards already had become a minor landed family of some note in the area around Bishop Auckland. Yet while they were not members of the rich peasantry who rose into the gentry after the Black Death, the family does appear to have belonged to what Nigel Saul has described as 'the class of lesser landowners who

---

[44] Ibid., pp. 54–5.
[45] R.F. Hunnisett, 'The Reliability of Inquisitions as Historical Evidence', in *The Study of Medieval Records: Essays in honour of Kathleen Major*, ed. D.A. Bullough and R.L. Storey (Oxford, 1971), pp. 206–35; N. Saul, *Knights and Esquires: The Gloucestershire Gentry in the Fourteenth Century* (Oxford, 1981), p. 206.
[46] The approximate value of Dionisia's estate is calculated from PRO, DURH 3/2, fols. 283r–v and 284v–285r.
[47] PRO, DURH 3/12, fols. 83v and 164v.
[48] Fraser, *History of Antony Bek*, p. 106.
[49] *Records of Antony Bek*, pp. 32, 42–4, 79–80. See also the later reference to thirty acres of wasteland in Bishop Auckland *quondam Nicholai Pollard*: *HS*, p. 41.

were doing well for themselves in the post-Black Death world'.[50] John Pollard jr. benefited from the policy of demesne leases pursued by the bishop. Thus, from around 1381 until his death by 1392 he leased, for £5 9s. *per annum*, the manor of Woodhouses, a demesne farm comprising 100 acres, an estate which previously had been granted by Bishop Hatfield to, among others, John de Popham, the bishop's kinsman and the chief forester of Weardale.[51] Like his father, John also leased the borough of Bishop Auckland from the bishop in partnership with others.[52] In fact, by the later fourteenth century and probably earlier the Pollards were farmers in both the medieval and modern senses of the word, for the family held a sheep-fold close to Bishop Auckland.[53]

Why were the Pollards doing well in the second half of the fourteenth century? Although the evidence is indirect and largely circumstantial, there is a strong likelihood that John Pollard jr. was an estate official of the bishop in the vicinity of Bishop Auckland. Among the previous farmers of the Woodhouses estate held by John Pollard from 1381 to 1392 was one Roger de Tickhill, a bailiff of the episcopal manor of Auckland and of the bishop's property of Coundon Grange in the mid-fourteenth century, with whom John's father had farmed the profits of the borough of Bishop Auckland in the 1350s.[54] If John Pollard jr. were an official of some kind on the bishop's estate at Bishop Auckland, he would have known what land was available for purchase and could have taken advantage of the active land market in the Auckland area, as land became cheaper and changed hands with increasing rapidity after the Black Death. Even a cursory reading of the Hatfield Survey reveals John Pollard jr. to be an omnipresent figure in the early 1380s, holding a wide variety of land, including freeholdings, leases of demesne land, cotland and former bondland (two forms of customary tenure), and exchequer land, a type of land of uncertain status, but which largely consisted of small waste enclosures.[55] Much of John's property recorded in the Hatfield Survey consisted of small parcels of land, ranging from one to two acres to around twenty acres, and, for a large proportion of it, the estate survey provides the names of its previous occupiers, suggesting perhaps that John was able to buy out smaller landowners after the Black Death.[56]

So what did the Pollard estate look like by the early fifteenth century? Using the IPMs of the grandson of John jr., another John, who died in 1415, and of this John's widowed mother, Isabel, who died two years later, it is evident that the Pollard estate consisted of over 350 'Durham acres' as well as seventeen burgages in the borough of Bishop Auckland.[57] The estate included several dispersed farmsteads carved from the neighbouring woodland, such as the close called 'le Frith', and from the moorland, such as the property known as Brack's Farm, but it largely comprised a series of small

---

[50] Saul, *Knights and Esquires*, p. 19.
[51] *HS*, p. 33; PRO, DURH 3/2, fols. 118v–119r. For Popham, see PRO, DURH 3/31, m. 10d.; 3/32, m. 3r.
[52] *HS*, p. 39.
[53] Ibid., pp. 33–4; PRO, SC 12/21/29, p. 43.
[54] PRO, DURH 3/31, m. 14d.; *HS*, pp. 211, 216; PRO, DURH 3/12, fo. 83v.
[55] *HS*, pp. 33–5, 37, 39–40.
[56] Although it should be noted that some of the previous named incumbents held this property a long time before the compilation of the Hatfield Survey. For example, John Pollard held a freeholding described as *quondam Umfridi Smyth* and Humphrey the smith was named in the Boldon Book: *HS*, p. 33; *BB*, p. 24.
[57] PRO, DURH 3/2, fols. 172v–173r and 285v. See also PRO, DURH 3/2, fo. 129r–v.

enclosures taken not only from the waste but also from the townfields of Bishop Auckland. These types of enclosures are revealed in the names of the individual pieces of property held by the family in the late fourteenth and early fifteenth centuries, such as 'Moreflate', 'Gawnlesflate', 'Langeflate', 'Hurnflat', 'Chapelthornflate', 'flat' being a Middle English word meaning a 'division of the open field'.[58] This pattern of landholding was maintained into the late sixteenth century when, on the death of the then head of the Pollard family, Leonard Pollard, his IPM in 1589 recorded that he possessed land in and around Bishop Auckland in 'various closes' including 'Meadow close' and 'Chappelthorne close'.[59]

A better indication of what the Pollards' property might have looked like by the early fifteenth century comes from the six inch First Edition Ordnance Survey map produced in the mid-nineteenth century, by which date the Pollard estate had become a separate township known as 'Pollards Lands'.[60] The acreage of Pollards Lands given by the tithe commissioners who assessed the township in the 1840s was just over 475 royal statute acres.[61] The Pollard estate in the early fifteenth century amounted to the equivalent of approaching 550 statute acres. Yet if the boundaries of the township in the nineteenth century were a slight contraction of the limits of the Pollard holdings in the early fifteenth century, the Ordnance Survey map of Pollards Lands shows clearly the piecemeal nature of the Pollards' acquisition of property. The estate essentially took the form of two consolidated blocks of land comprising, on the right bordering Auckland Park, a moorland farm called Brack's Farm, and on the left, a large piece of land enclosed from the townfields of Bishop Auckland. In these two areas the Pollard estate was sufficiently coherent that, when the episcopal estate between the Tyne and the Tees was surveyed for very different purposes in 1647 and 1662, the surveyors could refer first to land 'lying upon Pollards' and then to the freehold rents due from 'Pollards Lands'.[62]

In fact, the Pollard estate, according to the Ordnance Survey map, comprised the township itself and eleven associated detached portions of land. How was the property managed in the second half of the fourteenth and early fifteenth centuries? The chief residence of the Pollards seems to have been a property on the south side of the market place in Bishop Auckland, close to the gateway to Auckland Palace, which, by the 1580s and probably earlier, was known as 'Pollard Hall' and which survived until 1808, when Bishop Barrington purchased the property and demolished the building to make way for Barrington School.[63] Without any single sizeable rural estate of their own, it probably made sense for the Pollards to administer their estates from an urban residence, separate from their rural property, which was a patchwork of dispersed small-scale enclosures.[64]

---

[58] PRO, DURH 3/2, fols. 139r, 162r–v, 285v; Watts, *County Durham Place-Names*, p. 152.
[59] PRO, DURH 3/5, fo. 18v.
[60] See map 5.1.
[61] DUL, DDR, Tithe: Pollards Lands.
[62] *Parliamentary Surveys of the Bishopric of Durham*, ed. D.A. Kirby (2 vols., Surtees Society 183, 185, 1968–72), I, 24; DUL, Sharp MS 167, p. 7.
[63] See figure 5.2; M. Richley, *History and Characteristics of Bishop Auckland* (Bishop Auckland, 1872), p. 124.
[64] For a useful comparison, see Rosemary Horrox's important observation that some urban gentlemen 'may have remained in town from necessity' since the 'acquisition of land piecemeal often produced a

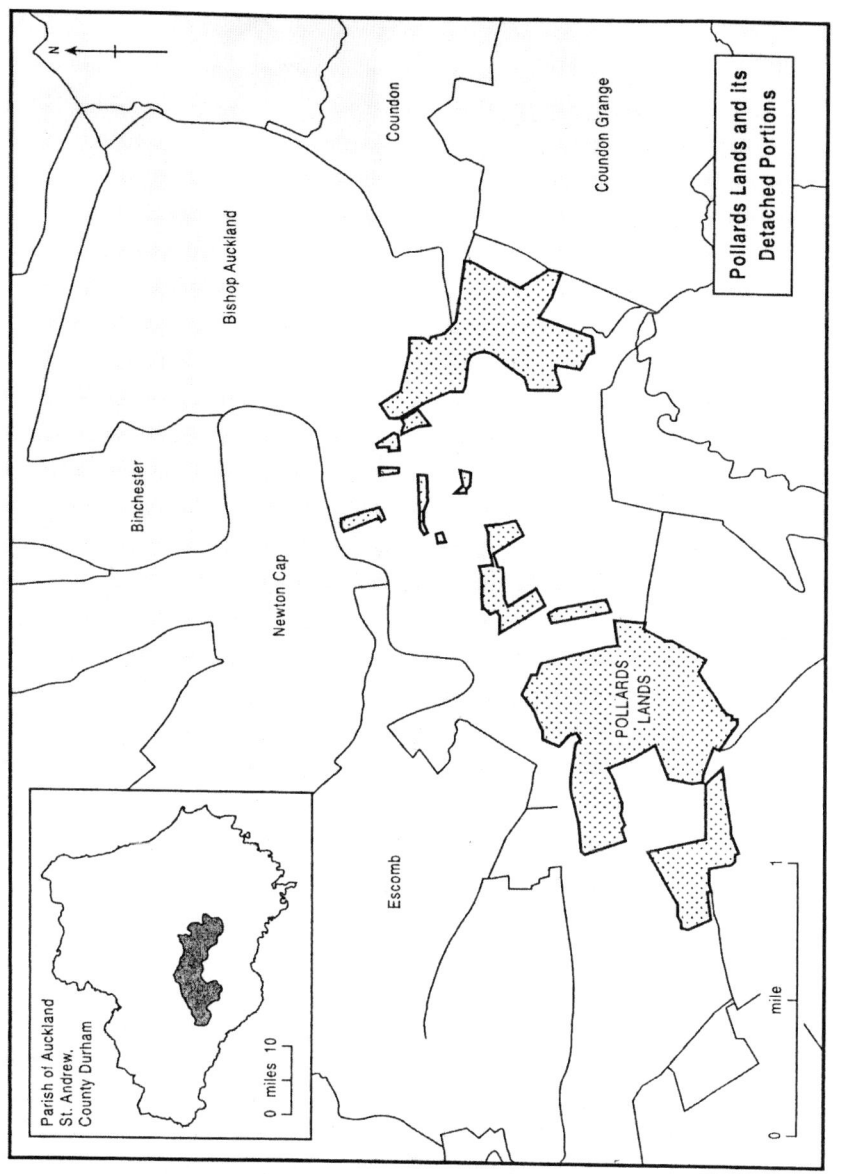

Map 5.1 Township of Pollards Lands, Co. Durham

The second half of the fourteenth century, then, saw the Pollards extend their landed base around Bishop Auckland. They were acquisitive and ambitious, building up their estates when the opportunities arose. One expression of their social aspirations was their bearing of a coat of arms, the right to which, during the fifteenth century, was beginning to sharpen contemporary definitions of gentility.[65] The evidence that the Pollards were armigerous in the fourteenth century is admittedly slight and relies upon the evidence of a 1584–5 heraldic visitation of the North Riding of Yorkshire, which, by this date, was where the main landed interests of the family were located. During the course of his investigations into the family's pedigree, Robert Glover, Somerset herald, was presented with what he described as 'an ancient seal of John Pollard, engraved in silver' (*sigillum Johannis Pollard antiquum ex argento sculptum*): presumably *sigillum Johannis Pollard* was the legend around the circumference of the seal. This John Pollard was the same person from whom the late sixteenth-century family traced its ancestry.[66] The last five generations of the family tree, from the later fifteenth century onwards, are accurate, but the 'John Pollard, of Pollard Hall, in Bishop Auckland' at the apex of the genealogy, from whom the later Pollards ultimately claimed their origin, was not William's father. This John Pollard was either John sr., who died by 1362, or his son, John jr., who was dead by 1392. In his study of the Gloucestershire gentry, Nigel Saul noted that it was significant that 'it was to the late fourteenth or early fifteenth century that several gentry families whose pedigrees were compiled in the late sixteenth century traced their origin' since it was in this period that these families 'came to be of some consequence'.[67] If title is a good indication of status, it is true that William Pollard, from the moment he became the head of the family in the 1430s after a series of minorities, was dignified with the title of 'esquire'.[68]

To what did William Pollard owe this title? The significance of the Pollards and the extent of their social ascent should not be exaggerated. Despite the growth of their estate in the second half of the fourteenth century, the Pollards remained 'parish gentry', only holding lesser administrative offices within the county. Thus, John Pollard jr. served as a juror in inquisitions held in the county court at Durham in 1388 and 1392 to inquire into cases of grants of land in *mortmain*.[69] Moreover, deed evidence, thin though it is relating to the Pollards, does emphasise the way in which the family's sphere of influence continued to focus upon the parish of Auckland St Andrew and particularly Bishop Auckland. In 1377 John Pollard jr. headed the list of witnesses to a grant of a messuage in Newgate in Bishop Auckland, while his

---

scattered estate with no very obvious focus': R. Horrox, 'The Urban Gentry in the Fifteenth Century', in *Towns and Townspeople in the Fifteenth Century*, ed. J.A.F. Thomson (Gloucester 1988), p. 26.

65 Saul, *Knights and Esquires*, pp. 26–8.
66 See figure 5.2.
67 Saul, *Knights and Esquires*, p. 249.
68 *The Register of Thomas Langley, Bishop of Durham, 1406–1437*, ed. R.L. Storey (6 vols., Surtees Society 164–82, 1949–67), IV, 15. See also, for example, the deed evidence in PRO, DURH 3/47, m. 13d. (1449), and the title accorded William Pollard on his death *c.*1495 in PRO, DURH 3/62, m. 1r. The minorities occurred after the death first of William's father, another William, in 1412, and then of William's elder brother, John, in 1415 (PRO, DURH 3/2, fols. 282r–283r and 284v–285r). William sought to enter his inheritance in 1431, as he had reached his majority, but there were complications which were not fully resolved until 1449 (PRO, DURH 3/36, m. 4r; 3/37, m. 14r–d.; 3/44, m. 6d.).
69 DCM, 1.10.Pont.5 and 1.11.Pont.3. For evidence of the county court in medieval Durham, see K. Emsley and C.M. Fraser, *The Courts of the County Palatine of Durham* (Durham, 1984), pp. 12–16.

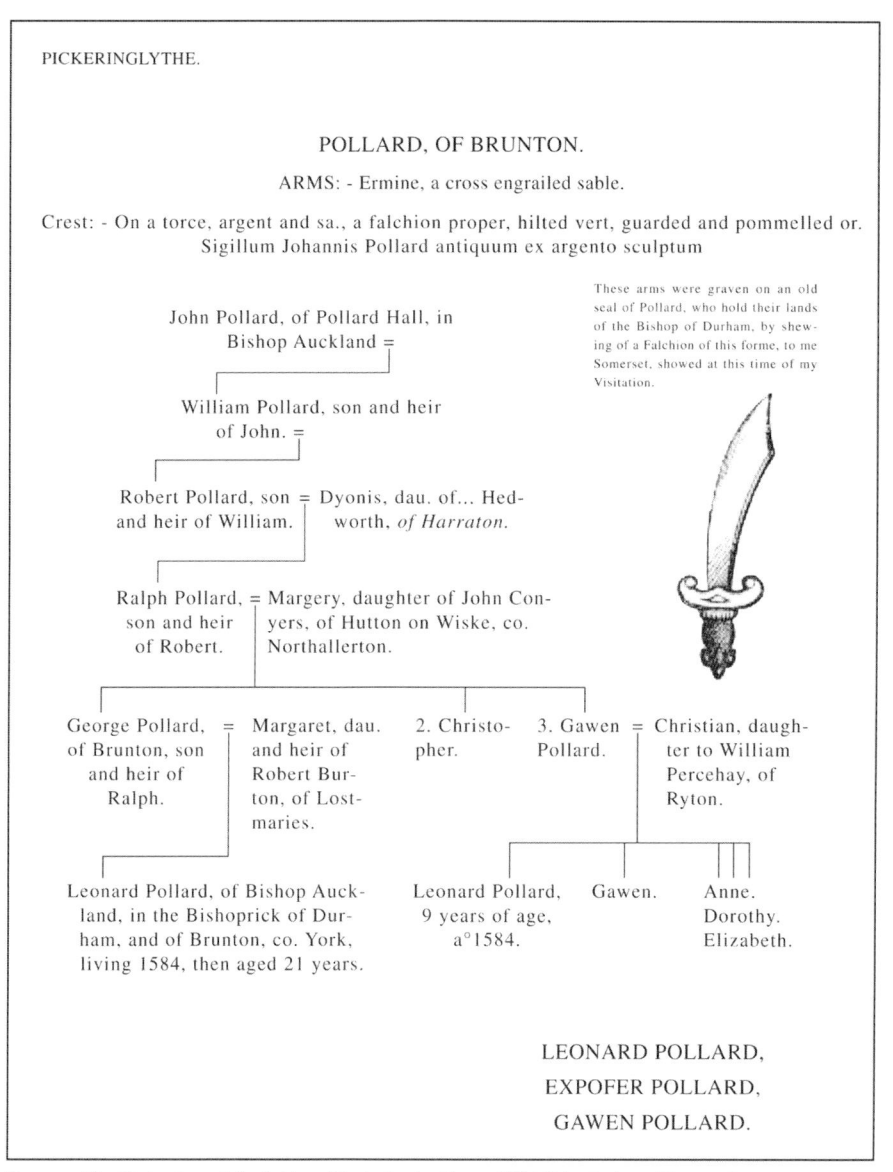

THE POLLARDS OF POLLARD HALL 87

PICKERINGLYTHE.

POLLARD, OF BRUNTON.

ARMS: - Ermine, a cross engrailed sable.

Crest: - On a torce, argent and sa., a falchion proper, hilted vert, guarded and pommelled or.
Sigillum Johannis Pollard antiquum ex argento sculptum

John Pollard, of Pollard Hall, in Bishop Auckland =

These arms were graven on an old seal of Pollard, who hold their lands of the Bishop of Durham, by shewing of a Falchion of this forme, to me Somerset, showed at this time of my Visitation.

William Pollard, son and heir of John. =

Robert Pollard, son and heir of William. = Dyonis, dau. of... Hedworth, *of Harraton.*

Ralph Pollard, son and heir of Robert. = Margery, daughter of John Conyers, of Hutton on Wiske, co. Northallerton.

George Pollard, of Brunton, son and heir of Ralph. = Margaret, dau. and heir of Robert Burton, of Lostmaries.

2. Christopher.

3. Gawen Pollard. = Christian, daughter to William Percehay, of Ryton.

Leonard Pollard, of Bishop Auckland, in the Bishoprick of Durham, and of Brunton, co. York, living 1584, then aged 21 years.

Leonard Pollard, 9 years of age, a° 1584.

Gawen.

Anne. Dorothy. Elizabeth.

LEONARD POLLARD,
EXPOFER POLLARD,
GAWEN POLLARD.

Source: *The Visitation of Yorkshire, Made in the Years 1584/5 by Robert Glover, Somerset Herald,* ed. J. Foster (London, 1875), p. 188

Fig. 5.2 Pollard family arms produced for the 1584–5 Yorkshire heraldic visitation

grandson, William Pollard Esq., who died around 1495, was among the witnesses to a 1449 quitclaim by Sir Robert Claxton of his manor of Wadley next to Harperley in Weardale, just over five miles north-west of Bishop Auckland.[70] Equally, the family's wealth, at least by the early fifteenth century, while greater than its income in the mid-fourteenth century in relative terms, was not exceptional. William's

[70] DRO, D/X 201/1; PRO, DURH 3/47, m. 13d.

inheritance in the 1430s, when he reached his majority, amounted to a net income of over £12 *per annum* from land and rents.[71] He was a very low-income esquire in a period when historians have argued that esquires were expected to enjoy an annual landed income of at least £20 and that an income of £10 a year was the minimum qualification for gentry status.[72]

In large part, the answer lies in the structure of landed society in the region of the county palatine which the Pollards inhabited. Even accounting for the rhetorical flourish of William Camden's description of Durham as a land of two halves, divided into western and eastern parts, there is a great deal of truth in his vivid sketch of the palatinate. In the west, the highest ground, where 'the fields are naked and barraine, the woods very thinne, the hilles bare without grasse', the land was less inviting, while in the east, where 'the ground being well manured, is very fruitfull', the land was 'well garnished with meddowes, pastures, and corn-fields'.[73] Durham's sharply contrasting topography between the east and west greatly influenced the process of settlement and colonisation of the land.[74] The south and east, particularly the south east along the Tees valley, an area of open countryside containing highly fertile land, were colonised first. Along the eastern seaboard of Durham and in the Tees valley especially was a series of large and rich manors, each often containing more than 400 acres of demesne arable and worth in excess of £20 a year, such as the manor of Elwick in the parish of Hart, valued at almost £50 in 1432.[75] In the south and east, especially in the south east, there also seems to have been a manorial estate structure which included a court and which conformed to the pattern of manorialisation found in the southern and midland counties of England.[76] With one or two exceptions, such as the Eures of Witton-le-Wear, it was in the south and east, particularly along the Tees valley, that most of the wealthy knights and esquires of the county palatine, such as the Hyltons, the Lumleys, the Claxtons, the Surtees, the Blakestons, the Bowes and the Conyers, resided in the fourteenth and fifteenth centuries.

In sharp contrast, the western part of Durham, in particular the foothills of the Pennines, which included the parish of Auckland St Andrew where the Pollards were resident, was an area of late colonisation. It was also a region more suited to pastoral than arable farming where, with the notable exception of the enormous Neville estate of Brancepeth, which in 1432 was said to be worth £100 *per annum* and included five sub-manors,[77] the small estate was the norm. The information drawn from the IPMs indicates that there were around forty properties in the western half of Durham which were described as manors and which were valued at around as little as £1 *per annum*. Only a few lay in the most westerly parts of Durham, in the parishes of Stanhope and Wolsingham; the vast majority were in the parishes of Auckland St Andrew,

---

[71] This calculation is based on PRO, DURH 3/2, fols. 283r–v, 284v–285r, and 285v.
[72] D.A.L. Morgan, 'The Individual Style of the English Gentlemen', in *Gentry and Lesser Nobility in Late Medieval Europe*, ed. M. Jones (Gloucester, 1986), p. 16.
[73] Camden, *Britannia*, p. 599, in Camden, *Britain*, p. 735.
[74] P. Dickinson and W.B. Fisher, *The Medieval Land Surveys of County Durham* (Department of Geography, University of Durham, Research Papers Series 2, 1959), p. 15; Roberts, *Green Villages of County Durham*, pp. 8–10.
[75] PRO, DURH 3/2, fo. 263r–v.
[76] This is a complex subject upon which I am currently working.
[77] PRO, DURH 3/2, fols. 264r–265r.

Brancepeth, Lanchester and Chester-le-Street.[78] Many of the so-called 'manors' seem to have been manors in name only and were in actual fact small sub-manors and isolated farmsteads, without either a court or a dependent tenantry. Few major Durham families inhabited this part of the county palatine, which instead produced several minor gentry, such as the Featherstones of Stanhope, another sub-manorial gentry family like the Pollards,[79] or the Marleys of Unthank in the parish of Stanhope and the Belasis family of Henknowle, neighbours of the Pollards in the parish of Auckland St Andrew, both of whom enjoyed similar levels of income to the Pollards.[80] In the large parish of Auckland St Andrew, which was dominated by the episcopal vills of Escomb and Newton Cap and by the bishop's demesne estates of the manor of Auckland and Coundon Grange, the only major resident gentry was the Eure family of Witton-le-Wear. In this rugged landscape of small estates, scattered settlement and single farmsteads, perhaps the Pollards' ambitions were not hindered by their lack of manorial lordship. The work of Christine Carpenter on gentry society in the Arden region of Warwickshire, an area also of 'late colonisation and small manorial fragments', surely has relevance to the Pollards' position in the county palatine of Durham.[81] In particular, Carpenter's illuminating discussion of the relationship between environment and status, specifically her suggestion that the absence of a major gentry in the Arden region of Warwickshire meant that it was 'all the more likely that there would be an inflation of rank that would give rise to small-scale esquires', can help to explain the Pollards' claims to gentility, rooted firmly as they were in the locality of Bishop Auckland.[82]

Nonetheless, the distinctive social and tenurial structure of the area around Bishop Auckland is not the only explanation why William Pollard was confident enough to claim the title of esquire from the second quarter of the fifteenth century. Gentility, ultimately, was an expression of an individual's standing within local society, and it is in this context that the Pollard falchion is important. The first known reference to the Pollards' possession of a falchion is from the IPM of Dionisia, the widow of John Pollard sr., which was held in 1400. According to the record of the inquisition, among the property she held in chief of the bishop on the day she died was a piece of land next to Auckland Park 'by the service of showing to the lord bishop a falchion on his first arrival at Auckland after his consecration' (*per servicium ostendendi domino Episcopo unum Fawchonem in primo adventu suo apud Aukland post consecracionem suam*).[83] How long had such a falchion been in the custody of the Pollard family and, perhaps most intriguingly, what was its purpose?

The recent work of Michael Clanchy on the growth of literacy in medieval

---

[78] PRO, DURH 3/2, passim. These properties will be discussed in more detail in my forthcoming monograph, *The Land of the Prince Bishops: The Palatinate of Durham, 1345–1437*.
[79] PRO, DURH 3/2, fo. 185r–v. William de Featherstone's son and heir, Alexander, was one of the Durham esquires who swore an oath to the bishop in Durham Cathedral to maintain the peace locally in 1434: *Register of Thomas Langley*, IV, 143.
[80] For the Marleys, see PRO, DURH 3/2, fols. 130r and 178v–179r; for the Belasis family, see PRO, DURH 3/2, fo. 194r–v and *Register of Thomas Langley*, IV, 143.
[81] C. Carpenter, *Locality and Polity: A Study of Warwickshire Landed Society, 1401–1499* (Cambridge, 1992), p. 70. See also the important article by B.K. Roberts, 'A Study of Medieval Colonization in the Forest of Arden', *AgHR* 16 (1968), 101–13.
[82] Carpenter, *Locality and Polity*, p. 70.
[83] PRO, DURH 3/2, fo. 129r–v.

England has provided an important reminder that 'it had been usual practice, before charters became common, to preserve the memory of a title to property in the object which had symbolized the conveyance'.[84] In fact, a wide range of objects was used to symbolise the transmission of both land and office in the Anglo-Norman period, including knives, cups, rings and hunting horns. A good example of the latter comes from a 1266 inquisition concerning the custody of the forest of Bernwood in Buckinghamshire, in which it was found that John Fitz Nigel and his ancestors had held the land from the king from before the Norman Conquest 'by a horn, which is a charter for the aforesaid forest'.[85] Knives were fairly common as a symbol of conveyance in the eleventh and twelfth centuries and, even when charters did become more prevalent, knives could still be attached to them as a means of authentication.[86] Swords and falchions, in particular, were more unusual as evidence of title to property. One notable exception is the famous account of the Earl Warenne's response to Edward I's *quo warranto* proceedings in the *Chronicle of Walter of Guisborough*. According to the chronicler, when asked by Edward's judges by what warrant he held his lands, Warenne 'produced in their midst an ancient and rusty sword and said: "Look at this, my lords, this is my warrant!"'[87] Roger Mortimer of Wigmore, first Earl of March, was one of the Contrariants who rebelled against Edward II and whose property was declared forfeit to the crown in 1322. When an inventory of all of Mortimer's property was drawn up, among the items preserved in the lord's wardrobe in Wigmore Abbey, close to the castle which the family had held since just after the Norman Conquest, was 'a bronze horn which, together with a certain falchion, is, it is said, the charter for the land of Wigmore' (*uno cornu eneo quod una cum quodam Fauchone est ut dicitur carta terre de Wygemor*).[88]

The Conyers falchion was a similar kind of title deed to the manor of Sockburn, which the Conyers family had held of the bishop of Durham from the pontificate of Ranulf Flambard in the early twelfth century.[89] The Conyers falchion was always returned to its owner after its presentation, presumably for safekeeping in the family archive. Indeed, this was the condition of its delivery to the bishop: in the IPM of Sir John Conyers in 1396, it was stated that the knight held the manor of Sockburn 'by the service of showing to the lord bishop a falchion provided that after the lord bishop sees it, he should return it to the shower' (*per servicium demonstrandi domino Episcopo unum Fawchonem ita quod postquam dominus Episcopus illud videre restituat ostendenti*).[90] As evidence of title, the power of physical objects resided not just in their continued possession by their beneficiaries, but also in their repeated use as an aid to memory. It was perhaps in this context that the practice began by which the Conyers family presented the falchion to the bishop of Durham upon his first entry

---

[84] Clanchy, *Memory to Written Record*, p. 38.
[85] For the horn, see Cherry, 'Medieval Horns of Tenure', 113, plate xix. For further discussion, see P.D.A. Harvey, 'Boarstall, Buckinghamshire, 1444x1446', in *Local Maps and Plans from Medieval England*, ed. R.A. Skelton and P.D.A. Harvey (Oxford, 1986), pp. 211–19.
[86] F. Pollock and F.W. Maitland, *The History of English Law Before the Time of Edward I* (2 vols., Cambridge, 1895), II, 87–8; Clanchy, *Memory to Written Record*, pp. 38–9, 258–9.
[87] *The Chronicle of Walter of Guisborough*, ed. H. Rothwell (Camden Society 3rd ser. 89, 1957), p. 216, translated with discussion in Clanchy, *Memory to Written Record*, pp. 35–43.
[88] PRO, E 358/14, m. 6d.; *Dictionary of Medieval Latin from British Sources* (London, 1975–), p. 897.
[89] Aird, *St Cuthbert and the Normans*, pp. 211–12.
[90] PRO, DURH 3/2, fo. 124r.

into his bishopric over the River Tees as he passed by the family's manor of Sockburn. In the case of the Conyers the falchion was demonstrably not the original object which conveyed the manor of Sockburn to the family in the early twelfth century. The falchion itself, a type of sword wider at the point than at the tip, although known from antiquity, only became popular in England in the thirteenth century in response to changes in the design of armour, a popularity attested in the numerous representations of the falchion in the Douce Apocalypse MS and in the lost murals containing Old Testament scenes in the Painted Chamber at Westminster Palace.[91] Indeed, the imagery on the Conyers falchion suggests a date for this particular weapon of the third quarter of the thirteenth century.[92] Rather like the 'Boarstall Horn', embellished with fifteenth-century silver gilt mountings but which allegedly was given by Edward the Confessor to Nigel, a forester,[93] there can be little doubt that the Conyers similarly chose to replace their original object of conveyance with an artefact far more prestigious, in this case a weapon bearing upon the pommel the arms of England and the arms of the Holy Roman Empire, which perhaps once belonged to Richard Earl of Cornwall, King of the Romans from 1257.[94]

Why, though, did the Pollards have a falchion in their possession? In the fourteenth and fifteenth centuries the falchion was always associated with a small piece of land consisting of fifteen acres next to Auckland Park.[95] This smallholding may have been the same as the property belonging to the family in the early thirteenth century and recorded in Boldon Book,[96] and it is quite conceivable that the initial grant was made by the bishop through the conveyance of a physical object such as a knife. Yet the falchion was a very unusual symbol of title, and the available evidence indicates that, in those few instances where it was preserved as proof of title, the object belonged to those in the upper strata of landed society. The Pollards, a minor gentry family in north-east England, were in exalted company. It is tempting to see the Pollards' acquisition of a falchion as a highly self-conscious attempt to emulate the Conyers in order to bolster the family's credentials. The families certainly were acquainted with each other by the early fourteenth century, when the then head of the Conyers, Sir John Conyers, held land in Auckland St Helen and Bishop Auckland.[97] It was at Brusselton in the parish of Auckland St Helen, of which Sir John Conyers was lord, that William Pollard was murdered in the late thirteenth century.[98] In 1321 Sir John Conyers headed a witness list to an episcopal charter granting land in Coundon, which also included Nicholas Pollard, and among the land held by John Pollard jr. at the time of the Hatfield Survey was a fourteen-acre holding *quondam appruatas per dominum Johannem Coniers* called 'Burtonbankes'.[99] If the Pollards knew the Conyers, there is a good chance that they were also aware of their falchion.

[91] M. Prestwich, *Armies and Warfare in the Middle Ages: The English Experience* (New Haven, 1996), pp. 28–30; P. Binski, *The Painted Chamber at Westminster* (London, 1986), p. 48. The earliest reference in Latin to a falchion in England is from 1266: *Dictionary of Medieval Latin*, p. 897.
[92] *Age of Chivalry*, p. 259.
[93] Harvey, 'Boarstall', p. 217.
[94] On the heraldry, see *Age of Chivalry*, p. 259. It remains to be seen how and why this sword should have entered the family's custody.
[95] PRO, DURH 3/2, fols. 129r–v, 139r, 172v–173r, 282r–283r, 284v–285r.
[96] *BB*, p. 24.
[97] *RPD*, II, 1187; III, 33.
[98] See above, p. 80, and *RPD*, III, 33.
[99] DRO, D/St/D7/2; *HS*, p. 39.

For present purposes, the most interesting aspect of the Pollard falchion lies less in its origin, about which it is impossible to be absolutely confident, and more in the way the falchion was perceived by the family and by others in the fourteenth and fifteenth centuries. This, of course, is another difficult subject, but a few suggestions can be made. In part, the falchion was of practical use to a family such as the Pollards who had built up their estate in small purchases of land and enclosures for which they may have had no written proof of title. Associated with one piece of land next to Auckland Park in the late fourteenth and early fifteenth centuries, the IPM of Leonard Pollard in 1589 reveals that, by this date, the falchion had become the title deed to the entire Pollard estate: all of the Pollards' numerous portions of land in and around Bishop Auckland were held in chief of the bishop for knight's service and 'by the service of showing to the lord bishop a falchion on his first coming to Auckland after his consecration'.[100]

In essence, however, the falchion was of symbolic importance to the Pollards. The armorial seal of the Pollard family in the second half of the fourteenth century, according to the evidence produced for the 1584–5 heraldic visitation, incorporated the image of the falchion above the family's arms.[101] Engraved in the Pollards' seal, the falchion was both central to the family's self-image and an expression of the way in which the Pollards wanted to be seen by others. In particular, the sword was both a symbol of knightly power and, in the case of the Pollards, a family without a tradition of military service in either the Scottish or French wars, whose members served instead as administrators on the bishop of Durham's estate, a statement of knightly aspirations.[102] By the early fifteenth century, moreover, there is some evidence that the family was embellishing its association with the sword, for on the death of John Pollard as a minor in 1415 he was recorded as holding land from the bishop *per servicium unius vetus Fauchonis*.[103] Like the Earl Warenne's production of his 'ancient and rusty sword' before Edward I's justices, the Pollard falchion was evidence of the longevity of the family's possession of its estates. Ancient landownership was an important quality of gentility.[104] Indeed, in the late sixteenth century, when the family was visited by one of the royal heralds, the Pollards were only too eager to display the family heirloom, the falchion, 'by shewing' of which, the herald recorded, they 'hold their lands of the Bishop of Durham'. The herald completed his visit with a drawing of the sword.[105] The Pollards saw their continued possession of the sword as a mark of distinction.

In fact, just like the Conyers, the Pollards' ownership of an ancient falchion had, by the seventeenth century, become the basis of a local legend surrounding the origins of the family and its estate. When the bishopric of Durham was surveyed on the orders of the Commonwealth Parliament to see how much the lands were worth before their sale in 1647, by which date the Pollards had become extinct, the surveyors discovered that several freeholds in Bondgate in Bishop Auckland had 'been given by some of

---

[100] PRO, DURH 3/2, fo. 18v.
[101] See figure 5.2.
[102] On the symbolism of the sword, see Clanchy, *Memory to Written Record*, pp. 39, 41.
[103] PRO, DURH 3/2, fols. 172v–173r.
[104] P. Morgan, 'Making the English Gentry', in *Thirteenth Century England V*, ed. P.R. Coss and S.D. Lloyd (Woodbridge, 1995), pp. 21–8.
[105] See figure 5.2.

the Bishops to one Pollard for killing a wild Boar', for which 'the owners of this land are to doe at every Bishop's first coming to be Bishop here to present him with the Falchon with which the Bore was slayne'.[106] The beginning of this legend is unknown. Was it a late development? It is interesting to note that a similar myth developed around the 'Boarstall Horn', according to which a wild boar had roamed free in the forest of Bernwood until a huntsman by the name of Nigel slew it, presenting the creature's head to Edward the Confessor and receiving in return land and the custody of Bernwood Forest.[107] The story of the boar was depicted in the map of the village of Boarstall contained in a mid-fifteenth-century cartulary belonging to a Buckinghamshire esquire by the name of Edmund Rede, and Paul Harvey has concluded that it 'no doubt originated – perhaps even with Edmund Rede himself – in a false etymology of the name Boarstall'. There is good reason to believe this particular connection, yet the Boarstall legend clearly fits into a much broader tradition of gentry self-fashioning linking chivalric ideals of prowess and bravery to the possession of land. The evidence of the Boarstall cartulary suggests that it would perhaps be a mistake to assume that the story of the Pollard boar was a post-medieval creation. Whatever the case, the most significant point is that the tradition was situated firmly in the locality, presenting the Pollard family as heroic figures, the saviours of the people of Bishop Auckland whom the animal had terrorised. The presentation of the Pollard falchion continued until the second half of the nineteenth century, by which time the myth of the martial endeavours of the founder of the Pollard family had become fully developed. Thus, William Fordyce, in his two-volume *History and Antiquities of the County Palatine of Durham*, could explain the existence of the township of Pollards Lands by recounting the 'tradition' of 'a champion knight' by the name of Pollard who, 'for slaying a wild boar, had as much land granted to him by one of the bishops as he could ride round whilst the grantor dined'.[108]

Perhaps this is a rather frivolous note upon which to end. Instead, it may be useful to draw attention to two issues arising from this study which need further examination. The first point is that the Pollard falchion, like the Conyers falchion, seems to have been both a symbol of title and a distinctive form of tenure, hovering between a service rendered for a piece of land such as a serjeanty and an object embodying the right to it.[109] Tim Thornton has suggested that the 'myths surrounding the Conyers of Sockburn family', coupled with the cult of St Cuthbert, should be considered as evidence of 'a no-less-impressive set of cultural traditions supportive of the palatine community and its privileges' than those found in the palatinate of Chester.[110] Certainly, there is much to be said for viewing the presentation of falchions as an

---

[106] *Parliamentary Surveys of the Bishopric of Durham*, p. 15.
[107] For this and what follows, see Harvey, 'Boarstall', p. 217 and n. 3.
[108] W. Fordyce, *The History and Antiquities of the County Palatine of Durham* (2 vols., Newcastle, 1855–7), I, 564.
[109] I would like to thank Robert Bartlett for discussion of this issue. On tenure by serjeanty, see Pollock and Maitland, *History of English Law*, I, 262–71, and A.L. Poole, *Obligations of Society in the XII and XIII Centuries* (Oxford, 1945), ch. 4. An example of a medieval horn of tenure from Lancashire provides an interesting parallel; one Roger de Heysham held two carucates of land by sounding his horn whenever the king entered and departed the county: T. Blount, *Fragmenta Antiquitatis: Antient Tenures of Land* (London, 1679), p. 58.
[110] T. Thornton, 'Fifteenth-Century Durham and the Problem of Provincial Liberties in England and the Wider Territories of the English Crown', *TRHS*, 6th ser. 11 (2001), 85.

integral part of the distinctive cultural traditions of the Durham palatinate. The IPMs of members of the Pollard family in the early fifteenth century make it abundantly clear that, by this time, the Pollards did regard the production of the falchion before the bishop of Durham as a form of service, which they were only too eager to point out released them from other obligations. For example, the second IPM of Dionisia, John Pollard sr.'s widow, referred to the land next to Auckland Park as held *per unum Fawchonem quiete de omnio alio servicio*, while William Pollard, appearing before chancery at Durham in 1435, claimed that this property was held of the bishop by the service of a falchion *tantum quiete de omnibus aliis serviciis et demandis*.[111]

In the 1660s Bishop Cosin saw the presentation of the falchions as a traditional and distinctive element in the process of episcopal inauguration within the county palatine. Indeed, Cosin's insistence that, with the demise of the Pollards, the freeholders of Bondgate in Bishop Auckland should present the falchion instead, is surely revealing.[112] Given the dissolution and subsequent revival of the palatinate with the Restoration, there may have been a particular concern at this time to see restored some of the traditional rituals associated with the liberty.[113] Whether it really is possible to read backwards from the peculiar circumstances of the mid-seventeenth century to see a continuous tradition stretching back to the late Middle Ages remains to be proven. It is hard to believe, though, that the bishops of Durham were not aware of the symbolism of receiving swords from two of their lay tenants as they first entered the liberty from the south, passing by the Conyers' manor of Sockburn, and then came to reside in Auckland Palace, from its construction in the late thirteenth century the main episcopal residence in the palatinate.[114] The idea that the falchion should be presented to the bishop 'on his first arrival at Auckland after his consecration',[115] the ceremony which specifically conferred spiritual power, is suggestive. The Pollard and Conyers falchions were delivered to and returned by the bishops of Durham in a ritual which acknowledged the bishops' temporal powers as overlords within the palatinate, from whom all tenants in the liberty ultimately held their land. The swords were part of the episcopal rites of passage in Durham, providing further evidence that the bishops enjoyed dual status as both ecclesiastics in respect of their spiritualities and earls palatine as to their temporalities.[116] The rituals surrounding the falchions may also have helped to delineate the boundaries of the palatinate and to mark it out as a separate entity, with which not only the bishop but also his tenants could identify.

Secondly, this case study, in its exploration of the hitherto largely neglected process of gentrification in the county palatine of Durham, has highlighted the need to extend the parameters of the traditional *foci* of studies of the late medieval English gentry to incorporate the lesser, sub-manorial landed figures in the shires, who were, after all, far more numerous than the county gentry.[117] How did the minor gentry build

---

[111] PRO, DURH 3/2, fo. 139r; 3/37, m. 14r.
[112] DUL, Sharp MS 167, p. 2.
[113] For the fate of the palatinate in the mid-seventeenth century, see Lapsley, *County Palatine*, pp. 199–200.
[114] J. Raine, *A Brief Historical Account of the Episcopal Castle, or Palace, of Auckland* (Durham, 1852), passim.
[115] PRO, DURH 3/2, fols. 129r–v, 282r–283v, 284v–285r.
[116] Fraser, *History of Antony Bek*, p. 95.
[117] C. Given-Wilson, *The English Nobility in the Late Middle Ages* (2nd edn., London, 1996), pp. 72–3.

up their estates, converting and amalgamating their small properties into manors? Work on Warwickshire landed society has sought to address this question, but it is important also to expand the geographical range of gentry studies, which have tended to focus almost exclusively upon the midland counties.[118] The Pollards only seem to have acquired manorial lordship in the second half of the sixteenth century when Ralph Pollard of Pollard Hall bought a share of the manors of West Ayton and Brompton in the wapentake of Pickering Lythe in the North Riding of Yorkshire. In an ironic postscript, the owners of the other moiety of the manor of Brompton were the Conyers of Sockburn.[119] Yet the Pollards of Pollard Hall, though only visible sporadically in the historical record, were a family of no little note and no little history in the county palatine of Durham. When an inquiry was held in the later fourteenth century regarding the terms of a final concord made in 1298 involving a member of the family, the Pollards were sufficiently well known for the *antiquiores totius Episcopatus Dunelmensis* to be able to testify accurately to their genealogical history from the early thirteenth century.[120] They, and other lesser landowners like them, warrant greater consideration.

---

[118] Roberts, 'Medieval Colonization in the Forest of Arden', 101–13; Carpenter, *Locality and Polity*, pp. 22–3. This point about the geographical bias is noted in Carpenter, 'Gentry and Community', 349.
[119] *VCH North Riding*, II, 426–7.
[120] DCM, 3.9.Spec. 31. I would like to thank Matthew Holford for this reference.

6

Local Law Courts in Late Medieval Durham

PETER L. LARSON

By the thirteenth century local justice in rural England was embodied primarily in two courts: those of the manor and hundred (or wapentake). The manor court was a seigniorial instrument, regulating the lord's estate but also providing to the villein tenants a basic forum for civil litigation that otherwise they would be denied. The hundred and wapentake courts were royal or public courts, and the jurisdiction often was described as leet jurisdiction, or the view of frankpledge.[1] Historians have assumed that these same courts functioned across England, with minor variations (and then more in name or shape than actual competence). However, like the manor, which historians once assumed to have a common, standard form, the rural local courts were quite diverse, perhaps more so than has been thought. In Durham, at least, local justice differed greatly from what would be found in Suffolk or Cambridgeshire. This cannot be questioned. The larger implications are far less clear. Has the uniformity of the local courts been exaggerated like the manor? Or, if Durham is an aberration, to what is this due?

A satisfactorily comprehensive answer to this question may be completely elusive, since many records do not survive. Still, there are at least three avenues of approach to this question, three starting points for fresh investigations. First, it is clear that, as a result of landlords exercising public functions on their estates, the divisions between manorial and hundredal jurisdiction were not always original but were imposed later, at times artificially. Separate hundred and manorial courts from the time of the Norman Conquest and before were not uncommon, but frequently a single court exercised a more plenary competence. Parallel to developments in the common law, the *quo warranto* inquests of the late thirteenth century firmly established the separation of these two courts in theory: a lord required a specific royal grant to claim hundred jurisdiction. The 'public' and 'private' spheres now were separate, even if only according to the jurists. To what extent was this separation true throughout all of England, or was there a gap between theory and practice? The jurists of Edward I often effected the division of local judicial competence in contravention of existing practices. Had Edward I had his way, local justice would have been regularised, most of it in the king's hand; but he was forced to back down on his claims. Changes to the system did occur, at least in some places, but often gradually, and perhaps only

---

[1] The frankpledge system was not adopted in northern England: W.A. Morris, *The Frankpledge System* (New York, 1910), p. 45.

superficially. It is quite likely that historians have granted too much importance to this theoretical distinction. It would well be worth investigating the timing of the practical effects of *quo warranto* inquests, to discover how much time elapsed between the statement of theory and its full implementation.[2]

Secondly, not all areas of England began with the same set of local institutions and divisions. The division of counties into hundreds (or wapentakes) was restricted to certain regions only. Peripheral areas such as the North continued to possess different local divisions, and, consequently, local institutions. The effects of *quo warranto* inquests and similar common law developments on these regions must be studied further.[3] This is especially true for the Scottish and Welsh border areas, regions traditionally portrayed as fiercely independent from royal interference. Even if this independence has been overstated, as it often has, these regions were still replete with liberties of varying stature, the greatest of all being the county palatine of Durham. How far did the theoretical division of local rural courts penetrate into these liberties?

Thirdly, as anyone who has read them knows, nearly all medieval English court proceedings were recorded using heavily formulaic and grammatically imprecise Latin. The few surviving rolls in English confirm the existence of a considerable difference between what was said in court and what was written down. This idea of filtering may be taken one logical step further. Clerks may have not merely translated the language of the proceedings into legal Latin, but may have translated the proceedings themselves into a standard idiom. This process has its modern equivalents; consider the ways that our words and ideas today are translated, in form and concept, into 'official' forms such as memoranda and minutes. Thus, unique courts may have been rendered into ones more consistent with widely accepted legal principles.[4]

Perhaps it is time that historians provide the manor court with the same treatment as the manor, looking past labels to the substance underneath. While the first approach, of examining the local effects of *quo warranto* inquests, is a long-term project, the second and third approaches may yield results more quickly. A test case is needed to demonstrate the need for and the utility of such a new inquiry. Durham is such an example. As a county palatine with its own legal apparatus, it is the one county in England most likely to have been insulated from the developments of the common law. Although conforming to the general model of English justice and administration, Durham was nonetheless unique in a number of ways. One of these is the organisation of local justice. How exactly did the local court network function in Durham, and to what extent does it follow the 'typical' model? Was there even a standard local law court in late medieval Durham?

Most of the evidence for the functioning of local Durham courts comes from the two great ecclesiastical estates, Durham Priory's main estate and the estate of the

---

[2] See H.M. Cam, 'Manerium cum Hundredo: The Hundred and the Hundredal Manor', and 'The Quo Warranto Proceedings under Edward I', in idem, *Liberties and Communities in Medieval England* (London, 1963), pp. 64–90 and 174 respectively.

[3] Those studies looking at northern England have focused on tracing the institutions back to their British or Celtic roots: J.E.A. Jolliffe, 'Northumbrian Institutions', *EHR* 41 (1926), 1–42; G.R.J. Jones, 'Basic Patterns of Settlement Distribution in Northern England', *Advancement of Science* 18 (1961), 192–200.

[4] The many arguments regarding the interpretation of Domesday Book alone should leave us sceptical of accepting concepts and institutions at face value.

bishops of Durham.[5] Together, the records from these courts cover more than one hundred settlements. Each series is reasonably complete from the Black Death into the sixteenth century (and for the bishopric, well beyond). This combination of geographical coverage and record survival makes Durham one of the most well-represented counties in England, albeit one that few historians have considered, and none comprehensively.[6] In stark contrast to the abundance of material in the bishopric and priory archives, however, evidence about courts held by lay lords is surprisingly rare. The right to hold courts must have been implied by the terms *sake* and *soke* in the charters, despite the arguments of the lawyers of Edward I to the contrary. However, only a handful of records survives for villages in lay hands, covering only a few years, and references to courts being held, or to the right to hold courts, either in charters or inquisitions *post mortem*, are few.[7] Accordingly, we know very little about the courts of lay estates in Durham. What does survive largely conforms to the picture drawn from the bishopric and priory courts.

Herein lies a crucial difference between Durham and the rest of England. In the rest of the country, there was a marked difference in social and judicial organisation even within counties. Two neighbouring vills might have very different court systems and organisations, so that we cannot really talk about a typical manor or manor court. Great estates and honours were spread piecemeal over multiple counties, and a large block of concentrated jurisdiction was extremely rare. Because of record survival, our knowledge of a county is based on only a small proportion of its manors and vills, and rarely is there sufficient evidence to account for variations in estate administration. Durham is different. Even given the virtual absence of lay court records, the amount of settled territory covered by the available evidence is vast. Thus we know more about the county, and generalisations are less dangerous. Durham was remarkably homogenous in terms of society and more so of custom than the rest of England, a homogeneity derived in large part from the original unity of the two estates and reinforced by parallel development elsewhere. Consequently, it is possible in Durham to speak of typical villages and typical customs, because the histories of the different villages as revealed in the halmote courts are often indistinguishable. The study of a small number of villages provides a picture of the local courts of the palatinate as a whole, something nearly impossible to achieve for other counties.

In Durham, there is no evidence of any court equivalent to the hundred courts, by any name, nor of any non-borough 'public' court other than the higher courts concerned with life and limb. Disputes between men of different estates were settled in the home court of the plaintiff or through special arbitration.[8] On the two major franchisal estates, where one might expect a form of delegated lesser public jurisdiction, the only local court was the halmote, which scholars usually have described as a manorial court. In the post-medieval period it certainly was; but this is an inadequate description of the medieval halmote, and it occludes the solution to the absent 'public'

---

[5] As found in DCM, Priory Halmote Rolls; PRO, DURH 3/12 and following (Bishopric Halmote Books). Selected extracts of the priory rolls to 1385 have been published as *HPD*.
[6] The volume of records may well be a factor, as is their relatively late start. In addition, the records are not capable of supporting the more demographically-oriented analyses favoured over the past few decades.
[7] I owe this information to a personal communication from Christian Liddy.
[8] K. Emsley and C.M. Fraser, *The Courts of the County Palatine of Durham* (Durham, 1984), pp. 7–9.

jurisdiction. These halmotes had greater competence than most manorial courts. Even more, describing them as 'manorial' classifies them according to a judicial system that, while similar to the one operating in Durham, was nevertheless alien to it. First, Durham possessed a somewhat different approach to the provision of justice at the local level, one that was more functional and organic, rather than one based on juristic organisation. Equity and dispute resolution were more important than procedures and judgments according to the strict hierarchies and legal principles assumed to have operated at all levels of medieval English law, high and low.[9] Secondly, the normal boundaries between courts did not always hold in Durham. The halmotes were commonly the *fora* for more business than should be found in a manorial court. Neither was there a clear path for appeals. Finally, as we shall see, the attitude of the bishops, who in Durham stood *in loco regis*, was different from that of the English kings whom they are often believed to have aped.[10]

It is necessary to take a quick look at the mechanics of these halmotes before examining their competence and origins. They were held three times a year, in the summer, autumn, and early spring. There is no evidence of formal courts meeting any other time, and it is doubtful whether more frequent meetings would have been profitable or even useful. Deadlines for performance were often set in between court sessions.[11] There are isolated incidents of villages holding their own moots independently of the courts, but these were highly irregular and quickly suppressed.[12] Courts were held in several places on different days as their senior officers progressed through the county. They were held in the same locations every tourn, with occasional exceptions. These locations were usually parish or estate centres, such as Easington and Pittington; the court itself met in the hall of a manor in or near these estate vills, or sometimes in the parish church.[13] The priory halmotes were held at Jarrow, Fulwell, Monk Wearmouth, Pittington, Beaulieu, and Merrington. The bishopric tourns stopped at Easington, Bishop Middleham, Sadberge, Bishop Auckland, Darlington, Chester-le-Street, Houghton-le-Spring, Wolsingham, Lanchester, and Stockton. At each of these court centres, several villages would come to the central court; for example, three vills owed suit to the bishopric halmote at Bishop Middleham. Business was heard village by village, with all the business for one vill heard before moving on to the next. Each village showed up at an appointed time, and usually was dismissed

---

[9] Lloyd Bonfield argues that all manorial courts functioned based on equity and dispute resolution rather than on substantive principles: L. Bonfield, 'The Nature of Customary Law in the Manor Courts of Medieval England', *Comparative Studies of Society and History* 31 (1989), 514–34. However, this view is contested.

[10] The widely-accepted misconception of Durham as a constitutional and legal microcosm of England is encapsulated in the classic work on Durham constitutional history by G.T. Lapsley, *The County Palatine of Durham: A Study in Constitutional History* (Cambridge, Mass., 1900). Although often challenged in detail, many of his views have been echoed by later scholars.

[11] In some cases, the results were never recorded, so it must be assumed that the ministers were satisfied with the results. At other times, however, the results were reported at the next tourn, even if performed, so the level of enforcement, or at least monitoring, varied.

[12] Two bishopric villages were amerced in 1394 for holding a court amongst themselves and making their own regulations, and similar events transpired elsewhere in 1396 and 1397: PRO, DURH 3/13, fols. 135v, 136v, 205v, 240v.

[13] Specific references as to the physical location of the court are quite rare, and often late. For references to payments made in court held in the hall at Pittington and the church at Merrington, see *Durham Cathedral Priory Rentals: Vol. 1, Bursar's Rentals*, ed. R.A. Lomas and A.J. Piper (Surtees Society 198, 1986), pp. 151–2, 168, 172.

before the business of the next vill was heard; villagers were fined if they arrived late or left early.

A jury of between three and five men represented each village. It is not clear whether the jury had any role in presenting offences, or if this was left to the officers of the estates. It is also unclear whether they functioned as a trial jury as well, or if judgment was in the hands of the court presidents. The jury did determine damages, inquire into facts, advise the court, and deliver occasional pronouncements on custom. On the priory estate, some cases never went to judgment by the jury or steward, but were settled by oath-helpers.[14] The jurors were not always considered co-operative, and were often called 'false' and 'perjurers'. Nevertheless, men held the position of juror for long periods of time, and sons often joined or succeeded their fathers. Along with the reeve (who was himself almost always a juror, and often the head juror), the jury functioned on behalf of the lord and their village. When the village as a whole leased land, or was involved in litigation with a third party, the jury represented the village as a corporate entity.

In the bishopric halmotes the bishop's steward presided over the sessions, assisted by the bailiffs and even the county coroners, who had a wider role than their colleagues elsewhere; in addition to the standard duties of the coroner, they acted as bailiffs in the courts, collected certain free rents, and were responsible for capturing and returning fugitive *nativi*. In the late Middle Ages, the bishopric steward was usually a senior clerk or else a member of a leading northern gentry family bordering on the nobility, such as Sir Thomas Gray or Sir Ralph Eure. Men such as these had wider interests than the palatinate, serving as members of parliament and justices of the peace for neighbouring counties, campaigning for the king, and performing other royally appointed tasks in the North and elsewhere. On the priory main estate, the stewards were drawn from the lesser county gentry and were relegated to a minor role on the estate. The obedientiaries concerned with the estate, the bursar and terrar, ran the court as well as the estate.[15] The prior certainly had extensive knowledge of what was occurring on the estate and in the courts; many concessions and pardons were recorded as being authorised by him. Tough questions and unclear points in the bishopric halmotes were referred to the bishop's council; and the bishops in their court received humble suitors and personally heard business on minor matters, such as an extension on a few pennies rent.[16] Thus the major officers, and even the lords, were in close contact with the ordinary villagers, and were well informed about local affairs and conditions, perhaps surprisingly given the size of each estate. Negotiation rather than conflict marked the relations between lord and tenant, with principles upheld but softened by practical concessions. Late medieval Durham was surprisingly free of open conflict between lords and tenants, and the close connection between the two through the courts may have been an essential factor in these developments.

---

14 This question of the functioning of the court requires further investigation.
15 The priory's main estate is often referred to as the bursar's estate. Certain other obedientiaries had smaller endowments for specific tasks in the cathedral, but the main estate provided for the everyday needs of the monks and the priory: R.A. Lomas, 'Durham Cathedral Priory as a Landowner and a Landlord, 1290–1540' (unpublished Ph.D. thesis, University of Durham, 1973), pp. 27–8; E.M. Halcrow, 'Administration and Agrarian Policy of the Manors of Durham Cathedral Priory' (unpublished B.Litt. thesis, University of Oxford, 1949), p. 4.
16 DUL, CCB B/23/1 (221160), 7, 10, 22, 26, 27, 34, 36, 66.

While we know much about the business in the halmotes, we do not have the original records of the courts. Rather, we have fair copies that do not contain all the information in the originals. The amount of information lost is indeterminable. There are numerous memoranda in the court records to the effect that the clerk has failed to note something and that the reader should go back to the original roll.[17] A variety of letters, writs, and schedules were attached to the original record and presumably were lost with it. Other information may have gone into other derivatory record series. For example, certain sums (including the perquisites of the court) appear in certain final copies but not in others. Another example of this is fines and reliefs for free land taken in the bishop's halmotes. In the 1340s and 1350s lists of these were appended to the end of the halmote records for each tourn, and they indicate that this business was transacted within the halmotes. When the series begins again after a gap in the late 1380s, these lists are gone, but the halmote books contain references to other rolls that had the information. There is no reason to assume that anything had changed except the record system. A third example concerns the halmote books on the priory main estate, which are not of the same type as the bishopric books. Instead of being a fair copy of the court record, the priory halmote books are a record of land transfers alone, and survive only from 1400 (though possibly having begun before then).[18] In the extant priory court rolls, information regarding these land transfers initially matches the entries in the books, but, over time, the detail decreases, since there was little need to copy the long and tedious formulae more than once. In one final example regarding gaps in the records, there are indications that the priory court of the marshalsea, which had jurisdiction over weights and measures, may have been held at the same time as the halmotes. There is a scrap of paper, which appears to be a draft copy of the halmote court from autumn 1395 for the villages of Pittington and East and West Rainton.[19] Comparison with the halmote roll for the same tourn demonstrates that the two are nearly identical and were based on the same original. However, it also reveals several differences between the two: most notably, the draft contains information pertaining to the marshalsea court, specifically regulation of measures, whereas the halmote roll omits this information. What we have, then, is a record that is neither complete, nor even one where we know what exactly is missing. Thus, any conclusions drawn from the halmote records must be treated with caution.

On the surface, halmotes appear to be the same as manorial courts with hundred or leet jurisdiction elsewhere in England. That is, they combine seigniorial affairs, such as servile dues and land conveyance, with public concerns such as minor peace-keeping functions and the assize of ale. Additionally, the halmotes served as village moots to determine local affairs such as stints and grazing periods.[20] There are a number of differences, however.

The first is the nature of the business. Elsewhere, the extent of this mixed manorial and public jurisdiction was limited. It was essentially petty business, minor debts, and scuffles. Most actions regarding land in the manorial courts were limited to unfree or customary land; after all, the major distinction between customary and free land was

---

[17] Among the clearest are PRO, DURH 3/12, fols. 10r, 11r, 16v, 19r, 63v; 3/13, fo. 187r.
[18] DCM, Priory Halmote Books I, II, III.
[19] DCM, Priory Halmote Roll for Autumn 1395, m. 4d.; Loc.IV:250.
[20] F. Pollock and F.W. Maitland, *The History of English Law Before the Time of Edward I* (2 vols., 2nd edn., Cambridge, 1898), I, 531–2.

that those with the latter had access to the royal courts regarding that free land. Because of the limits of competence in manorial courts, most of these local courts began to decline after the Black Death, and the quarter sessions absorbed more of the 'civil' litigation. The amount of information in fifteenth-century manorial court rolls is much smaller and more limited than those of the thirteenth and fourteenth centuries, and for many places no records survive at all. I am of course generalising about other manorial courts here; there is no real 'standard' manorial court just as there are no 'typical' manors. It is easier to say that the Durham halmotes exceeded what would be considered the limits of manorial competence in the rest of England; more business was conducted than would be legally permissible in other courts. For this reason, the halmotes continued to be viable, well-used courts even when manorial courts elsewhere began to atrophy.

What follows is a selection of some of the more conspicuous examples of this extraordinary business, which for Durham was quite ordinary. Most come from the bishop's halmote courts, since the record in the bishopric books is often fuller, and the bishopric courts catered to a larger population over a wider area, and with a greater variation in wealth and status. Nevertheless, the other halmotes also shared in these peculiarities to varying extents, and this will be returned to later.

The first matter is debt. In the rest of the country, debts of forty shillings and over had to go before the royal courts, a practice based on a not-quite-straightforward interpretation of the 1278 Statute of Gloucester.[21] This may not always have been strictly followed in practice in the manor courts of England. In Durham, both the halmotes as well as the county court ignored the limitation, in such a way that there is no implication that they were bound by it. For example, in the bishopric halmote, John Galon sued a certain Thomas for £9, a debt assigned to him by the earl of Northumberland. The executors of Bishop Walter Skirlaw (d. 1406) pursued numerous debtors for large sums over several years, some for sums even over £100.[22] These are exceptional. Most debts were small, but there are sufficient instances of large debts to demonstrate the lack of legal limitation.

The second instance of unusual competence is free land. Matters touching free land should have been heard in a free court, if not in a royal court. Elsewhere, free land could come before a manorial court, but this was at the discretion of the holder; a free tenant could not be compelled to answer regarding free land in a villein court. Again, in Durham, this was not the case, although some of this turns upon the classification of the halmotes themselves, as we shall see below. Most unexpectedly, there were several cases of *mortmain*, the practice of giving land to the 'dead hand' of the church, forbidden by the Statute of Mortmain in 1279.[23] In the early fifteenth century the

---

[21] Ibid., I, 553–4. The simplest reading of the statute would be that one could only plead a debt in a royal court with a writ if the debt was greater than forty shillings.

[22] PRO, DURH 3/13, fo. 28v; see also 3/13, fo. 211v, and 3/14, fo. 60v and following.

[23] The history of royal statute in medieval Durham is in need of elucidation. Most historians appear to have silently assumed that these statutes applied to Durham just as to the rest of the country. Bishop Hatfield (exceptionally) copied the 1351 Statute of Labourers into his register: R.H. Britnell, 'Feudal Reaction after the Black Death in the Palatinate of Durham', *P&P* 128 (1990), 29. This is one of the few, perhaps the only, instance of a statute being recorded in the Durham archives. Certainly, the issue is clouded by the lack of record survival, compounded by the assumption of medieval writers that the audience knew what they implied and so did not explicitly state the subject of their writing. Despite this, the role of statutes in Durham needs to be defined. Did Durham's palatine status result in limited or

bishop's steward charged several tenants in the Stanhope area of granting free lands held of the bishop to the church in violation of the statute. The grantee is not stated. Further action on these breaches is not recorded, but the very fact that it appears more than once in the halmotes is sufficient to justify the conclusion that *mortmain* was justiciable in the halmotes.[24] Pleas regarding free land in other respects were sometimes heard in the halmotes, though usually for lesser properties. The steward, sometimes regularly, took fines and reliefs for free land in court, and certain dringage tenures, although explicitly considered free land, were continually dealt with in the halmotes throughout the period. Transactions involving small parcels of free land were common, even some held in chief of the bishop by military service. Though uncommon, it by no means was unusual to have free land transacted in the halmotes.

The halmote court was also used to combat the continuing problems of labour shortage after the Black Death. This was not merely an instance of employers suing servants for breach of contract. Instead, there are numerous cases in which a tenant is fined for taking a servant away from another; he is found guilty of extracting the servant from the service of another.[25] Furthermore, one offence, when Stephen Gerying was fined sixpence for enticing away the servant (*garcio*) of Robert Kyrkeman late in 1353, was recorded explicitly as against the Statute (*contra Statutum*); this can only refer to the Statute of Labourers.[26] Even if, technically, many of these cases were not associated with either the 1349 Ordinance of Labourers or the 1351 Statute of Labourers, they do show a concern over employers stealing workers from others.[27] It further proves that the halmotes were seen as an acceptable place to seek justice; again, not the sort of occurrence one would expect to find in a manorial court.

A fourth set of examples relates to the hundredal or leet jurisdiction. The halmotes regulated the peace, as did many manor courts and all the hundred courts. Most breaches of the peace were minor scuffles and arguments; but some were quite violent: deliberate ambushes from hiding, or gangs attacking a single person. Officers of the lord were assaulted, and many victims complained that they were wounded so grievously, they despaired of their lives. Anything short of murder could go before the halmotes, unless the victim wished to pursue it as a trespass in a higher court. In the rest of England, many of these cases undoubtedly would have gone before other courts. In addition to prosecuting breakers of the bishop's peace, the halmotes often went to great lengths to preserve the peace. In times of perceived disorder, injunctions were issued against carrying weapons and drawing them, or from hosting strangers on the lord's demesne.[28] The priory even forbade gambling and football games in these

---

selective adoption of the statutes, or in different enforcement of them? Are the oddities and differences in justice at the lowest level mirrored or matched at the 'royal' and 'statute' levels as well?

[24] PRO, DURH 3/14, fols. 97r, 109r.

[25] PRO, DURH 3/12, fo. 187r (Bishopley, 1358).

[26] PRO, DURH 3/12, fo. 89r (Cornforth).

[27] The 1349 Ordinance specifically forbade employers from employing workers who had left their earlier position before the expiration of the agreement: B.H. Putnam, *The Enforcement of the Statute of Labourers* (New York, 1908), appendix, p. 9; *SR*, I, 307. Although not specified in the 1351 Statute, the earlier clause would still have been enforceable as the Ordinance was regarded through the later fourteenth century as having 'all the force of statute law': Putnam, *Enforcement*, p. 179.

[28] For example, see PRO, DURH 3/135, m. 1r (Sedgefield), and DCM, Priory Halmote Roll for Spring 1384, m. 3d. (Dalton).

times, as the games often led to quarrels and brawls.[29] One late injunction against football allowed it to be played twice a year, but explicitly stated that 'he who makes an affray on those days forfeits to the lord forty shillings'.[30] When a dispute between two parties became violent, the quarrelling parties could be bound over to keep the peace, many times at £20 per person. While perhaps not as impressive a sum for a bond as others have found elsewhere, most studies of violence have focused on the gentry and nobility. For peasants, even rich peasants, such sums would have been high, and clearly were meant to deter them from breaking the peace in future.

A final example of the unusual business and competence of the halmotes is proof of personal status. A man claiming to be free should have gone before royal courts to prove his status; even the county court was no longer sufficient.[31] In Durham, this fell to the halmotes. There are numerous inquests in the late fourteenth century asking whether a specific man was free or a *nativus*, a serf. In the summer of 1375 a jury of twelve men declared,[32] in the presence of the prior and others, 'that Thomas son of John Wydouson of West Rainton is free and of free condition and of free status, and is not a *nativus* of the said Lord Prior'.[33] The priory even began compiling lists of its serfs through the mechanism of the halmote courts; the jury would list all the *nativi*, sometimes including children, who pertained to a set of villages and where they were now living.[34] No special jury was used, only the regular halmote juries from the neighbouring townships. The only other reference to an inquest concerning personal status comes from the palatine chancery rolls. This is a record of a commission to determine the status of two men who had appealed, to the bishop and his council, the decision in the halmotes that they were not free.[35]

The question of status leads to the second unusual feature of the halmotes, the people who used these courts. The common assumption, especially among those who are not social historians, is that if this were a manorial court in, say, Suffolk, one would expect only those who held customary lands to attend; by extension, most if not all of these men would be unfree tenants. Free men would, even should, take their business elsewhere unless it had to do with customary land that they held.[36] Not so in

---

[29] *Injunctum est Johanni Heddon, Johanni Henrison, Thome Patonson, Johanni Patonson, Willelmi Raynton, Nichole Colson, Thome Miller, Thome Robynson, et omnibus aliis quod nullus eorum decetero ludat ad talos, cardes, pilam pedalem, et alios ludos prohibitos sub pena . . . xx s.*: DCM, Priory Halmote Roll for Spring 1478, m. 1 (Aycliffe).

[30] DCM, Priory Halmote Roll for Spring 1492, m. 2d. (Billingham).

[31] P.R. Hyams, *Kings, Lords, and Peasants in Medieval England: The Common Law of Villeinage in the Twelfth and Thirteenth Centuries* (Oxford, 1980), pp. 162–3.

[32] This is not the standard jury of three to five men of the halmote courts mentioned above. It would seem that for more important matters, and for matters touching multiple vills, larger juries were empanelled; and from the names found in these larger juries, they drew heavily, if not exclusively, on the smaller village jury of the halmotes.

[33] *Est liber et liberi condicionis ac liberi status et non nativus dicti domini Prioris*: DCM, Priory Halmote Roll for Summer 1375, m. 1 (Pittington). There is no clearer statement of freedom possible. Similar inquests can be found throughout the halmote records of the main estates of both priory and bishopric for this period.

[34] These begin in 1378, and the last surviving inquest is from 1470: DCM, Priory Halmote Book II, fols. 112v–113. For treatment and enrolment of serfs by other monastic houses, see E.D. Jones, 'The Exploitation of its Serfs by Spalding Priory before the Black Death', *Nottingham Medieval Studies*, 43 (1999), 147–9.

[35] PRO, DURH 3/31, fo. 14v.

[36] Bonfield makes villein tenure part of the integral definition of a manor court: Bonfield, 'Nature of Customary Law', 517–18. This misconception – that the majority of peasants were villeins – seems

Durham. To begin with, *nativi* made up approximately ten to twenty per cent of the customary tenants in the late fourteenth century. The rest were personally free, even though dependent on their lords because they held customary lands. In the case cited earlier, the man who was declared to be 'free and of free condition and of free status' would not have been counted as one of the priory's 'free tenants', and would not have had access to the prior's free court. He was a customary tenant, a man of low but free status who held customary land. The simplistic, juristic divide between free and unfree, found in the rest of England, did not operate in Durham, where an older, three-tiered status system continued in conjunction with a simple division in status of land. Free men who were not free tenants served on the juries along with the serfs, held local offices, and in all ways mixed with the *nativi*; but they could go to higher courts if they pleased, and give testimony in Courts Christian.[37] Yet, they frequently preferred to use the halmotes for their business. In doing so, they were joined by greater free men, usually ordinary free tenants, but even knights and the occasional lord. Nevertheless, tenants of free land (*terra libera*) had the right to use the free court of their lord. It is difficult to determine how often this right was *not* exercised, because the status of the person in question often is indeterminable. Some free tenants chose to use the free courts, especially on the priory estate, even for minor business. It was their right, and some must have felt insecure enough about their status to exercise it whenever possible.[38] Serious business went before justices or the bishop himself, but for many minor matters the halmotes were perfect. One did not have to travel all the way to Durham from the edges of the county to receive justice. The local courts were probably cheaper, and maybe even faster; as will be soon discussed, the halmotes insisted on fewer legal hurdles. The halmotes seemed to have little stigma other than being a minor court. Certainly no one refused to plead in the existing records, citing the halmotes as an unfree court, because it was not. Halmotes are never called villein courts.[39] Could free men of lower status have made greater use of the manor courts than we have given them credit?

The procedures followed in the Durham halmotes were remarkable as well. The royal courts of England, and many honorial or free courts, were procedure-driven and followed strict rules. An error in pleading could cost a litigant the case; if the exact formula were not recited, if the proper procedures were not followed precisely, the case would be thrown out and he who made the error amerced. Judgments relied more on legal principles and precedents. There is an ongoing debate about the penetration of royal law and procedures into the manorial courts of England. Even though manorial courts did not put the same emphasis as royal courts on precise formulation during pleading, there was an increasing sophistication and possibly the development of

---

incredibly difficult to dispel; see also P.R. Hyams, 'What did Edwardian Villagers Understand by Law?', in *Medieval Society and the Manor Court*, ed. Z. Razi and R.M. Smith (Oxford, 1996), pp. 70–1.

[37] But not to the free courts (*libere curie*), which were reserved for men who held free land.

[38] One example regarding the assize of ale may be seen in DCM, Priory Halmote Roll for 1389, m. 3d. (Cowpen).

[39] One of the complaints against Bishop Antony Bek, answered in his charter of liberties, was that he and his officers compelled free men to plead in the halmote courts 'among the villeins (*entre les vileins*)': *Records of Antony Bek, Bishop and Patriarch, 1283–1311*, ed. C.M. Fraser (Surtees Society 162, 1947), p. 94. Given the small percentage of *nativi* in the bishopric, 'villagers' must be the preferred translation for 'villeins'.

substantive legal principles and categories.[40] The Durham halmotes provide no examples of cases dismissed because of procedural or formula errors.[41] Many of the entries are formulaic, of course; but since the records are in Latin, there is no reason to believe that they are exact translations. Rarely are the cases phrased to include direct speech. When defendants 'put themselves on the country' or request a jury verdict, the exact wording in the records varies; if specific formulae were required, the scribes saw no need to translate them consistently.

Nor did there seem to be any special concern with categories of pleas, or the rejection of a complaint because it did not fit into the right, precise category. Not only was language used more loosely than in royal courts and even many manorial courts, but procedures were as well. One example is debt. To record a monetary debt, one should have made a plea of debt (*debiti*). This was the phrase used most of the time in the priory halmotes. In the bishopric halmotes, one could plead a monetary debt thus, but frequently litigants were involved in a plea of detinue (*detentionis*). This should only have applied not to monetary sums, but to specific goods whose return was desired. In the bishopric courts, however, debt and detinue were used interchangeably. This possibly could be seen as evidence of archaic practice; the two were originally equivalent in common law, as seen in Glanvill.[42] Given the unexpected competence of the halmotes demonstrated above, it seems that procedures were not strictly adhered to in the halmotes. Instead it would appear to be the case that they were not fixed. This is reminiscent of the 'equity' jurisdiction of the royal chancery, although I am cautious in using the term. Justice in the halmotes did not follow rigid, juristic principles, but focused on solving disputes fairly; hence, the resemblance to equity. Arbitration was a common feature of the courts; the halmotes sought to settle problems, not rule according to legal principle. Likewise, justice was quick. Unlike the Durham county court, where it seems a case could be delayed endlessly with ease and often it seems the only way a case could end was in default, in the halmotes litigation rarely dragged on.[43] An unfinished case in the halmotes was exceptional. In fact, it would seem as if the courts had evolved organically to be almost omni-competent (with some limitations, of course). While this may seem like a manor court out of control, bear in mind that those presiding over the courts were powerful and experienced men, well-versed in law. They often sat on commissions of the peace in Durham and other counties, and were no stranger to procedure. Yet, their main concern lay not in preserving legal principles, but in maintaining law and order, and keeping their estate running smoothly. Unconstrained by common law and the royal courts, it really is no surprise that they chose to execute justice expeditiously and equitably.

This unusual competence and attendance requires an explanation. The simple answer is that the halmotes were not manor courts as they are usually defined. The full

---

[40] See Hyams, 'What did Edwardian Villagers Understand by Law?', pp. 79–85, for a brief introduction to the question of royal law in manorial courts. On the other hand, Bonfield argues that what historians have seen as substantive legal principles in customary law were not; instead of ruling on principles, juries made decisions based on factors other than custom, in much the same way as equity jurisdiction.

[41] This was not the case with the priory free court, however: see the contribution by C.M. Fraser to this volume.

[42] F.W. Maitland, *The Forms of Action at Common Law*, ed. A.H. Chaytor and W.J. Whittaker (Cambridge, 1910), p. 48.

[43] Only one (previously overlooked) county court roll survives, as DCM, Misc. Ch. 5722, for the year 1403–4.

answer lies in two parts, and is connected with the 'manorial' history of the county, and also with its palatine status. Although Durham was never divided into hundreds or wapentakes, it did have shires such as Aucklandshire and Staindropshire. These shires may reflect an old, royal estate system.[44] The system of the four wards of the palatinate would not be complete until the early fourteenth century.[45] Other than the halmotes, there is no evidence of any local court in the county akin to the hundred or wapentake court, the wapentake of Sadberge excepted.[46] G.T. Lapsley's claims for a court for each of the wards is unfounded; in the fourteenth and fifteenth centuries there is no evidence for any local courts other than the halmotes, either in clerical or lay hands.[47] Although not provable, it is very possible that the halmote was the original 'local' court in Durham, the equivalent of the hundred or wapentake elsewhere, and all the halmotes had come into private hands. To help explain this, it first should be pointed out that in most of England the manor was seldom coterminous with the village. It was because the two were separate, and because the grants to lords could contain different rights and appurtenances, that a separation of jurisdictions often was required. Private, manorial jurisdiction covered the manor; public jurisdiction – the hundred or wapentake – covered the village. As we have seen, lawyers of Edward I in the *quo warranto* proceedings had hardened this division of the public and the manorial.[48] The distinction was generally accepted well before the Black Death.

In Durham there never was such distinction, since estates were never composed of less than a village. This was identified by Jolliffe as a general characteristic of the north east; he noted of Northumbrian communities that they '[appear] at once a mediatized hundred and a private estate, and we are puzzled to draw the line between public and private rights'.[49] So far as I have seen, in the various records of the palatinate, all lords had both jurisdictions. When a lord was granted an estate, he received full local jurisdiction, the same as the bishop had in his 'regalian' or 'palatine' vills. Since there were no manors that were only part of a vill, there was no need for the separation of competence. Unlike Edward I, the bishops of Durham saw no reason to reassert their rights to this jurisdiction; in fact, there was no internal *quo warranto* until the very end of the fifteenth century.[50] Because there are so few records for lay estates, and because charters rarely covered specific judicial rights, we have to rely on the negative evidence of the records we have. The bishopric and priory halmotes

---

[44] Jolliffe, 'Northumbrian Institutions', 1–42; W.E. Kapelle, *The Norman Conquest of the North: The Region and its Transformation, 1000–1135* (Chapel Hill, 1979), pp. 53–84. Compare the 'small scir' in R. Faith, *The English Peasantry and the Growth of Lordship* (Leicester, 1997), pp. 8–14.

[45] There were only three wards in the 1293 *quo warranto* proceedings for Durham (under Northumberland): Emsley and Fraser, *Courts of the County Palatine*, p. 14. The earliest mention of four wards is from a gaol delivery roll of 1330: DCM, Misc. Ch. 2640.

[46] Sadberge is foreign to Durham; having been purchased by one of the bishops, it retained its own free court as well as its own coroner, sheriff, and other officials.

[47] Lapsley, *County Palatine*, p. 194, claims that ward courts were held every three weeks, citing the *quo warranto* proceedings as proof of ward courts, which later became the sheriff's tourn. The *quo warranto* text mentions the *existence* of three wards; it does not mention ward courts, and it is difficult to construe such an implication from the records. Neither is there mention of ward courts in any bishopric, priory, or palatinate record.

[48] *Select Pleas in Manorial Courts, I: The Reigns of Henry III and Edward I*, ed. F.W. Maitland (Selden Society 2, 1888), pp. xvii–xxii; Cam, 'Quo Warranto Proceedings under Edward I'.

[49] Jolliffe, 'Northumbrian Institutions', 2.

[50] PRO, DURH 3/61, m. 11.

occasionally had outsiders coming into court, but tenants of other lords were decidedly rare. They must have received comparable judgment in their own lord's court. Thus, essentially, all lordships in Durham were franchises in this regard, although again this is imposing an alien category.

Alternatively, there may never have been a 'shire' court that later developed into the halmote. It has been argued convincingly that Durham was never fully divided into shires.[51] In this case, the exceptional features of the halmote are easily explained. Because there was no hierarchy of public courts as in the rest of the country, even theoretically,[52] and free from many of the constraints of the common law, and more so of common law jurists, the local courts were free to develop organically. They were able to add ways of dealing with important problems without requiring a fiat from above, or the creation of new and complicated procedures, or even new courts. Similarities between the halmotes and the other 'manorial' courts in Durham are attributable either to independent parallel development, or to the active adoption of loose procedures. Variations are explained as independent solutions to the same need, or to different needs.

While the various halmotes may originally have been the court of a territorial unit, the Durham shire, this was no longer the case by 1300 at the latest. Still, a common origin is feasible; it could well be that the halmotes evolved completely separately from each other to fulfill certain functions or needs specific to an estate. Either way, this would explain the many similarities within the courts, while also accounting for the differences in evolution – the prevalence of oaths on the priory estate compared to a preference for juries on the bishopric estate, for example.[53] What kept the halmotes going strong into the late fifteenth century, and beyond, was their organic development, based more on fulfilling need than following strict judicial definitions. The ability to accept different cases, without complicated procedure, and judgments based on compromise more than points of law, provided quick and fair justice for the majority of the Durham population. The lords certainly saw the halmotes as sufficient; access to Courts Christian was prevented when the matter could be resolved in the halmotes, with similar regulations regarding access to the borough courts.[54] Generally, the bishop as earl palatine seemed little concerned with the execution of local justice within the county except on his own estates.[55] Next to the continued fullness of the records, this is the best proof that the halmote courts, and the administration of justice on the local level, continued to be satisfactory.

---

[51] Kapelle, *Norman Conquest*, pp. 76–7.
[52] The appeals mentioned previously were all appeals to the bishop as seignior, not as earl palatine.
[53] These differences, which range from the trivially unimportant to those of strikingly great import, need to be mapped out and their full implications explored. While this is to some extent beyond the scope of my current project, I hope to investigate these issues in the near future.
[54] It seems that the greater lords, at least, were flexible if not uncaring about which of their courts a tenant used, so long as the tenant did not use the court of another lord.
[55] Of course, the bishop had little to fear of competition from other courts, unlike the king; a treaty of 1229, called *le Convenit*, had settled the relation of the bishop's courts to those of the priory: Emsley and Fraser, *Courts of the County Palatine*, pp. 7–9.

7

The Free Court of the Priors of Durham

CONSTANCE M. FRASER

In April 2000 Cynthia J. Neville published an article in *History* focusing on the complicated web of courts in the medieval county palatine of Durham. She listed these as the bishop's halmote court, the priory halmote court, the free court of the prior of Durham, the county court, the borough courts, and local customary courts, three prerogative courts (forest, admiralty and marshalsea), and the court of chancery. 'All these were in addition to the courts which administered, according to Common Law principles and procedures, the law familiar to and available throughout all medieval England'.[1] This essay examines in detail one of the threads, the free court of the priors of Durham. It seeks evidence regarding the truth of the assertion that free courts were strangled by the inability of feudal lords to require their free tenants to provide evidence on oath, as would be necessary in many actions originally heard in courts baron. It was one of the charges brought against Bishop Bek in 1303, that he was requiring free men to answer in his halmote courts as opposed to his 'free court'.[2] (The bishop's free court was presumably the ancestor of the Durham Court of Pleas, which survived until 1873.) Jean Scammell has argued that the bishop himself was hamstrung by an inability to use statute law in his 'free court', but I believe that there is adequate evidence that cases were brought in Durham after 1279 which required writs based on statute.[3]

Between Tyne and Tees the bishops of Durham claimed during the Middle Ages to exercise palatine powers. The priors of the Benedictine priory of Durham claimed to exercise similar powers over their own tenants by virtue of a written agreement, *le Convenit*, reached between Bishop Richard le Poore and Prior Ralph Kerneth in 1229. During succeeding centuries the bishops tried to limit the prior's jurisdiction to matters specified in the agreement, while the priors claimed increasing jurisdiction to keep in step with changes in legal procedure. Evidence for this development may be found in various recognitions of competence granted by bishops of Durham to the priors, and in the broken series of court rolls which survive for the prior's 'free court'.

The prior of Durham claimed by virtue of this agreement of 1229 to have a free

---

[1] C.J. Neville, 'The Courts of the Prior and the Bishop of Durham in the Later Middle Ages', *History* 85 (2000), 221.
[2] *RPD*, III, 42.
[3] J. Scammell, 'The Origin and Limitations of the Liberty of Durham', *EHR* 81 (1966), 461–73; *Northern Petitions*, ed. C.M. Fraser (Surtees Society 194, 1981), pp. 160, 232–40. Cf. K. Emsley and C.M. Fraser, *The Courts of the County Palatine of Durham* (Durham, 1984), pp. 8–12.

court 'with sac and soc, tol and team and infangenetheof'. While the prior accepted the fact that the bishop alone had a gallows, pillory and tumbrel, it was expected that he would allow free access for the prior's officers to use them. The bishop alone had a prison, and jurisdiction over pleas of the crown, assizes, and suits originating with a writ of the bishop (or of the king *sede vacante*) other than the writ of right. Provision was made for cases where a priory tenant turned approver, for such cases could be brought only in the bishop's court. Where a priory tenant was found guilty in the bishop's court, whereby he fell into the bishop's mercy, it was provided that his fine be assessed by two free men on behalf of the bishop and two free men on behalf of the prior. The prior claimed, however, to share equally with the bishop the profits of justice arising from the condemnation of priory tenants after trial, namely half the forfeited goods and chattels of felons, half of the revenues derived from forfeiture of their lands for a year and a day, and half the amercements.

Superficially the agreement gave little encouragement to the prior to enlarge his jurisdiction. The only ambiguity came after the recognition of the prior's free court, where it was stated that 'if any of the land or fee of the Prior be attached by the bishop's bailiffs for anything appurtaining to the prior's court, the prior or his bailiff should sue his right of court and have it without contradiction, if the request be made at the due time and place'. Rolls surviving in the archives of the Dean and Chapter of Durham testify to the legal ingenuity which enabled the prior's officers to enhance the scope of the priory jurisdiction.[4]

When its rolls emerge in 1302, the prior's free court was held once every two weeks on a Tuesday. From 1349 it is specifically described as being held at Durham, although the precise site of the court-room is unknown. Courts held nearest after Christmas, Easter and Michaelmas were often called a 'head court' (*curia capitalis*), when those tenants who held their lands by three suits of court were expected to appear. Otherwise the court was attended (or not) by the prior's free tenants in general, who were amerced at the rate of 6d. a default, unless they had provided an attorney to present their apologies for absence. These suitors provided the members of juries, were pledges for prosecution or bail, and frequently were litigants. For instance, Richard Ayre served as juror at an inquisition *post mortem* in 1330. He subsequently appeared as a juror in various cases of assault, breach of the peace, and theft. In 1331 he was charged with casting stones onto the prior's land and damaging his grain, also with encroaching on the prior's land, removing the soil at various places, and rescuing livestock impounded by the prior's bailiff. In 1334 he excused his presence in court several times, but also acted as pledge for prosecution in a case of trespass. In 1335 he was fined for failure to have other persons in court for whom he had stood surety.[5] It should be emphasised that the prior's court in question here was

---

[4] The earliest evidence of the bishop's court survives in the archives of the Dean and Chapter of Durham as successors to the prior and convent, with endorsements noting the presence or absence of reference therein to the claiming of the prior's court. These records relate to the episcopate of Bishop Beaumont (1317–33), although the run of records surviving in the PRO begins with Beaumont's successor, Bishop Richard de Bury. Apparently, some agent of the prior, rummaging through the palatinate archives, appropriated some of the earliest surviving rolls of the bishop's courts for more leisurely research within the priory, and omitted to replace them. Cf. DCM, Loc.IV:157, Loc.V:25, 33, 36, 41, 43, 52, Misc. Chs. 2640, 7023.

[5] DCM, Loc.IV:86, 54, 43, 20, 52, 2.

his free court. Thomas Currour in 1337 was stopped in his prosecution in a plea of debt 'because the terrar [of Durham] and the steward were unwilling to allow Thomas to implead William of Ludworth and Roger son of Scolastica because they were the prior's bondsmen: therefore he was instructed to pursue them in the halmotes if that seems to him worthwhile'.[6]

The presence of jurors in the prior's free court may be a cause for surprise. According to Pollock and Maitland, it was the inability of the ordinary lord to compel his free tenants to act under oath that brought to an end his court for land cases, because he could not employ royal assize procedure. The prior certainly had his difficulties in securing the presence of jurors. In May 1324 four suitors were fined for defaulting when summoned 'to deliver gaol', and in April 1338 nine jurors were fined for their failure to appear at the previous court when summoned to testify about a breach of the peace: yet the bishop on occasion had similar difficulties in assembling panels.[7]

Parties and jurors were summoned to appear in court by an officer sometimes described as bailiff, sometimes as coroner, and in the later fourteenth century as *cursor scaccarii*.[8] Where there were too many defaults the officer concerned might be threatened with a fine. Procedure consisted of the normal allowance of three summonses and three attachments, with essoins including absence on the bishop's service. Postponements might be allowed at the request of the parties, or through lack of jurors, and once because the bishop's justices were sitting on the same day. The need for a pledge for prosecution was once waived where the plaintiff was a poor man.[9] The main difference in procedure from the bishop's court was the absence of the sheriff, although as the steward of Durham Priory who presided sometimes was the sheriff of Durham there may have been an overlap in practice. Twice at least the steward acted as prosecutor, and in 1346 he presided in gaol delivery cases.[10]

The only criminal jurisdiction specifically acknowledged by the bishop to belong to the prior of Durham was over thieves, and such cases occur in 1313, 1321, 1324, 1332, 1335, 1337, 1338, 1355 and 1376.[11] The accused normally put himself on his country, and the jurors testified as to his guilt or innocence; but it is a curious fact that in the rare cases where the accused was found guilty the value of the goods in one case was less than a shilling, the minimum for a capital offence, and in another he was a clerk, and so was remanded to the bishop's gaol (*ideo remittitur gaole episcopi*).[12] A less happy outcome was recorded at the free court held on 26 August 1337. Hugh Talkan of Westoe, with his daughter and granddaughter and a neighbour, was taken for a burglary of the prior's grange at Westoe and other thefts. They appeared in court and put themselves on their country. A jury was empanelled, which found all but the granddaughter guilty as charged, and they were duly hanged. Hugh's chattels were valued at 40s. and the neighbour, William Bodi of Westoe, had chattels worth 8s.[13]

---

6   DCM, Loc.IV:2 m. 2: *Ideo dictum est ei quod sequatur versus eos in halmotis si sibi viderit expedire*.
7   DCM, Loc.IV:79, 2 m. 3 (cf. Loc.IV:68); F. Pollock and F.W. Maitland, *The History of English Law Before the Time of Edward I* (2 vols., 2nd edn., Cambridge, 1898), II, 584–94.
8   DCM, Loc.IV:203 m. 1, 2 m. 1, 65, 144d, 83, 152.
9   DCM, Loc.IV:2 m. 4, 6, 79, 65.
10 DCM, Loc.IV:44, 52, 203 m. l, 60.
11 DCM, Loc.IV:86, 4, 79, 2, 152; *FPD*, p. 215.
12 Cf. DCM, Loc.IV:234, where three convicted felons were hanged (1337).
13 DCM, Loc.IV:234.

Exercise of peace jurisdiction by the prior's court could find no justification by reference to *le Convenit*. If in Durham the situation was clouded by the problem of whether the peace was of the king or the bishop, nevertheless by 1334 such cases were being entertained in the prior's court, despite the contention of royal lawyers that any trespass alleging an offence against the king's peace (*contra pacem regis*) was a plea of the crown.[14] Normally they were cases of assault, where damages were claimed, the plaintiffs asking for sums ranging from 20s. to £40, while a severely realistic jury assessed the damage between 6s. 8d. and £2. In November 1337 William Ryton of Willington accused John son of Emma of wounding 'by force and arms' (*vi et armis*), and the jurors testified that John was indeed guilty and awarded interim damages of 40s., with the recommendation that they should be increased to ten marks if it were found later that William had suffered permanent damage (*mahemiatus de vulneracione predicta*). In another case a fortnight later William del Kirk, the prior's pinder at Billingham, claimed that while he was enforcing the halmote ordinance that the west meadows be left ungrazed under pain of 6d. fine, and tried to impound animals depasturing there, Alan Bisshop had attacked and maltreated him. The jurors duly found Alan to be guilty, awarding 26s. 8d. in damages, and Alan was in the prior's mercy. But Alan brought a counter-claim against William, similarly upheld, and was himself awarded 6s. 8d. in damages.[15] In two cases breaches of the peace were the result of *hamsoken*, the first being a burglary and the second an aggravation of assault, the defendant having thrown stones at the plaintiff's doors and windows. By 1348 the notion of what constituted a breach of the peace had broadened, and between November of that year and February 1356 there were five such cases involving livestock depasturing grass and standing crops, an overworking of horses, and another case where a master claimed damages of 40s. arising from loss of services as the result of a brawl between the servants of plaintiff and defendant.[16]

The generality of actions in the prior's free court were less exciting. In 1336 Thomas Freman of Middridge demanded compensation for a horse sold to him by John of Merrington as 'good, useful and without fault', but which had proved unsuitable. He was awarded 20s. damages by a jury, and the defendant was amerced for breach of covenant. Another breach of agreement was pleaded in 1376, when William Gaugi of Ferryhill complained that whereas he was granted a nine-year lease of a messuage and eighteen acres by Robert Dicenson, he was turned out before the expiry of his term in favour of an Isabel of Ferryhill, for which he claimed £5 in damages. Dicenson admitted breaking his own agreement and a jury assessed damages of 13s. 4d.[17] Most, however, of the suits in covenant, debt and detinue were never brought to trial and presumably were intended to bring pressure on the defendant to give satisfaction out of court. Of some interest is a case of debt in 1349, where the plaintiff, Hugh Bakester of Wolviston, sold a horse to John of Bellasis for 7s. and two quarters of wheat, payable the following Christmas. Bellasis admitted the failure to pay and was amerced, while Hugh recovered damages of 6d. Another plea of debt concerned arrears of wages, where the executors had no money to make repayment and the

---

[14] DCM, Loc.IV:52 ; Pollock and Maitland, *History of English Law*, II, 464.
[15] DCM, Loc.IV:52 m. 1, 2 m. 1, 78 m. 3, 29.
[16] DCM, Loc.IV:78, 65, 34, 26 m. 1, 29.
[17] DCM, Loc.IV:52, 152.

plaintiff sought recovery from a third party, who successfully disclaimed liability. A more complicated case arose in 1348, when John son of Alan of Merrington charged his vicar with detention of 39s. 11d., being a forfeited bond for 40s. Apparently there had been previous disputes between the two, and on 24 February 1348 the vicar had entered into a bond to pay 40s. should he subsequently commit any trespass against John. On 21 April following the vicar had driven his livestock onto John's standing crops and meadow-land. The vicar wagered his law that he was innocent of any offence, but in the event was unable to find any supporters and was amerced by the court. Not content with recovering the 39s. 11d., John then attempted to sue the vicar in covenant for the same transaction, which the vicar traversed on the grounds that he had already recovered damages. The court's decision is not recorded.[18]

Wagering of law occurred on a number of occasions. Thomas son of John son of Robert of Merrington was charged in debt and detinue in December 1350, namely, failure to pay 10s. for an iron-bound cart and the retaining of three sheets, two blankets, a coverlet, a tripod, a pair of ploughshares, two great barrels, an iron barrel and a set of cart gear, valued together at 10s. He wagered his law, then defaulted, and the plaintiff recovered damages totalling 13s. 4d., the debt of 10s., and the chattels enumerated. Thomas was amerced on both counts. Previously, in 1335, the court had required that certain brewers, charged with using unauthorised measures, should prove their innocence on the oath of twelve pledges each.[19]

In the foregoing actions the prior's free court leaned heavily on royal procedure. Other business might more properly be described as baronial. Enquiries were held as to the terms on which free tenements were held of the prior. Homage and fealty were received on the prior's behalf, and cases were heard concerning dower. Here too actions were brought by the bishop's writ of right to decide ownership of land.[20] There was also an undercurrent of cases concerning management of the priory estates. These ranged from punishment of assaults made on manorial officials, through encroachment on the prior's soil and removal of boundary stones, to ownership of dogs responsible for worrying sheep.[21] In a case brought in 1351 it was the prior who, having brought a charge of breaking into the pound and removing livestock, lost his case and was amerced for his false claim, the defendant having successfully wagered his law.[22] This was the court in which the prior enforced his rights to licence the cutting of timber, supervise the assize of ale, and maintain his monopoly of mill and bakehouse in Durham. Old farming practices were upheld, including that of restoring walls demolished to enable farm carts to pass laden with grain. A curious case concerned William Gynour, who was charged with impounding the livestock of priory tenants making their way along the king's highway (*via regia*) leading to the prior's mine at

---

[18] DCM, Loc.IV:28, 144, 65 m. 3.
[19] DCM, Loc.IV:26 m. 2, 52 m. 1d.
[20] DCM, Loc.IV:1 m. 2, 44, 52 m. 2d, 54, 65 m. 3, 78 m. 4. On 20 May 1348 Bishop Hatfield issued a writ of right to Prior John Fossor in favour of Geoffrey Hunter, who claimed to hold of the prior twenty-two acres in Wolviston. The writ was received at the free court held on 3 June, and the parties were summoned to appear in court on 17 June. The four defendants entered essoins, and Hunter pleaded these were inadmissible as there should be only one. The case was then adjourned successively to 1, 15 and 29 July, until on 4 November Hunter failed to pursue his case and the matter was dropped. Two cases begun by a writ of right were brought on 5 May 1349: DCM, Loc.IV:65 m. 5d, 78 m. 2.
[21] DCM, Loc.IV:4, 52, 68.
[22] DCM, Loc.IV:26 m. 4.

Rainton. The prior recovered 12s. in damages and William was fined 6d., but the reason for Gynour's original act is obscure.[23]

So much for the practice of the prior's free court at Durham as developed from *le Convenit* of 1229, where the prior was grudgingly allowed half the profits of justice and cognisance of the writ of right. (By 1376 the prior's coroner was pleading for the right to transfer to the prior's court not only the cases of tenants who were thieves but also of those who were debtors).[24] The right to this jurisdiction had been patiently won by successive priors from the bishop of Durham, stages in the process being marked by a writ of Bishop Kellawe in December 1311 recognising the right of the prior to judge his tenants, whether or not they were captured on priory lands, a writ of Bishop Beaumont (the date unfortunately omitted in the copy) confirming the same, and another of Bishop Hatfield of May 1381 (the month of his death) allowing the prior his court in Norhamshire. These rights, however, were exercised subject to the vigilance of the bishop's officers, since there is a memorandum of 1381 recording the presentation before the bishop's council of evidence found in the treasury of Durham Priory, joined with a petition for 50s., namely the half of the fine imposed on the township of Billingham by the bishop's justices of gaol delivery for permitting the escape of a prisoner delivered to its custody. Also in the prior's register about 1435 is another memorandum touching the prior's rights to half the profits of justice coupled with the text of a petition on this subject from Prior Wessington to Bishop Langley.[25]

Rolls of proceedings survive in the archives of the Dean and Chapter of Durham, as successors of the Prior and Convent, spanning the years 1302 to 1426. If the volume of business in the free court was not as great as in the halmote, this merely reflected the smaller number of free men eligible to use the former court. The type of business heard was analogous to the English hundred court but tempered with local peculiarities such as frequency and the numbers of suitors.[26] The only business outside its range was homicide and the possessory assizes, both firmly reserved to the bishop's justices. Cynthia Neville considers that the prior 'doggedly' maintained his free court for reasons of prestige.[27] In practice, his free tenants increasingly refused to attend the court. Competition from the bishop's court may have been too great. Certainly the prior himself was using the bishop's court of pleas for his own litigation. On 20 September 1390 in the bishop's court the prior sued various people for debts. Among these, he sued John de Tours of Brafferton for a debt of £12. Tours appeared on 4 January 1391 to answer the charge that be had bought the tithes of Preston le Skerne for five marks and the tithes of Brafferton and Hurworth for £8 13s. 4d., payable half on 2 February and half on 20 March, and had failed to pay. Tours denied the terms of the agreement, and was required to wager his law by twelve hands. The prior subsequently failed to prosecute and was amerced. During the same year he also sued William Hoton, parson of St Nicholas, Durham, and five others for their refusal

---

[23] DCM, Loc.IV:26 m. 4, 68, 78 m. 3, 65, 2 m. 5, 26 mm. 2 and 4, 83, 152, 28, 34.
[24] DCM, Loc.IV:152.
[25] DCM, Misc. Ch. 5640, Reg.III, fols. 178–88. Cf. DCM, Cart.I, fols. 186–9, and Neville, 'Courts of the Prior', 223–5.
[26] H.M. Cam, *The Hundred and the Hundred Rolls: An Outline of Local Government in Medieval England* (London, 1930), p. 18.
[27] Neville, 'Courts of the Prior', 231.

to admit his candidate to the chantry of St James on Elvet Bridge, and Richard Joy and two others for digging coal to the value of £100 on his land at Tursdale.[28]

The final rolls of the prior's free court simply record the compositions and armercements of suitors for failure to attend court, with notes that 'proceedings were adjourned', 'the bailiff defaulted', 'nothing was done'.[29] It was 'ane end of ane old song'.

---

[28] PRO, DURH 13/223, passim.
[29] DCM, Loc.IV:27.

8

Church Discipline in Late Medieval Durham City: The Prior as Archdeacon

MARGARET HARVEY

The prior of Durham claimed the right to exercise archidiaconal jurisdiction over all the churches appropriated to the priory in Durham and Northumberland and by 1435 certainly was using his rights regularly, both to visit and to correct his flock in his court.[1] The object of this essay is to ask a few questions about the exercise of the jurisdiction in the city itself.

The evidence concerning the archdeacon's court is very good. There are two court books: *Capitula generalia*, 1435–56, and the Court Book of the Prior's Official, 1487–98.[2] There are also references in the letter-books of the priory.[3] In addition, we have some records of the secular courts so that sometimes one can see persons litigating or being dealt with in both types of court and often one can know more about them.

From at least 1435 the court met in Durham, usually in St Oswald's Church, every three weeks on Thursdays, and by the later period every week.[4] The court book records of the sessions are typically summary but include some witness statements, documents issued by the court, monitions and even a few visitation records.[5] The prior seldom sat in person but used a series of officials and commissaries.

All the usual archidiaconal cases occur.[6] Both court books include many cases of sexual misconduct, fornication, adultery, keeping a woman, matrimonial disputes – either claiming that one had occurred or attempting annulment. The later volume has many more cases of *lesio fidei*, concerning debts.[7] The first contains a few cases about

---

1 See my essay in *Retribution, Repentance and Reconciliation*, ed. K. Cooper and J. Gregory (Studies in Church History 40, 2004), pp. 95–105 for the details of this exercise and its origins.
2 Both are in the DCM. *Capitula generalia*, 1435–56, will hereafter be cited as 'Capitula' and the Court Book of the Prior's Official, 1487–98, will be cited as 'Official'. DCM, Crossgate Court Book, 1498–1524, will be cited as 'Crossgate'. For other local secular courts, see also M. Bonney, *Lordship and the Urban Community: Durham and its Overlords* (Cambridge, 1990), pp. 199–205.
3 See below, p. 123.
4 For further details see my essay as n. 1.
5 For typical records the latest example is *Lower Ecclesiastical Jurisdiction in Late-Medieval England: The Courts of the Dean and Chapter of Lincoln, 1336–1349, and the Deanery of Wisbech, 1458–1484*, ed. L.R. Poos (Records of Social and Economic History, New Series 32, Oxford, 2001).
6 See list of cases in Poos: subject index under cases.
7 R.H. Helmholz, 'Assumpsit and fidei lesio', *Law Quarterly Review* 91 (1975), 406–32.

sorcery, whereas the second has none.[8] Both contain breaches of the Sabbath, failure to attend church on Sundays or holydays (or working on these same days), and failure to receive the Eucharist in the parish church at Easter.[9] Although some business came *ex officio*, sometimes from visitations,[10] plenty did not.

The prior and his obedientiaries brought claims about rents and dues, and defended other rights there. So the hostillar claimed one quarter of barley,[11] or the sacrist tithes from some parishioners of Edlingham and Lemmington, where he was the rector.[12] The almoner claimed rent from a widow, which her husband had owed.[13] In 1455 Thomas Halyday was accused of poaching in Bearpark, thereby incurring a sentence of major excommunication as violator of church goods and immunities,[14] but he was also accused of being a common *objurgator* of his neighbours and of defaming the inquisitors and the Official with certain contumelious and opprobrious words. When caught he had probably been foolishly loquacious.[15]

There is little evidence of anti-clericalism. Many people were punished for obstinacy in their sins, of course, but few persons were cited for rude words to the clergy or about the court. John Thomson of Witton Gilbert in December 1449 was accused of going about the chapel during mass saying rude things, and preaching in a tavern.[16] A man in South Shields in 1492 attacked the priest and the holy water clerk who was attempting to read out his excommunication.[17] But such cases were rare.

That the authorities were not frightened of too much lay criticism is revealed by the very public way the erring clergy were made to do penance. Of course, an unchaste cleric was very hard to stop, just as no doubt an unchaste layman. The clergy were also vulnerable to defamation. In October 1494 *Dominus* Thomas Thomlynson, *capellanus de Dighton*, was cited for fornication, and, 'because the judge did not find from his demeanour that he was defamed concerning the said woman by good and serious people but rather from malice', he was let off.[18] But when the court was satisfied, or when the man confessed, the penance was public and very unpleasant. In 1455 Robert Segefeld, *capellanus*, confessed to fornication with Joan Bell. He had to stand on Friday at the font of St Margaret's Church, Durham city, bare-headed, reading his psalter at the time of the main mass; and on Sunday, at the time of high mass, he was to come to the choir of Durham Cathedral offering a candle at the high altar, as well as giving 6s. 8d. to the feretrary of St Cuthbert and avoiding all suspect places under pain of a 40s. fine and suspension.[19]

Among the more telling examples of the stresses and strains of this kind of jurisdiction are the cases about wills, mortuaries and tithes. In some respects these

---

[8] All defamation cases.
[9] See below, p. 124.
[10] For these, see *Lower Ecclesiastical Jurisdiction*, pp. xxi–xxiv.
[11] DCM, Capitula, fo. 70v.
[12] DCM, Capitula, fo. 106.
[13] DCM, Capitula, fo. 101.
[14] W. Lyndwood, *Constitutiones Provinciales Ecclesiae Anglicanae* (Oxford, 1679), III, tit. 28, pp. 257–9.
[15] DCM, Capitula, fo. 141v.
[16] DCM, Capitula, fo. 83v.
[17] DCM, Official, fols. 52, 54r–v.
[18] DCM, Official, fo. 73v: *quia judex non invenit ex animo suo quod penes bonos et graves fuit diffamatus erga mulierem predictam sed ex malitia*.
[19] DCM, Capitula, fo. 140.

Durham courts seem to have been sensitive to local feelings. When in 1436 the proctors of the fabric of St Oswald's, Durham, asked that the court should force the villagers (*villani*) of Croxdale and Sunderland Bridge to pay their share to the fabric of St Oswald's, a payment of which the villagers said they owed only half, the court gave them time to produce proof and meanwhile ordered them to discuss the matter with the old men of the parish (*ad deliberandum cum senioribus parochie*).[20] There are a few tithe cases in the court books but none seems to have caused enormous problems. There were some group prosecutions, for instance in 1497 by *Dominus* Robert Segefeld as proctor, probably for the priory.[21] But some were between laymen. In December 1443 and January 1444 John Smyrk sued William Cornforth about the tithes of Castle Eden. He claimed that he had bought the tithe of sheaves of the seventeen acres of wheat which William Cornforth had there but that Cornforth had given him only ten acres worth from that place and the other seven from elsewhere. In the end the parties were ordered to sort out their quarrel.[22]

Mortuaries were probably more sensitive. The notorious Hunne case has made mortuaries a test case for the revelation of both anti-clericalism and of the bad behaviour of the church courts.[23] In the Durham courts in the later period there were several cases, and the preservation of many of the depositions of witnesses suggests that they were contentious, though not always against the church. In April 1497 Thomas Williamson, clearly acting for St Margaret's, Durham, brought a case against John Farwell, of St Margaret's, for a mortuary. Farwell declared that the collar which was claimed was not his wife's but his daughter's.[24] John Hall and John Babyngton were his witnesses.[25] Babyngton described the collar as a 'gown collar' for a gown newly made with one ribbon (*rebayn*) and no other collar. It was delivered as a mortuary to the chapel of St Margaret. The gown had been new about the time of his marriage twelve years ago or more. He did not know of a gift made to the daughter of John Farwell by her mother, Farwell's first wife. John Hall alleged that the gown had first been the mortuary of Farwell's mother-in-law. It was newly made for their marriage, bound with one *rebayn* around the gown as a present and was thus given to St Margaret's. He had never heard at any time of the first wife giving the collar to her daughter during her life but often heard the daughter demanding it and blaming the (second) wife for using it, saying that her mother had given it to her in her life-time. She often complained against her step-mother using it against her mother's last will. He knew the lately-dead wife of John Farwell often used a collar of green colour and that Farwell had this collar from the first wife of George Dobson, though whether it was a gift or purchase he did not know. He knew that she used it during her life but did not know whether or not John gave it to her. The outcome is unclear but at issue was a quarrel between a step-daughter and step-mother.[26] An interesting point is the custom of buying back a mortuary. John Hall said that the gown in question had been the

---

20 DCM, Capitula, fo. 7.
21 DCM, Official, fo. 105v.
22 DCM, Capitula, fols. 51v, 52r–v; for other examples, see Capitula, fols. 114v, 121v.
23 For Hunne, see P. Gwynn, *The King's Cardinal: The Rise and Fall of Cardinal Wolsey* (London, 1990), pp. 34–40.
24 DCM, Official, fols. 104v, 105.
25 DCM, Official, fols. 105r–v, 106v.
26 For other mortuary cases, see DCM, Official, fols. 100, 103v, 108, 115r–v.

mortuary of the mother of Farwell's first wife, but that his wife had bought it back, and it had subsequently been altered about the time of their wedding.[27]

Some cases were clearly worse because they occurred at a time of plague. In early 1498 Crossgate secular court forbade anyone from Bishop Auckland, where there was plague, to be lodged in Durham,[28] but the prior's court books show that there was plague in Durham in the previous two years. One very sad case comes from April 1497. Alice, wife of William Dawson, a well-known butcher, sued Joan, wife of Richard Barne, for *lesio fidei* for the goods of Alice Hyne, dead of plague, which Alice Dawson said were left to her. She produced witnesses and a list representing the last will of the dead woman, but the parish chaplain of St Margaret's, William Fabian, alleged another later will and also produced witnesses.[29] All witnesses professed to know the parties well. Stephen Thomas said that he was not present when Alice Hyne was *in extremis* but that Alice Dawson, then in service to the widow of Robert Cokyn, had specially asked him to go with her to hear what Alice Hyne wished to say. They went and called Alice Hyne outside into the street before the house and stood far off for fear of the plague which was then rife, though she was not ill and did not feel infected at that time. They asked her how she wanted to dispose of her goods 'if God perhaps should visit her' (*si Deus eam forte visitaret*). Alice replied that she wished to give the clothes in which she was then dressed to the wife of William Johnson: one chemise, one white kirtle, one green kirtle, one cap, one *cornchaffe* one *neckcornchaffe*, and one pair of shoes and stockings. Thomas had heard her saying that she gave one kirtle for her soul, to have masses said for her.[30] The rest of her goods she gave to the wife of William Dawson, that is one cover with all her other goods. This happened on a Saturday before Alice Dawson left the service of Cokyn's widow and entered the home of Robert Farne. Michael Preston and William Tadcaster together went to the woman when she was lying sick in the house of Richard Barne, in which she afterwards died of plague. Preston there heard Barne's wife ask how she wished to dispose of her goods if God perhaps should visit her and take her from this life and whether she gave her best kirtle to *Dominus* William Fabian or not. She said she wanted to give the kirtle and other things if Fabian consented. Thus it appeared that she gave the kirtle to Fabian. The witness also asked if she gave her other goods to some other of her friends and she said not. He especially asked her what she left to the wife of William Dawson, her friend. She replied, nothing, because she had bought one new kerchief (*kirchaffe*) when she was well and had given it to her friend for hemming (*le hemyng*) and *surfelyng* and Dawson's wife kept it, so she had never wanted to give her anything again because of the ingratitude. This happened about seven weeks after she left the service of the widow. William Tadcaster[31] confirmed that he had gone with Preston to Richard Barne's house where the woman lay sick and heard Preston ask her whether he had any goods of hers in his keeping and she said clearly no; before she was ill she had had all her goods from him. When they were standing in the house

---

[27] DCM, Official, fo. 106v: *Illa toga que iam offertur in mortuarium erat primo mortuarium matris eiusdem uxoris sue et ipsa re-emebat eandem togam, que toga erat noviter aptata circa nuptias eorundem.*
[28] DCM, Crossgate, fo. 1v.
[29] DCM, Official, fo. 105, and witnesses fo. 106v, continued fo. 132.
[30] The document is unclear.
[31] The 'Tadcastell' of the manuscript is almost certainly wrong.

he heard Barne's wife asking her who was to have her goods after her death and the sick woman said that she wished those looking after her in her sickness to have them, but on condition that a kirtle went to William Fabian, parochial chaplain of the chapel of St Margaret. He had not heard the sick woman make any other disposition of her goods.[32] Almost certainly, therefore, Alice Dawson would lose this grisly plea.

In Durham the question of parish allegiance could be problematic. St Margaret's Chapel was for many years only a chapel-of-ease of St Oswald's. This caused problems over mortuaries and other matters. In June 1384 John Legge, parishioner of St Oswald's, contested the obligation to give a mortuary (apparently a horse) for his dead wife, whose executor he was. He was supported by a group of parishioners and appealed from the consistory court of Durham, to the court of York, through the bishop's official.[33] A copy of the final agreement was entered in the convent's register about 1431, when St Margaret's was becoming in effect an independent parish.[34] After much contention the parties in 1384 agreed by arbitration that the prior and convent had the right to claim one animal from every man and unmarried woman in the parish at the time of death, with the choice to be made by the proctor of the prior and convent if the parishioner had more than one animal. At the death of a married woman the second best animal was to be taken from either the husband's goods or their jointly held goods, though the inhabitants of Framwellgate were exempted for animals held in Framwellgate unless they left a beast by will or had animals elsewhere in the parish. Almost certainly this case had been brought to sort out some of the rights of St Margaret's.

The contentious question of place of death and of parochial status comes out clearly in 1496. *Dominus* Thomas Williamson, proctor for St Margaret's, brought a case against William Hogson of Earl's House for *lesio fidei* about keeping back one gown (*toga*) as a mortuary for a young girl dead in Northumberland.[35] The young woman, Joan, had gone off into Northumberland and was not hired by anyone at the time, so Hogson must have been claiming that she was a parishioner where she had died and not, as Williamson alleged, in Durham. Both parties agreed to stand by the decision (*laudum*) of Richard Smyrke, a most respected figure, often called on to adjudicate in such arguments and in this case very central since Joan had been his servant. Smyrke's decision is recorded in detail.[36] Joan had had his permission just before Pentecost last to go to Rothbury. He had been unwilling because he had no one else to prepare and serve his meals but she had arranged that her sister would serve him in her absence. The length of Joan's absence was not fixed; she promised to return, but died of plague at Pentecost. Therefore, presumably, she still counted at death as a St Margaret's parishioner so her gown would come to it as a mortuary.

The possibility of cheating over mortuaries is also clear. Thomas Williamson prosecuted Thomas Armestrong (under *lesio fidei*) beginning on 1 December 1497 for a mortuary for Isabella Dixson. Armestrong denied the debt and pleaded that Isabella

---

[32] The end is torn.
[33] DCM, Reg.II, fo. 208v. There is a great deal of further material on this matter which I shall use in a forthcoming book.
[34] DCM, Reg.III, fols. 177–8.
[35] DCM, Official fo. 90.
[36] DCM, Official fols. 91, 92v.

had sold her *ornamenta* before she died to pay for food (*pro victu suo*).[37] At the second hearing Armestrong, who should have brought his witnesses, did not appear, whereas on 15 December Williamson came with Thomas Colman, Thomas Burdale and John Hall and seems to have won his case.

There is no evidence for heresy in the city of Durham in this period but parishioners failed to attend church and the parish clergy and archidiaconal visitors were assiduous in accusing them. Easter Day in 1492 was 22 April. The court was thus very quick off the mark when on 4 May Joan Peirson and Agnes Johnson or Levynston of St Margaret's were cited because without licence of their curate they had not received communion in the church. Both appeared. Joan said that she had received in St Nicholas's Church, Newcastle and was given a day to return with proof.[38] Agnes said that she had received at St Oswald's. She was required to prove it but also was given a penance of three floggings around the chapel for withdrawal from her church without permission.[39] When, at her next appearance, Agnes failed to prove her claim, she was given three floggings around St Margaret's and three around St Oswald's. On 11 January 1448 John Robynson, 'walker' (that is, a fuller), of Elvet, was warned not to exercise his art on festival days (in this case on the Epiphany just passed).[40] Richard Smyrke, whom we met above, was accused in November 1494 of fulling on Sundays and feast-days.[41]

Equally, those who received communion when they should not, were noticed. Easter Day in 1440 was 27 March, so someone again had acted fast when on 6 April 1440 Thomas Cok of St Margaret's was accused of receiving communion whilst suspended and not absolved. He tried to plead that on the day he was cited the court did not sit.[42] In April 1455 a series of parishioners of St Margaret's were prosecuted for various offences, including John Coxhoe for not receiving the Eucharist while he was staying at Witton Gilbert. He had to find six oath-helpers to purge himself.[43]

Finally there were many cases concerning sexual offences and marriage. Two points about this are striking. The first is the intrusion into the lives of the laity, which would now be considered oppressive but probably was much more acceptable than we suppose. The abundant presentment of sexual sins by fellow parishioners at visitations might be thought to be ecclesiastical pressure but there was plenty of the same in the secular courts. A man might be indicted in the Crossgate court because he entertained a loose woman (*hospitat quamdam mulierem non bone gubernacionis*),[44] and the halmotes regularly fined women for *leyrwit*.[45]

But the laity knew exactly how to use these mechanisms to their own ends. One of the best examples is a suit between Joan Hansell of St Margaret's parish, and John Porter, who was probably the actual janitor of the abbey; he was certainly an abbey

---

[37] DCM, Official, fols. 115–16, for the whole case.
[38] DCM, Official, fo. 35v.
[39] DCM, Official, fo. 36v.
[40] DCM, Capitula, fo. 71v.
[41] DCM, Official, fo. 74.
[42] DCM, Capitula, fo. 29v.
[43] DCM, Capitula, fo. 141.
[44] DCM, Crossgate, fo. 60.
[45] For example, DCM, Loc.IV:112 (Shincliffe Halmote), 20–22 Richard II (1396–99).

servant.[46] A John Porter held a tenement in North Bailey in 1454. The parties were accused of fornication. On 27 October 1440, Joan Hansell confessed to sleeping with John but claimed they were married. John was said to be outside the jurisdiction, which might simply mean away but probably meant that his resident parish was not under the prior's jurisdiction.[47] In November both appeared. Joan claimed that they had contracted marriage on 24 June a year ago (1439?). The words she alleged that they had exchanged were that if she would wait a year for him he wished to marry her. John said under oath that if Joan had not been defamed and could have her father's consent he wished to have her. On that understanding he had slept with her. The judge warned Porter that until the case was settled he should abstain from Joan and from suspect places *sub pena nubendi* (that is, that if he did sleep with her marriage would be automatic).[48] On 2 December, in St Andrew's Chapel, Elizabeth Carr swore that Porter had stayed with her since he was warned to avoid Joan.[49] Joan came with her witnesses and also a letter, in three pages with a sign (which the text reproduces). Joan Cuthbert said under oath that on a Saturday a year ago, about June 24, at night, John, in bed with Joan, said that he wanted Joan as his wife more than other women in the world and Joan said the same. He lay the following two nights with her. Cuthbert knew this because she was lying in a bed nearby. She said that it had long been thought in Durham that they were married. William Lascy said that this year in summer, near 24 June, John Porter entered his house and he asked John if he did not wish to marry Joan. John replied that he did not need to because he had already contracted marriage with her. Joan confessed the same in William's presence. John Gervase, who may be John Gervaux, an important mercer and spicer of Durham, who supplied the priory for years,[50] was asked by John Porter if Joan had been respectable (*bone conversacionis*) when she was in Hull. He said yes and asked Porter why he wanted to know, who replied that Joan was his wife. Gervase then sent Joan the letter shown in court. John Haldwell said that a year ago John Porter had asked him if he knew Joan Hansell and he said he did. Porter then asked about her respectability (*conversacio*) and Haldwell said it was good. Asked why he wanted to know, Porter said that she was his wife and that her father was against the marriage but that he wished to have her whether her father wished it or not. Sentence in favour of Joan was pronounced on 12 January 1441 in St Oswald's Church; the couple were therefore declared married and the definitive sentence is given.[51] The court record, however, says that they were warned to solemnise the marriage within three weeks, on pain of excommunication.[52] This was almost certainly a case carefully orchestrated by the parties and their supporters to validate a marriage opposed by the parents of the girl.

The evidence given here is simply a small taste of what is available from the abbey

---

[46] For the position, see M. Camsell, 'The Development of a Northern Town: Durham *c.*1250–1540' (3 vols., unpublished D.Phil. thesis, University of York, 1985), II (ii), 260–1, 418, III, 557.
[47] DCM, Capitula, fo. 31v.
[48] DCM, Capitula, fo. 32.
[49] DCM, Capitula, fo. 28.
[50] Camsell, 'Development', II (ii), 418; R.B. Dobson, *Durham Priory, 1400–1450* (Cambridge, 1973), p. 58 n. 4.
[51] DCM, Capitula, fols. 29, 33.
[52] DCM, Capitula, fo. 33.

archives for anyone wishing to investigate an aspect of late medieval law and order in Durham city and area. So far they have been under-exploited but they are a very rich source for social and religious history of the area and need to be more widely known and used.

9

Economy and Society in North-Eastern Market Towns: Darlington and Northallerton in the Later Middle Ages[1]

CHRISTINE M. NEWMAN

The economic history of north-eastern England in the fifteenth and early sixteenth centuries is characterised by decline, with the region scarcely recovering from the economic and demographic ravages of the Black Death and subsequent outbreaks of plague before being plunged back into long-term recession.[2] The main urban centres of the region, York and Newcastle-upon-Tyne, suffered considerable dislocation in the fifteenth century and remained in recession until well into the sixteenth.[3] A major factor in the decline of York was the contraction of its cloth making industry, largely as a result of increased competition from the textile towns of the West Riding of Yorkshire, such as Leeds, Wakefield and Halifax.[4] Smaller centres also suffered in this respect. John Leland's later description (c.1538) of Ripon as a town 'where idleness is sore increased' bore testimony to the fate of one such small town whose prosperity had once been founded upon the cloth trade.[5] Another market town in decline was Richmond in the North Riding of Yorkshire. Its economy, too, was partially based upon the textile industry, although it was also an important marketing centre for corn and wool, being advantageously placed between the pastoral highlands of the Pennines and the lowland agricultural dales. However, the town suffered, apparently as a result of the great pestilence and agrarian crisis, which further undermined the north-eastern economy in the period 1438–40. By 1440, the burgesses of Richmond felt compelled to appeal to the crown for a reduction in the town's fee farm, citing a contracting population and competition from the numerous neighbouring markets

---

[1] My research on Darlington forms part of a study conducted under the auspices of the *Victoria County History of Durham*.
[2] A.J. Pollard, *North-Eastern England during the Wars of the Roses: Lay Society, War and Politics, 1450–1500* (Oxford, 1990), chs. 2–3.
[3] J.N. Bartlett, 'The Expansion and Decline of York in the Later Middle Ages', *EcHR*, 2nd ser. 12 (1959), 17–33; D.M. Palliser, 'A Crisis in English Towns? The Case of York, 1460–1640', *NH* 14 (1978), 108–25; A.F. Butcher, 'Rent, Population and Economic Change in Late Medieval Newcastle', *NH* 14 (1978), 67–77.
[4] D.M. Palliser, *Tudor York* (Oxford, 1979), pp. 208–9; *The Manor and Borough of Leeds, 1425–1662: An Edition of Documents*, ed. J.W. Kirby (Thoresby Society 57, 1983), pp. 3–37.
[5] Pollard, *North-Eastern England*, pp. 72–3; *The Itinerary of John Leland in or about the years 1535–1543*, ed. L.T. Smith (5 vols., London, 1907–10), I, 82.

(which were, undoubtedly, vying for the limited amount of trade) as the main reasons for the town's decline.[6]

Nevertheless, the region maintained the principal elements of its marketing structure, as this had developed during the two centuries before 1300. Margaret Bonney's study of Durham, for instance, illustrates how that city managed to maintain a reasonable level of economic stability because there was no significant export industry to suffer from native or foreign competition. Durham, indeed, functioned primarily as a service centre for the twin ecclesiastical administrations of the priory and the bishop, as well as providing marketing facilities for the rural hinterland.[7] Other, less well-known urban communities which also managed to survive as viable marketing centres at this time were the small north-eastern market towns of Darlington and Northallerton. In the later fifteenth and early sixteenth centuries both displayed the visible signs of urban decay and economic contraction which characterised the region as a whole. Yet both continued to function as marketing and trading centres despite the vagaries of the north-eastern economy. This discussion will seek to explore the nature of these towns and of their trading mechanisms before going on to identify possible reasons for their survival during the worst years of contraction and decline.

The boroughs of Darlington, in the palatinate of Durham, and Northallerton, in the North Riding of Yorkshire, both belonged to the bishop of Durham. In terms of trade and local economy, the two were similar, although Darlington was larger and more prominent. It was one of the six medieval boroughs in the palatinate 'between Tyne and Tees' over which the bishop exerted direct control, the others being the boroughs of Durham, Bishop Auckland, Gateshead, Stockton and Sunderland.[8] In respect of its status within the palatinate, Darlington was second only to Durham. In 1197, in the pipe roll of 8 Richard I, in which Durham was noted as *civitas*, Darlington was the only Durham town designated *burgus*.[9] Over three hundred years later, in the late 1530s, the Tudor antiquary, John Leland, remarked that Darlington was still 'the best market town in the bisshoprick, saving Duresme'.[10]

The smaller mesne borough of Northallerton was also in the hands of the bishop of Durham. However, it stood as the focal point of his outlying liberty of Allertonshire in the North Riding of Yorkshire where, although the bishop exercised the normal powers of lordship, he did not enjoy the quasi-regal authority he exerted within the

---

[6] Pollard, *North-Eastern England*, pp. 40–1, 51; *VCH North Riding*, I, 24.

[7] M. Bonney, *Lordship and the Urban Community: Durham and its Overlords, 1250–1540* (Cambridge 1990), pp. 145, 229.

[8] Of the remaining episcopal boroughs within the palatinate, those of Elvet (or Elvethaugh) and St Giles had been granted, respectively, to the priory and the hospital of St Giles at Kepier. The boroughs of Barnard Castle and Hartlepool lay within the lordships of Barnard Castle and Hart respectively and remained the subject of disputed overlordship between the crown and the bishop for much of the later Middle Ages: M.H. Dodds, 'The Bishops' Boroughs', *AA*, 3rd ser. 12 (1915), 81–185; *VCH Durham*, II, 253–6, III, 54–62, 270–2, 354; Bonney, *Lordship and the Urban Community*, pp. 41–9; R. Lomas, *North-East England in the Middle Ages* (Edinburgh 1992), pp. 163–8; G.T. Lapsley, *The County Palatine of Durham: A Study in Constitutional History* (London, 1900), pp. 42–4; Pollard, *North-Eastern England*, pp. 147–9; A.J. Pollard, 'The Crown and the County Palatine of Durham, 1437–94', in *The North of England in the Age of Richard III*, ed. A.J. Pollard (Stroud, 1996), p. 69.

[9] *BB*, appendix, p. vi; Dodds, 'Bishops' Boroughs', 84.

[10] *Itinerary of John Leland*, I, 69.

palatine of Durham.[11] Although not designated a borough in 1197,[12] the town's borough status was certainly in place by the end of the thirteenth century when Northallerton was granted representation in the York parliament of 1298.[13]

Comparisons of sixteenth-century population sources indicate that Northallerton was considerably smaller than Darlington. The chantry certificates of the late 1540s indicate a figure of 700 communicants for the parish of Northallerton, which included four outlying townships.[14] When the figures are adjusted upwards to take account of those below communicant age,[15] it suggests a parish total of around 900. Since the majority of these would have been concentrated in Northallerton, this would indicate a town population of between 600 and 700 inhabitants. The population of the town would have been less in the later fifteenth and early sixteenth centuries, before the onset of the demographic upturn, which probably began in the north from the 1530s.[16] In respect of Darlington, the chantry certificates, although extant, lack details of communicant numbers.[17] However, the ecclesiastical census of households, taken in 1563, reveals that there were 366 households in the parish of Darlington. The parish included the township of Darlington, which encompassed the borough and the vill of Bondgate, as well as three outlying vills.[18] This figure suggests a parish population of around 1,600 or 1,700 inhabitants.[19] Since the outlying vills remained far less populous throughout the period and beyond,[20] it seems likely that the majority of the households enumerated were concentrated in the township of Darlington itself, indicating a population of around 1,200 inhabitants, although the distribution of households between the borough and Bondgate is impossible to determine.[21] Literature pertaining to the great fire which swept through Darlington in 1585 suggests that much of the town, some 273 houses in all, had been destroyed, providing a figure not incompatible with the 1563 census return.[22] As

---

[11] C.M. Newman, *Late Medieval Northallerton* (Stamford, 1999), pp. 1–8, 17; R.L. Storey, *Thomas Langley and the Bishopric of Durham, 1406–1437* (London, 1961), p. 52.

[12] *BB*, appendix, p. vi.

[13] This privilege was thereafter discontinued until representation was restored in 1640: *VCH North Riding*, I, 422; C.J.D. Inglelew, *The History and Antiquities of North Allerton* (London, 1858), pp. 126–8.

[14] *The Certificates of the Commissioners Appointed to Survey the Chantries, Guilds, Hospitals, etc., in the County of York*, ed. W. Page (2 vols., Surtees Society 91–2, 1892–3), II, 485.

[15] E.A. Wrigley and R.S. Schofield, *The Population History of England, 1541–1871* (London 1981), pp. 565–6; M.K. McIntosh, *A Community Transformed: The Manor and Liberty of Havering, 1500–1620* (Cambridge, 1991), p. 10.

[16] Pollard, *North-Eastern England*, p. 48; I.S. Blanchard, 'Population, Change, Enclosure and the Early Tudor Economy', *EcHR*, 2nd ser. 23 (1970), 428–9.

[17] *The Injunctions and other Ecclesiastical Proceedings of Richard Barnes, Bishop of Durham, from 1575 to 1587*, ed. J. Raine (Surtees Society 22, 1850), appendix, p. lxx.

[18] BL, Harleian MS 594, fols. 186–95; for a transcript of the Durham return, see B.J.D. Harrison, 'A Census of Households in County Durham, 1563', *Cleveland and Teesside Local History Society Bulletin* 11 (1970), 16.

[19] Working on a mean household size of between 4.3 and 4.75. See, for example, McIntosh, *Manor and Liberty of Havering*, p. 40; P. Laslett, 'Size and Structure of the Household in England over Three Centuries', *Population Studies* 23 (1969), 200. See also M.J. Tillbrook, 'Aspects of the Government and Society of County Durham, 1558–1642' (unpublished Ph.D. thesis, University of Liverpool, 1981), pp. 43–4.

[20] D.A. Kirby, 'Population Density and Land Values in County Durham during the mid-17th Century', *Transactions of the Institute of British Geographers* 57 (1972), 92.

[21] The division of Darlington into the borough and vill of Bondgate is discussed below, p. 131.

[22] *Lamentable N[ewes] from the Towne of Darnton in the Bishopricke of Durham* (London, 1585). A copy

with Northallerton, the population of Darlington would have been lower in the later fifteenth and early sixteenth centuries.

Darlington and Northallerton were both sites of ancient settlement and were situated at adjacent, strategic points along the main route to the north. Darlington's position was even more favoured in that it stood close to the main crossing point over the River Tees, between Yorkshire and Durham. Prehistoric, Iron Age, and Roman artefacts have been found in and around Darlington. The Roman fort at Piercebridge was located only a few miles to the west. Moreover, the discovery of an Anglian burial site on the town's Greenbank estate indicates some form of settlement in Darlington itself by the latter part of the sixth century.[23] The earliest surviving documentary reference to Darlington concerns a grant of land made to the newly established see of Durham by one Styr, the son of Ulf. It was by virtue of this grant, made around the beginning of the eleventh century, that the bishop of Durham first acquired the vill called 'Dearthingtun', together with its dependent townships and the sac and soc of the same.[24] The construction of Darlington's most important building, the collegiate church of St Cuthbert, was begun c.1192, in the closing years of the episcopate of Bishop Hugh du Puiset.[25] However, the discovery of several Anglo-Saxon sculptures during restoration work upon the church in the mid-nineteenth century has led historians to conclude that an earlier structure existed within the vicinity of the present twelfth-century building. Evidence from late twentieth-century archaeological excavations of the market place, suggesting the presence of a Saxon church, with a graveyard containing remains dating from the mid-eleventh century, has further reinforced this theory.[26] The fact that a church with burial rights was located in the town in this period lends weight to the view that Darlington was not merely a parochial centre but had developed into the administrative and economic focal point, or 'chief place', of one of the pre-Conquest shires which existed in Durham.[27] As such, Darlington probably functioned as one of the 'informal centres of trade' which existed in the north by the eleventh century.[28]

The vill of Darlington, as granted to the bishop of Durham at the beginning of the

---

of this publication is held in the BL. N. Sunderland, *A History of Darlington* (Darlington, 1967, reprint. Manchester, 1972), pp. 35–6; N. Sunderland, *Tudor Darlington* (2 parts, Durham, 1974–6), I, 13.

[23] For the town's early history, see C.M. Newman, 'Darlington before 1600', in G. Cookson, *The Townscape of Darlington* (Woodbridge, 2003), pp. 5–10.

[24] Symeon of Durham, *Libellus De Exordio atque Procursu istius, hoc est Dunhelmensis, Ecclesie: Tract on the Origins and Progress of this the Church of Durham*, ed. and transl. D. Rollason (Oxford, 2000), pp. 152–3. The precise date of the grant is not clear. The year 1003 is given in Dodds, 'Bishops' Boroughs', 84. A similar date of c.1003–16 is suggested in C. Hart, *The Early Charters of Northern England and the North Midlands* (Leicester, 1975), pp. 126–7.

[25] R. Surtees, *The History and Antiquities of the County Palatine of Durham* (4 vols., London, 1816–40), III, 350.

[26] E. Wooler and A.C. Boyd, *Historic Darlington* (London, 1913), pp. 75–6; P.J. Carne and M. Adams, *Darlington Market Place: Archaeological Excavations 1994* (Archaeological Services, University of Durham, 1995), pp. 4, 11; Newman, 'Darlington before 1600', p. 10.

[27] Newman, 'Darlington before 1600', p. 10; P.A.G. Clack and N.F. Pearson, *Darlington: A Topographical Study* (Durham, 1978), p. 8. On this topic, see also E. Cambridge, 'The Early Church in County Durham: A Reassessment', *Journal of the British Archaeological Association* 137 (1984), 79–80; B.K. Roberts, *The Green Villages of County Durham* (Durham, 1977), pp. 8, 13–18; *VCH Durham*, I, 263–8; Lomas, *North-East England*, p. 105.

[28] R. Britnell, 'Boroughs, Markets and Trade in Northern England, 1000–1216', in *Progress and Problems in Medieval England: Essays in Honour of Edward Miller*, ed. R. Britnell and J. Hatcher (Cambridge, 1996), pp. 58–9.

eleventh century, was, at some early stage, subdivided into two entities, with one becoming the borough of Darlington and the other being known as the vill of Bondgate in Darlington.[29] The division had certainly taken place by the end of the twelfth century since the borough gained a brief mention in Boldon Book, Bishop du Puiset's survey of the Durham episcopal estate, compiled *c.*1183.[30] The original Boldon Book has not survived and historians are forced to rely upon later medieval copies of the text, the earliest of which dates from the early fourteenth century. Doubts have been raised as to whether the borough actually appeared in the original version.[31] However, the borough was certainly in evidence a few years later when, in 1197, it was referred to in the pipe roll of 8 Richard I, which detailed the revenues of the bishopric during the vacancy of the see following du Puiset's death.[32]

It is probable that du Puiset was responsible for the creation of the borough and that he did grant Darlington a charter, which is now lost.[33] As with other similar creations in the palatinate, the borough of Darlington seems to have been founded in order to complement the episcopal palace which had been built in the vicinity.[34] Not only would this have provided a suitable focal point for the provision of foodstuffs, goods and services, but it would also have served to create extra revenue in terms of rents, tolls and market dues.[35] As illustrated in Boldon Book, dyers were already operating in the town, suggesting signs of an early cloth industry. Commodities such as wine, salt and herrings were also being brought into the town. Wine was a principal import of Wearmouth and Hartlepool on the eastern seaboard of the palatinate. Salt and herrings were probably also drawn from the same source. The reference, in Boldon Book, to the obligations of the Darlington cotmen to carry fruit indicates, also, that some type of fruit cultivation seems to have been established in the locality.[36] If, as appears to be the case, Darlington was already a 'place of consequence' by the time of the Norman Conquest, it is hardly surprising that a vigorous and politically ambitious bishop such as Hugh du Puiset should seek to impose his influence there more effectively.[37] This he did, not only in visible terms, through the building of an episcopal palace and church, but also through the enhancement of the town's role within the locality.[38] With Darlington more clearly defined as the focal point of administrative and economic life within the locality, the bishop was thus able to strengthen and consolidate his own authority within the region.

Northallerton was also a 'chief place', standing as it did at the focal point of the pre-Conquest manor of 'Alluertune', which extended to some forty-four carucates of

---

[29] Dodds, 'Bishops' Boroughs', 100.
[30] *BB*, p. 17.
[31] For a discussion of the manuscript sources, see G.T. Lapsley's detailed analysis in *VCH Durham*, I, 321–6, which has been surpassed by H.S. Offler, 'Re-reading Boldon Book', in idem, *North of the Tees: Studies in Medieval British History*, ed. A.J. Piper and A.I. Doyle (Aldershot, 1996), ch. 12. A modern translation of the oldest surviving text (known as Manuscript A), appears in *Boldon Book: Northumberland and Durham*, ed. D. Austin (Chichester, 1982).
[32] *BB*, appendix, p. vi.
[33] *English Episcopal Acta 24: Durham 1153–1195*, ed. M.G. Snape (Oxford, 2002), pp. 176–7.
[34] *BB*, p. 17; *VCH Durham*, I, 339.
[35] Lomas, *North-East England*, p. 163.
[36] This reference is not contained in all of the surviving MSS of Boldon Book: *BB*, p. 16; *VCH Durham*, I, 302.
[37] *VCH Durham*, I, 312–13.
[38] Dodds, 'Bishops' Boroughs', 91.

land. The manor had been worth £80 a year, although by the time of the Domesday survey it was wasted.[39] To the manor belonged eleven berewicks and the soke of the lands in twenty-four outlying localities. Much of this land was later incorporated into the bishop of Durham's liberty of Allertonshire. The town was, reputedly, the site of a Roman settlement, although little evidence of this has survived.[40] There was, however, some Anglo-Saxon activity in the area, fragments of late eighth- to early ninth-century Anglian sculptures having been found in the vicinity of the church.[41] These add weight to the suggestion that the town's earliest known church, of twelfth-century origins, was built on the foundations of a pre-Conquest church.[42] The earliest documentary evidence is that concerning the c.1088 grant of the manor of Allerton to Bishop William of St Calais by King William II.[43] The earliest mention of the town of Northallerton occurs only in 1197, in the pipe roll of 8 Richard I. Like Darlington, the town probably developed under the auspices of Bishop du Puiset, who had built a castle there by 1174. The castle was razed to the ground following du Puiset's support for the rebellion against Henry II, but the bishop's palace or manor house was erected there shortly afterwards.[44]

The bishops' boroughs, even those with charters, enjoyed little in the way of autonomy.[45] In Darlington, the town's chief official, the bailiff of the borough, was the bishop's appointee and the visible source of episcopal authority within the town. Moreover, the borough farm was granted out in the bishop's halmote court, signifying the extent of the lord's control over the town and its privileges.[46] Nevertheless, much of the administration of the town was undertaken in the borough court which was jointly convened by the bailiff and the burgesses of the town. Through the medium of the court, the townsmen were thus able to exercise a certain amount of initiative in terms of the day-to-day governance of the borough. Local interests may also have been served by the fact that officials and holders of the borough farm were often drawn from members of the local landed elite. In 1395, for example, the borough farm was granted to Ingelram Gentill, William de Werdale and Thomas Casson.[47] Of these, Casson was certainly a member of a local landholding family.[48] There are no contemporary local references to Gentill and Werdale. However, if they were not already part of the local elite, they and their families quickly became so.[49] In the closing decades

---

[39] *VCH York*, II, 196.
[40] *VCH North Riding*, I, 418.
[41] E. Cambridge, 'Why did the Community of St Cuthbert settle at Chester-le-Street?', in *St Cuthbert, His Cult and His Community to AD 1200*, ed. G. Bonner et al. (Woodbridge, 1989), pp. 382–5.
[42] *VCH North Riding*, I, 426.
[43] *Scriptores Tres*, appendix, no. CCCCXXV.
[44] *VCH North Riding*, I, 418.
[45] Dodds, 'Bishops' Boroughs', 97–8; *VCH Durham*, II, 254.
[46] See, for instance, PRO, DURH 3/12, fols. 62v, 83, 98, 166v, and 3/13 fo. 165v (re-numbered 160v).
[47] *HS*, p. 6; Dodds, 'Bishops' Boroughs', 137.
[48] The Cassons were free tenants of the bishop in his vill of Coatham Mundeville and of Durham Priory in its township of Burdon, near Haughton le Skerne: *HS*, p. 7; *Durham Cathedral Priory Rentals: Vol. 1, Bursar's Rentals*, ed. R.A. Lomas and A.J. Piper (Surtees Society 198, 1986), p. 109.
[49] Several references to Ingelram and John Gentill appear in the palatine chancery rolls of Bishop Langley's episcopate. Moreover, John Gentill was appointed one of the commissioners of array for the ward of Darlington in 1415. By the 1420s the Werdales, too, were holding land in Darlington: 'Durham Records: Calendar of the Cursitor's Records: Chancery Enrolments', in *The Thirty-Third Annual Report of the Deputy Keeper of the Public Records* (1872), pp. 91, 93, 168.

of the fifteenth century two successive borough bailiffs and holders of the farm, Stephen Bland,[50] and William Betts,[51] were members of local landholding families.

The evidence from Allertonshire in the later fifteenth and early sixteenth centuries suggests that here, too, the local community enjoyed a degree of involvement in the day-to-day running of local government. In the liberty the chief official was the bishop's steward, the office being held by successive members of the Strangways family during this period.[52] However, much of the daily administration was undertaken by the bailiff of the liberty, another episcopal appointee.[53] In the later fifteenth and early sixteenth centuries this official was drawn from amongst the ranks of the Northallerton burgesses. From the mid-1490s to the 1520s the bailiff of Allertonshire was Edmund Skarlett who, from 1506, also held the office of receiver of Allertonshire.[54] Certainly during Skarlett's period of tenure, overall administrative control within both borough and liberty resided, largely, within his hands. Moreover, in 1522 Edmund Skarlett, together with his son, Thomas, acquired the lease of the borough farm, for the annual sum of £7, for a period of thirty years.[55] The date at which the borough of Northallerton was initially granted at farm is not clear, although in a royal inquisition of 1334, following the townsmen's appeal to the crown for the clarification of their rights and privileges, the borough was valued at forty marks. The inquisition had been set up to investigate the townsmen's complaint against unjust financial exactions made by the bishop and the crown during vacancies of the see of Durham. The inquisition found that the men of Northallerton were free and of free condition and that they held their tofts and crofts of the bishop in fee, together with the market and fair and all profits arising from the same, for the annual sum of forty silver marks. The inquisition also confirmed the privilege of holding the borough court, in which a panel of townsmen was empowered, together with the bailiff of Allertonshire, to adjudicate in all pleas pertaining to lands and tenements within the borough.[56] Chief sessions of the borough court were held biannually, in conjunction with a view of frankpledge, which gave the townsmen the authority to punish those who committed minor offences and misdemeanours.[57] Supervision of economic affairs within the town and the passing of bye-laws were also undertaken in the court.[58]

---

50 DUL, CCB B/48/6 (188791). This was probably the same Stephen Bland, a yeoman, mentioned in a memorandum regarding the surrender of lands in Darlington, entered in the palatine chancery rolls in 1503–4: PRO, DURH 3/65, m. 2d.

51 *Letters of Richard Fox, 1486–1527*, ed. P.S. and H.M. Allen (Oxford 1929), pp. 24–6; 'Durham Records: Calendar of the Cursitor's Records: Inquisitions Post Mortem', in *The Forty-Fourth Annual Report of the Deputy Keeper of the Public Records* (1883), p. 328.

52 Newman, *Late Medieval Northallerton*, pp. 19–20, 42–3.

53 A borough bailiff seems also to have been elected annually in the borough court. He was probably responsible for the routine administration of the town, although evidence concerning his precise role is scant. See, for example, the election of Robert Hede as bailiff in the chief session of the borough court, held at Easter, 1500: NYCRO, ZBD 52/25 (189449); *VCH North Riding*, I, 422.

54 Newman, *Late Medieval Northallerton*, pp. 21–3; PRO, DURH 3/61, m. 14. In 1500 Bishop Fox granted the office to Skarlett for life. A copy of the patent is attached to the Allertonshire receiver's account of 1500–1: DUL, CCB B/84/8 (189299).

55 PRO, DURH 3/70, m. 34.

56 *CCR, 1333–7*, pp. 189–90; Ingledew, *North Allerton*, pp. 98–103.

57 It has been suggested that, whilst the frankpledge system seems not to have operated in the north, the term, nevertheless, came to denote the existence of leet jurisdiction: W. Morris, *The Frankpledge System* (New York, 1910), pp. 51–2.

58 Newman, *Late Medieval Northallerton*, pp. 94–8.

Both towns had fairs from the early thirteenth century and were holding regular markets by the beginning of the fourteenth. In Northallerton the grant of a fair on the feast of St Laurence was made to the bishop by King John in March 1200, although this was not, apparently, in existence by the early fourteenth century. Indeed, in 1306–7 the bishop laid claim only to the right to hold a fair on the feast of St Bartholomew. The holding of a market, together with the right to its profits, was another privilege claimed by the bishop at that time, although by 1334, this right had passed to the townsmen.[59] Darlington's marketing economy probably had its roots in the pre-Conquest period although first mention of its fair occurs in 1217,[60] whilst evidence from the account rolls of Durham Priory shows that, by the later part of the century, the market was also thriving. According to the *quo warranto* proceedings of 1293 Darlington was one of only three boroughs on the Durham episcopal estate with recorded regular markets and fairs, the other two being Durham and Norham.[61] The account rolls of Durham Priory reveal that by this period the obedientiaries were in the habit of making purchases of cattle, cloth and other commodities from the town.[62] By 1315 the market was becoming increasingly important and was attracting visitors from far beyond the immediate locale.[63] This was a time of instability when the palatinate was subjected to the ravages of Scottish incursions.[64] In order to ensure the safety of travelling merchants, given the uncertain conditions at that time, the bishop issued a mandate threatening to excommunicate anyone who obstructed visitors to the Darlington market and fair.[65]

Darlington's cloth industry was in existence before the end of the twelfth century, for Boldon Book noted the existence of a dyeworks in the town. By the later thirteenth century the town was an important cloth trading centre. Merchants such as John de Graham, who in 1295 had several bales of cloth confiscated by the bishop's bailiffs, frequented the fair in order to sell their wares.[66] The monks of Durham Priory were regular customers. As early as 1292 purchases of cloth from Darlington fair were being noted in the bursar's accounts. 'Bluett' (blue woollen cloth), worth 32s., was similarly purchased at the fair of 1299.[67] Later accounts show further evidence of purchases of other cloths in various colours, both plain (i.e. green) and striped.[68] Northallerton, too, had a cloth manufacturing industry, although its trading concerns were more limited and localised. Nevertheless, there is evidence of its vitality during the fourteenth century. Dyers and a fuller appeared among the taxpayers noted in the 1301 lay subsidy assessment.[69] At the end of the fourteenth century the town was still

---

[59] *Rotuli Chartarum in Turri Londinensi Asservati*, ed. T.D. Hardy (London, 1837), p. 37; *RPD*, III, 48–9; Ingledew, *North Allerton*, pp. 101, 103; J.L. Saywell, *The History and Annals of Northallerton* (Northallerton, 1885), pp. 32–3.
[60] Dodds, 'Bishops' Boroughs', 86; *FPD*, p. 148.
[61] *Placita De Quo Warranto*, ed. W. Illingworth (London, 1818), p. 604.
[62] *DAR*, II, 484, 494.
[63] Dodds, 'Bishops' Boroughs', 111.
[64] Lomas, *North-East England*, pp. 159–60; C. McNamee, *The Wars of the Bruces: Scotland, England and Ireland 1306–1328* (East Linton, 1997), pp. 107–8.
[65] *RPD*, II, 222.
[66] C.M. Fraser, *A History of Antony Bek, Bishop of Durham, 1283–1311* (Oxford, 1957), p. 97.
[67] *DAR*, II, 492, 494.
[68] Ibid., III, 577, 633.
[69] *Yorkshire Lay Subsidy, being a Fifteenth collected 30 Edward I, 1301*, ed. W. Brown (Yorkshire Archaeological and Record Society 21, 1897), pp. 69–70.

marketing a certain amount of cloth, since it appeared in the ulnage account of 1395–6, in company with the nearby cloth making centres of Bedale and Richmond.[70]

By the fourteenth century Darlington merchants were also engaged in the international wool trade. Details have survived of an inquisition, set up in 1337, to make enquiry into the confiscation, by the count of Flanders, of wool worth £60, which had been exported to Bruges by John and William de Durham of Darlington. The two men, who shipped their wares through the ports of Hartlepool, Newcastle and Kingston-upon-Hull, were prominent merchants.[71] John de Durham was named as a member of the consortium of wool merchants who, by the indenture of July 1337, gave backing to the royal purveyance of wool designed to provide funding for Edward III's war effort. He was later appointed to oversee the purchase of wool in the palatinate.[72] William was appointed controller of the customs of wool, wine, hides and woolfells in Hartlepool in 1338,[73] and in 1339 he was among a number of merchants summoned to Westminster to offer advice on the wool trade.[74] These were not the only Darlington men to trade internationally in wool. In 1348 John Slaver of Darlington had his consignment of wool, shipped via Newcastle on board a ship called the *Cuthbert*, confiscated by the king's agents in Bruges because it lacked official documentation regarding customs payments. The mayor and bailiff of Newcastle were ordered to investigate, subsequently obtaining proof that customs had been paid, and thus resolving the matter.[75]

The impact of the Black Death and subsequent plagues upon the region is well documented and both towns suffered from the demographic and economic upheavals of the period.[76] Northallerton's cloth manufacturing industry, in company with those of York and other, less substantial North and East Riding towns, declined as a result of competition from the West Riding. By the later part of the fourteenth century Darlington's cloth trade was probably also in decline. In the early years of the sixteenth century Darlington's fulling mill, the first evidence for which dates from the late fourteenth century, ceased to operate.[77] Although its dyeworks remained in occupation, at an annual rent of 26s. 6d., it, too, had fallen into decay by 1516.[78] Nonetheless, local inhabitants probably undertook cloth production as a secondary occupation and there is a great deal of evidence to suggest that, even though the industry was in decline, small-scale production continued throughout the sixteenth century. A number of late fifteenth- and early sixteenth-century Allertonshire wills and inventories survive, and several of these contain references to cloth making implements and resources, such as looms, spinning wheels, linen seed and hemp.[79] Similarly, several late sixteenth- and early seventeenth-century Darlington wills and inventories

---

70 H. Heaton, *The Yorkshire Woollen and Worsted Industries* (Oxford 1920), pp. 7, 70.
71 *CCR, 1337–9*, p. 432.
72 *CCR, 1337–9*, pp. 148, 270; PRO, DURH 3/12, fo. 31v.
73 The grant was renewed in 1339: *CPR, 1338–40*, pp. 163, 392.
74 *CCR, 1339–41*, p. 341.
75 *CCR, 1346–9*, pp. 471–2, 514–5.
76 Pollard, *North-Eastern England*, pp. 43–59, 71–80.
77 By 1506 the fulling mill was noted as being 'out of tenants': DUL, CCB B/48/8 (188791B). In 1509 timber from the 'old walk' mill was being used to repair the bishop's corn mill at Blackwell: Sunderland, *Tudor Darlington*, I, 70.
78 DUL, CCB B/68/8 (189065A).
79 DCM, Loc.VIII:1, 4, 17.

contain references to linen looms, flax and other linen making equipment, thus providing early evidence of the rise of the town's later linen industry.[80]

Both towns also had leather working industries. In late fifteenth-century Northallerton the tradesmen of the town included tanners, shoemakers, glovers and saddlers. Indeed, several freemen of the borough, who appeared regularly as borough court jurors, were engaged in one or other of these trades.[81] The leather trade of Darlington which, by the sixteenth century was outstripping the cloth industry, had been in evidence since at least the fourteenth century. An early fourteenth-century charter records the presence of a cobbler in Houndgate, whilst the street named Skinnergate, dating from the mid- to later fourteenth century, provides an early indication of the leather working which ran in association with the town's livestock trade. An early resident of that street was one William Skinner. The Clervaux chartulary, which gives details of several fourteenth- and fifteenth-century street names, refers also to a limekiln, essential to the tanning trade, in Skinnergate. This appears to have been adjacent to a well, water being another essential prerequisite of the trade.[82] In the fifteenth century the marketing of leather goods in the town was sufficiently well-established to the extent that the saddler's guild of York, which actively forbade its members from trading at fairs and markets within a forty-league radius, exempted Darlington from this ban.[83]

As already indicated, the late fifteenth and early sixteenth centuries were characterised by continued economic constraint within north-east England, unlike parts of the south which had begun to show signs of regeneration following the demographic and economic upheavals of the fourteenth and fifteenth centuries.[84] Darlington and Northallerton suffered along with the rest of the north east. The Allertonshire receivers' accounts show evidence of stagnant rents and farms and soaring arrears totals. The 1490s, in particular, were years of economic difficulties in the liberty. Plague ravaged Northallerton in this decade and analysis of the small plea litigation within the liberty's courts shows evidence of the short-term sudden upsurge in prosecutions for debt associated with periods of credit crisis.[85] Whilst by the 1520s the economy was beginning, slowly, to stabilise, there was no evidence of any significant recovery. Indeed the 1555 grant sanctioning the holding of a St George's Day fair and fortnightly cattle market noted how the town, 'on account of the poverty of its inhabitants is now in great ruin and decay'.[86] In Darlington, too, the borough bailiff's accounts illustrate the level of visible decline within the town. A particularly detailed account, that of 1477–8, indicates that the tollhouse – the focal point of the marketplace – was in a state of near dereliction. Of the twelve shops situated in the lower part of the building the farms of only two were capable of being levied. The town's granary, also situated in the tollhouse, was unoccupied, with its rent in decay, as was another shop, situated under the pillory.[87] By 1516 the decay had deepened, the shops under the

---

[80] Sunderland, *Tudor Darlington*, I, 72; *Darlington Wills and Inventories, 1600–25*, ed. J.A. Atkinson et al. (Surtees Society 201, 1993), pp. 39, 103, 108, 137.
[81] Newman, *Late Medieval Northallerton*, pp. 94, 122.
[82] A.H. Thompson, 'The Clervaux Chartulary', *AA*, 3rd ser. 17 (1920), 200, 208–9.
[83] Sunderland, *Tudor Darlington*, I, 44; Pollard, *North-Eastern England*, p. 41.
[84] Pollard, *North-Eastern England*, pp. 53–80.
[85] Newman, *Late Medieval Northallerton*, pp. 81–92.
[86] *CPR, 1554–5*, p. 183.
[87] DUL, CCB B/68/1 (188916).

tollhouse being difficult to let due to the poor repair of the building. The common oven was unoccupied for want of repair, its 40s. farm in decay.[88]

Despite the sluggish nature of the later medieval economy, however, the marketing functions of both towns continued to operate. Darlington's weekly market was, as now, held on Monday, with the borough bailiffs' accounts recording the total profits drawn from this and from the holding of the fairs. These remained fairly stable, at around £4 or £5 *per annum*. The 1477–8 bailiff's account noted a profit of £4 13s. 4d., whilst in 1505–6 a similar sum of £4 11s. 5d. was collected. In 1515–16 the profits of the town's four fairs and markets stood slightly higher at £5 16s. 8d.[89] Independent sources confirm this impression of continuity. In 1467–8 the earl of Warwick's farm at Middleham was stocked with cattle from Darlington.[90] The priory of Durham also continued to purchase stock from Darlington throughout the period. Particularly detailed references in the bursars' accounts of 1507–12 enumerate the expenses of officials travelling to various localities throughout the region, including Darlington, for this purpose.[91] In the early sixteenth century four fairs were held annually. Although the dates of these are not given in the accounts, it seems likely that one took place at some point in February, with others at Easter, Whitsuntide and Martinmas.[92] The Martinmas fair was famed for the sale of livestock – especially horned cattle – and attracted customers from across the region.[93] The Durham bursar's household books for 1530–4, for example, show purchases of stock in Darlington at both the Whitsuntide and Martinmas fairs.[94]

In Northallerton, too, the market and fair continued to function. Here the weekly market was held on a Wednesday; a custom which, as with that at Darlington, has also survived to the present day. The fair of St Bartholomew, noted in 1306–7,[95] was still held two hundred years later. By the later sixteenth century Northallerton's St Bartholomew's fair was famous, attracting dealers from as far afield as Middlesex. The Elizabethan antiquary, William Camden, noted how it was the 'greatest Faire of Kine & Oxen'.[96] Whether the fair was quite as bustling, in the economically-stagnant years surrounding the turn of the sixteenth century, is not made clear in the available sources. Nevertheless, from the evidence concerning the collection of the town's tolls, it appears that Northallerton's marketing activity continued unabated throughout the period. The profits of the markets and fairs were included in the borough farm which was let, in this period, for £7 *per annum*, and this amount appeared annually in the accounts. On only two occasions during the period under consideration was the farmer of the borough granted a rebate. The first time was in 1493–4, when the town

---

[88] DUL, CCB B/68/8 (189065A).
[89] DUL, CCB B/68/1 (188916); B/68/2 (188918); B/68/7 (188921).
[90] Pollard, *North-Eastern England*, pp. 12, 41.
[91] DCM, Bursar's Account Rolls, 1507–8, detailing the 'expenses of Anthony Thomson, Roland Busby and others working with them riding to Alnwick, Morpeth, Newcastle, Corbridge, Hexham, Darlington, Stokesley, Barnard Castle and elsewhere for purchase of animals, in the time of this account'. See also Bursar's Account Rolls, 1508–9, 1509–10, 1510–11, 1511–12, 1512–13.
[92] Dodds, 'Bishops' Boroughs', 109.
[93] W.H.D. Longstaffe, *The History and Antiquities of the Parish of Darlington, in the Bishoprick* (Darlington, 1854), p. 275; Pollard, *North-Eastern England*, p. 41.
[94] *Durham Household Book; or, the Accounts of the Bursar of the Monastery of Durham from Pentecost 1530 to Pentecost 1534*, ed. J. Raine (Surtees Society 18, 1844), pp. 71–2, 202, 301.
[95] *RPD*, III, 48–9.
[96] W. Camden, *Britain* (London, 1610), p. 723.

and liberty were badly hit by a 'great pestilence'.[97] The second occasion was in 1536–7, in the aftermath of the Pilgrimage of Grace, when the lessee was granted a rebate of £2 because of the problems he had encountered in collecting his dues 'in the commotion time'.[98]

It seems, therefore, that the trading mechanisms of both Northallerton and Darlington continued to operate despite the stagnant nature of the late medieval north-eastern economy. This was in contrast to the experiences of some of the other market centres in the region. In the North Riding the towns of Wensley, Catterick and Boroughbridge were all struggling. Within the palatinate, Wolsingham market was also in abeyance.[99] So how did the two boroughs, as well as their trade, market and fairs, manage to ride out the economic storms of the later Middle Ages? They were fortunate in several respects. In the first place, they both stood at strategic positions along the great northern route from York. Travellers on that route passed through Northallerton, crossing the Tees, either at Croft Bridge or Neasham ford,[100] and thence to Darlington. Passing trade therefore generated a regular income. Northallerton certainly received its fair share of travellers, although not all were welcome. Indeed, cases in the borough court rolls of the late fifteenth and early sixteenth centuries illustrate the extent to which Northallerton provided a convenient stopping point, along the main route between York and the north, for vagrants, itinerant Scots and other undesirable individuals.[101] The court records do not provide evidence of more socially acceptable travellers, but they must have been equally as numerous. There is early reference to the existence of a hostelry in Darlington in a case brought before the Durham court of pleas in 1390–1. This was prosecuted by the prior of Brinkburn and John de Stockton, a fellow monk, who sued John de Acle for goods worth £10 which had been stolen from Stockton whilst he had been lodging with Acle in the town.[102] Later, in 1585, one of the complaints expressed in the pamphlet which described the Darlington fire of that year was that the town, 'which was of good harbour to travellers to Barwicke or from thence to London . . . is not able to entertain the twentieth part of the passengers which heretofore it received'.[103]

Trading links between Darlington and Durham, the next major stopping place on the main route north, have already been mentioned.[104] However, the strategic position of Darlington along the national north-south thoroughfare was complemented by the fact that it was also well placed with respect to local trading routes. As such, it enjoyed close links with the smaller market towns in its vicinity. Indeed, the burgesses of the town were exempt from the payment of the tolls of the fair and market of Bishop Auckland as well as of Darlington itself.[105] Moreover, Darlington

---

[97] DUL, CCB B/84/1 (189330–189331). William Leek had held the farm since at least 1485 when he had been granted the demise, initially for a period of one year: NYCRO, ZBD 52/5 (189583).
[98] DUL, CCB B/85/29 (190132), B/85/30 (189426).
[99] *Itinerary of John Leland*, I, 84, IV, 26, V, 129.
[100] Ibid., I, 68–9.
[101] Newman, *Late Medieval Northallerton*, pp. 128–36.
[102] PRO, DURH 13/223, mm. 2, 4d., 7. I am grateful to Constance Fraser for providing me with these references.
[103] *Lamentable N[ewes] from the Towne of Darnton*, p. 6.
[104] See above, p. 137; Bonney, *Lordship and the Urban Community*, pp. 17, 157, 171, 193; C.M. Fraser, 'The Pattern of Trade in the North-East of England, 1265–1350', *NH* 4 (1969), 49–51.
[105] Durham Chapter Library, Allan MS 15, pp. 152–3.

stood directly on the main route running eastwards from Barnard Castle across the Tees valley. Darlington's famous stone bridge, which straddled the River Skerne, connected directly with the road to Yarm, thus opening up the routes to Stockton, Hartlepool, Guisborough and Stokesley, which were the main marketing centres of the Tees valley region.[106] In the twelfth and thirteenth centuries the River Tees seems to have been a viable waterway, with Yarm and Hartlepool, which stood at the river's mouth, both serving as thriving ports. The quantities of wine, salt and herrings that were transported to Darlington at the time of Boldon Book (c.1183) might well have been carried via this route.[107] As already noted, Darlington's fourteenth-century wool merchants were trading through Hartlepool as well as through Newcastle and Hull.[108] By the middle of the fourteenth century, however, both Hartlepool and Yarm were in decline due to the combined effects of the economic and demographic decline within the Tees valley and growing competition from the port of Newcastle.[109] The decline of nearby centres such as Yarm undoubtedly enabled Darlington to consolidate its position as a major marketing centre within the Tees valley region.[110]

Coal from the Durham pits was transported through Darlington into north Yorkshire. Leland, writing in the 1530s, noted how most of the coal used in Richmond was brought from the bishop of Durham's pits at Railey, near Bishop Auckland.[111] The coal was probably transported along the highway from West Auckland, known in later records as the 'coal road', which passed through Darlington and on to Piercebridge. This route was certainly in use by the middle of the fifteenth century, for an enrolment in the Durham chancery dated 1457 appointed commissioners to enquire into obstructions in the highway between West Auckland, Darlington and 'Percybridge'.[112] Coal from this source probably also found its way to Northallerton. In a plea of broken contract brought before the borough court in 1498 William Wadylove of Northallerton claimed that he had been sold a horse, by one Richard Stanes of Osmotherley, which, despite assurances to the contrary, had proved unfit to undertake Wadylove's regular wintertime journey to Darlington to collect coal.[113] Northallerton also had links with the Cleveland marketing centres, drawing fish supplies from the coastal towns of the region. As further pleas of debt in the borough court rolls show, Northallerton's cloth makers also traded with those of Bedale and Ripon.[114] Apart from its favourable geographical position with respect to other regional centres, Northallerton was also fortunate from a local perspective in that it stood at the focal point of the bishop's lordship of Allertonshire, which comprised more than thirty small townships and vills. As such, it was the administrative, social and economic centre of the locality, and, as an analysis of the borough court rolls has

---

[106] A.J. Pollard, ' "All Maks and Manders": The Local History of the Tees Valley in the later Middle Ages', *Cleveland History* 65 (1994), 17.
[107] *BB*, p. 16; *VCH Durham*, I, 302.
[108] See above, p. 135.
[109] Pollard, ' "All Maks and Manders" ', 24.
[110] Ibid., 25.
[111] *Itinerary of John Leland*, V, 140.
[112] PRO, DURH 3/45, m. 6.
[113] NYCRO, ZBD 52/22 (189447); Pollard, ' "All Maks and Manders" ', 17; Pollard, *North-Eastern England*, p. 76.
[114] Newman, *Late Medieval Northallerton*, pp. 110, 113; NYCRO, ZBD 53/4 (189588), ZBD 52/1 (189269), ZBD 52/29 (189586).

shown, the town's markets and fairs were regularly patronised by the inhabitants of its rural hinterland.[115]

The position of Darlington and Northallerton, on strategic trade and travel routes, undoubtedly contributed to their survival during the years of stagnation and decline, which characterised the late medieval north-eastern economy. Moreover, both lay at the centre of large pre-Conquest administrative units. As such, they had probably functioned as the 'chief places' of those localities, perhaps for several centuries before the emergence of the documentary sources upon which we rely for tangible evidence. As natural focal points, with longstanding trading and marketing traditions, they were, perhaps, better able to retain their footing in times of economic upheaval than less well placed centres, especially those lacking long-established trading links. Longevity of function, coupled with favourable location, may thus have contributed to the survival of towns such as Darlington and Northallerton, which managed to maintain some degree of economic momentum despite the vagaries of late medieval economic forces.

---

[115] Newman, *Late Medieval Northallerton*, pp. 100–2.

10

Newcastle Trade and Durham Priory, 1460–1520

MIRANDA THRELFALL-HOLMES

This essay uses the expenditure recorded in the Durham Priory obedientiary accounts to shed some light on regional trade in the north east in the late medieval period. Using the accounts of a substantial local consumer to investigate the extent and structure of trade in the area of Durham and Newcastle-upon-Tyne provides a fresh perspective on these issues. The evidence available for the history of medieval Newcastle in particular is notoriously limited, with only a handful of municipal records having survived from before the sixteenth century. Despite this limitation, a substantial body of work has been built up by the resourceful use of what does remain, such as customs accounts.[1] The official nature of the surviving evidence, however, has meant that little is known about Newcastle's trade from the consumers' point of view, and so it has not been possible to quantify the relative importance of Newcastle as a supply centre to local purchasers. The wide range of purchasing information from a substantial series of years which is detailed in the Durham obedientiary accounts can go some way towards redressing this balance, giving valuable insights into the range and extent of trading activity both in Newcastle itself and throughout the north-east region.[2]

In this essay it is argued that the evidence from Durham Priory indicates Newcastle's considerable importance as a centre for trade and distribution in the late medieval period, and moreover that this importance increased over the course of the fifteenth and early sixteenth centuries. In addition, the priory's relationship with, and use of, the marketplace as a source of supply will be considered. The priory acquired goods in two main and distinctive ways, either via tenurial links or via market purchasing. Here the priory's use of these two methods of acquisition is briefly

---

[1] J.F. Wade, 'The Overseas Trade of Newcastle upon Tyne in the late Middle Ages', *NH* 30 (1994), 31–48; *The Customs Accounts of Newcastle upon Tyne*, ed. J.F. Wade (Surtees Society 202, 1995); *The Accounts of the Chamberlains of Newcastle upon Tyne 1508–1511*, ed. C.M. Fraser (Society of Antiquaries of Newcastle upon Tyne Record Series 3, 1987). Valuable work on the earlier period includes J. Conway Davies, 'Shipping and Trade in Newcastle upon Tyne, 1294–1296', *AA*, 4th ser. 31 (1953), 175–204, idem, 'The Wool Customs Accounts of Newcastle upon Tyne for the Reign of Edward I', *AA*, 4th ser. 32 (1954), 220–308, and C.M. Fraser, 'The Pattern of Trade in the North East of England, 1265–1350', *NH* 4 (1969), 44–66.

[2] C.M. Fraser first realised the potential of the Durham obedientiary account material for the history of the region's trading activity in 'The Pattern of Trade', in which she drew upon the Durham account material published in *DAR*. This essay draws largely upon DCM, Bursar's Account Rolls. For a more detailed discussion of the source material, see my 'The Import Merchants of Newcastle upon Tyne, 1464–1520: Some Evidence from Durham Cathedral Priory', *NH* 40 (2003), 73–4.

outlined, and its use of the market is then discussed in more detail. The analysis will clarify which markets supplied the priory, the priory's use of agents in the purchasing process and the impact or otherwise of transport considerations on purchasing decisions. The priory's purchases of wine and cloth will be the main focus of discussion here, since these bulky and high-value items, about which we have most information in the accounts concerning their provenance, accounted for a high proportion of the priory's market purchasing. Finally, the merchants from whom the priory made its purchases, and the extent and types of the priory's relationships with them, are also examined.[3]

Tenurial and Market Supply

Two distinct modes of operation can be seen in the provisioning of the priory. Much of the local agricultural produce and other items of local manufacture or provenance which the priory acquired was bought via the priory's network of tenurial relationships. Over ninety-five per cent of the grain which entered the priory was acquired in this way, as well as around half of the meat and fish, and varying amounts of certain other goods such as honey, salt, oil, and locally-produced cloth. These items were not 'bought' in the usual sense of the word but were given to the priory as payments in kind for the rents which their tenants owed, or occasionally for other payments due such as that for the purchase of a tithe. Such payments in kind were in widespread use at Durham, being used to some extent in fifty-seven per cent of the rental payments made in 1495–6.[4]

The market was by no means redundant, however. It was used both for other goods – mainly manufactured, processed or imported items – and for top-up purchases of the commodities which were mainly bought using the tenurial system. For example, grain was almost entirely acquired from tenants of the priory as payment in kind, but additional small amounts were bought on the open market in most years, and the market was resorted to on a large scale in years of dearth such as the early 1480s, when grain could be bought from outside the region at significantly lower prices. Around half of the fish and livestock which entered the priory was also bought, often from the same individuals who also supplied some in the form of rental payments, and this demonstrates the lack of any sharp dividing line between either the goods or suppliers involved in these two methods of supply.

Whilst the priory only sourced grain from outside the immediate region in exceptional circumstances, it might be expected that other commodities such as luxuries, imported or manufactured goods would be sourced from a wider area, perhaps including the major fairs, and certainly including London. In fact, whilst to some

---

[3] Details concerning the priory's purchases of a wider range of commodities can be found in M. Threlfall-Holmes, 'Provisioning a Medieval Monastery: Durham Cathedral Priory's Purchases of Imported Goods, 1464–1520' (unpublished M.A. thesis, University of Durham, 1997). A comprehensive survey of the priory's two modes of purchasing is contained in M. Threlfall-Holmes, *Monks and Markets: Durham Cathedral Priory, 1460–1520* (Oxford, 2005), pp. 136–91. For a fuller discussion of the merchants from whom the priory purchased goods, see Threlfall-Holmes, 'Import Merchants of Newcastle upon Tyne', 71–87.

[4] R.A. Lomas, 'A Priory and its Tenants', in *Daily Life in the Late Middle Ages*, ed. R.H. Britnell (Stroud, 1998), pp. 117–19.

extent this was the case in an earlier period, one of the major long-term changes that these accounts reveal is the increasing proportion of the priory's business in luxuries and imports that went to Newcastle merchants over the medieval period. The immediate north-east region supplied virtually all of the priory's requirements by the beginning of the sixteenth century, with Newcastle assuming an increasingly dominant role.

This is well illustrated by the history of the priory's wine purchases. Margaret Bonney has shown that, in the thirteenth and fourteenth centuries, local middlemen supplied the priory with wine which they probably purchased in turn from London wholesalers. By the mid-fourteenth century, the emphasis had shifted to the fairs of Durham, Darlington and Boston, and by the late fourteenth century to the merchants of Durham, Newcastle, Hartlepool, Darlington, York, and Hull. By the first years of the fifteenth century, the majority of the priory's wine came from Newcastle.[5] The evidence from the fifteenth century indicates that this trend towards Newcastle continued over the century, with Newcastle merchants claiming an increasing share of the priory's business.

Between 1460 and 1520, the bursar paid out over £2,000 on wine, and ninety-four per cent was spent with Newcastle merchants. Nearly six per cent was spent with the merchants of Hull, and negligible amounts were spent with merchants of York (£36 3s. 4d.), London (£17 0s. 6d.) and Durham (£9 6s. 8d.). The proportion of the priory's trade that was given to York, in particular, had declined noticeably since the first half of the century, when eleven per cent of the bursar's wine had come from that city compared to less than half of one per cent by the later period.[6] This reflects the decreasing numbers of York merchants participating in overseas trade over the fifteenth century, an important feature of the recession that lasted there from c.1420 to the early decades of the sixteenth century.[7] The pattern of the priory's purchases from York merchants suggests that its increasing focus on Newcastle suppliers was a response, rather than a contribution, to this decline; there was no sudden abandonment of the York market (indeed, in 1471–2, forty-nine per cent of the bursar's wine purchases were made there). In the first half of the fifteenth century the bursar had occasionally purchased wine not simply at the four towns used in the second half of the century, but also from South Shields and Hartlepool; by the sixteenth century, no wine was bought from even Hull, York or Durham merchants. Apart from the purchase of a butt of malmsey from London in 1500–1 and 1506–7, Newcastle merchants supplied all of the priory's wine after 1497–8, even the luxury wines such as malmsey, generally considered to have been the preserve of London merchants.[8]

A different pattern may be seen in the priory's purchases of livery cloths, although the north east as a whole still predominates. For most of the cloth purchases recorded

---

5   M. Bonney, *Lordship and the Urban Community: Durham and its Overlords, 1250–1540* (Cambridge, 1990), pp. 169–174; for the wide range of luxury goods available in Durham in the late thirteenth and fourteenth centuries, see also Fraser, 'Pattern of Trade', 46, 50.
6   N. Morimoto, 'The Demand and Purchases of Wine of Durham Cathedral Priory in the First Half of the Fifteenth Century', *The Nagoya Gakuin University Review* 20 (1983), 101.
7   J.I. Kermode, 'Merchants, Overseas Trade and Urban Decline: York, Beverley and Hull, c.1380–1500', *NH* 23 (1987), 51–73.
8   Newcastle was the centre of the wine trade for the northern region of England by the sixteenth century, sending wine throughout Northumberland and even on occasion into Scotland: A.L. Simon, *The History of the Wine Trade in England* (2 vols., London, 1906–7), II, 122–3.

in these accounts no indication of location is given, except the negative evidence of silence which might be taken to imply cloth of local manufacture and/or supply. However, most of the purchases were also of small importance in terms of the quantity or value involved. In contrast, the livery cloths bought by the bursar were of very high value and represented a high proportion of the priory's total expenditure on cloth in each year. The account entries recording these purchases are accompanied in almost every year by an item of expenditure for the carrying of that cloth from the hometown of the cloth merchant (or the place where the cloth was bought, if different) to Durham. This makes it clear that these transactions were in fact conducted in the town mentioned, and thus implies that the merchants were in fact residents of the towns associated with them in the accounts, rather than being Durham or Newcastle-based tradesmen originally hailing from elsewhere. More importantly, the existence of these carriage charges in the bursar's accounts confirms that it is valid to trace the movement of the priory's cloth purchasing by reference to these place-names.

In the period in question, up to and including 1482–3, the cloth purchased by the bursar for liveries was bought in York. In 1484–5 this cloth was bought in Halifax, and this was followed by three years (out of seven, four being missing) in which purchases were made in London. It should be noted that on one of these occasions the merchant supplying the cloth was specified to be a Colchester man selling in London, the locality of the sale being confirmed by the entry for carriage from London to Durham. From 1492–3 until 1505–6, purchases were made in Leeds. From 1505–6 until 1515–16, no carriage charges are mentioned in the account, the cloth being bought from a William Middley of Durham.

The changing location of the bursars' main cloth purchases thus mirror the trend, traced by several historians of the medieval textile industry, for the focus of cloth making activity to move from York itself to the West Riding towns over this period.[9] It is interesting to note in this context that the (remarkably abrupt) changeover found in these accounts was punctuated by an interval of purchasing in London, suggesting that York became an unsatisfactory source of supply before an alternative source in the West Riding had become established. It is also interesting that towards the end of this period cloth was sourced in Durham itself. It would seem likely that this cloth was bought from a middleman, that William Middley was a Durham merchant who sourced it from the West Riding, since we have no record of any large-scale woollen cloth industry in the Durham area in this period.

The pattern of these high-value cloths is rather different from that for wine, since the goods were being bought largely direct from their place of manufacture rather than from their place of import. Two things remain consistent for both commodities, however, and for the priory's supply as a whole. In the first place London, whilst mentioned occasionally in these accounts, played only a minor and fleeting part in supplying the priory. In addition to the wine already discussed above, the bursar made three purchases of linen there in these years, buying forty-one ells of Holland cloth in 1468–9 and fifty-four ells of 'Flemish' cloth in 1478–9 'at London', and purchasing a further thirty ells of unspecified linen 'from Thomas Ayer of London' in 1494–5.

---

[9] This has become virtually a truism in recent discussions of the subject. H. Heaton, *The Yorkshire Woollen and Worsted Industries, from the Earliest Times up to the Industrial Revolution* (2nd edn., Oxford, 1965), pp. 45–7 gives a clear account of the change.

There is no other reference to London amongst the goods looked at here; the majority of the goods purchased by the priory came directly from north-east suppliers. Although some goods (such as spices) may well have been purchased in London by middlemen and then brought to the north east to be retailed there, this was not the general pattern, as the number and variety of imports into Newcastle implies.[10]

Secondly, the area from which the goods bought by the priory were sourced shrank over this period. For wine the focus shifted increasingly to Newcastle at the expense both of London and of other regional centres such as York, Hull and even Durham itself; for cloth, though the most interesting point to note is the shift in manufacturing activity from York to the West Riding implied by the priory's changing purchases at the end of the fifteenth century, it is also notable that the priory chose to buy such cloth from a Durham merchant after 1505–6. These two trends were common to all the goods purchased by the priory on the open market.[11]

The Use of Agents

When purchases were made from a distance, the priory used agents to choose, purchase and pay for goods, and to transmit them back to the priory. Agents were also employed in transactions nearer to home, such as those in Newcastle. Although no explicit statements exist in the priory records about the way in which or the extent to which such agents were used, the obedientiary accounts give tantalising glimpses of a comprehensive system of purchasing agents employed by the priory.

Most of these references concern the payment of the expenses incurred by the agents, and it is clear from these entries that they could be involved at all stages of the procurement process. In particular, there is substantial evidence for the use of agents in the wine-buying process. For example, a typical entry under the bursar's 'necessary expenses' heading, that for 1495–6, reads 'Paid to William Wright and to Richard Wren for their expenses at Newcastle for the purchase and delivery of wine at different times – 3s.' Similarly, in 1487–8 a payment of 14s. 0d. 'for the expenses of William Wright and Richard Simpson at Newcastle and Hull' is recorded. Agents such as these were clearly involved in all stages of the wine purchasing process; an entry in the bursar's 'necessary expenses' section for 1535–6 records that Robert Whitehead was paid 2s. 7d. in 'expenses for choosing wine at Newcastle'. As the above examples show, agents arranged both the actual purchase and the delivery of the wine to the priory, and perhaps travelled between the different ports to ensure that the priory paid the best prices for its goods. Some of these men were evidently employed regularly, as the bursar's account for 1488–9 includes in the wine purchases for that year the cost of five tuns and one pipe of red wine bought from William Wright and Richard Simpson, 'with their expenses'. William Wright can be seen to have been associated with wine purchasing for the priory for at least eight years, and both he and Richard Simpson appear to have been wine merchants in their own right as well as agents employed by the priory. In general, however, the role of such agents seems to have been solely a facilitative one. None of their names appears

---

[10] *Customs Accounts*, passim.
[11] Examples of goods bought from outside the region in previous years can be found in Bonney, *Lordship and the Urban Community*, pp. 169–74.

in the Newcastle customs accounts as importers, and none other than the two mentioned above appears in the priory records as suppliers in his own right.

Agents such as these were apparently not used in connection with spice or imported iron purchases, for example. It is possible that the purchase of wine presented special difficulties for which agents were particularly valuable; in particular, the fact that only two consignments of wine were shipped to England each year, and that such wine was frequently sold from the boat as soon as it was docked, may well have meant that speed and being on the spot were uniquely important considerations in this case. The large quantities in which wine was bought might also have warranted the use of agents. However, it can be seen that agents were not only used by the priory for the purchase of wine, but also for other high-volume, high-value or perishable commodities. A surviving example of letters patent given to such an agent by the prior demonstrates the wide-ranging role that he fulfilled. This example comes from a slightly earlier period, being dated at Durham on 1 September 1410. John, the prior of Durham, states that he has appointed John de Hyndley as his attorney 'to supply and purchase for the prior's use all necessary grain and victuals as provisions for him and the church of Durham wherever, as seems most advantageous, the aforesaid attorney may travel in England'. The letter goes on to give John de Hyndley permission to do whatever he chooses in the prior's name, and calls upon all those who might come across him to let him travel freely and without toll.[12] Other examples of the use of agents come when large quantities of fresh fish were required for a feast. For example, in 1495–6 the bursar paid 2s. 8d. for the 'expenses of John Youle riding to York for eels, pike, tench and roach for the feast of St Cuthbert in March', and 1s. 6d. for the 'expenses of Antony Elison riding to Benwell, Ovingham and Ryton for fresh salmon for the same feast'.

Such examples suggest a class of men who were professional agents, but more informal contacts could also be used in this way. Several other documents indicate that a similar means of purchasing was to ask an employee, friend or acquaintance who was away on business to purchase items for the priory's use. For example, a letter dated 13 June 1456 survives from William, prior of Durham to an unknown addressee, apparently in London on business unconnected with the priory, including the request 'I pray you heartily provide for me 2 hogsheads of the best malmsey that you may buy in London.' The recipient of the letter is asked to buy the goods personally and arrange to send them, as his own goods, to his own place in Newcastle, and the prior promises that 'what money you pay therefore I shall content you again'.[13] The prior expected the individual concerned to comply with this request, and the impression is that such informal arrangements, based on personal relationships and propitious circumstances, were usual.

Some agents were entrusted with a great deal of responsibility and cash. A letter from the prior of Durham to his trusted steward, Robert Rhodes, who was in London on business in May 1456, asks him to purchase a full set of vestments for around £100. Rhodes had clearly sent a sample and quote in a previous letter, as the prior asks him to provide six copes of blue velvet and to ornament them with gold flowers as in the sample he sent; also to provide orphreys with embroidery to go with the said

---

[12] DCM, Reg. Parv.II, fo. 12v.
[13] DCM, Reg. Parv.III, fo. 84r.

copes, at the price of eight marks each, as he had quoted to the prior in a previous letter. Further, he is asked to provide an additional six copes of the same blue velvet and to have these latter embroidered with smaller and fewer gold flowers. This is presumably intended as an economy, as the prior goes on to specify that Robert should expect to pay 6d., or 7d. if necessary, per flower. The total sum available for spending on all these things is £103 6s. 8d., although the prior clearly anticipated there to be some change, as he requests that five marks be paid to a third party out of this sum, and that anything left be spent on providing additional vestments at Rhodes's discretion.[14]

Transport

It is necessary to address the question of whether or to what extent transport costs or difficulties impacted upon the priory's purchasing decisions and strategies. In the first place, it should be noted that there was probably no physical bar to travel and the transport of goods to and from the north east in this period. The infrastructure of roads and waterways to, from and within the north east of England was certainly adequately developed from early in the Middle Ages, and the main routes were well travelled by the fifteenth century. The first known medieval map of England, that of Matthew Paris from c.1250, shows the route from Dover to Newcastle via London, Doncaster, Northallerton and Durham, and known royal itineraries indicate a similar route from London to York and Newcastle via Durham in frequent use throughout the medieval period.[15] The coast and rivers provided an additional network of alternative routes, the importance of which is shown by the high proportion of prominent medieval towns built with ready access to navigable water.[16] Overall, all the evidence available about medieval travel and road systems indicates that the existing infrastructure was adequate well into the sixteenth century.[17] G.H. Martin's study of the fourteenth- and fifteenth-century journeys of the warden and fellows of Merton College, Oxford, whilst restricted by the lack of information which has survived about specific transport costs, concluded that travel in this period was 'systematic and regular, and . . . undertaken as a matter of course'.[18] Even winter weather does not appear to have posed a regular hindrance to the travel necessary for the conduct of trade or business; haulage could be carried on in the winter months without attracting undue comment or problems, and the royal household continued to travel around the country at all seasons.[19]

It is not possible to calculate the precise impact of transport costs upon the priory's purchasing decisions. Carriage costs are only rarely given, suggesting that at least non-bulky goods were frequently brought to the priory by someone making the

---

[14] DCM, Reg. Parv.III, fols. 79v–80r.
[15] B.P. Hindle, 'The Road Network of Medieval England and Wales', *JHG* 2 (1976), 209, 215.
[16] J.F. Edwards and B.P. Hindle, 'The Transportation System of Medieval England and Wales', *JHG* 17 (1991), 129.
[17] B.P. Hindle, 'Roads and Tracks', in *The English Medieval Landscape*, ed. L. Cantor (London, 1982), p. 214.
[18] G.H. Martin, 'Road Travel in the Middle Ages: Some Journeys of the Warden and Fellows of Merton College, Oxford, 1315–1470', *JTH*, new ser. 3 (1975–6), 172.
[19] B.P. Hindle, 'Seasonal Variations in Travel in Medieval England', *JTH*, new ser. 4 (1978), 170, 176–7.

journey for other reasons, so that they were not charged for separately. In addition, prices varied so much from year to year that total costs given for goods in different years, one of which included a carriage element, cannot be used with any certainty to assess the magnitude of the carriage element. A rare example of costs which are to some extent comparable comes in the bursar's purchases of Holland and Flemish cloths. Two such purchases were made at London, of forty-one ells in 1468–9 at a total cost of £1 17s. 8d. which was specified in the account to have included the cost of carriage, and of fifty-four ells in 1478–9 at 8d. per ell, a total cost of £1 16s. 0d. (without a carriage element). These cloths almost always cost 8d. per ell, and if it is assumed that those bought in 1468–9 were no exception then the carriage element of the total cost can be calculated to have been 10s. 4d. No other locations are given for the purchase of such cloths except for one purchase of five ells in 1466–7, which was specified to have been made at Pipewellgate in Gateshead; it seems likely that the remaining cloth was bought in Newcastle, particularly since many of the names which occur as suppliers (such as William Cornforth, William Shotton and John Farne) are those of well-known Newcastle merchants who appear many times in these accounts. That being so, there is no apparent reason why the Holland cloth bought in London in 1468–9 should have been purchased in London; and the presence of a significant carriage charge does not appear to have been a disincentive to such a purchase. It is possible that no Newcastle supplier happened to be able to supply the priory with the quantity or quality of cloth that it required on that one occasion; certainly the London purchase was the only purchase of such cloth in 1468–9, but then it was by no means unusual for only a single purchase of this nature to be made in any one year.

However, the infrequency with which goods were in fact sourced from outside the immediate region, even when price differentials clearly existed, suggests that powerful disincentives to such activity either were in fact in place or were at least perceived to be in place. Although letters clearly show that individuals in London were on occasion asked to purchase goods and forward them to the priory, and occasional purchases in London did take place, these were very much the exception. It is not surprising that a bulky, common and relatively low-value commodity such as grain was only purchased outside the region when failure of local supply occurred and the pressure of price differentials made transporting the large quantities needed worthwhile. Yet, the fact that even such luxury specialist goods as malmsey were generally purchased in Newcastle, and that even such high-value goods as livery cloths were purchased in Durham by the end of this period, suggests that supply was the key to this pattern. Local suppliers were more likely to be used providing they could supply the types, qualities and volumes that were required. Sourcing locally must have presented a range of advantages, such as the ability to assess and sample the goods more accurately before purchase and to negotiate quicker delivery; in addition, however, it seems probable that personal relationships with local suppliers would be an important factor.

Suppliers

The priory's purchasing was based on credit and trust, as the large proportion of purchases made from tenants demonstrates. As such, knowledge of and relationships with suppliers would have been at a premium.[20] When it was necessary to make purchases at a distance, the priory overcame the lack of such personal knowledge by using trusted agents who themselves had such relationships or access to the necessary networks to acquire them. Local suppliers could be known directly, and relationships could be cultivated with them so that the quality of their goods and their reliability could be assessed on the basis of past experience or personal trust. This was undoubtedly one advantage of the tenurial system of purchasing; the suppliers were by definition known, they were stable and certain (or very likely) to remain in business for the duration of the 'contract' with them, and issues of credit and payment were avoided by the adoption of a largely cashless system. In a system in which personal relationships and the individual supplier were of such importance, the detail and high degree of survival of the priory accounts can greatly illuminate both some of the individuals concerned and the cohort of priory suppliers as a whole.

Interestingly, the most immediately obvious feature of the suppliers of the priory is their number and the fact that very few entered into anything approaching a long-term or exclusive marketing relationship with the priory. Many names appear only once in the accounts, and only a select few appear more than twice. Most of the merchants who did secure repeated orders still appear in the accounts only occasionally. This pattern is comparable to that found by Christine Newman for the labourers and craftsmen used by the priory in this period.[21]

The priory's tendency was to spread its business between several suppliers in each product category in each year. A clear distinction is visible here between the pattern observed for imported and manufactured goods, purchased primarily via the market, and that for agricultural produce acquired largely via tenurial relationships. The average number of merchants from whom the bursar purchased wine in any one year was only five, varying between two and nine. A similar pattern can be seen in the bursar's purchases of iron, where the average was again five named merchants, varying from two to twelve. Cloth was purchased from an average of fifteen suppliers each year, although high-value livery cloths and the furs purchased to trim them were each bought from only a single merchant each in each year. Spices, too, were bought from one principal merchant in each year, although supplementary purchases were generally also made from several others. Salmon, a fish which appears to have been frequently bought via market transactions, was purchased from an average of ten suppliers per year, whilst other fish came from around twice as many; herring were purchased from an average of twenty suppliers per year, and dogdraves from eighteen. With the exception of sheep, which came from an average of fifteen suppliers per year, livestock was acquired much more widely than these other goods. On average, poultry was supplied to the priory by forty-five individuals each year, pigs by forty-eight and cattle by fifty-six. Grain, meanwhile, was supplied to the priory by 127 individuals in 1495–6 alone, and there is no reason to suspect that this was by any means an exceptional year; indeed, the rentals for 1507–10 show a similar pattern.

---

[20] C. Muldrew, *The Economy of Obligation* (London, 1998), pp. 4–5; D.C. North, 'Transaction Costs in History', *Journal of European Economic History* 14 (1985), 560.
[21] C.M. Newman, 'Work and Wages at Durham Priory and its Estates, 1494–1519', *Continuity and Change* 16 (2001), 357–78.

Wider Relationships between the Priory and its Suppliers

It is clear, though, that the priory did have closer relationships with some merchants than would appear to have been the case from a simple list such as that above of the number of transactions entered into with each one. The names of several Newcastle merchants and other suppliers of the priory are to be found in the *Liber Vitae*, a book of names which was kept upon the altar in Durham Cathedral and added to throughout the medieval period.[22] The exact significance of inclusion in this book is not clear, but it certainly argues a more complex relationship with the priory than one simply based on trading relationships or the occasional transaction, and many of the names included appear to have been those of the families of monks. In an attempt to quantify the extent to which these social relationships penetrated the priory's supply networks, a comparison has been made between the names of suppliers collected in the database used in the course of this research and those names recorded in the *Liber Vitae* which have been dated palaeographically to the late fifteenth or early sixteenth century.[23]

In all, seventy surnames are common to the two sources, and whilst the exact identification of individuals in one with those in the other is not possible, seventy-one individuals with exactly the same first name and surname combination are to be found. These represent six per cent of the suppliers looked at here. In addition, the *Liber Vitae* contains a further seventy individuals (whose names are written in hands which have been dated to this period) who can be identified as monks of Durham and who have surnames matching those of suppliers to the priory. For many of these cases it is explicitly spelt out in the *Liber Vitae* that the lay individuals listed were the family of the monks concerned, and indeed a link is sometimes made with individuals of different surnames. For example, John Robinson of Newcastle (probably the merchant of the same name who supplied wine to the priory in this period) and his wife Maiona are listed with the monk, Edward Hebburn, who is explicitly described as their son.[24] Entire family groupings are also described on occasion, as is the case with the entry for William Lawe, a monk of Durham in the second half of the fifteenth century, who is listed in the *Liber Vitae* with his father Thomas, his mother Agnes, and nine other members of his family.[25] In other cases, a monk's name is given and his parents are mentioned, but their names are not provided. For example Robert Spink, a monk of Durham who entered the monastery in the early sixteenth century, is listed 'with his parents' but no further details are included in the book.[26]

Whilst it is not possible to identify positively the names in the *Liber Vitae* with the suppliers' names to be found in the obedientiary accounts, it seems very likely that many of the names to be found in both sources denote the same individual or at least members of the same family. It is also worthy of note that several of the more prominent surnames in both sources are the same, suggesting the presence of families who

---

[22] *Liber Vitae Ecclesiae Dunelmensis: A Collotype Facsimile of the Original Manuscript*, ed. A.H. Thompson (Surtees Society 136, 1923). All subsequent references to the *Liber Vitae* are to the original MS: BL, Cotton MS Domitian VII.
[23] I am indebted to Lynda Rollason for her assistance with this comparison in the course of her doctoral research into the composition and significance of the *Liber Vitae*.
[24] Threlfall-Holmes, 'Provisioning', p. 96; BL, Cotton MS Domitian VII, fo. 83r.
[25] BL, Cotton MS Domitian VII, fo. 66v.
[26] BL, Cotton MS Domitian VII, fo. 81v.

were closely connected with the priory on a variety of levels. For example, the Willys were a prominent monastic family, whose name appears several times in the *Liber Vitae*. Individuals of that name recorded there included a monk named Robert and his father, Edward, and two other monks, Christopher Willy and Henry Willy, who were described as being the sons of Richard and Elizabeth Willy and the siblings of Roland, Thomas, Robert, William, Alice, Joan, William and Alice.[27] A large group of Willys (John, Ralph, Richard, Robert, Thomas and William) also supplied the priory with a range of livestock, poultry and grain, and these individuals were mainly described in the accounts as coming from Kirk Merrington and thus were almost certainly a family grouping. Other names which occur several times in each source include Coke, Duket, Forest, Lawson, Rakett, Richardson and Robinson, although the latter is so common that it almost certainly denoted the members of more than one family.

Further evidence from a different source of such a familial relationship between the monks and the suppliers of the priory comes in 1477, when a John Esyngton entered Durham College at Oxford, probably with the intention of later joining the monastery. This is known because his father entered into a bond with the prior which has survived in the Durham archive, in which he promised to pay a sum of money if his son misbehaved whilst at the college or left before taking his degree.[28] The boy is described specifically in the source as the son of the merchant of Newcastle-upon-Tyne of the same name. The merchant, John Esyngton of Newcastle, was a notable supplier of the priory, appearing at least ten times in the accounts between 1465–6 and 1485–6, selling a typical range of imported and processed goods; wine, Spanish iron, processed fish and oil.[29] Without being able to quantify precisely the degree of integration between the social or familial networks of the members of the priory and the supply networks which they drew upon, therefore, it is clear that there was a significant degree of overlap between the two.

Conclusion

It can be seen, then, that several interesting points emerge from a study of the priory's market purchases. In the first place, it is notable that the majority of the priory's needs could be and were supplied from the immediate Durham and Newcastle region. This was increasingly the case over the period 1460–1520, and Newcastle was increasingly the regional focus of the priory's purchasing. In particular, the subordinate place of London in the provisioning of the priory is significant, and this was the case even for luxury items such as malmsey and spices.

Secondly, it can be seen that the priory used agents extensively, even when purchasing goods from this immediate region. These agents could be priory servants, officials, monks or simply merchants or individuals known to the priory who happened to be in the right place at the right time, and they were used throughout the whole purchasing process, from collecting samples and transmitting them to the

---

[27] BL, Cotton MS Domitian VII, fo. 80.
[28] DCM, Reg. Parv.III, fo. 173r.
[29] John Esyngton appears in the bursar's accounts selling wine in 1472–3 and 1482–3 and Spanish iron in 1467–9, 1470–1 and 1472–4. He is also mentioned three times in the bursar/cellarer indentures, supplying oil in 1465–6, a barrel of sturgeon in 1467–8, and an aughtendell of salt eels in 1485–6.

priory, to choosing goods, paying for them and sometimes arranging for their carriage to Durham or bringing them back personally. Credit arrangements may well have also been one of the agents' responsibilities, and there must have been some element of credit involved in many transactions which were carried out at second- or third-hand, but the evidence for this is scanty since precise dates of transactions and payments are only rarely given in the priory records.

Acting as an agent for the priory was one of the ways in which some of the suppliers were involved in more complex relationships with the priory than simply those of supplier and customer. As has been seen, many of the priory's suppliers were also tenants; others clearly belonged to the families of monks, and still others are listed in the *Liber Vitae* for no apparent reason, but may well have had some sort of confraternal relationship with the priory which went beyond the purely mercantile.

Overall, however, the most notable feature of the priory's suppliers as a group was their number and variety. Well over 1,200 suppliers were involved in provisioning the priory over this period, and these individuals ranged from small tenants of the priory involved in a single transaction to major merchants supplying high-value items over a period of years. Most of the suppliers appear infrequently in the accounts; of the individuals identified here, over half appear only once and around two-thirds only once or twice. In each product category (with the sole exception of the livery cloths bought by the bursar) the priory tended to spread its business between multiple suppliers in each year, and this could involve as many as the 127 individuals who supplied grain in 1495–6. Even the priory's wine purchases were split between an average of five merchants in each year, and never less than two.

The large number of individuals whom these accounts reveal to have taken an active part in the provisioning of the priory implies that the north-east region was one in which competition flourished, and in which the state of trade was sufficiently healthy to enable the numbers involved to make a satisfactory living. This is particularly significant when looking at the state of the import and luxuries trade in Newcastle. The numbers involved in this trade, and the fact that the priory was able to increasingly source even the most expensive luxuries from there rather than from London suggests the existence of a regional economy which was afloat, if not positively buoyant.[30]

---

[30] This point is made in Threlfall-Holmes, 'Provisioning', pp. 70–1. The question of the economic health of Newcastle in this period is one which has been debated, but which remains unresolved due to the survival of so little direct evidence such as customs accounts or civic records. See, for example, W.G. Hoskins, 'English Provincial Towns in the Early Sixteenth Century', *TRHS*, 5th ser. 6 (1956), 4; R.B. Dobson, 'Urban Decline in Medieval England', *TRHS*, 5th ser. 27 (1977), 19; A.F. Butcher, 'Rent, Population and Economic Change in Late Medieval Newcastle', *NH* 14 (1978), 75; C. Phythian-Adams, *Desolation of a City: Coventry and the Urban Crisis of the Late Middle Ages* (Cambridge, 1979), pp. 16–18; and A.J. Pollard, *North-Eastern England during the Wars of the Roses: Lay Society, War and Politics, 1450–1500* (Oxford 1990), p. 74.

11

The Size and Shape of Durham's Monastic Community, 1274–1539

A.J. PIPER

The fourteenth century dawned ominously for the Durham monks. In the summer of 1297 war broke out between England and Scotland, but, as relations between the two kingdoms had been strained before, the monks had no reason to anticipate that this marked the outbreak of recurrent conflict which would eventually lead to the complete loss of their valuable possessions in south-east Scotland in the fifteenth century.[1] Similarly, their experience of disputes with successive bishops would not have made them appreciate just how costly was to be the one with Bishop Bek that ignited on 20 May 1300.[2] Yet these were the local preliminaries which introduced the Durham monks to a half-century of disasters that afflicted most of north-western Europe. No other period could approach it for sheer dreadfulness, but a major crisis befell the Durham monks in 1438, when a massive failure to collect the revenues of the main estate came to light, a crisis that was compounded by a severe outbreak of plague in northern England.[3]

It was perhaps in 1438 that the monks revised a statement of their tithe income.[4] This looked back to a golden age late in the thirteenth century: in 1436, an exceptionally poor year, tithe income was less than a quarter of what it had been in 1293, and under sixty per cent of the level in 1348. The monks were evidently well able to assess their financial circumstances in the context of a very long chronological perspective. If they concluded that there was little cause for optimism they were right, for their position worsened somewhat during the mid-fifteenth century. Decline ceased, however, during the 1470s, and for the rest of the community's history revenues stabilised at about two-thirds of the level found during the first half of the fourteenth century, with some signs of a modest improvement.[5] Broadly speaking, the size of the

---

[1] R.B. Dobson, *Durham Priory, 1400–1450* (Cambridge, 1973), pp. 316–27.
[2] An excellent account of this is given in C.M. Fraser, *A History of Antony Bek, Bishop of Durham, 1283–1311* (Oxford, 1957), chs. 7–8.
[3] Dobson, *Durham Priory*, pp. 285–7.
[4] *Scriptores Tres*, appendix, pp. ccxlviii–cclii. This is discussed in B. Dodds, 'Tithe and Agrarian Output between the Tyne and Tees, 1350–1450' (unpublished Ph.D. thesis, University of Durham, 2002), ch. 4, which is the source of much of the regional economic data that follows. I am indebted to Dr Dodds for sharing with me his current results on tithe revenues between 1300 and 1350, and 1450 and 1540.
[5] Figures for the income from the main monastic estate, for which the bursar accounted, are presented in the tables in R.A. Lomas, 'Durham Cathedral Priory as a Landowner and a Landlord, 1290–1540' (unpublished Ph.D. thesis, University of Durham, 1973).

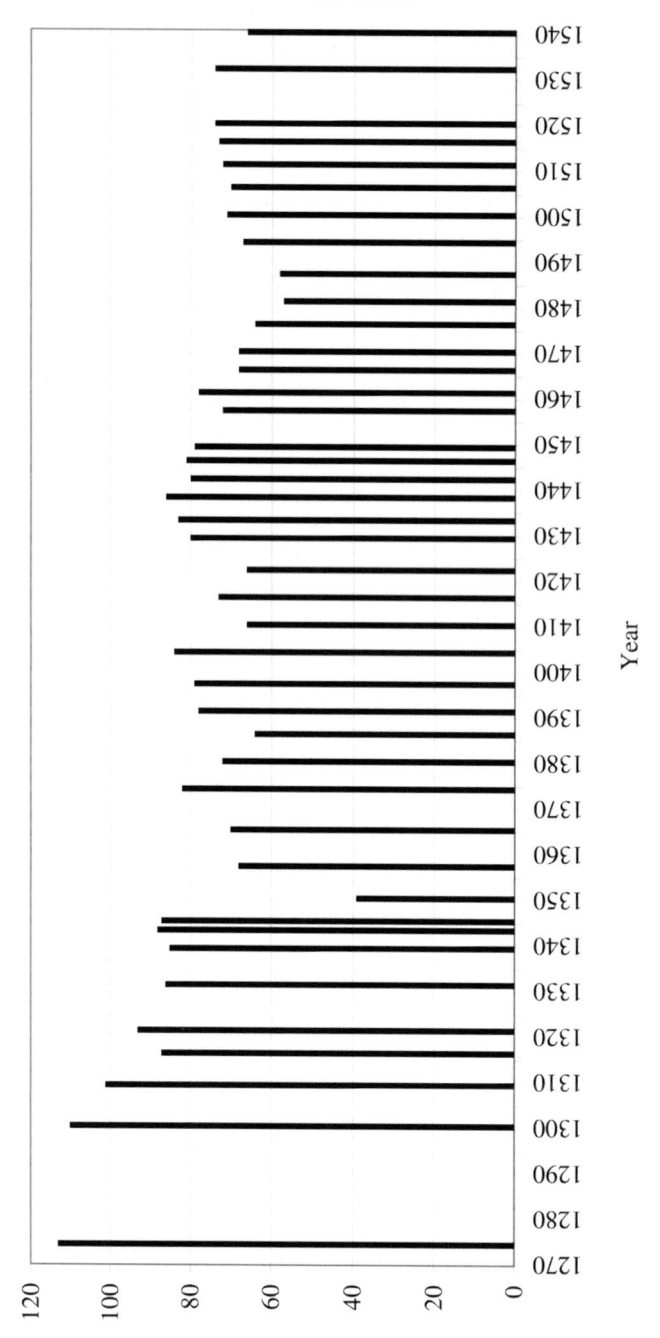

Fig. 11.1 Minimum number of Durham monks, 1274–1540

community reflected the serious decline in its resources, although not to the same extent (figure 11.1). How this equilibrium was achieved raises interesting questions, not least because there was no knowing what next year's harvest would bring, what devastating epidemic might break out.

The impact of catastrophes and changing economic circumstances on the size of the monastic community can be assessed thanks to the wealth of data contained in the priory's medieval archives and the *Liber Vitae* that makes it possible to achieve a close estimate of the number of Durham monks year by year from 1300. Numerous references to monks are found in the accounting material that survives in very considerable quantity from the early fourteenth century, but of particular significance are the long lists of monks present for elections, of bishops and of priors, and at visitations, for in these lists they are named in order of seniority.

Of even greater importance than the archives for basic knowledge of the members of the Durham community is the Durham *Liber Vitae*, in which their names were normally entered, again in order of seniority.[6] There were two periods, *c*.1315–65 and *c*.1482–1539, when the *Liber Vitae* was not regularly maintained. With the former, the problem is principally that groups of names, instead of following one after another, are instead scattered haphazardly; some names are also completely missing. The deficiences can very largely be made good by recourse to the long lists of monks present at the elections of 1313, 1321, 1345, 1374 and 1381, and at the visitation of 1343, although there is one piece of evidence suggesting that five names have escaped all record.[7] The problems with the later period are considerably greater, for the *Liber Vitae* contains only four groups of properly ordered names, and it is very largely a matter of compiling the list *ab initio*. Eighteen different documents contribute to this process, ranging from long lists of monks at elections in 1494 and 1520 and at visitations in 1501 and 1529 to records of payments to monks for saying mass in order of seniority at one of the four chantries that they served in the cathedral.[8] These materials fix the standing of 154 monks, leaving fifteen whose position cannot be established precisely; they can only be placed in the light of individual biographical circumstance.

A major problem in establishing the overall size of the community is the fact that Durham was the mother house of a number of cells. In 1274 there were nine, at Coldingham, Holy Island, Farne, Warkworth, Jarrow, Wearmouth, Finchale, Lytham and Stamford, but Warkworth ceased to exist shortly after 1300;[9] at about that time a

---

[6] *Liber Vitae Ecclesiae Dunelmensis: A Collotype Facsimile of the Original Manuscript*, ed. A.H. Thompson (Surtees Society 136, 1923). For a brief discussion of the purpose and contents of the book, see the contribution of Miranda Threlfall-Holmes to this volume, pp. 150–1. The commentary accompanying the forthcoming digital edition of the *Liber Vitae*, funded by the AHRB, will include my biographies of all the Durham monks.

[7] DCM, Reg.II, fo. 16r–v, Loc.XIII:3d., Misc. Ch. 2636, Loc.XIII:8a, Reg. Hatfield, fols. 102v, 103r, Reg.II, fo. 198r, 3.6.Pont.4. See n. 29 below.

[8] DCM, Loc.XIII:19a; Reg.V, fols. 184v–185r; York, Borthwick Institute of Historical Research, Register 25, fo. 146v; DCM, Reg.V, fo. 231v; DCM, Chamberlain's Accounts, 1494–5, 1521–2, 1523–4; DCM, Almoner's Rent-Book, 1532–7, fo. 77v; *The Registers of Cuthbert Tunstall, Bishop of Durham, 1530–59, and James Pilkington, Bishop of Durham, 1561–76*, ed. G. Hinde (Surtees Society 161, 1946), no. 376; Bursar's Rent-Books, 1507–11, fols. 142v, 212v, and 1516–18, fo. 86r; Bursar's Expenses, fols. 101v, 181v, 254r; Bursar's Rent-Books, 1538–9, fo. 118v, and 1539, fols. 146v, 155r.

[9] On the cell at Warkworth, see DCM, 1.8.Spec.33, dated 1274, J. Raine, *The History and Antiquities of North Durham* (London, 1852), appendix, no. DCCLXXXIX, *DAR*, II, 493 (DCM, Bursar's Account

study-house at Oxford was in the process of establishment, and Bishop Hatfield provided the means to transform this into Durham College late in the fourteenth century.[10] In normal circumstances these cells were never deliberately left without a monk present, and in consequence no list of the monks in Durham, for example at elections, was complete.[11] Nor can the total be made up by simply adding nine or ten to allow for the cells and the establishment in Oxford: one monk was excluded from Prior Wessington's election in 1416 on account of his disobedience, and the biographies of individual monks reveal that some might be absent from an election.[12] It is the biographies, therefore, that provide the most reliable evidence for the size of the community.[13]

The evidence of the biographies has one major shortcoming. If the Durham monks ever maintained a record of the deaths of their fellows, it has been lost. In many cases, however, the expenses associated with a monk's funeral were recorded, normally by the bursar, whose accounts have generally survived, but sometimes, for reasons that remain to be unravelled, the communar paid.[14] For monks whose deaths are not recorded it would be possible to make allowance, by adding on a number of years after their last occurrence, but this would introduce an undesirable element of uncertainty to the matter of the community's actual size, and so no monk is included in the total after he ceases to appear in the records.

Unfortunately, this could have the effect of concealing major leaps in mortality as a result of epidemic disease, most notably in the period 1345–50. Fortunately, late in the fourteenth century a note was added to the October page of a kalendar in a Durham breviary for the commemoration of fifty-two brothers *in prima pestilencia* 1349.[15] Since the careers of thirty-eight monks who occur after 1349 can be traced back before that in the records, the size of the community at the outbreak of the Black Death was at least ninety, but, with the names of fifty of the fifty-two who died as a result of it unrecorded,[16] most of them last appear in previous years, most commonly

---

Rolls, 1292–3), and DCM, Bursar's Account Rolls, 1300–1, with the last indication of the cell's existence. Its creation was envisaged by 1252: Raine, *North Durham*, appendix, pp. 140–1.

[10] Dobson, *Durham Priory*, pp. 343–9.

[11] Lists at visitations by the bishop of Durham were made further incomplete on occasion by the omission of the monks at Stamford; see A.J. Piper, 'St. Leonard's Priory, Stamford ii', *The Stamford Historian* 6 (1982), 7–8 and cf. 3–4.

[12] Dobson, *Durham Priory*, p. 74.

[13] No chronological compilation of the biographies was available to R.B. Dobson and so he was obliged to rely on the lists: ibid., pp. 52–5. The figures offered here are generally higher than those of Dobson, but do not call for a major revision of his account, except to shade the notion of 'numerical stability' for the later fifteenth century.

[14] The normal entry records the *distributio*, the dole to the poor. Apart from the cell at Finchale, whose accounts are well-preserved, deaths at the cells are rarely recorded, except for their heads. For the Finchale accounts, see *The Priory of Finchale: The Charters of Endowment, Inventories, and Account Rolls of the Priory of Finchale*, ed. J. Raine (Surtees Society 6, 1837).

[15] BL, Harleian MS 4664, fo. 130v. The figure can be confirmed as approximately correct from contemporary sources: B. Harbottle, 'Bishop Hatfield's Visitation of Durham Priory in 1354', *AA*, 4th ser. 36 (1958), 81–100, esp. 90.

[16] The thirty-eight include Jordan of Seaton, who apparently had a career of over forty years but appears in the records extremely rarely. Entering c.1318, he is listed for the 1321 election (DCM, Loc.XIII:3d), but is only mentioned once, in 1343 (DCM, 3.6.Pont.4), until one *dom. Jordanus* made loans to the cell at Jarrow in 1356–7 and 1365–6: *The Inventories and Account Rolls of the Benedictine Houses or Cells of Jarrow and Monk-Wearmouth* (Surtees Society 29, 1854), pp. 39, 49. Robert of Hallington died *in fine prime pestilencie* (DCM, 4.16.Spec.56a), probably also Hugh of Woodburn, who was alive in May

at the election of Bishop Hatfield in 1345. This would give rise to a seriously distorted picture, but, in this most important instance, it can be corrected.

There are a few further cases where a significant number of monks last appear in a single year, but with no clear evidence that a major epidemic was the cause. A typical instance arises in 1274 with the election of Bishop Robert de Insula. Ninety monks are listed as present and twenty-three others are known to have been alive at the time; a total of 113. Of these there are twenty-one monks who are never mentioned again. The explanation for this is lack of documentation between 1274 and the election of Bishop Bek in 1283, when the community numbered at least 103. Between those dates twenty-nine monks disappeared from the records, an unremarkable average of a little over three per year. The position is similar with the disappearance of twenty-six monks after the 1283 election, eleven after the controversies of 1300, and seventeen after the 1321 election. For the next two centuries, however, the documentation is much better and there are no sudden disappearances of large numbers of monks, except as already discussed in relation to the Black Death. The phenomenon recurs in the sixteenth century: ten monks disappeared after the election of Prior Whitehead in 1520, and sixteen last occur in 1522. With some justification it could be argued that this reflects a deterioration in record-keeping during the last two decades of the monastery's history, but the situation does not approach the paucity of documentation found in the late thirteenth century and the possibility that the mortality rate among the monks was particularly high during the 1520s certainly deserves consideration, even though the death rate for the period 1520–39 fell somewhat below three per year.[17]

A lesser problem concerns the date at which monks entered the community. Between 1353 and 1467 some groups of names in the *Liber Vitae* have dates noted beside them, in some instances a full date rather than the year alone. It is not clear whether this refers to tonsuring and clothing or to subsequent profession, but, if it was the latter, then it followed tonsuring so closely that the distinction is of virtually no significance in the present context;[18] although novices were not fully qualified as monks in every respect when they were first tonsured, at that point they certainly became an established charge on the community's resources.[19] Expenditure on

---

1349 and dead by early September (DCM, Chamberlain's Accounts, 1348–9, and Bursar's Account Rolls, 1348–9).

[17] Fifty-five monks died or disappeared in the twenty-year period.

[18] The point is discussed by Dobson, *Durham Priory*, p. 62; he assumes that the dates in the *Liber Vitae* refer to profession and draws attention to the fact that the chamberlain paid for the tonsuring of six monks between 21 May and 4 September 1414 and that they can be identified with the group dated 28 June 1414 in the *Liber Vitae*. A similar point could be made with the four names dated 8 September 1412 whose tonsuring expenses appear on the chamberlain's account opened on 16 May 1412. Given that the *Liber Vitae* lay on the High Altar, with those named in it implicitly benefiting from the masses offered there, it is hard to see why the names of monks should not have been entered as soon as they were tonsured. On making his profession a monk wrote out the requisite profession slip, which was then kept in a cupboard at St Cuthbert's shrine: *DAR*, II, 461.

[19] Junior novices were excluded from elections: when Bishop Hatfield was elected in 1345 the names of the five most junior monks were included in the list of those participating and then crossed out (DCM, Misc. Ch. 2636), while at the election of Bishop Neville in 1438 the eight most junior monks were recorded as being present in chapter but not participating in the election (DCM, Misc. Chs. 2637, 2639). The seven monks entered in the *Liber Vitae* (BL, Cotton MS Domitian VII, fo. 79r) with the date 6 November 1445 did not participate in the election of Prior William Ebchester on 30 June 1446 (DCM, Reg.IV, fo. 49r), but were recorded in chapter on 5 April 1446, although not on 2 January 1446 (DCM,

clothing for the novices was regularly recorded in the chamberlain's accounts, each receiving two sets of footwear a year throughout the novitiate for instance. Much fuller provision was made by the chamberlain when novices were tonsured; the number is given but not normally the names. It is often possible, however, to identify the monks involved from other biographical information: the earliest extant chamberlain's account reveals that thirteen novices were tonsured between July 1334 and July 1335 and they can be identified from the fact that nine of them were made acolytes on 23 December 1335.[20] Unfortunately, there are large gaps in the extant series of these accounts and some of those that survive are badly damaged.

The approximate date of tonsuring can be established for only a proportion of those who became monks between 1274 and 1539. For a few others their date of entry can be established from subsequent statements: for instance, Thomas of Bamburgh claimed as a witness in 1325 to be almost eighty and stated that he had first entered religion fifty-seven years before.[21] There remain, however, many monks whose date of entry can only be estimated from other occurrences early in their careers, although the fact that the *Liber Vitae* reveals the groups of monks admitted together does at least mean that a reference to any monk in a particular group provides a dating for all monks in the group.[22] The ground would be much firmer if the major steps in a novice's training had followed a set pattern, but even within a single group there was in fact considerable variation in the time that elapsed before each became an acolyte, a subdeacon, a deacon and finally a priest.[23] Nonetheless the quantity of evidence is such that an approximate date of entry can be assigned to every monk, a date that is probably correct to within one year either way in the great majority of cases.[24]

The problems of establishing at a detailed level the precise numbers of Durham monks between 1274 and 1539 are not so serious that the broad picture lacks credibility. The community stood at its largest known size at the beginning of the period,

---

Misc. Chs. 5638[1], 5638d). It has not been established at what point during the novitiate a monk became fully qualified, but the threshold was not apparently the priesthood: Richard Blackwell, who celebrated his first mass between May 1458 and May 1459 (DCM, Bursar's Account Rolls, 1458–9), had voted at the election of Prior Burnaby in October 1456 (DCM, Loc.XIII:13h). On the other hand, *pace* Dobson, *Durham Priory*, p. 63, ordination to the priesthood did not mark the end of the novitiate and a monk's emergence *de custodia*: five of the eight novices in 1440–1 were priests and they did not leave the novitiate until 1441–2 (DCM, Chamberlain's Accounts, 1440–1, 1441–2).

[20] *DAR*, I, 165–66 (misdated to 1324–5); *RPD*, III, 168; cf. BL, Cotton MS Domitian VII, fo. 75r. The group of monks immediately senior to these thirteen had been tonsured earlier. Two of them were priested on 26 March 1334: *RPD*, III, 151, 156; cf. BL, Cotton MS Domitian VII, fo. 71v.

[21] DCM, 3.6.Pont.10.

[22] For instance, the presence of John Swineshead in chapter on 24 July 1396 (DCM, Reg.II, fo. 320r) provides a *terminus ante quem* for the entry of the other four monks listed in the same group in the *Liber Vitae* (BL, Cotton MS Domitian VII, fo. 74r).

[23] See, for example, Dobson, *Durham Priory*, p. 63.

[24] Two exceptionally important pieces of evidence come at the beginning of the period under consideration. It is known that Thomas of Bamburgh became a monk in *c.*1268 (see above, n. 21) and that he was the most junior monk participating in the episcopal election of September 1274: *The Historians of the Church of York and its Archbishops*, ed. J. Raine (3 vols., Rolls Series, London, 1879–94), III, 191. It is also known that Geoffrey of Boston (de Botolf) was accepted as a monk in 1274 or 1275: *CIM*, I, no. 1582; to judge by the *Liber Vitae* (BL, Cotton MS Domitian VII, fo. 59v, col. c, ll. 4–6) two other monks entered at the same time. None of these, nor the ten monks who entered immediately before them, are recorded at the 1274 election, but it seems extremely unlikely that those ten were not already novices at the time of the election; they presumably fell into the category of junior novices not yet qualified to participate (see above, n. 19), who nonetheless should be counted as members of the community.

with at least 113 members in 1274. This figure is closely in line with a statute drawn up by the monks in 1235, that there should be seventy monks residing in Durham and thirty at Coldingham;[25] if allowance is made for a minimum complement of two at each of the other seven cells in existence in 1235, the total would rise to 114. Between 1274 and 1300 there is no sign of any significant change in size, and there are no factors known that might have prompted retrenchment.

On the other hand, between 1300, when there were at least 110 monks, and 1321, when there were at least ninety-three, an exceptionally sharp reduction in the community's size took place, a reduction that was never reversed. The reasons for this are not far to seek. If any year in the Durham community's history, from 1083 to 1539, deserved the title *annus horribilis* it was 1300. In the war that had already broken out between England and Scotland, Durham's major cell at Coldingham lay in a very vulnerable position, a few miles north of Berwick, while the cell on Holy Island was heavily dependent on tithe income from its parish which ran up to the border and lay wide open to Scottish incursions. Added to this came the most vicious and divisive dispute ever to affect the Durham community; this broke out in May 1300, when Prior Hoton refused Bishop Bek admission to conduct a visitation. The consequent protracted litigation was extremely costly and put the monks heavily in debt for a considerable period. Yet more was to befall. Scottish raiders reached Durham in 1312 and again in 1315, looting and burning; the disastrously heavy rains during the summers of 1315 and 1316 ruined the harvests, destroyed mills and mill-dams, and large numbers of sheep were carried off by the disease that followed. Although difficult to quantify precisely, there can be no doubt that the income available to the community must have been very significantly reduced by this combination of factors. Little wonder that William of Guisborough, elected prior after Geoffrey Burdon had been forced out of office in 1321, took only two days to decide that he preferred the quiet of the cloister to the burdens of high office.[26]

The community did not react hastily to the predicament in which it found itself; initially the monks probably regarded their problems as short-lived, and not warranting a permanent reduction in their numbers. It was perhaps only the resounding defeat of Edward II at Bannockburn in 1314 that brought home to them that Coldingham might never be the same again, and they would have been right, for, although they were often able to maintain some presence there, it was greatly reduced in scale and was finally abandoned to the Scots in 1478. In later years the losses in Scotland figured prominently in the community's case for increasing their revenues through the appropriation of Hemingbrough Church.[27]

The reduction in the community's size between 1300 and 1321 was achieved by the obvious means: limiting recruitment. Between *c.*1312 and *c.*1317 only two monks were admitted. This seems to have had the desired effect, for admissions then resumed at a more normal rate, which probably maintained numbers at a little above ninety for almost thirty years, to judge by the figure of at least ninety at the outbreak of the Black Death in 1349, with the highest detailed count giving at least eighty-six late

---

[25] *Scriptores Tres*, appendix, p. xliii.
[26] Ibid., p. 102.
[27] R.B. Dobson, 'The last English Monks on Scottish Soil', *SHR* 46 (1967), 1–25. Appropriation: DCM, 4.2.Archiep.2, dated 1356, but not put into effect.

in 1344. The death of fifty-two monks, over half the community, in a matter of weeks must have been shattering, but the survivors were not slow to respond. By 1353 twenty-nine new monks had been admitted, and the recording of the date in the *Liber Vitae* seems symptomatic of a certain pride at this achievement;[28] by *c*.1360 sixteen more had entered. Progress was maintained: there were no major losses during the 1360s and by 1374, when Prior Fossor died, there were at least eighty other monks, not so very far short of the total twenty-five years earlier. At his death John Fossor had been a monk for about sixty-five years, since *c*.1310 when the community had numbered at least 100, and he may well have felt that the great crisis of his priorate (1341–74) had very largely been surmounted, but the size of the community was only half of the picture.[29] Others saw the other side.

Sudden, shocking, mortality was one effect of the Black Death and of recurrences of the plague. Long-term deterioration in the economic position of major landlords was another, and it was Fossor's successor, Prior Walworth, who seems to have confronted the implications of this for the size of the community. He appears to have taken stock of the fact that the recovery of arable output of the 1350s had not been sustained, and indeed showed signs of faltering,[30] and so, following his election in 1374, some seven years passed without any monks being admitted. Such drastic action has no known parallel in Durham's history and it did not meet with the community's unanimous approval: complaints were made at a Benedictine visitation in 1384.[31] In its credible form the complaint may reveal Prior Walworth's aim: twenty-two monks had died but only twelve had been tonsured, a difference of ten. In

---

[28] BL, Cotton MS Domitian VII, fo. 73v: the names on the lower half of the page, Adam of Darlington-Robert of Claxton, with the date at the foot. The number matches Prior Fossor's claim in 1354: DCM, 2.8.Pont.5.

[29] The verse memorial to Fossor in *Scriptores Tres*, pp. 133–4, recorded him as *centenorum fuit effector monachorum ac vicenorum*. This figure of 120 is five more than the known total for Fossor's priorate, from John of Newcastle, at the head of the group including Uthred of Boldon whose *Vita* records that he took the habit in August 1341, to William Appleby, the most junior monk in 1374. Given that the *Liber Vitae* was not always regularly maintained during Fossor's priorate it is possible that five monks have completely escaped record, but for this to happen they cannot have been members of the community for long. A trace of one or two of these 'lost' monks may perhaps be recorded on DCM, Chamberlain's Accounts, 1357–8 (B), which is unique in naming those who were tonsured: *rasura R Clak R Syr W Elwet J Qwitd*. The third name is otherwise unknown at this period; the fourth may represent John de Whitrig and the others are presumably Robert of Claxton and Robert de Sireston, but there is real difficulty in taking the entry at face value, because all three belong to the '1353' group in the *Liber Vitae* (BL, Cotton MS Domitian VII, fo. 73v), a group whose presence precisely corroborates Fossor's statement in 1354 that twenty-nine monks had been admitted since the Black Death (DCM, 2.8.Pont.5).

[30] Dodds, 'Tithe and Agrarian Output', p. 189.

[31] *Documents illustrating the Activities of the General and Provincial Chapters of the English Black Monks, 1215–1540*, ed. W.A. Pantin (3 vols., Camden Society, 3rd ser. 45–54, 1931–7), III, 83 (cited in Dobson, *Durham Priory*, p. 55 n. 3), undated but with possible dates in 1384, 1387, 1390 and 1393. The complaint took two forms: that twenty-two monks had died with only twelve tonsured, or that twenty-six had died with only eight tonsured. So far as the latter goes the tonsuring of eight monks may have matched the situation in 1387, 1390 or 1393, referring to a group headed either by John Auckland or by Robert of Bolton in the *Liber Vitae* (BL, Cotton MS Domitian VII, fo. 74r), but the figure for deaths is grossly inflated. The other form of the complaint is entirely compatible with the situation in 1384: twelve monks, Thomas Staplay-William Drax in the *Liber Vitae* (BL, Cotton MS, Domitian VII, fo. 74r), had been admitted in the previous ten years, and during that period sixteen monks are known to have died, with a further thirteen disappearing from the records. There is no difficulty in supposing that seven of those who disappeared were still alive at the time of the visitation: that is the number who last appear in the records in 1383.

terms of actual numbers this would point to a reduction from *c*.85 to *c*.75.[32] In fact, in 1384 Walworth was in a strong position to give a reassuring response: the recent establishment of Durham College, Oxford provided support for a significant increase in the numbers of monks studying in Oxford, and so for the enlargement of the community as a whole. More frequent admissions were resumed and this, combined with a very low death-rate in a community that had very few old members, brought the numbers up to at least seventy-six when Walworth retired through ill-health in 1391. Nonetheless, the rate of admissions during Walworth's seventeen-year priorate was the lowest in the whole of the period 1274–1539.

For the monks of Durham the extreme vicissitudes of the fourteenth century were not repeated in the century that followed. Overall it saw the community significantly reduced in size, from at least seventy-eight in 1401 to at least sixty-four in 1500, in parallel with a similar reduction in income from the main monastic estate.[33] Within this pattern there were some fluctuations, but it is not always easy to identify factors that may have prompted these changes. John Hemingbrough's priorate (1391–1416) fell into two parts: numbers built up to at least seventy-eight in 1400 and then drifted downwards to at least seventy-two in October 1414. This came about because it was not until 1410 that the rate of admissions rose to keep pace with the marked increase in mortality between 1404 and 1410 when twenty monks died and a further five disappeared from the records. This increase was predictable, reflecting as it did the high proportion of older monks, those who had been members of the community for thirty years and more, but a prudent prior would hardly have started filling places before they had been vacated, and Hemingbrough's caution may have been reinforced by a cluster of years with poor arable outputs between 1394 and 1400.[34]

During the first twelve years of John Wessington's priorate (1416–46) the admission rate was kept high, but not high enough to maintain stability. When he was elected the community still included a large group of aged members: five men who had been monks for over fifty years and a further six who had been monks for over forty years. Not surprisingly they were all dead by 1426, and this, combined with other losses, outweighed admissions. By 1426 the band of *antiquiores* was very greatly reduced, and with it the mortality rate: during the five years between 1426 and 1431 not a single member of the community is known to have died or disappeared from the records, a happy situation quite without parallel. Admissions slowed, from thirty-four in the 1420s to fourteen in the 1430s, but up to 1438 this was more than enough to match the very low mortality rate, and at the start of that year the community numbered at least eighty-three, its highest known level since the Black Death in 1349 and never attained again. If this was cause for satisfaction it must also have become cause for concern when it came to light during 1438 that the monastery's chief accounting officer, the bursar, had conducted himself with extreme incompetence and improvidence for the past six years, failing to collect rents and covering this by running up a huge concealed debt of £1,210, although in mitigation it has to be said

---

[32] Support for this estimate comes from the number of deaths reported in the complaint (see n. 31): to the sixty-seven monks known to have been alive when it was made, seven of those who had previously disappeared should be added.
[33] Dobson, *Durham Priory*, p. 292; Lomas, 'Durham Cathedral Priory', p. 179.
[34] Dodds, 'Tithe and Agrarian Output', p. 195.

that he was operating against a background of exceptionally low arable outputs.[35] It is no surprise that between 1437 and 1445 only eight new monks were admitted; retrenchment was assisted by a return to a more normal rate of mortality, with fifteen monks dying and four disappearing from the records during that period. On 6 November 1445 Wessington admitted seven monks, the last of his priorate; they brought the size of the community up to at least eighty-one, considerably more than when he was elected in 1416, and very close to the number achieved seventy years before by Prior Fossor. To an extent it could be said that he had been flying in the face of economic reality, and it may be concluded that adjusting the number of monks in line with dwindling resources was not Wessington's highest priority, in seeming contrast to Prior Walworth (1374–91) and perhaps the next prior.

Following the election of William Ebchester as prior in 1446 a small but significant change took place in the treatment of admissions: monks continued to be admitted in groups, as before, but the groups were smaller. Under Wessington eight monks had commonly been admitted together, even ten in 1423; between 1446 and c.1481, when it becomes impossible in all cases to identify the groups, the largest was six. Given variation in the spacing of admissions, smaller groups could provide the means of restricting fluctuations in the size of the community.

During his ten years (1446–56) as prior William Ebchester admitted twenty monks, in four groups, two of six and two of four. This was not a markedly low rate, but it was outstripped by the mortality rate, with numbers of very old men in the community again, and the total figure fell back from at least eighty-one late in 1445 to at least seventy-two in 1456. The reduction in the community's size under William Ebchester was quite marked; if this was the result of deliberate policy it may perhaps reflect a toughening of approach that seems to characterise Ebchester as against his predecessor Wessington.[36] Under Prior Burnaby (1456–64) admissions continued at almost exactly the same rate, seventeen in eight years, but his early years were marked by fewer losses, with the result that the community grew; it fell back to at least seventy-three at about the time of his death late in 1464, and it was observed at the annual chapter earlier that year that there were eight fewer monks than a few years previously.[37] Under his successor, Richard Bell (1464–78), matters were handled in a different way at times. Six monks were admitted between c.1471 and c.1477: three together, then one by himself and finally two together.[38] Such a pattern was extremely unusual, but there is no knowing whether it was adopted for reasons related to the size of the community. Bell admitted twenty-six monks over fourteen years, only a slight reduction in the rate of about two a year under his two immediate predecessors, but fewer than were needed to maintain the community's size at a time when monks were dying significantly younger than before.[39] Bell left in 1478, to become bishop of Carlisle, and had recently admitted six monks, bringing the total to at least sixty-six. Apart from the situation immediately after the Black Death the number of monks was smaller than it had been for well over two centuries.

---

[35] Dobson, *Durham Priory*, pp. 285–7; Dodds, 'Tithe and Agrarian Output', p. 205, and figures 5.05, 5.06.
[36] Cf. Dobson, *Durham Priory*, p. 76 (the case of Robert Erghowe).
[37] DCM, Loc.XXVII:29.
[38] *Liber Vitae* (BL, Cotton MS Domitian VII, fo. 79v): the top six names in col. a.
[39] The demographic data based on the biographies of Durham monks will appear shortly.

Towards the end of Robert Ebchester's priorate (1478–84) the regular listing of monks' names in groups in the *Liber Vitae* ceased, making variations in the pattern of admissions much harder to discern. Nonetheless, there is sufficient biographical information to establish approximate admission dates, and hence to estimate the size of the community. Under Robert Ebchester the admission rate rose slightly, with at least fourteen monks admitted in six years, but the total slipped further, to at least sixty-two. His successor, John Auckland (1484–94), saw an increase in the rate of almost fifty per cent, with thirty-two monks admitted in ten years; this brought the community back up to at least sixty-six before his death in 1494.

The next priorate (1494–1519), that of Thomas Castell, was twenty-five years long and the admission rate rose still higher, to 3.44 a year, with eighty-six monks joining the community, a truly remarkable position; in the whole of the period under consideration it has no parallel over any length of time except for the twenty-five years immediately following the Black Death.[40] An apparently rather high mortality rate reduced the impact, but it was still enough to turn the clock back almost sixty years, with a total of at least seventy-four monks before Castell's death in 1519. The last prior of Durham, Hugh Whitehead (1520–39), was in office for twenty years; he admitted forty-seven monks, a rate of 2.35 a year, but thirty-nine of these were admitted before 1532, giving a rate of 3.25 a year, only about two monks fewer per decade than under his predecessor. A high loss rate meant that this did not suffice to maintain the position achieved by 1519 and the community numbered at least sixty-seven in June 1529.

It is hard to know how to view the last decade of the monastic community's existence. It is easy to read the fact that after 1532 only eight more monks were admitted, in *c*.1535, as a symptom of foreboding, of waning confidence. This is not justified: if those monks were admitted by the autumn of 1535, then the known size of the community at the end of that year was at least seventy-one, and if a further eight men had been ready for admission early in 1540 that would have brought the total to seventy. The impression that the community was being allowed to dwindle in the later 1530s very largely rests on the assumption that no young men were being prepared to join it; there is no good warrant for that. It would be more defensible to characterise the whole of the period 1500–39 as one of significant growth leading to impressive stability. Certainly, it was a period in which the health of the community, judged by its size, was considerably stronger than during the preceding forty years, 1460–99.

In describing the changes in the size of the Durham community over a period of 265 years it has been tacitly assumed that the community itself was in control. There were in fact two constraints on its freedom: the availability of suitable recruits to replace monks who had died, and the actions enjoined as a result of visitations. The matter of recruitment is one that the surviving evidence illuminates hardly at all, but there are questions worth raising, even if firm answers cannot be given. The most basic concerns the availability of suitable recruits. Perhaps, for a house with such manifold attractions and so distant from any alternative avenue for pursuing a Benedictine vocation,[41] the possibility that such recruits were not available can be

---

40 During Hugh of Darlington's second short priorate (1286–90) fifteen monks may have been admitted, an average of 3.75 a year.
41 For a fine evocation, see Dobson, *Durham Priory*, ch. 1.

immediately dismissed, but the decline in the community's size during the latter part of the fifteenth century leaves the question open; here the fact that there was no apparent difficulty in raising the recruitment rate from 1484 onwards suggests that suitable candidates could normally be found when wanted. On the other hand, when they were needed in very large numbers, following the Black Death in 1349, there was said to have been some difficulty, although the evidence for this is Prior Fossor's attempt to rebut a complaint about his derelictions in the matter of recruitment.[42]

A more complex question concerns the flexibility of the process of preparing young men for admission in the almonry school.[43] There seems to be no evidence to show whether candidates reached a point in their preparation when, barring scandal, the community was irrevocably committed to admitting them, but, if that was the situation, it would have reduced the speed with which a wish to cut back on admissions could be implemented. Even if that was not strictly the position, some candidates had influential sponsors, who would need to be approached sensitively if their expectations were to be disappointed in some way.[44] On the other hand, by the mid-fifteenth century candidates were expected to be recommended principally by Durham monks, commonly on the basis of kinship,[45] and the monks were well aware that the quality of their communal life would deteriorate if the numbers outgrew the financial resources available. A cynic might attribute the decline in admissions after 1446 to the community consulting its own comfort. Rather earlier it was Prior Walworth's good fortune that his predecessor, Prior Fossor, had admitted a huge group of fifteen novices shortly before his death in 1374, probably leaving no candidates in the pipeline; Walworth was then free to put a complete and immediate brake on admissions that lasted for some seven years.

The sharp change in admissions policy following Fossor's death points clearly to the prior having control over this. Earlier, in 1354, when replying to a complaint about the numbers admitted, Fossor had made no attempt to shift the blame elsewhere but answered in terms showing that he accepted personal responsibility.[46] Previously, Prior Burdon had expressed his readiness to consult the community over raising numbers in a way that indicates that he was proposing to act in an exceptional manner.[47] Thus one of the things that could be put to a prior's credit was the number of monks that he had admitted.[48] Equally, it was the prior who chose the men whose professions he would receive, and it was against the prior that allegations were made about their qualifications and the considerations involved.[49] It was to the prior that correspondence about the admission of individuals was addressed.[50]

The degree to which the existing community's own interests were consulted in fixing the rate of admissions was limited by the fact that the house was subject to visitation by the bishop and by fellow Benedictines appointed for the purpose. Reference

---

[42] See below.
[43] Dobson, *Durham Priory*, p. 60. It is worth noting that in 1354 Prior Fossor gave no hint that preparing large numbers of men for admission presented him with any difficulty.
[44] Ibid., p. 59, citing the example of the earl of Northumberland.
[45] Ibid., pp. 59–60.
[46] DCM, 2.8.Pont.5, more fully discussed below at p. 167.
[47] DCM, Loc.XXVII:31, art. 45. Note especially the force of *tamen*.
[48] For Prior Wessington, see Dobson, *Durham Priory*, p. 55.
[49] DCM, 2.8.Pont.5, 2.8.Pont.12, discussed more fully below at pp. 167–8.
[50] Dobson, *Durham Priory*, p. 59.

has already been made to a complaint about admissions voiced in the latter context in 1384; the articles of enquiry for Benedictine visitations composed some twenty years earlier addressed the matter of whether there were the ancient and due (*antiquus et debitus*) numbers of monks, in line with the constitutions of Pope Benedict XII dated 1336.[51] Equally, while it is well established that diocesan bishops were already concerning themselves with monastic numbers by the thirteenth century, there is evidence as late as 1314 that bishops of Durham did not invariably do so.[52]

Articles of enquiry copied in the earlier fourteenth century and addressed by the bishop to the Durham community asked how many monks there were and how many *conversi*, whether there was the customary (*solitus*) number of monks and what this was, how many monks there could be given good sound (*legalis*) administration, and also whether all the revenues of the monastery and cells were turned to the use and needs of the monks.[53] When Bishop Langley conducted a visitation in 1408 his sixty-six articles of enquiry were based on existing models.[54] The fourth article expanded on the question of how many monks there were and how many *conversi* by asking whether the set and customary (*statutus et solitus*) numbers were observed in the monastery and the cells, while subsequent articles concerned the revenues of the house and whether they were all used for the monks' needs; the suitability of those admitted to the community was not raised.

The earliest document setting out detailed complaints about the running of the monastery was not produced in the course of a visitation but in the wake of the violent dispute between Bishop Bek and Prior Hoton that broke out in 1300. In seeking the prior's suspension by the pope, an endeavour crowned with success in March 1306, Bek set out nineteen articles against Hoton's administration.[55] Given the extreme bitterness engendered by the dispute the failure to mention the size of the community or other aspects of admissions suggests strongly that in this matter Hoton had not laid himself open to criticism, particularly as his stewardship of the monastic estates, on which the community depended, was roundly condemned at some length.

Bishop Kellawe (1311–16) conducted a visitation in 1314. Neither the many articles set down for examination nor those for correction refer to the matter of the size of the community.[56] This is all the more significant since Kellawe was especially well-equipped to probe possible defects: he was the last member of the Durham

---

51 *Chapters of the English Black Monks*, II, 82–9, surviving in two Durham copies and one from St Albans; for numbers, see ibid., II, 87, art. 33 and II, 232.
52 See C.R. Cheney, *Episcopal Visitation of Monasteries in the Thirteenth Century* (Manchester, 1983), pp. 22, 73, 146, 165–6.
53 DCM, 2.9.Pont.4. The dating is based on the script; also of significance may be the fact that these articles were not those by Bishop Kellawe in 1314, and there is also reason to think that the matter of numbers was not raised at the visitation undertaken by Bishop Beaumont in 1319 (for which, see below). Although there are references to *statuta Capituli generalis*, the visitation was clearly episcopal, not Benedictine, since *testamenta predecessorum nostrorum* and their anniversaries are mentioned. References to Howdenshire, Jarrow and Wearmouth show that the enquiries related specifically to the Durham community.
54 *The Register of Thomas Langley, Bishop of Durham, 1406–1437*, ed. R.L. Storey (6 vols., Surtees Society, 164–82, 1949–67), I, 66–76, esp. 72, 75; for the house's badly damaged copy of the articles of enquiry, see DCM, Loc.XXVII:36. The details are close to those found in DCM, 2.9.Pont.4.
55 *Records of Antony Bek, Bishop and Patriarch, 1283–1311*, ed. C.M. Fraser (Surtees Society 162, 1947), pp. 113–18; Fraser, *History of Antony Bek*, p. 166.
56 DCM, Reg.II, fols. 49v–51r.

community to be successfully elected as bishop by his fellows. Equally, he would have been particularly well aware that the curtailment of recruitment at this time was prompted by acute financial difficulties.

Bishop Beaumont opened his primary visitation in October 1319, but Prior Burdon failed to obey the subsequent injunctions, which led a group of monks to petition the bishop with a list of articles that the prior should be enjoined to observe; at this stage the matter of the number of monks was not raised.[57] The bishop launched an investigation and it seems that a fuller list of *positiones* against Burdon was drawn up, relating back to the articles following the visitation; again the number of monks was not mentioned, suggesting that this had not been raised at the visitation, although the sharp decrease in admissions between *c*.1312 and *c*.1317 must have been very obvious by then.[58] It is only in the record of Burdon's replies to the articles laid against him that reference to numbers appears, suggesting that this was by no means the most immediate or clear-cut charge; he answered by claiming that the church's obligations were being properly met, and that, although the exhaustion of its goods in many ways made them insufficient for the customary number of monks, he was ready to increase the number with the community's counsel as opportune.[59] From what is known of the house's financial predicament this was an entirely reasonable rejoinder, but it is significant for its references to a customary number and, as already discussed,[60] to consultation of the community. In 1354 a later prior would deny that there was a customary number, but Burdon did not; there was, after all, the statute of 1235 which set down figures for Durham and Coldingham,[61] but also there appears to have been a long period, between 1273 and *c*.1310, when the community's size was quite stable, and in 1320 there were at least seven monks who could remember the whole of that period and may well have regarded the situation prevailing then as a set norm.

Prior Burdon was obliged to resign in 1321 as a result of the investigation. After one abortive attempt William of Cowton was elected in his place, and it was probably as part of the visitation initiated by Bishop Beaumont late in 1332 that William gave his answers to eleven articles.[62] None of these concerned the size of the community or admissions.

---

[57] DCM, 2.9.Pont.2. The process against Burdon is described in J. Scammell, 'Some Aspects of Medieval English Monastic Government: The Case of Geoffrey Burdon Prior of Durham (1313–1321)', *Revue Bénédictine* 68 (1958), 226–50.

[58] DCM, Loc.XXVII:30.

[59] DCM, Loc.XXVII:31.

[60] See above at p. 164.

[61] See n. 25 above.

[62] DCM, 2.7.Pont.1d, Loc.XXVII:12 and 2.9.Pont.6. Only the first of these documents is dated, while the second is addressed to Bishop Louis and the third is another version of it. References in the second establish a dating between *c*.1332 and 1337: to Simon of Rothbury as master of Farne, first attested by DCM, Bursar's Account Rolls, 1332–3, and to John of Seaton, whose death is evidenced by DCM, Bursar's Account Rolls, 1336–7. An interesting but fragmentary list of complaints (DCM, Misc. Ch. 7288) by individual monks, against their fellows and officeholders rather than the prior, makes no mention of the size of the community or admissions, and concerns matters not obviously connected with those known to have been raised in 1332; the fragment is to be dated by its references to William de Scaccario, who entered *c*.1322, and Robert of Kingston, who died between November 1342 and November 1343 (DCM, Bursar's Account Rolls, 1342, 3A). Injunctions (DCM, 2.9.Pont.10) mentioning Simon of Rothbury as master of Farne, and so to be dated to the 1330s, are silent on the subject of the number of monks, but two out of over thirty depositions recorded in *c*.1331 (DCM, Misc.

At Bishop Hatfield's visitation in 1354 one of the allegations against Prior Fossor was that the number of monks was smaller than it customarily used to be and smaller than the revenues could support.[63] To this the prior responded that the number had never been fixed but went up and down in line with fluctuations in the house's resources, and he indicated that recruitment had been constrained by want of clerks surviving the plague, with some of those admitted being of a different quality from previous recruits because of the urgent necessity; he stated that the numbers matched the resources available and were sufficient to sustain the round of services, but acknowledged that numbers were reduced, just as the revenues had been reduced, as a result of the plague. The prior's case was accepted by the bishop and no reference to the size of the community was made in the subsequent injunctions.[64] In view of the exceedingly difficult and distressing circumstances that had confronted Prior Fossor it is hard to suppose that he did not regard this complaint as singularly ill-judged. Yet for the members of his community there was indeed urgent need that the losses be made good: quite apart from the round of services, they had to keep the whole elaborate administrative machinery of the monastery in operation and staff the cells, putting virtually every one of them under pressure that could only end when numbers were restored.[65]

Bishop Hatfield initiated a third and final visitation of his cathedral priory in 1371.[66] A long list of fifty-eight carefully phrased complaints probably formed part of this process.[67] The matter of the community's size surfaced yet again, but in a more

---

Ch. 2645) do allude to the matter: *Vicesimus sextus. Numerus fratrum in conuentu deberet esse sufficiens pro seruicio diuino nec dum est iuxta facultates monasterii et eius statum antiquum [!]. . . . Tricesimus primus. In claustro nostro non sunt iam fratres virtute potentes et numero sufficientes pro diuino seruicio in choro et eius labore.*

63 Harbottle, 'Hatfield's Visitation of Durham Priory', 81–100, esp. 92–3.

64 For the text, see ibid., 98–100. Concern over the question of numbers does not seem to have been stilled: the damaged first entry among the draft replies to one enquiry reads *Dominus prior dicit quod...habent in numero xxxiij M[onachos] professos* (DCM, 1.9.Pont.1b). This is to be dated between 11 November 1357 and 26 May 1358, from the fact that Richard of Birtley was bursar (DCM, Reg.III, fo.183r–v; Bursar's Vouchers, 1356–7, with Adam of Darlington bursar; Bursar's Account Rolls, 1357–8; and the extract on the dorse of the Pittington Accounts, 1285–6) and Robert of Walworth hostiller (DCM, Hostiller's Accounts, 1358, 1358–9). If the document was prompted by a triennial Benedictine visitation, 1357 would fit into the pattern (*Chapters of the English Black Monks*, III, 82 note to no. 236). More difficult to establish is the question to which 'thirty monks' was the answer. It was certainly not the total, since this was at least sixty-eight by early 1357, following the admission of Reginald of Wearmouth, ordained acolyte in April 1357 (DCM, Reg. Hatfield, fo. 101v), nor was it the number admitted since the Black Death, since Reginald's admission brought this to thirty-eight, of whom at least thirty-six were alive in 1357; possibly it was the total in Durham, but this would imply at least thirty-five at the cells, an improbably high figure, and considerably more than was the case during the earlier fifteenth century after the founding of Durham College, Oxford (Dobson, *Durham Priory*, p. 300 n. 1).

65 Symptoms of the strain can be seen in some of the allegations laid against Prior Fossor in 1354, namely that the master of the cell at Wearmouth had no fellow monk, that the prior appointed to Stamford was improvident and lacking in judgement, that too many older and more responsible monks had been sent to the cells, that young and inexperienced monks had been appointed to offices (DCM, 1.8.Pont.1); none of these matters found a place in Bishop Hatfield's injunctions.

66 DCM, 2.7.Pont.4, 2.7.Pont.1h; his first was in 1346 (DCM, 2.7.Pont.1h), followed by 1354 (see above). That initiated in 1369 (DCM, 2.7.Pont.2e) apparently came to nothing.

67 DCM, 2.8.Pont.12. The rather fulsome heading is addressed *reuerende pater* and the first complaint refers to the prior of Durham. The dating is between 1349 and 1375: one article (49) refers to the situation *ante pestilenciam*, and others (53, 54–55) mention John of Shaftoe, who died in 1374 or 1375 (*Priory of Finchale*, appendix, p. xcii).

subtle form: the notion of a customary number had become 'the old number' and it was claimed that the resources would support this if they were well administered.[68] Poor estate management is thus directly connected to its most serious consequence: fewer monks. In his defence Prior Fossor would presumably have referred to the widespread difficulties experienced by landlords as a result of the plague. Another complaint appears to criticise the quality of some of those received into the community, as wanting in knowledge and social status, often being admitted as a result of pressure rather than rational consideration, and causing damage to the church and shame.[69] In 1354 Prior Fossor had more or less acknowledged that he had been obliged to lower entry requirements after the Black Death, and in *c.*1368 he admitted one monk subsequently described as a cousin of the earl of March, a possible instance of bowing to influence.[70]

In 1384, at a Benedictine visitation, yet further complaint was made about numbers.[71] The notion of a customary number (*numerus solitus*) was revived and it was again claimed that there were not as many monks as the resources could support if they were well regulated. Six years later the point was further elaborated: in June 1390, again at a Benedictine visitation, it was argued that the onerous multitude of secular clerks assisting at services, needed because there were too few monks, should be reduced and the number of monks increased, with those admitted being especially those who would remain in the monastery, to 'bear the heat of the day', and who knew how to read and sing.[72] With the community numbering between seventy and eighty the picture presented may seem unreal, but those available for the full round of daily worship would have been much smaller, with some thirty monks away at the cells and perhaps ten or more officeholders in Durham escaping full participation in the liturgy; the core of monks in choir at all hours was probably no more than thirty, including eight novices, without taking account of any confined to the infirmary.[73] Whether 1390 saw the end of a period of almost seventy years during which members of the community sought repeatedly to enlist a visitor's powers to increase their number is impossible to tell; the next visitation for which detailed records survive is

---

[68] DCM, 2.8.Pont.12.
[69] DCM, 2.8.Pont.12. The complaint does not refer explicitly to the admission of monks, but it is very hard to provide a satisfactory alternative interpretation; the next two complaints refer to novices and to young monks respectively. Social status was a sensitive matter among the monks: in 1446 John Oll went to considerable lengths to rebut a malicious slander by a fellow monk that 'he was a bondman and nott of fre condicion' (*Scriptores Tres*, appendix, pp. cclxxviii–cclxxxiv, cited in Dobson, *Durham Priory*, p. 74 n. 1).
[70] William Trollopp: BL, Cotton MS Faustina A. VI, fols. 87v, 69r.
[71] See n. 31 above.
[72] Article 48, defective, on DCM, Loc.XXVII:35, two damaged sheets of paper containing articles numbered up to 55 but with 18–37 missing. The visitation, with its references to the constitutions of Northampton in articles 5 and 53, was presumably a triennial Benedictine visitation; Bishop Skirlaw (1388–1406) embarked upon his primary visitation in March 1391 (DCM, 2.7.Pont.2d, 2.8.Pont.2)
[73] For numbers at the cells, see Dobson, *Durham Priory*, p. 300 n. 1; officeholders likely to be absent frequently included the prior and his chaplain, the terrar, bursar, cellarer, hostiller and almoner, while the granator, chamberlain, chancellor and sacrist all had responsibilities that took them away from Durham at times. What is obscure, however, is how far the latter, together with the communar and the infirmarer, played a reduced part in the liturgical round simply because they held office. In 1442 sixteen officeholders were said to have been excused from Matins, when only the terrar should have been; the reply was that this applied to only six every night *exceptis principalibus* (DCM, 1.9.Pont.3, 1.8.Pont.2).

not until 1442, and then the *detecta* make no mention of the community's size or admissions.[74]

After 1442 the process of episcopal visitation has left very little trace;[75] if it was neglected, that can hardly be the whole explanation for the decline in numbers after 1446, for the round of triennial Benedictine visitations was not allowed to languish.[76] On the other hand, even if Benedictine visitors addressed the matter, they may have been more readily persuaded than bishops that an increase in numbers was undesirable, as a threat to the comfort of the existing community, whereas bishops, with their manifest interest in the keeping of their predecessors' anniversaries,[77] were likely to share the more general view, namely that the more monks participating in divine service, the more masses they said, then the more efficacious these activities would be on behalf of those for whom they were offered. Awareness that a bishop might well concern himself with the total number of monks may well have influenced those responsible for admissions, but this also gave those liable to dissent a ready rod with which to attempt to beat a superior's back. To a degree the frequency of complaints about the size of the community during the fourteenth century may be symptomatic of a fractious spirit engendered by repeated crises.

Occasional reference has already been made to times when there were an unusual number of aged monks in the community. It was a consequence of varying rates of admission that the proportion of experienced to inexperienced monks changed over time, so that the community did not always have the same shape. So, for example, the effect of the suspension of admissions for some seven years after 1373 can be observed through the following period until it was the prime reason why there were no members of the community with more than fifty years' experience between 1425 and 1431, when the first monk admitted by Prior Walworth attained his jubilee.[78] In sharp contrast only a few years earlier, at the beginning of 1415, there had been six monks in this category, a long-term effect of Prior Fossor's efforts to restore numbers after the Black Death in 1349.

Admission rates were the main factor determining the shape of the community because mortality rates were normally random across the ages represented. This was not invariably the case: during the period 1500–20 mortality among the junior monks was unusually high, with all four who died of the plague early in September 1508 having been admitted less than twelve years before. Conversely, three monks with more than fifty years' experience died in 1437 or 1438 and the same number in 1462 or 1463; perhaps they were particularly vulnerable to some virulent respiratory infection. The number who survived to attain sixty years' experience was small: out of 639 monks only seven are known to have achieved it between 1300 and 1539, and it is striking that three of these were priors, among them John Fossor, who died aged ninety, the greatest age known to have been reached by any Durham monk.[79] These

---

74 DCM, 1.9.Pont.3, 1.9.Pont.1c, 1.8.Pont.2, Loc.XXVII:19, 39. A fragment of injunctions, in a late fourteenth-century hand (DCM, Loc.XXVII:34), contains no mention of numbers.
75 DCM, 4.6.Pont.14 and 15, 2.7.Pont.16, concern the formalities of visitations initiated by Bishop Booth in 1459 and 1464.
76 *Chapters of the English Black Monks*, III, 236–45.
77 *Register of Thomas Langley*, I, 74.
78 William Pocklington, who did not die until 1442 or 1443 (DCM, Bursar's Account Rolls, 1442–3).
79 639 is arrived at by adding the number of admissions in that period (595) to the number already monks

three priors present the temptation to speculate that some aspect of the office which they held increased their life expectancy, but it is equally possible that the community was quite good at judging potential longevity when it elected a prior; it certainly had an interest in avoiding frequent elections, not least because of the expense involved.

One less conspicuous phenomenon produced by the randomness of mortality is the survival of entire groups of monks: all ten men admitted on 2 November 1368, most of whom were probably small children at the time of the Black Death, were still alive at the start of 1404, thirty-six years later, while the entire group of eight who had entered by early 1438 survived for at least thirty-four years, until early 1472. If a certain fellow-feeling existed among monks admitted together, it is difficult to imagine that the dynamics of the community were not influenced by the presence of groups of such longevity. It was after all the case, when every member of a group attended a chapter meeting, that at least one of his neighbours would have been the same year by year, decade by decade.

The most conspicuous general feature of the shape of the community between 1300 and 1539 is the fact that it usually included members who could bring to it experience stretching back for fifty years and more. There were times when this was probably not the case:[80] for almost the whole of the 1380s, as a direct result of the losses at the Black Death; between 1425 and 1430, because of the prolonged suspension of admissions fifty years earlier; and 1465–73, 1502–9 and 1523–33, largely because of raised mortality among the older monks. Except for the period 1465–73 these were also times when the number of monks with more than forty years' experience was small, making the length of the community's living memory considerably shorter than usual.

The most striking individual feature of the shape of the community was caused by the effort to restore numbers after the massive losses from the Black Death in 1349. Initially, of course, this meant that there was a very high proportion of inexperienced monks, and some of them had to be given administrative responsibilities much more rapidly than was normal. As time passed and these men moved into the middle years of their careers the imbalance in the community shifted, an effect considerably exaggerated by the suspension of admissions in 1374. Finally, during the first two decades of the fifteenth century, the proportion of aged monks rose exceptionally high.

Major changes in the rate of admissions had predictable consequences for the shape of the community, but there is no evidence that these were ever taken into consideration. Prior Fossor doubtless saw no alternative to speedy recruitment after 1349, and, when his successor put this into complete reverse in 1374, he probably felt that the financial position did not allow a more gradual approach to be adopted. A balanced community was not the highest priority, and everything points to size being the governing consideration. In itself size was not, however, an uncontested matter. In

---

in 1300 (110) and subtracting those who survived the Dissolution (sixty-six). For those with an exceptionally long monastic career, see A.J. Piper, 'The Monks of Durham and Patterns of Activity in Old Age', in *The Church and Learning in Later Medieval Society*, ed. C.M. Barron and J. Stratford (Donington, 2002), pp. 51–63.

[80] It can only be 'probably' because monks who disappear from the records before the periods in question may in fact have lived on into them. This could well be the case for three short periods between 1338 and 1360.

the fourteenth century some held tenaciously to the idea of a customary number,[81] but others, who faced up to the house's diminished finances, sought to adjust numbers to resources, and they eventually won the argument. With the notion of an ideal number apparently abandoned, the fact that a reduction in numbers was put into reverse late in the fifteenth century is all the more remarkable. Possibly, there was pressure for this at visitations, either episcopal or Benedictine, but no doubt a determined prior could have found reasons for resisting such pressure if he had wished to do so. Between 1478 and 1519, under the guidance of three successive priors, the size of the Durham community grew, in line with improved economic circumstances. Growth was the deliberate policy, and it was a policy that succeeded because the community could attract a sufficient supply of young men who wanted to join it. As the clouds of the Reformation gathered, monastic life at Durham was apparently marked by renewed vitality.

---

[81] Between 1375 and 1529 the number of Westminster monks was in principle fixed: B. Harvey, *Living and Dying in England, 1100–1540: The Monastic Experience* (Oxford, 1993), pp. 73–4.

12

Peasants, Landlords and Production between the Tyne and the Tees, 1349–1450

BEN DODDS

Historians of economic and social change in the Middle Ages have developed explanatory frameworks spanning several centuries. These models depend on the gradually altering balance between the number of consumers and the resources available to meet their demands or the slow tightening and loosening of landlords' ties over the peasantry.[1] The problem with such long-term analysis is that the available evidence comes from much more limited time periods. For the agrarian economy, series of manorial accounts or court rolls are usually patchy and at best stretch for a few decades. The problem is particularly acute for the agrarian history of the century after the Black Death when manorial demesnes were increasingly leased out, meaning that fewer highly informative accounts were produced. One type of evidence, however, produces much longer series of indicators than the others: tithe.[2]

By the fourteenth century religious corporations had often appropriated more than one parish from which they were owed tithe and, unable or unwilling to collect the grain themselves, the practice of selling tithes for cash became widespread. On the basis that tithe was supposed to represent one tenth of total output, French historians of the 1960s and 1970s developed methods for using cash tithe receipts as indicators of production levels.[3] Up to now, this approach has not been used by historians of England but the resources here are abundant. In particular, the Durham Priory accounting material contains around 6,000 tithe receipts for the period 1349–1450 alone. These were collected and a technique developed for indexing and deflating receipts by price in order to convert them into approximations of arable output. The results of these calculations are shown in figure 12.1.[4]

---

[1] J. Hatcher, 'The Great Slump of the Mid-Fifteenth Century', in *Progress and Problems in Medieval England: Essays in Honour of Edward Miller*, ed. R. Britnell and J. Hatcher (Cambridge, 1996), pp. 237–72; J. Hatcher and M. Bailey, *Modelling the Middle Ages: The History and Theory of England's Economic Development* (Oxford, 2001), pp. 21–120; E. Le Roy Ladurie, 'A Reply to Robert Brenner', in *The Brenner Debate: Agrarian Class Structure and Economic Developments in Pre-Industrial Europe*, ed. T.H. Aston and C.H.E. Philpin (Cambridge, 1985), pp. 101–6.

[2] E. Le Roy Ladurie and J. Goy, *Tithe and Agrarian History from the Fourteenth to the Nineteenth Centuries: An Essay in Comparative History* (Cambridge, 1982), p. 26.

[3] For example, E. Le Roy Ladurie, *The Peasants of Languedoc* (Urbana, 1974), pp. 77–80.

[4] A detailed description of the method by which the output indices were obtained can be found in B. Dodds, 'Tithe and Agrarian Output between the Tyne and Tees, 1350–1450' (unpublished Ph.D. thesis, University of Durham, 2002), pp. 138–67. See also B. Dodds, 'Estimating Arable Output Using

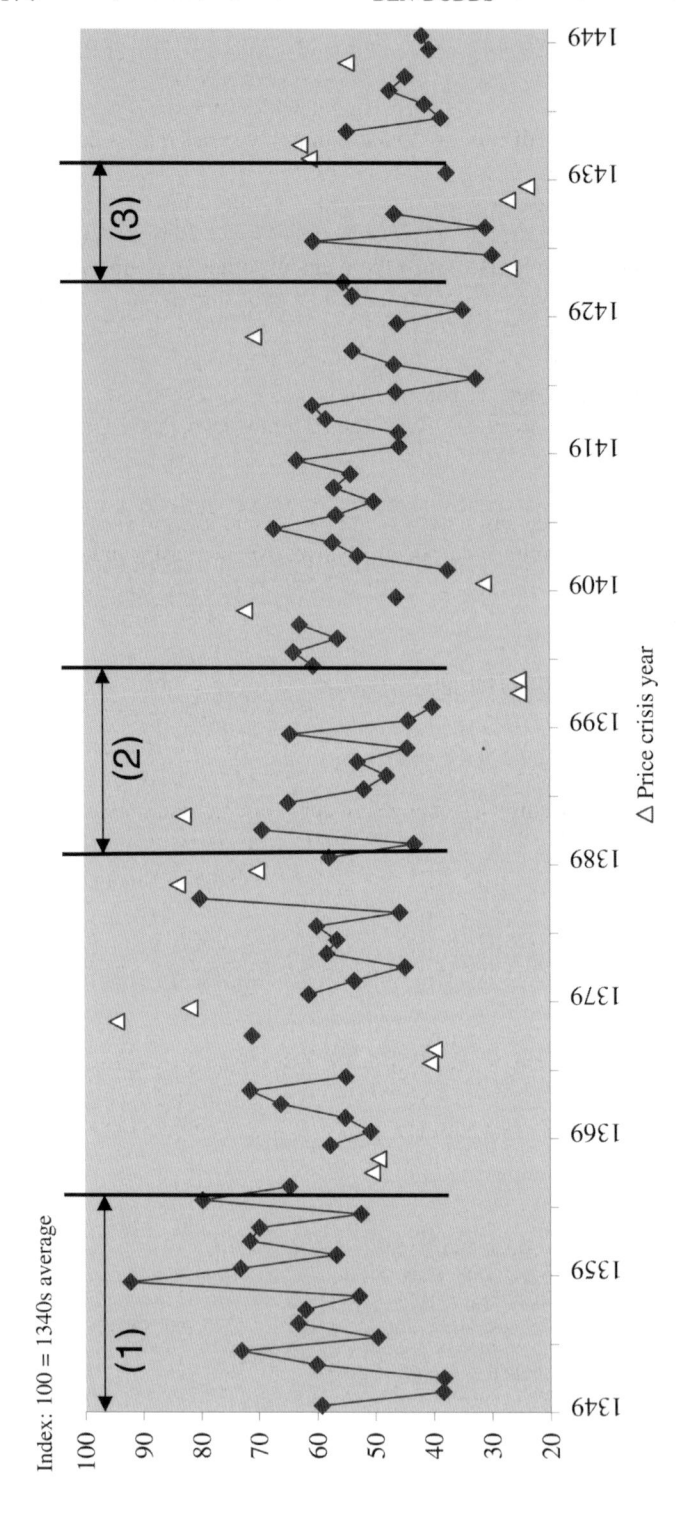

Fig. 12.1 Estimated arable output from Durham Priory parishes between Tyne and Tees

Note: price crisis years are singled out because of the likelihood that the process of price deflation would not work so well when prices were exceptionally high or low. Tithe purchasers negotiated their offer price prior to the harvest and therefore must have estimated the value of grain over the coming year. It has been assumed that their estimates would be less accurate for years of exceptional prices. In this instance, price crisis years are arbitrarily defined as the ten years of the highest prices and the ten years of the lowest prices.

This unique series of indicators affords the historian an unprecedented opportunity to examine the detailed chronology of agrarian change over this period. However, despite the unusually large number of individual figures which make up the series, the tithe evidence must be treated with caution. In particular, the series makes no allowance for changes in tithe collection costs or the profits made by the tithe purchasers. The data for these factors are insufficiently consistent to enable them to be incorporated in the calculations. It is the purpose of this essay not only to describe the patterns of change shown in figure 12.1 but also to test them against other Durham evidence. This consists mainly of manorial and rental evidence. The former gives detailed insights into agricultural practice but only on seigniorial lands. The latter is difficult to interpret but, like tithes, can shed light on developments outside the demesne sector. Similarly, the tithe data derive from arable production levels and therefore only one aspect of the agrarian economy. Evidence of trends in pastoral farming is much more scarce but will be examined in conjunction with the arable series when available.

This discussion of agrarian transition between the Tyne and Tees will be centred on the two themes of demographic and social change. An increasing number of studies and weight of scholarly opinion agree that the century following the Black Death was one of population decline. The case was made by M.M. Postan in 1950 using indirect indicators, and a number of local studies have exploited pockets of exceptional evidence in support.[5] The Durham tithe evidence enables the demographic indicators we do have to be compared with production levels. Historians have also emphasised the profound social ramifications of the economic changes undergone in the late fourteenth and fifteenth centuries. The comparison of the tithe series with other Durham evidence illuminates changes in consumption and labour supply during this period. The length of the Durham output series favours a case-study approach. Three periods of particularly rapid change in production levels have been identified and numbered on figure 12.1. These will be discussed in turn, and a detailed examination of associated evidence made. The three case studies will yield an overall interpretation and suggest possible patterns relating production levels to demographic and social change.

The Black Death crossed the River Tees towards the end of the summer of 1349.[6] Figure 12.1 suggests that output was very seriously affected: the index for 1349 is only 59.3 per cent of 1340s levels and then plunges further to 38.4 per cent and 38.2

Durham Priory Tithe Receipts, 1349–1450', *EcHR*, 57 (2004), 245–85. The indices draw on around 500 individual accounts, inventories and sale of tithe lists contained in DCM.

[5] M.M. Postan, 'Some Economic Evidence of Declining Population in the Later Middle Ages', *EcHR*, 2nd ser. 2 (1950), 221–46; J. Hatcher, *Plague, Population and the English Economy, 1348–1530* (London, 1977), pp. 12, 21–54. Local studies include L.R. Poos, *A Rural Society after the Black Death: Essex 1350–1525* (Cambridge, 1991), pp. 90, 108–9; Z. Razi, *Life, Marriage and Death in a Medieval Parish: Economy, Society and Demography in Halesowen, 1270–1400* (Cambridge, 1980), p. 117; D. Postles, 'Demographic Change in Kibworth Harcourt, Leicestershire, in the Later Middle Ages', *Local Population Studies* 48 (1992), 41–8; J. Hatcher, 'Mortality in the Fifteenth Century: Some New Evidence', *EcHR*, 2nd ser. 39 (1986), 19–38.

[6] Some of the evidence discussed in this case study is also referred to in my article, 'Durham Priory Tithes and the Black Death between Tyne and Tees', *NH* 39 (2002), 17–21. Evidence for the precise timing of the Black Death between Tyne and Tees can be found in F.A. Gasquet, *The Black Death of*

per cent in the two subsequent years. Over the following thirteen years, there was a sustained rise in production levels. In 1358 estimated output reached 92.3 per cent of 1340s levels, the second highest index of the series. Growth was slightly slower during the early 1360s but the 1364 index is nearly eighty per cent of 1340s levels. In some vills, estimated output recovered in an even more spectacular way. Heighington, for example, produced an estimated 65.3q. on average during the 1340s, which fell to 11.0q. in 1350 but was as high as 66.4q. in 1358 and 67.7q. in 1362. Only a handful of small vills showed a continued decrease in output during the 1350s.

The rapid recovery of overall production levels in the decade following the Black Death is not completely unexpected given widespread evidence for the 'Indian summer of demesne farming'.[7] Sown acreages of demesne land often recovered quickly and the main phase of leasing only began on many estates in the 1370s.[8] Evidence for such an Indian summer in Durham is sparse because there are no manorial accounts from the 1350s and most of the 1360s.[9] Certainly the timing of leasing on priory manors suggests that they did not cease to be profitable enterprises for the monks immediately after the Black Death. The priors of the dependent cell at Finchale and the bursar and terrar at the mother house made their first new manorial leases since the Black Death in the early 1370s.[10] The only scraps of more detailed information so far uncovered are from inventories made by the almoners recording sown acreages on their manors. These data are collected in table 12.1.

Table 12.1: Total sown acreages on the almoner's manors, 1340–54

Almoner's 'status'	*Maudleyns*[11]	Witton Gilbert	Total
8 May 1340	14	84	98
30 April 1341	14	77	91
1345	10	71	81
30 May 1351	15.5	96	111.5
21 May 1352	18	89	107
26 May 1354	15	91.5	106.5

The table shows that sown acreage actually increased on these fairly small manors during the 1340s and early 1350s. Such flimsy evidence is hardly proof of an Indian summer but, in conjunction with the timing of the manor leases, it suggests

1348 and 1349 (2nd edn., London, 1908), p. 185; F. Bradshaw, 'Social and Economic History', in *VCH Durham*, II, 210–11; R.H. Britnell, 'Feudal Reaction after the Black Death in the Palatinate of Durham', *P&P* 128 (1990), 31.

[7] A.R. Bridbury, 'The Black Death', *EcHR*, 2nd ser. 26 (1973), 584.
[8] For example, M. Saaler, 'The Manor of Tillingdown: The Changing Economy of the Demesne 1325–71', *Surrey Archaeological Collections* 81 (1991–2), 28; E. Miller, 'Tenant Farming and Farmers: Southern Counties', in *The Agrarian History of England and Wales, III: 1348–1500*, ed. E. Miller (Cambridge, 1991), p. 704; P.D.A. Harvey, 'Tenant Farming and Farmers: Home Counties', in *The Agrarian History of England and Wales, III: 1348–1500*, ed. E. Miller (Cambridge, 1991), p. 663.
[9] A.J. Piper, *Muniments of the Dean and Chapter of Durham: Medieval Accounting Material* (Durham University Library, Archives and Special Collections, Searchroom Handlist, 1995).
[10] Richard de Birtley, prior of Finchale, leased Wingate manor in 1372–3: *The Priory of Finchale: The Charters of Endowment, Inventories, and Account Rolls of the Priory of Finchale*, ed. J. Raine (Surtees Society 6, 1837), appendix, p. lxxiv; R.A. Lomas, 'The Priory of Durham and its Demesnes in the Fourteenth and Fifteenth Centuries', *EcHR*, 2nd ser. 31 (1978), 345.

production levels on Durham manors may have recovered like those in many parts of the south.

Rental evidence can be used to assess the occupation of land in the fifteen years following the Black Death. John Hatcher judged that 'within a few years of 1350 the land of England was almost fully reoccupied, and at rents which seemingly stood comparison with former years'.[12] On the Oxfordshire manor of Cuxham all the holdings which had been vacant in 1349 were tenanted again by May 1355.[13] Not only was it possible to let tenements on the manors of the duchy of Cornwall, but by 1356 it was often possible to raise rents to 'pre-plague levels'.[14] Richard Lomas used the rolls recording the deaths of Durham Priory customary and free tenants in the 'Great Pestilence' to suggest that around sixty-nine per cent of holdings were re-let by the early to mid-1350s.[15] Despite this apparently rapid take-up of tenements in the immediate aftermath of the plague, Lomas argued, on the basis of unpaid rent for waste holdings in the bursars' accounts, that 'there was no stampede on the part of the survivors to take up vacant holdings and that, even after ten years, there was still plenty of untenanted land'.[16] Reiterating this evidence some years later, however, he was sceptical of the significance of the bursars' vacant holdings. On the basis of a 1396 list of decayed rents, he observed that the vacancies tended to be 'urban properties, Spennymoor assarts . . . or holdings of a minor and peripheral sort'.[17] It seems reasonable to reinterpret Lomas's evidence. Nearly seventy per cent of vacated priory holdings were re-let within months of the Black Death. In his study of bishopric court records, R.H. Britnell charted a very large number of entry fines paid around the time of the plague suggesting many bishopric holdings were successfully re-let. Whether the take-up of holdings around Durham constituted a 'stampede' is doubtful: the bishops at least filled their vacancies by offering tempting favourable terms and, failing that, through coercion.[18] What is clear, however, is that the agricultural land between the Tyne and Tees was not left deserted in the aftermath of the plague.

A full-scale study of the rental evidence in the bursars' accounts of the 1350s and 1360s might further our understanding of the reoccupation of agricultural tenements after the Black Death. This would be a huge task and it has been decided, instead, to use a pilot study of rent collection on the lands of Finchale Priory, a dependency of the Durham Benedictines a few miles up the River Wear. The accounts of the Finchale priors, part of the Durham monastic archive, are much shorter than those of the bursars. Following the usual medieval practice, the Finchale priors entered what should have been received from their rents in the main body of their accounts and then made allowances at the end of each document for rents which were not collected.

---

[11] For the location of this manor, see R.A. Lomas, 'Durham Cathedral Priory as a Landowner and a Landlord, 1290–1540' (unpublished Ph.D. thesis, University of Durham, 1973), p. 218.
[12] J. Hatcher, 'England in the Aftermath of the Black Death', *P&P* 144 (1994), 6.
[13] P.D.A. Harvey, *A Medieval Oxfordshire Village: Cuxham 1240–1400* (London, 1965), p. 44.
[14] J. Hatcher, *Rural Economy and Society in the Duchy of Cornwall* (Cambridge, 1970), pp. 122, 128.
[15] R.A. Lomas, 'The Black Death in County Durham', *JMH* 15 (1989), 131. This seems to be a revision of his earlier estimate that 'less than two-thirds' of holdings were re-let: Lomas, 'Durham Cathedral Priory', p. 29.
[16] Lomas, 'Durham Cathedral Priory', p. 30.
[17] R.A. Lomas, 'Developments in Land Tenure on the Prior of Durham's Estate in the Later Middle Ages', *NH* 13 (1977), 38.
[18] Britnell, 'Feudal Reaction', 31–6.

These allowances fell into one of three categories: arrears, waste and decay. The first applied to rents which the tenant failed to pay. Sometimes the accountants despaired of ever collecting certain arrears (*de quibus non es spes*), as in the case of those from the year of the Black Death whose debtors had 'escaped through death' (*quia debitores evanuerunt per mortalitatem*).[19] Sometimes there was hope of recovering the arrears. In 1354, 55s. 0½d. were owed for tenements at Yokefleet (East Riding, Yorkshire) and the Finchale prior's 'collector of farms' was convinced he would receive the money, even if the accountant was more sceptical.[20] Arrears are an ambiguous indicator for the historian interested in levels of agricultural activity. They suggest tenants were unwilling to pay rents, which could indicate low profits from their fields. On the other hand, if a tenant was in arrears he was still a tenant: the lands were occupied. Despite Lomas's scepticism, mentioned above, wasted rents are a more promising indicator if used with care. Rents were allowed as waste when the tenement lay vacant. At the end of the fourteenth century, for example, the Finchale prior noted that 5s. should have been received from a waste tenement in Durham Bailey and the same from a waste tenement in Elvet.[21] Decays, often accounted for together with waste rents, appear to refer to tenements for which a reduction in rent has been agreed but the accountant still hopes a reversion to the older higher sum may be possible.

The Finchale accounts from the period of rising output indices give ample evidence for difficulties in the collection of rents immediately after the Black Death. The first surviving precisely datable post-plague account, from 1354–5, records arrears of £24 12s. 3½d. from 1349 and £27 1s. 7d. from 1350. These high levels of arrears quickly fell. In his final account William de Goldsburgh answered for £26 15s. 7d. in arrears which he had hoped to collect at the beginning of the accounting period; by the end of the account, he answered for only £15 14s. 4d. He appears to have successfully collected old arrears and avoided accumulating new ones.[22] The first account of John de Tickhill, beginning on 15 May 1363, lists only £9 13s. 9½d. in arrears from the whole of Goldsburgh's priorate which stretched over the second half of the 1350s.[23] This evidence suggests that rent collection became much easier after the beginning of the 1350s, which could confirm the agrarian recovery indicated by the tithe evidence. However, rents and their arrears are notoriously deceptive economic indicators: it is difficult, and sometimes impossible, to tell from the accounts if and when certain arrears were written off and no longer entered.

More persuasive supporting evidence for the recovery in production is the level of waste recorded in the Finchale priors' accounts. No sums of money were 'exonerated' in the series of surviving accounts on grounds of wasted or decayed rents between

---

[19] *Priory of Finchale*, appendix, p. xxxvi.
[20] Ibid., appendix, p. xxxvii: 'Item lv s. ob. de arreragiis de Yukflet, de tempore domini Johannis de Norton, qui levari poterint si fidelitas Johannis de Lynton [later described as *collector firmarum*] cum sua industria conveniret'.
[21] Ibid., appendix, p. cxxiv.
[22] Ibid., appendix, pp. xlix, li.
[23] Ibid., appendix, p. lxii. On the basis of the periods of account, Goldsburgh's priorate seems to have run from 1 March 1355 to 18 May 1360: ibid., appendix, pp. xxxix–liv; Piper, *Medieval Accounting Material*.

1347–8 and 1361–2.[24] This contrasts starkly with the higher waste and decay figures of the 1430s and 1440s (see below) and suggests that tenements were filled during the period of rising production levels in the aftermath of the Black Death. If tenements were occupied, as the lack of reference to waste suggests, and rents increasingly collected, as the falling arrears levels suggest, then the figure 12.1 evidence for rising production levels is supported.

The tithe sections of the Durham accounts can also be used to test the implied pattern of high occupation of tenements in the Finchale priors' accounts of the 1350s and early 1360s. Just as auditors were interested in the failure of accountants to produce money owed for rented property, so they concerned themselves with vills from which an expected tithe was not received. The Durham Priory parishes between Tyne and Tees each consisted of several vills and sometimes a situation arose where tithe could not be collected from one or more of these units because they were 'waste' or 'unsown'. In 1390–1, for example, the bursar recorded receipts from the Aycliffe parish vills of Aycliffe, Heworth, Preston le Skerne, Newton Ketton, Brafferton, Nunstainton, Woodham and Newhouse; the vills of Ricknall Grange and Grindon, however, produced no receipts because they were waste.[25] Figure 12.2 shows the percentage of vills entered in the accounts and described as 'waste' or 'unsown'. The number of surviving accounts varies from year to year and not all accountants were equally rigorous: for this reason decennial averages were used. The pattern in which tithing vills fell waste closely resembles that for the vacant Finchale tenements in the aftermath of the Black Death. There is no record of waste during the 1350s but entries begin to appear in the following decade.

Evidence of Black Death mortality contained in the priory's lists of tenants who died in the *pestilencia magna* indicates a death rate of slightly over fifty per cent. The worst-affected township was Jarrow where seventy-eight per cent of tenants succumbed and the least affected, despite its proximity, was Monkton where only twenty-one per cent perished.[26] The demographic evidence for the impact of the plague suggests a fall of both population and production of over half by 1350 and yet between 1358 and 1364 production levels were over seventy per cent of pre-plague levels. It would have been impossible for population to recover in so short a time so there must have been an increase in arable output per head.

The simple comparison between Lomas's mortality figures and the pattern of output shown in figure 12.1 (period 1) seems to confirm suggestions made by Postan. He argued that, in the wake of the Black Death, cultivation contracted from marginal areas to the fertile core: as fewer mouths needed feeding, plots of land newly cultivated in the thirteenth and fourteenth centuries were left unsown. Naturally, husbandmen abandoned the least fertile land first which meant that overall production fell but production per acre increased.[27] He also emphasised the under-employment of labour during the period of higher population in the early fourteenth century. Following Ricardo's argument, it is implied that this process would be reversed when

---

[24] *Priory of Finchale*, appendix, pp. xxvii–lviii.
[25] DCM, Bursar's Account Rolls, 1390–1, *Decime* (Aycliffe).
[26] Lomas, 'Black Death', 127–40.
[27] M.M. Postan, 'The Economic Foundations of Medieval Society', in idem, *Essays on Medieval Agriculture and General Problems of the Medieval Economy* (Cambridge, 1973), p. 14.

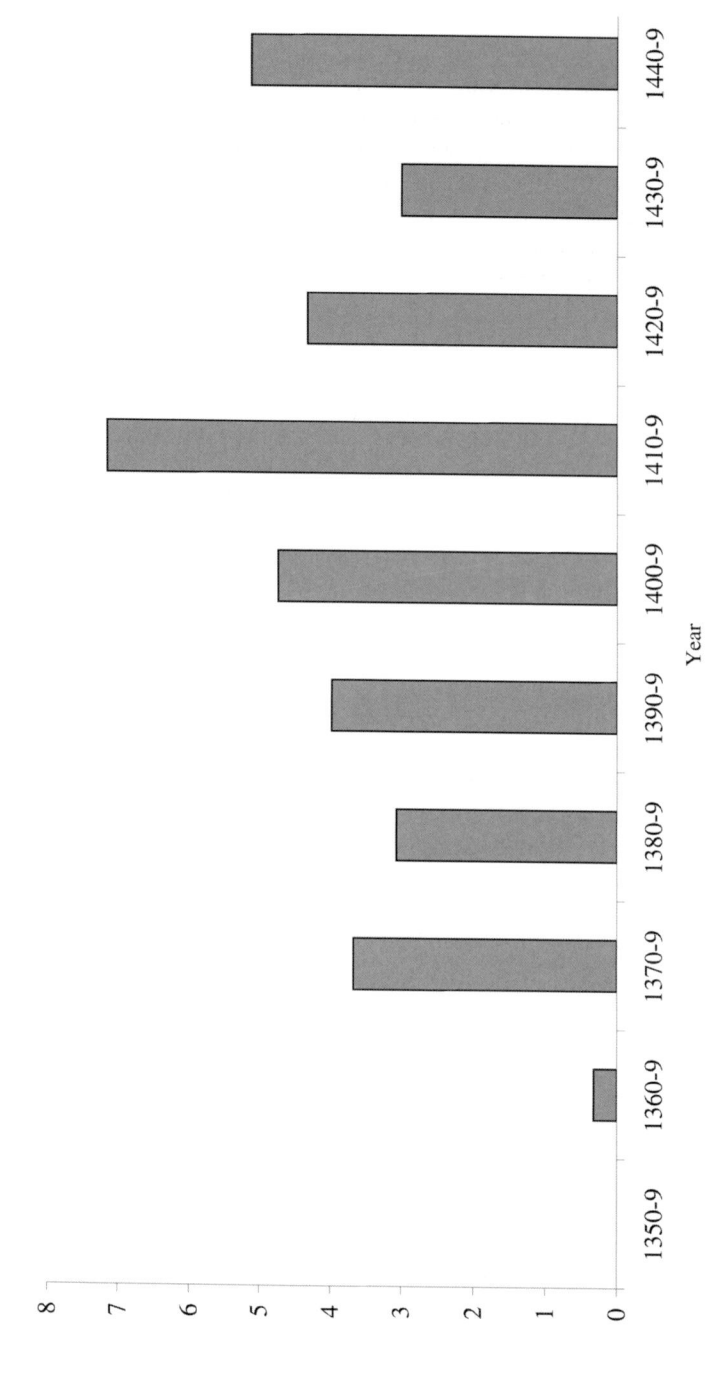

Fig. 12.2 Decennial average percentage of vills recorded as 'waste' or 'not sown' in the Durham Priory bursars' accounts

population declined: overall production levels would fall but the marginal product of labour would increase.[28]

Closer interpretation of the tithe waste evidence in figure 12.2 enables Postan's hypothesis to be tested. A vill in which the cultivated area declined was not necessarily laid waste. Each vill contained a number of holdings and would have yielded a tithe even if only one of these were occupied. Figure 12.2 does not preclude a retreat from the margin to the fertile core during the 1350s. In fact, court roll evidence suggests that this is exactly what did happen. In 1352 the bishop's steward had to force the peasants of Sedgefield to leave one-third of their land fallow, as had been their traditional practice. It seems that they had begun to sow even the third field with grain in the early 1350s. Bradshaw explained this apparently bizarre behaviour as follows:

> It seems probable that as each man had more land at his disposal while labour was dear, the peasants had decided to go in for 'extensive' as opposed to 'intensive' cultivation, or at any rate only to sow the most fertile patches of each field.[29]

Later priory halmote evidence supports this suggestion: in 1367 the West Merrington peasants refused to sow the outer parts of their arable land (*exteriores partes campi*).[30] Although outside the period under consideration, and therefore too late to explain the 1350s recovery in output levels directly, this example shows the type of device by which a reduced number of peasants may have expanded their *per capita* output.

The post-Black Death recovery in output levels may have been achieved in part by a retreat from the margin to the fertile core. Other evidence suggests, however, that this did not operate in quite the way originally envisaged by Ricardo. It has long been observed that the chronology was not simple and that the Black Death not necessarily the sudden turning point from demographic expansion to decline.[31] Affected by the famines in the second decade of the fourteenth century, Durham had also suffered severe disruption because of Anglo-Scottish hostilities. The Durham monks themselves calculated that their tithe income had fallen to forty-two per cent of its 1293 level by 1348.[32] Nevertheless, for parts of southern England, it is maintained that there was sufficient over-capacity before 1347–9 to enable a speedy recovery despite demographic disaster: A.R. Bridbury's famous 'submerged and pullulating throng' of landless labourers and vagrants suddenly grasped a golden opportunity.[33]

Even before the ravages of the early fourteenth century, however, Durham could hardly have been described as 'overpopulated'. Britnell's work on the Haswell

---

[28] M.M. Postan, 'Medieval Agrarian Society in its Prime: England', in *The Cambridge Economic History of Europe, I: The Agrarian Life of the Middle Ages*, ed. M.M. Postan (2nd edn., Cambridge, 1966), pp. 622–32; Hatcher and Bailey, *Modelling the Middle Ages*, pp. 24–5, 38–9; B.M.S. Campbell, *English Seigniorial Agriculture 1250–1450* (Cambridge, 2000), p. 24.

[29] Bradshaw, 'Social and Economic History', p. 216.

[30] Ibid., p. 217; *HPD*, p. 65.

[31] B.F. Harvey, 'Introduction: The 'Crisis' of the Early Fourteenth Century', in *Before the Black Death: Studies in the 'Crisis' of the Early Fourteenth Century*, ed. B.M.S. Campbell (Manchester, 1991), pp. 1–24.

[32] *Scriptores Tres*, appendix, p. ccl.

[33] Bridbury, 'Black Death', 590; C. Dyer, *Making a Living in the Middle Ages: The People of Britain 850–1520* (New Haven, 2002), pp. 279, 293–4. See also J. Kanzaka, 'Villein Rents in Thirteenth-Century England: An Analysis of the Hundred Rolls of 1279–80', *EcHR* 55 (2002), 598.

charters suggests that there never ceased to be an abundance of moorland and pasture in this lightly populated area; moreover, this is confirmed by the 'informality' of arrangements for farming these lands 'that could hardly have been tolerated in a large Midland village'.[34] The mapping work of Simon Harris and Helen Dunsford has revealed great tracts of wasteland in Durham in the seventeenth century which, they argue, was probably largely uncultivated during the Middle Ages. Evidence from charters and from the exchequer land sections of the Hatfield Survey indicates the timing of expansion of the cultivated area between the Tyne and Tees. After a limited initial phase in the second half of the twelfth century, there is a substantial collection of waste grants from the pontificates of Walter de Kirkham and Richard Kellawe, that is, from the mid-thirteenth century until 1316. This is late by comparison with southern evidence. In the light of colonisation of waste at so late a date and the probable continued existence of tracts of wasteland, it seems inconceivable that there could have been a floating mass of landless labourers in Durham who were desperate to take on holdings in the 1340s.[35]

The enigmatic rise in productivity after the Black Death, supported by both tithe and rental evidence, cannot be explained solely in terms of a liberation of the supply of land. Land had always been available and tenants were not necessarily found even before the plague. Nevertheless, the 1350s saw a drastic change in the relationship between population and resources and those cultivating the land responded to this change. Tenants were able to use land in a different way and, in so doing, achieve greater productivity. Of course, increased productivity would only be achieved in circumstances of increasing *per capita* demand. One indicator of the buoyancy of demand is the rise in prices which followed the plague, as shown in figure 12.3. Given that it is unlikely that significantly greater quantities of grain were exported from north-eastern England in the 1350s and early 1360s, the only possible explanation for the maintenance of demand levels is an increase in consumption per head. Evidence for peasant diets is scanty, but Christopher Dyer's work on liveries to harvest workers suggests grain consumption did increase in the aftermath of the plague: more wheat was used for the baking of bread and more barley for the brewing of ale. The grinding of grain to produce flour, and especially the brewing of grain to produce ale, were more roundabout means of preparing cereals for consumption than cooking less-processed grain in the form of pottage. More grain was needed to provide the same kilocalorie output.[36] These dietary changes were long-term but they appear to have been sharpest in the decades immediately following the Black Death.[37] In this way, fewer people could have enjoyed a better diet through using more grain.

This detailed analysis of period 1 in figure 12.1 indicates, in the first place, that the post-Black Death recovery in production levels was a real phenomenon. The manorial

---

Kanzaka's research demonstrates population pressure in the late thirteenth century but considerably modifies the classic Postan interpretation.

[34] R.H. Britnell, 'Between Durham and the Sea, 1100–1300' (University of Durham, Inaugural Lecture, 25 October 2000).

[35] H.M. Dunsford and S.J. Harris, 'Colonization of the Wasteland in County Durham, 1100–1400', *EcHR* 56 (2003), 34–56.

[36] Campbell, *Seigniorial Agriculture*, pp. 387, 398.

[37] C. Dyer, *Standards of Living in the Later Middle Ages* (revised edn., Cambridge, 1998), pp. 158–9.

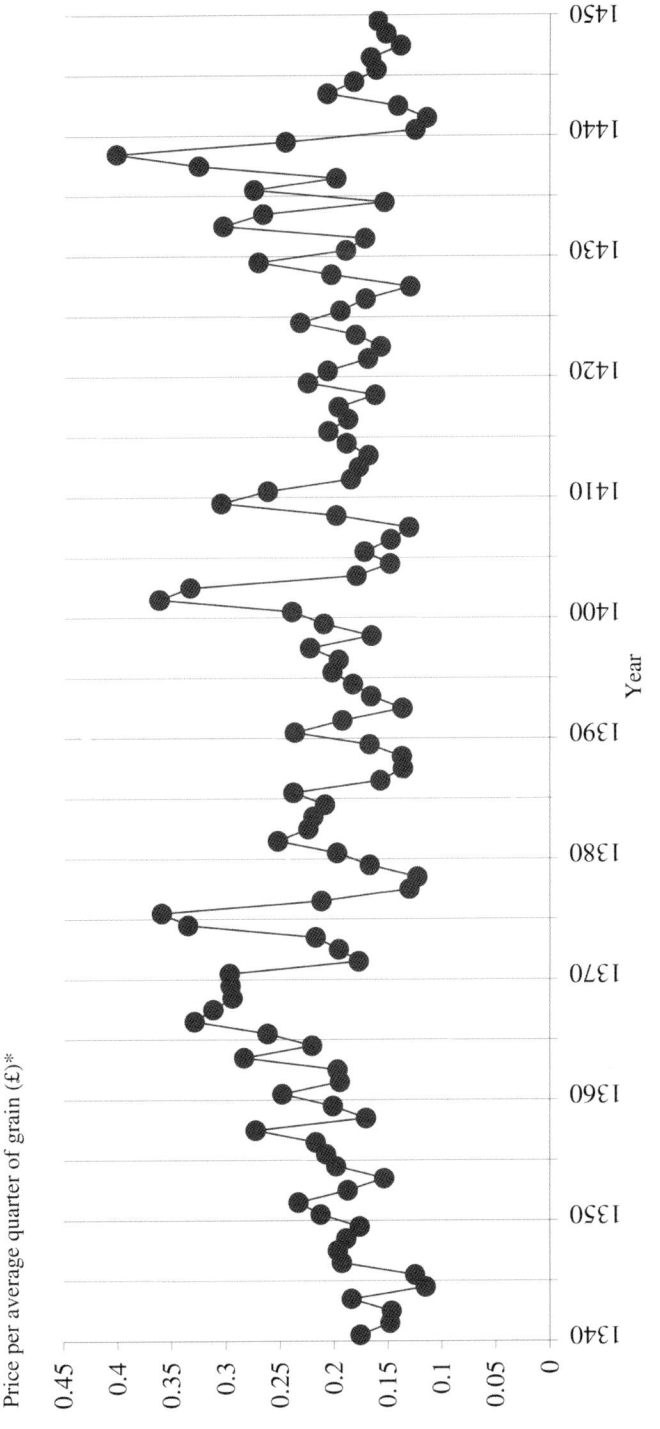

Fig. 12.3 Durham grain price data collected by Lord Beveridge's International Committee on Wages and Prices

Note: * the composition of an average quarter of grain is based on grain tithe receipts, i.e. grain received from appropriated parishes where the tithes were not sold.

Source: boxes C1, C2, C3, C4, C5, C6, C7, C8(i) and C8(ii), The Beveridge Price History Archive (British Library of Political and Economic Science).

and rental figures confirm the pattern suggested by the tithe evidence. Rising productivity is explicable in terms of the changing relationship between population and resources. Whilst land had never been scarce between Tyne and Tees, the 'Great Pestilence' bequeathed a new abundance of the county's most fertile land to its survivors. The growth in *per capita* demand needed to consume the grain output is conceivable within the bounds of the evidence. Most striking, however, is the adaptability of those cultivating the land. In his survey of statistical and chronicle evidence, Dyer judged that '[t]here may have been despondency after the plague, but the survivors appreciated the new opportunities'.[38] This is exactly what the Durham peasants did: they were able to use their resources more efficiently and, in so doing, improved their own standards of living. This apparent adaptability of peasant cultivators has been observed in other contexts. David Stone discovered the managers of the backwater Suffolk demesne of Hinderclay employing sophisticated yield-raising techniques when the market conditions were encouraging. He speculated that this commercial and technological awareness must have filtered through to peasant farmers some of whom, after all, managed the demesne land.[39] In a different context, N. Plack observed the responsiveness to demand of eighteenth-century peasants in southern France who took advantage of the developing Mediterranean wine trade and turned their lands over to vines.[40] Though on a smaller scale, peasant cultivators in parts of Castile showed similar adaptability by turning to viticulture in the late Middle Ages.[41] The Durham tithe evidence for the period 1350–64 throws light on the mentality of peasant cultivators who were able to seize an economic opportunity in the wake of serious human catastrophe.

Period 2 in figure 12.1 was chosen for detailed analysis because it presents one of the sharpest downturns of the whole series. Four decades had passed since the Black Death. Production levels now fell below fifty-three per cent of 1340s levels for nine harvests between 1390 and 1402. The bursars' practice of listing grain receipts from tithes which were not sold, introduced in the late 1370s, means we also have grain receipts with which to test the validity of the deflated cash receipts in figure 12.1.[42] Figures 12.4, 12.5, 12.6 and 12.7 confirm that output had reached low, and sometimes very low levels, around the turn of the century in Billingham parish. All four graphs also show a broad downward trend from 1396. Most usefully, these direct output graphs confirm the very low output levels in 1402 for which the estimated index in figure 12.1 is unreliable because of the exceptionally high grain prices in that year. South Sherburn is the only vill from which we have grain tithe receipts from 1349 with which to compare the turn of the century crisis. The vill produced 32.3q. as tithe

---

[38] Dyer, *Making a Living*, p. 74.
[39] D. Stone, 'Medieval Farm Management and Technological Mentalities: Hinderclay before the Black Death', *EcHR* 54 (2001), 612, 634.
[40] N. Plack, 'Viticulture and Wine Trade in 18th-Century Languedoc' (paper presented to the Economic History Society Conference, April 2002).
[41] J. Valdeón Baruque, 'Parte Primera: Los Países de la Corona de Castilla', in *Historia de España Menéndez Pidal, tomo XII: La Baja Edad Media peninsular siglos XIII al XV: La Población, la Economía, la Sociedad*, ed. J. Valdeón Baruque and J.L. Martín Rodríguez (Madrid, 1996), pp. 136–8.
[42] The introduction of a new system for recording grain tithe receipts in the accounts of the Durham bursars is described in detail in Dodds, 'Tithe and Agrarian Output', pp. 98–104.

PEASANTS, LANDLORDS & PRODUCTION BETWEEN THE TYNE & TEES 185

Fig. 12.4 Total grain tithe receipts from Billingham

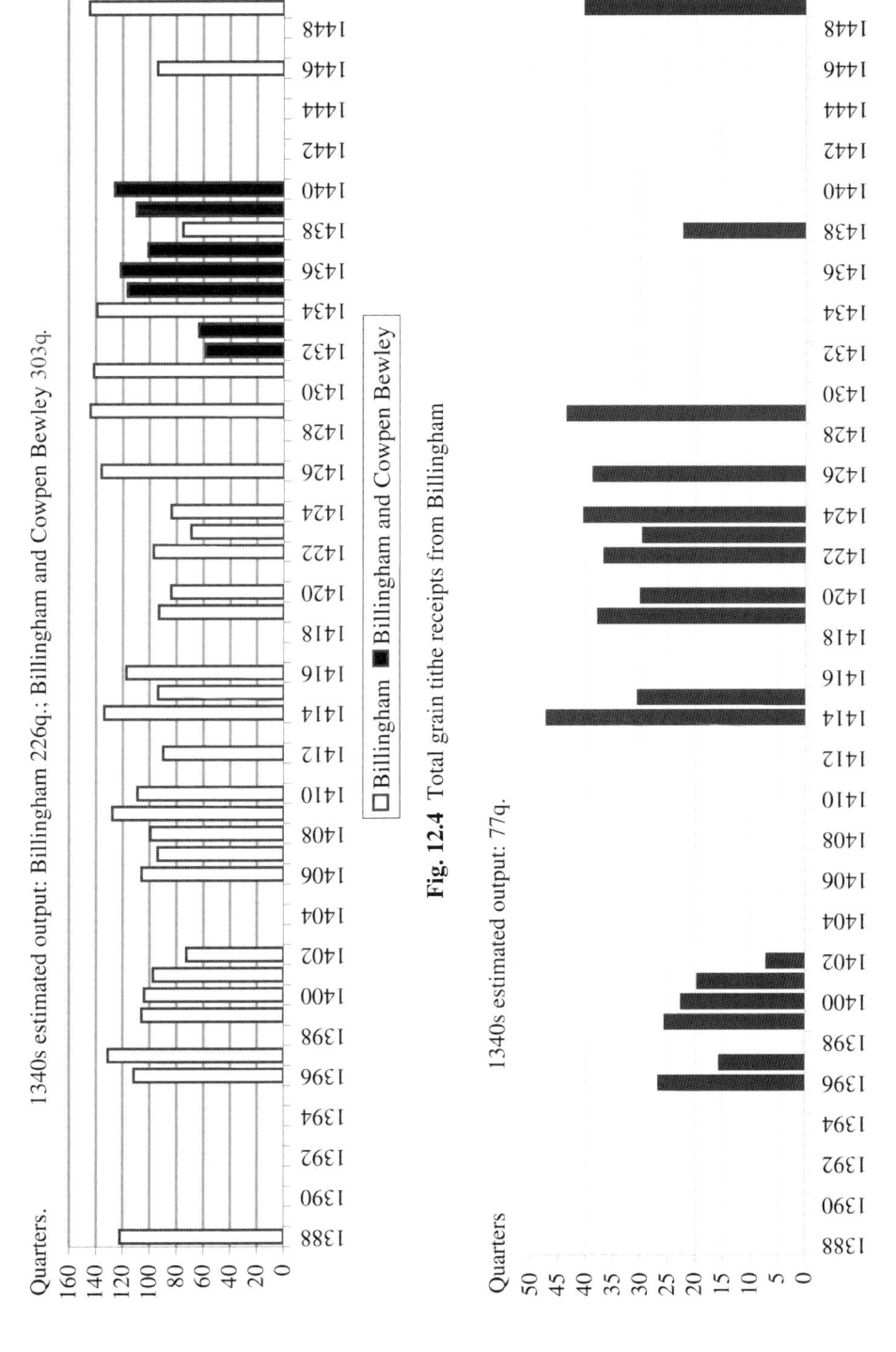

Fig. 12.5 Total grain tithe receipts from Cowpen Bewley (Billingham parish)

186 BEN DODDS

Fig. 12.6 Total grain tithe receipts from Newton Bewley (Billingham parish)

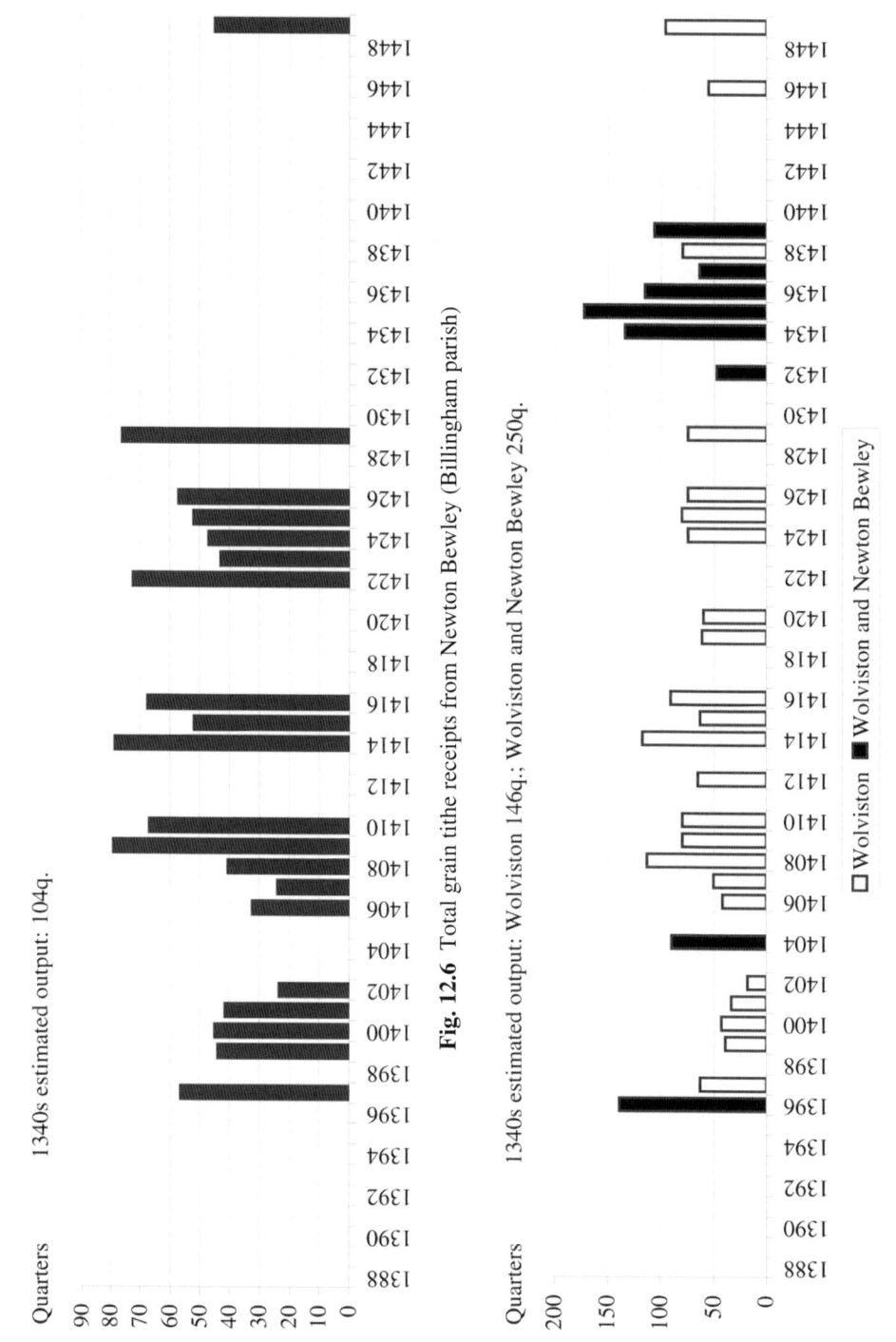

Fig. 12.7 Total grain tithe receipts from Wolviston (Billingham parish)

in 1349 but in 1402 this was two-thirds lower at only 9.9q. There is a strong body of tithe evidence demonstrating low arable output levels at the turn of the century.

The pattern in figure 12.1 is confirmed by demesne and rental evidence. When demesne farming became unprofitable, landlords often resorted to leasing their manors. Leasing became increasingly frequent after the Black Death and especially at the end of the fourteenth century.[43] Durham was no exception to this pattern: only one of Durham Priory's demesnes was newly leased between 1350 and 1373 but between the latter date and 1416 ten more were rented out.[44] Production was severely curtailed on those manors which remained in hand. Figure 12.8 shows that the cultivated area at the manor of Pittington, which accounted to the bursar and terrar, was cut back during the 1390s to levels low by comparison with those of the previous two decades. Difficulties in rent collection also increased in the 1390s. Allowances for wasted and decayed rents were almost totally absent from the Finchale priors' accounts of the 1370s, but they reappear in the 1390s.[45] Rent collection became exceptionally difficult by the end of the decade. When he took over the Finchale priorate in 1397, Robert Ripon answered for the second highest arrears sum from the printed series of accounts of the second half of the fourteenth century.[46] Lomas's examination of the terms under which tenants of the Durham Priory held their land also indicates the landlords' desperation to fill vacant holdings during the 1390s.[47] The agricultural landscape must have looked increasingly deserted, as is also apparent from the lists of waste tithing vills. Figure 12.2 shows a significant increase during the 1370s, a slight fall in the 1380s, and then an explosion in the number of vills recorded as waste over the following three decades.

By the end of the fourteenth century, society had been ravaged not just by the Black Death but by repeated outbreaks of pestilence.[48] The demographic effect of endemic plague is complicated but it appears population levels may have sustained some recovery in the wake of the Black Death but then fallen again and floundered at between one-third and one-half of pre-plague levels.[49] This may have been the result of the specific biological nature of the plague: the lottery of genetics meant that if an individual survived one outbreak then he was likely to survive the next. The result would be a larger proportion of children and young adults decimated in post-1349 outbreaks; by the end of the century, these missing generations would have an effect not only on economic productivity but also replacement rates. The best English evidence for this comes from Halesowen in the West Midlands, where Z. Razi discovered that people were on average much older in 1393 than in 1350.[50]

---

[43] B. Harvey, *Westminster Abbey and its Estates in the Middle Ages* (Oxford, 1977), p. 151; C. Dyer, *Lords and Peasants in a Changing Society: The Estates of the Bishopric of Worcester, 680–1540* (Cambridge, 1980), pp. 147–8; D.V. Stern and C. Thornton, *A Hertfordshire Demesne of Westminster Abbey: Profits, Productivity and Weather* (Hatfield, 2000), p. 54; G.A. Holmes, *The Estates of the Higher Nobility in Fourteenth Century England* (Cambridge, 1957), p. 116.
[44] Lomas, 'Durham Cathedral Priory', pp. 117–24; Lomas, 'Priory of Durham and its Demesnes', 345.
[45] *Priory of Finchale*, appendix, pp. lxxxiv–cii, cvii, cix, cxi, cxiii, cxvi, cxxi, cxxiii.
[46] Ibid., appendix, p. cxxiii. The highest level was answered for by John de Tickhill in 1365–6: ibid., appendix, p. lxxi.
[47] Lomas, 'Black Death', 135.
[48] Hatcher, *Plague, Population and the English Economy*, pp. 23–5; Dyer, *Making a Living*, pp. 274–5.
[49] Hatcher, *Plague, Population and the English Economy*, p. 31; Poos, *Rural Society*, p. 96; Postles, 'Demographic Change in Kibworth Harcourt', 46.
[50] Razi, *Life, Marriage and Death*, p. 151. More wide-ranging evidence of the same phenomenon in Italy

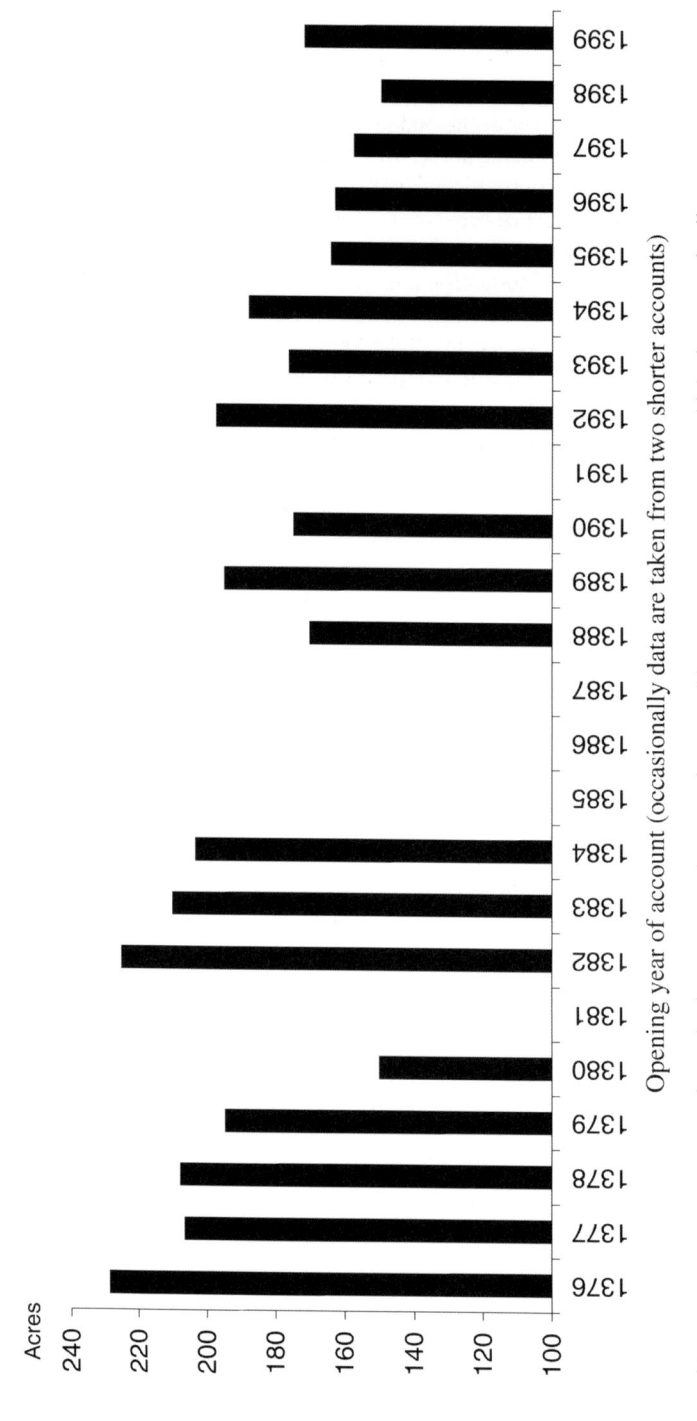

Fig. 12.8 Estimated total sown acreage on Pittington demesne, 1376–1399

Note: sown acreages were estimated using mean sowing rates from the fifteenth-century accounts (occasionally data are taken from two shorter accounts which give more details).

Source: DCM, Pittington manor accounts, 1376–7, 1377–8, 1378–9, 1379–80, 1380, 1380–1, 1382, 1382–3, 1383–4, 1384–5, 1388–9, 1398–90, 1390–1, 1392–3, 1393–4, 1394–5, 1395–6, 1396–7, 1397–8, 1398–9, 1399–1400.

Durham was badly affected by further plague outbreaks but there is no direct evidence for population levels around the turn of the century. Certainly, plague mortality had been high in the early 1390s.[51] Lomas described the fall in the number of tenants between the 1347–8 bursar's rental and that from 1396–7 as '[t]he hint that the population was about 45% lower at the end of the century than it was just before the plague of 1349'.[52] The possibility that this was caused by age-specific outbreaks of plague is suggested by the demographic evidence from the community of Benedictine monks at Durham: if a member of the community survived one outbreak, then he stood a better chance of surviving the next.[53]

The relationship between low production and population levels is clarified by an examination of the labour sections of the Pittington manorial accounts, as the case of one individual worker will serve to illustrate.[54] William Coatham lived in a cottage in Pittington and had his own garden for which he paid 18d. in 1396–7.[55] For over fifteen years, between 1393 and 1410, Coatham worked as a servant (*famulus*) on the Pittington manor. His main role was as a ploughman but he also assisted in threshing, mowing, weeding and harvesting. When Coatham began work he was paid an annual cash stipend of 14s. At least as valuable as his cash stipend was his wheat livery which was paid at a rate of a quarter of grain every twelve weeks. If baked as bread, this wheat would have provided sufficient calories for a small family to survive:[56] the existence of such a family is suggested by the appearance of a Robert Coatham in the Pittington accounts of 1408–9 and 1409–10. There were additional perks from which William also benefited such as a pair of harvest gloves and the shared harvest '*ladegoose*' feast. It is not clear from the accounts, but he may have eaten and drunk at his employer's expense at other times. During the final decade of the fourteenth century, William Coatham and his family must have experienced a significant rise in their standard of living. Whilst his wheat livery remained at the same level, his cash stipend rose steadily. Having started on 14s., his stipend rose to 15s. and then 16s. by 1400. Unfortunately there are no Pittington manor accounts between 1399–1400 and 1405–6 but, by the latter year, he earned 18s. During the 1390s alone, Coatham's cash income increased by nearly fifteen per cent; when he had worked on the demesne for twelve years, it was nearly thirty per cent higher than when he started. Prices in this

---

can be found in D. Herlihy, *Medieval and Renaissance Pistoia: The Social History of an Italian Town 1207–1430* (New Haven, 1967), p. 100, and D. Herlihy and C. Klapisch-Zuber, *Tuscans and Their Families: A Study of the Florentine Catasto of 1427* (New Haven, 1985).

51 Chronicle evidence: *Polychronicon Ranulphi Higden Monachis Cestrensis*, ed. C. Babington and J. Rawson (9 vols., Rolls Series, London, 1865–6), IX, 237–8, 259; C. Creighton, *A History of Epidemics in Britain from A.D. 664 to the Extinction of the Plague* (2 vols., Cambridge, 1891), I, 220. The widespread election of reeves in the Durham priory and bishopric halmotes suggests that there was high mortality during these years between the Tyne and Tees (I am grateful to Peter Larson for supplying me with this information).

52 Lomas, 'Black Death', 135.

53 A personal communication from A.J. Piper.

54 Unless otherwise stated, the following details have been taken from DCM, Pittington Manor Accounts, 1393–4, 1394–5, 1395–6, 1396–7, 1397–8, 1398–9, 1399–1400, 1405–6, 1406–7, 1407–8, 1408–9, 1409–10.

55 *Durham Cathedral Priory Rentals: Vol. 1, Bursar's Rentals*, ed. R.A. Lomas and A.J. Piper (Surtees Society 198, 1986), p. 91.

56 Coatham received 4.33q. of wheat each year. Dyer estimated that one person needed twelve bushels each year, with which he would have enough corn to make 1½ or 1¾ lbs. of bread daily, yielding almost 2,000 calories: Dyer, *Standards of Living*, p. 153.

period had shown no offsetting increase; a representative basket of consumables cost much the same in 1406 as in 1393.[57] Payments made to all the Pittington *famuli* show a rise in the modal cash stipend from 12s. in 1376–7 to 16s. in 1399–1400. Whilst the stipends continued their upward trend into the 1440s, the last quarter of the fourteenth century saw the steepest rises. The payments made to other workers on the demesne also rose.[58]

This period of sharply increasing wages is well known from other English evidence: a steep rise from the mid-1390s is apparent in D.L. Farmer's aggregate data.[59] The story of William Coatham is good indirect evidence for low population levels around the turn of the century.[60] The rising cost of labour is also good reason for the cutback in sown acreages on demesnes, and the increasing number of leases, but it is not such an obvious explanation for falling production levels on peasant land. It has been suggested, for example, that peasant production would be less susceptible to the problem of rising wages since more unpaid family labour would be used on non-seigniorial strips. This does not appear to have militated against low production levels between the Tyne and Tees at the end of the fourteenth century. Either peasant cultivators were using paid labour and forced to curtail sown acreages as this became increasingly expensive, like the lords, or the high wage levels obtainable meant they neglected their own lands. Around the turn of the century, peasants must have been faced with new decisions: opportunities elsewhere were good. However, too much weight should not be given to the very low output levels of the late 1390s. After the end of period 2 on figure 12.1 production levels enjoyed some recovery. It appears that the short-term disruption caused by high mortality, possibly combined with poor weather conditions, was responsible for the exceptionally low levels of 1400–2.

The association between low population, the desertion of lands and falling production around half a century after the Black Death seems to be strong on the basis of tithe, manorial and rental evidence. However, the precise relationship between production and population is more complicated. Lomas warned that a collapse in tithe income may not translate to an equivalent drop in population. He observed that tithe receipts from Aycliffe parish fell more between 1348 and 1396 than did income from mills and the number of tenants. This he attributed to the fact that 'the priory had no way of directing the farming policies of most of the farmers of the parish'. He justified this statement by comparing a vill which belonged to the priory to one which did not (but still owed tithes to the priory). He found that income from the latter fell far more between 1348 and 1396. This he attributed to the substitution of arable cultivation for pastoral.[61] Indeed, the monks themselves partly blamed the fall in their tithe revenues on lords who had turned arable land over to pasture.[62]

It is possible that increased numbers of livestock compensated for the fall in grain production meaning that the total output from the land did not fall as much as figure

---

[57] D.L. Farmer, 'Prices and Wages, 1350–1500', in *The Agrarian History of England and Wales, III: 1348–1500*, ed. E. Miller (Cambridge, 1991), pp. 521–2.
[58] B. Dodds, 'Workers on the Pittington Demesne in the Late Middle Ages', *AA*, 5th ser. 28 (2000), 151–2.
[59] Farmer, 'Prices and Wages, 1350–1500', p. 437.
[60] Hatcher, *Plague, Population and the English Economy*, p. 48.
[61] Lomas, 'Black Death', 136.
[62] *Scriptores Tres*, appendix, p. ccl.

12.1 suggests. The evidence for levels of pastoral production between the Tyne and Tees is thin. There are hardly any references to livestock tithes from this area in the priory accounting material and even the demesne evidence is difficult to interpret. Whilst the priory kept stock on many of its manors, the flocks and herds were accounted for through two centres at Muggleswick and Saltholme, near Billingham.[63] We have a dozen enrolled stock accounts from between 1340 and the end of the century. The existence of at least thirty-nine different stock centres managed from Muggleswick and Saltholme makes the collection of a series of comparable figures for the priory's flocks and herds very difficult to compile.[64] Muggleswick, although well represented in the accounting material, was really a group of stock centres since it was connected with at least sixteen different places.[65] Given the incomplete state of many of the enrolled accounts, it is not possible to put together a list of Muggleswick stock in which all these centres are fully represented for each year. Saltholme, on the other hand, was a less sprawling operation. The livestock accounts only mention its connections with 'Bartoncotes' and 'Hoggecote', and it is possible to extract a useful series of sheep numbers from both the enrolled and individual stock accounts. Figure 12.9 presents the number of breeding ewes recorded as remaining at the beginning of the accounting period at Saltholme. Unfortunately the survival of accounts is very poor for the second half of the fourteenth century. However, it appears that there was only a slight fall in the number of breeding ewes after the Black Death and that numbers were buoyant at the end of the 1380s and 1390s. The sheep operation at Saltholme was not scaled down to the same extent as the sown acreage at Pittington (figure 12.8) or the overall arable output index (figure 12.1).

The increasing importance of livestock operations on demesnes in southern England during the late fourteenth century is well established.[66] Although in parts of northern England the agrarian economy was primarily pastoral before the Black Death, in the lowland parishes appropriated to Durham Priory between Tyne and Tees, the mid-fourteenth-century economy was primarily arable.[67] The Saltholme sheep evidence, supported by the monks' own mention of land turned over to pasture, suggests the second half of the fourteenth century may have seen flocks and herds increase at the expense of arable. It seems certain that the low arable output indices of the 1390s reflect demographic decline but they may also reflect shifting agricultural practice. Flocks of sheep, after all, were a much less expensive means of deriving some return from land than arable cultivation during a period of acute labour shortage.

---

[63] E.M. Halcrow, 'Administration and Agrarian Policy of the Manors of Durham Cathedral Priory' (unpublished B.Litt. thesis, University of Oxford, 1949), pp. 2, 10, 69. The documents themselves refer to 'Le Holme', as does Piper, *Medieval Accounting Material*. The gazetteer in *Durham Cathedral Priory Rentals*, however, describes 'the separate manor of Saltholme in marshland to the east [which] was let for a corn-rent until 1350, when it became the priory's principal lowland centre of sheep-farming' (p. 208). Modern maps identify Salt Holme to the east of Billingham new town. Although identification of modern Salt Holme with medieval 'Le Holme' is probably not exact, the term 'Saltholme' has been used here for convenience

[64] This figure is taken from Piper, *Medieval Accounting Material*.

[65] *Durham Cathedral Priory Rentals*, p. 218; Piper, *Medieval Accounting Material*.

[66] Campbell, *Seigniorial Agriculture*, p. 178.

[67] Lomas, 'Black Death', 132.

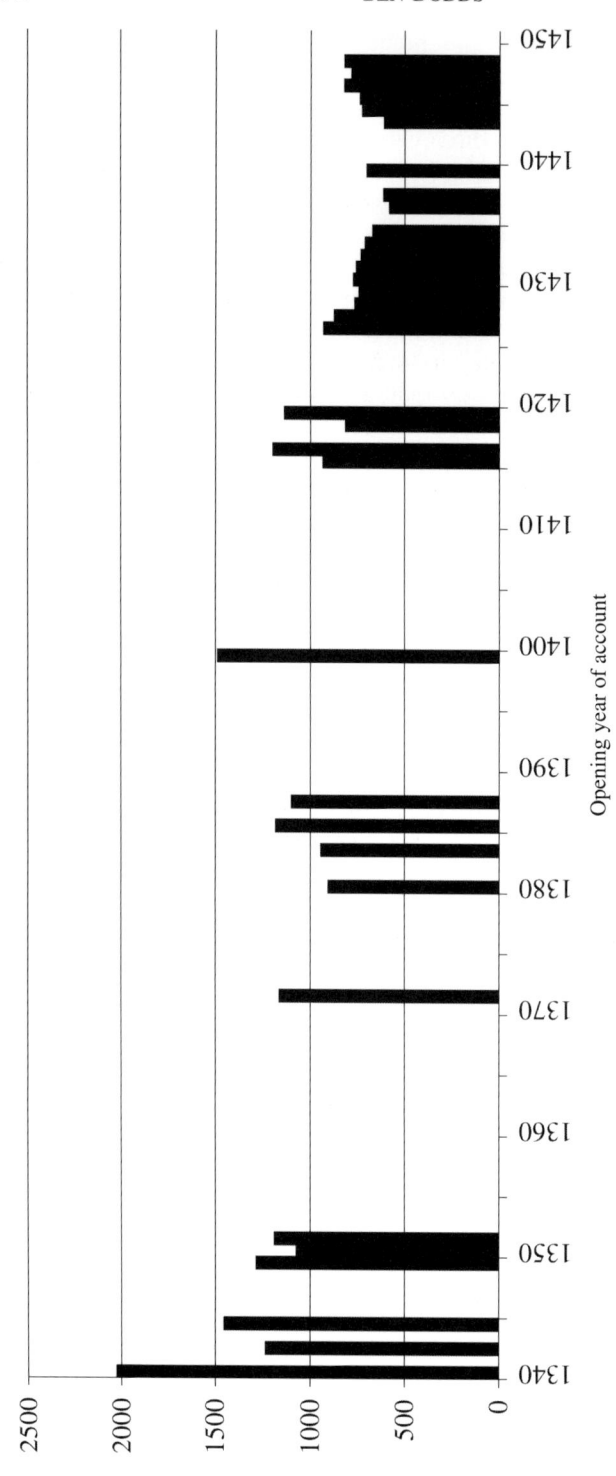

Fig. 12.9 Number of breeding ewes at Saltholme, near Billingham

Source: DCM, enrolled livestock accounts, 1340–1, 1342–3, 1343–4, 1344–5, 1349–50, 1350–1, 1351–2, 1371–2, 1380–1, 1383–4, 1385–6, 1387–8, 1399–1400, 1416–17, 1420–1; DCM Holme livestock accounts, 1415–16, 1418–19, 1419–20, 1420–1, 1426–7, 1427–8, 1428–9, 1429–30, 1430–1, 1431–2, 1432–3, 1433–4, 1434–5, 1435–6, 1436–7, 1437–8, 1439–40, 1443–4, 1444–5, 1445–6, 1447–8, 1448–9.

*

Period 3 in figure 12.1 encloses the worst crisis in arable production in the whole series. It contains the two lowest arable output indices, if price crisis years are excluded, and five of the lowest of the years of very high grain prices are included. The only years of comparably low output indices are those of the crisis at the turn of the century. The wild fluctuation of prices throughout the 1430s (figure 12.3) confirms the likelihood of agrarian disruption but does not inspire confidence in the precision of figure 12.1. Figures 12.4 and 12.7 confirm that output levels did fall very low in Billingham parish during that decade. In particular, Billingham and Cowpen Bewley produced very little in 1432 and 1433; the Wolviston and Newton Bewley combined receipt was also very low in 1432. In Billingham parish, at least, the harvests at the end of the decade were not quite as disastrous as those at the beginning although output levels were very low. Other vills, with patchier series of grain tithe receipts, do show very low production levels at the end of the decade. Aycliffe, in particular, produced less than a third of its 1433 level in 1438.

Following the lease of nearly all the priory manors by the middle of the second decade of the fifteenth century, we have little demesne evidence to support the pattern shown in figure 12.1. However, the 1430s and 1440s did see the worst concentration of rental arrears in the whole series of accounts from Finchale Priory. William Barry did not allow for any arrears from the current accounting year in 1430–1 but in the following year he was owed £39 2s. 4d.[68] In 1436–7 he was owed the astronomical sum of £53 18s. 3¾d. for payments due in the accounting year which had just ended: this constituted nearly one-third of the amount he should have received in assized rents, mill rents and tithes.[69] Rental arrears spiralled out of control on the prior of Finchale's properties during the 1430s and 1440s and must have precipitated a cash flow crisis in the monastery. Debt lists do not appear in William Barry's accounts of the 1430s but when he ceased to be prior in 1439 a rental was produced listing £109 11s. 9d. of unpaid debts.[70]

The 1430s saw an unusual conjunction of exceptionally poor weather conditions and high mortality. The Crowland Chronicle, for example, mentions three wet harvests in succession at the end of the 1430s and other evidence suggests conditions were exceptionally bad from Scotland to France.[71] No direct evidence for population levels during the first half of the fifteenth century between the Tyne and Tees has yet been uncovered. The series from elsewhere in the country also begins to peter out, although the consensus is that numbers had stagnated somewhere below half of pre-Black Death peak levels.[72] The continued rise in the cost of labour on the Pittington demesne is evidence that the labour shortage was not alleviated between Tyne and Tees.[73] There is also evidence for high mortality in the years coinciding

---

[68] *Priory of Finchale*, appendix, pp. ccvi, ccviii.
[69] Ibid., appendix, pp. ccxx–ccxxii.
[70] Ibid., appendix, p. ccxxx. The comparative ease with which Durham's officeholders could conceal the borrowing of large amounts of money from the auditors of their annual accounts caused problems at the mother house during the 1430s when the bursar, Thomas Lawson, seems to have left debts of £1,210: R.B. Dobson, *Durham Priory, 1400–1450* (Cambridge, 1973), p. 286.
[71] Creighton, *History of Epidemics*, I, 223.
[72] Poos, *Rural Society*, p. 90; J.C. Russell, *British Medieval Population* (Albuquerque, 1948), pp. 260–70; Hatcher, *Plague, Population and the English Economy*, pp. 27–30.
[73] Dodds, 'Workers on the Pittington Demesne', 152

with period 3 on figure 12.1.[74] The agrarian crisis of the 1430s has already attracted the attention of A.J. Pollard who linked difficulties in rent collection with 'a spate of high mortality and failed harvests'.[75] His rental evidence presents a complex picture of agrarian change in the first decades of the fifteenth century. He observed that the crisis of the 1430s was 'all the more painful because it followed two decades of relative stability'.[76] Whilst he observed some improvement in rental income from lowland arable areas during the 1410s and 1420s, his evidence highlighted a mini-boom in the pastoral sector during these years.[77] When crisis did arrive in the early 1430s both sectors were affected but the arable worse than the pastoral.[78] Pollard's article is important for our understanding of the origins of 'what must constitute one of the deepest, most pervasive and enduring of all depressions' in the mid-fifteenth century.[79] He even went so far as to argue that the mid-century difficulties were 'largely the result of this [crisis] and not the end point of a slow remorseless contraction'.[80]

The improvement Pollard commented on in lowland areas of the north east between 1410 and 1430 is amply confirmed by the Durham tithe series. The rallying of the estimated output indices after the turn of the century low is clear in figure 12.1 from the indices between period 2 and period 3. Overall estimated output exceeded its 1390s levels throughout most of the 1410s and 1420s, although there were very bad harvests in 1424 and 1429. Figures 12.5, 12.6 and 12.7 show strong recovery in these decades in most Billingham parish vills, although curiously it was not so marked in Billingham itself (figure 12.4). The Finchale rental evidence uncovers a similar pattern. Levels of waste and decay remained high throughout the first half of the fifteenth century, but arrears were low during the 1410s and 1420s. The priors were not able to let all their holdings but could at least collect the rents. The agrarian economy appears to have readjusted to the changed conditions during the second and third decades of the fifteenth century. Output was still very low but did not show the instability of the period 1370 to 1410. This is demonstrated by table 12.2. The indices of the second decade of the fifteenth century have the lowest standard deviation of the series. The preceding decade has the second highest standard deviation.

Readjustment before period 3 on figure 12.1 in another sector of the agrarian economy is suggested by Pollard's evidence of buoyancy in the rents received from properties used for cattle rearing.[81] Pollard's rental evidence is supported by the cluster of Saltholme data from 1415–19: numbers of breeding ewes were certainly lower than in the 1340s but had not fallen as much as estimated arable production. Population must have been scarcely half pre-Black Death levels but the stable arable output levels and comparatively strong pastoral sector indicate an economy adapting to a shortage of labour but high *per capita* consumption of meat and dairy products. In

---

[74] P.J.P. Goldberg, 'Mortality and Economic Change in the Diocese of York, 1390–1514', *NH* 24 (1988), 45.
[75] A.J. Pollard, 'The North-Eastern Economy and the Agrarian Crisis of 1438–40', *NH* 25 (1989), 93.
[76] Ibid., 105.
[77] Ibid., 89, 92–3.
[78] Ibid., 99–100.
[79] Hatcher, 'Great Slump', p. 270.
[80] Pollard, 'North-Eastern Economy', 103.
[81] Ibid., 89, 91–2.

Table 12.2: Decennial standard deviation of output indices, 1350–1449

Decade	Standard deviation of output indices (rank low to high)
1350–9	16.68 (8)
1360–9	10.55 (3)
1370–9	17.19 (10)
1380–9	13.20 (5)
1390–9	13.24 (6)
1400–9	17.15 (9)
1410–9	8.46 (1)
1420–9	11.57 (4)
1430–9	13.58 (7)
1440–9	8.83 (2)

other words, the changing balance between population and resources of the second half of the fourteenth century was stabilising.

Described in these terms, and in keeping with Pollard's conclusions, the difficulties of the 1430s look more like crisis restarted rather than crisis deepening. Figure 12.1 and figure 12.9 suggest a double crisis in the arable and pastoral sectors. Pollard's evidence, whilst showing difficulties in the pastoral sector, suggested it was less affected than the arable.[82] This may have been the case, but the good series of Saltholme data from 1426 to 1436 shows the seriousness of the pastoral crisis on this manor at least. This is consistent with the extreme difficulties faced by landlords during these years. While William Barry saw the gap widen between receipts and expenditure at Finchale Priory, John Wessington, prior of Durham, became so desperate that he divided the office of bursar into three. This was a daring administrative experiment which Wessington went to considerable lengths to justify to the visiting bishop in 1442 in terms of falling income not attributable to the prior's negligence (*negligentia dicti Prioris*).[83]

Tithe evidence of the sort presented in figure 12.1 is ideal for identifying the turning points in long-term economic change. With the series as it currently stands, the 1440s appear somewhat enigmatic. Arable output was desperately low but much more stable than in the preceding decade. This gives little clue as to whether the difficulties of the 1430s precipitated further recession. The Finchale priors did not succeed in cutting back levels of waste and decay to the levels of the late fourteenth- and early fifteenth-centuries until around 1480.[84] This implies that Pollard's view of the significance of the crisis of the 1430s may be justified. The best way to test this on a wider scale will be through an extension of the tithe output series.

---

[82] Ibid., 99–100.
[83] DCM, Loc.XXI:20b; Dobson, *Durham Priory*, pp. 233–5, 267, 285–90.
[84] Allowances for waste and decay fell from £9 in 1477–8 to £5 3s. 2d. in 1480–1 and remained at around this level at least until the end of the decade: *Priory of Finchale*, appendix, pp. cccxlii–ccclxxxviii.

*

Through the study of three short periods, a possible long-term pattern of economic change in the north east between 1349 and 1450 can be suggested. The most obvious conclusion is that arable output never fully recovered from the catastrophe of the Black Death. In fact, production levels became steadily lower and may have fallen to under one-third of 1340s levels during the 1430s. However, within this long-term decline there were two periods of recovery. The best documented and most certain is that of the 1350s and the other began in the second decade of the fifteenth century and lasted until the crisis of the 1430s. Production during these years did not reach the heights of the 1350s but regained stability. This highlights the most important conclusion about the causation of this change. Although we do not have a demographic indicator so direct and precise as the tithes for arable output, it appears that, whilst the failure of population to recover after the Black Death underlies the century's low arable output, the relationship between the two is not simple. The economy seems to have undergone more than one phase of major readjustment. After each recovery, renewed stability was once more set back by further crisis, probably of a demographic character. Pestilence returned at the beginning of the 1360s and disabled the recovering arable economy of the 1350s. Perhaps ever present thereafter, it returned with renewed vigour at the beginning of the 1430s and put an end to the stability of the arable and possible buoyancy of the pastoral sectors of the 1410s and 1420s.

Whilst the indicators used here are primarily economic, they shed light on social change during the same period. To some extent, the fortunes of peasants and landlords moved together. The reduced population of the 1350s still succeeded in filling most of the tenements vacated by the plague's first victims. Likewise, the 1430s must have spelled disaster for both: prices reached famine levels and rents were impossible to collect. In broad terms, however, the fate of the two social groups diverged. Thorold Rogers long ago characterised the fifteenth century as 'the golden age of the English labourer' and the output evidence throws the meaning of this epithet into sharp relief.[85] Labourers benefited with whirlwind rapidity in the 1350s: tithe evidence, supported by rents, implies a sharp rise in standards of living. This relative abundance and freedom from want almost certainly continued and increased. The Coathams of Pittington seem to have enjoyed an almost annual increase in income around the turn of the century. The hints that the pastoral sector burgeoned until the 1430s, and especially in the first decades of the fifteenth century, may translate to further improvements in diet.

Tithe data represent a valuable source for historians of the English economy in the late Middle Ages which is only just beginning to be tapped. Their interpretation is complicated by certain unknown factors, but these can be overcome by comparison with other indicators. In the absence of equally long and detailed series of rental, manorial and demographic indicators, the case-study approach is effective. This essay has demonstrated that the detailed examination of 'islands', for which a greater volume of evidence can be produced, is a useful means of developing hypotheses and arriving at overall interpretation. As more tithe data are collected, these islands will grow and it will be possible to advance conclusions with greater certainty.

---

[85] J.E. Thorold Rogers, *Six Centuries of Work and Wages: The History of English Labour* (5th edn., London, 1901), p. 326.

13

Wastes, the Margins and the Abandonment of Land: The Bishop of Durham's Estate, 1350–1480[1]

SIMON J. HARRIS

The period from the Black Death to the later fifteenth century has presented many problems for social and economic historians. For M.M. Postan it was 'an age of recession, arrested economic development and declining national income'.[2] But for others such as A.R. Bridbury the period was not at all this world of economic gloom. Certain groups did suffer, but for Bridbury this was a period of 'fundamental buoyancy and resilience'.[3] Such extreme and contradictory views are no longer accepted. A whole plethora of work, recently summarised by John Hatcher, has suggested that the period should in fact be seen as a progression of sub-periods where quite differing economic conditions prevailed, and different groups within the economy and different sectors of the economy could and did have widely differing experiences.[4]

There is nevertheless no doubt that this was a period of momentous change, particularly on the land, following the first visitation of the plague in 1349 and perhaps earlier. It has long been recognised that there was a fundamental change in the relationship of lords to their tenantry, and in the way that the land was managed, which reflected the impact of depopulation. The period was marked by a general withdrawal of lords from the direct exploitation of their estates. With a smaller population and the concomitant strengthening of the position of tenants, demesne farming became economically unviable. This was by no means a sudden change – the retreat was managed over a period of many decades – but by the mid-fifteenth century most lords had permanently let their demesnes, and only a few vestigial elements such as parks and home farms remained on the majority of estates. For example, on the Percy estates, which lay throughout the northern counties, Yorkshire and Sussex, there was

---

1   I would like to thank Richard Britnell and Ben Dodds for reading and commenting on an earlier draft of this essay. I would also like to thank Brian Roberts for his advice and for permission to use his map of Steward Shield Meadow. I am also grateful to Helen Dunsford for the production of the other maps in this essay.
2   M.M. Postan, 'The Fifteenth Century', in idem, *Essays on Medieval Agriculture and General Problems of the Medieval Economy* (Cambridge, 1973), p. 42.
3   A.R. Bridbury, *Economic Growth: England in the Later Middle Ages* (London, 1962), p. 82.
4   J. Hatcher, 'The Great Slump of the Mid-Fifteenth Century', in *Progress and Problems in Medieval England: Essays in Honour of Edward Miller*, ed. R. Britnell and J. Hatcher (Cambridge, 1996), pp. 237–72. The widely differing experiences of this period are perhaps exemplified by two very different studies: R.H. Britnell, 'The Pastons and their Norfolk', *AgHR* 36 (1988), 132–44; C. Dyer, 'A Small Landowner in the Fifteenth Century', *MH* 1 (1972), 1–14.

a retreat from demesne farming so that by 1416 even on the estates in Yorkshire and Sussex, well away from the periodic instability of the Scottish border, demesnes were let at farm. Only at Alnwick, the chief seat of the family, was any land still directly managed at this time.[5] On the large West Midlands estate of Ramsey Abbey, there was a slow retreat from demesne farming in the period from the 1370s until the 1390s when a widespread agricultural depression saw the collapse of the manorial economy.[6] This shift impacted inevitably on the relationship between lords and their customary tenants. With scarcely any demesne left to justify the maintenance of customary services, and with an increasingly truculent tenantry, there was widespread commutation of services, and a modification of the relationship of lord to tenant. Customary tenures on many estates were converted to shorter leases and copyholds, with an accompanying substitution of money rents for labour and other services.[7] In addition, because of the steep decline in the number of tenants, and a lower demand for land, landlords found it more difficult to find tenants on any terms, especially for unrewarding properties.

The north east of England shared in the social and economic changes experienced elsewhere in the country. R.H. Britnell's analysis of the response of Bishop Hatfield and his administration to the post-plague difficulties on the episcopal estate has shown the uncompromising stance he adopted. Lands left untenanted were forced upon other tenants and groups of tenants, and there was a reluctance to grant reductions in rents and services. However, the bishop was fighting a losing battle and his 'feudal reaction' ultimately failed to arrest change on his estate, so that the resolution of estate officials to protect episcopal rights was swept away by 'tenant resistance and economic realism'.[8] In the end, the bishop's administration retreated from direct exploitation of the demesne, so that almost all of the episcopal demesne was in the hands of farmers by 1381. The extensive customary services, still recorded in detail in the Hatfield Survey, had effectively been commuted. Although the early fifteenth century was a period of declining income for the bishops of Durham, it was also a period of relative stability on the episcopal estate.[9] Yet, following the agrarian crisis of 1438–40, it would appear that the north east suffered in an even more pronounced manner; the stability and modest growth enjoyed prior to 1438 collapsed, so that depopulation, according to A.J. Pollard, 'led to abandonment of arable, conversion to pasture and a fall in revenues from land of approximately one third over the first fifty years of the fifteenth century'.[10] In response, the bishop's administration was forced to make further concessions, and Mark Arvanigian has shown that the administration

---

[5] J.M.W. Bean, *The Estates of the Percy Family 1416–1537* (Oxford, 1958).

[6] A. Raftis, 'Peasants and the Collapse of the Manorial Economy on some Ramsey Abbey Estates', in *Progress and Problems in Medieval England: Essays in Honour of Edward Miller*, ed. R. Britnell and J. Hatcher (Cambridge, 1996), pp. 191–206.

[7] C. Dyer, *Lords and Peasants in a Changing Society: The Estates of the Bishopric of Worcester, 680–1540* (Cambridge, 1980), especially chs. 5 and 6, where it is shown that a combination of declining arable prices, demographic change and the growing assertiveness of the tenantry saw a retreat from demesne farming, conversion of arable to pasture, and ultimately abandonment of land.

[8] R.H. Britnell, 'Feudal Reaction after the Black Death in the Palatinate of Durham', *P&P* 128 (1990), 46–7.

[9] R.L. Storey, *Thomas Langley and the Bishopric of Durham, 1406–1437* (London, 1961), esp. pp. 67–91.

[10] A.J. Pollard, 'The North-Eastern Economy and the Agrarian Crisis of 1438–1440', *NH* 35 (1989), 88.

encountered increasing difficulties in collecting rents from its free tenants, who themselves may well have been facing similar problems.[11]

Durham Priory's estate underwent similar change. Indeed the changes initiated there were even more fundamental. The work of E.M. Halcrow, R.B. Dobson, and Richard Lomas has revealed that most of the demesne had been let by 1370 and that, although certain manors appurtenant to the major residences of the prior at Pittington and Bearpark, or held by obedientaries, were retained longer, the changes were rendered irreversible by the conversion of customary tenures to copyholds and leaseholds.[12] But despite these changes the priory still faced serious problems. The work of Ben Dodds on the tithes belonging to the priory has shown that in the later fourteenth and earlier fifteenth centuries abandoned arable land became increasingly widespread.[13] Timothy Lomas's study of the peasant land market on the episcopal and priory estates in south-east Durham has highlighted the disruption to peasant society and economy in the later fourteenth and fifteenth centuries, especially the considerable depopulation of many substantial peasant communities, the increasing descent of peasant estates outside the family, and the growing importance of pastoral agriculture in the arable heartland of the palatinate.[14] The north east, then, was by no means unusual in the problems that it faced in the later fourteenth and fifteenth centuries or in the response that its greater landholders adopted.

This essay addresses the extent to which land was in fact abandoned and the nature of that land which was left untenanted or which had to be let at heavily discounted rents. Historians have long emphasised the 'marginal' nature of the land abandoned first in the wake of fourteenth-century depopulation. This land was marginal in both location and in quality, and was thought to have been colonised because of the pressures on resources in the later thirteenth century. Although recent work has challenged this definition, the model of retreat from the margin in the later fourteenth and fifteenth centuries still provides a useful foundation for discussion and comparison.[15] Discussion will focus on a study of the episcopal estate in the palatinate of Durham. Durham makes a good subject of study because of work already extant, the survival of a good series of records for the episcopal estate, and the diversity of landscapes from the rich lands of the Tees Lowlands in the east of the county, to the difficult terrain of the High Pennines in the west.[16] The essay will use the documentary evidence to

---

[11] M.E. Arvanigian, 'Free Rents in the Palatinate of Durham, and the Crisis of the Late 1430s', *AA*, 5th ser. 24 (1996), 99–108.

[12] E.M. Halcrow, 'The Decline of Demesne Farming on the Estates of Durham Cathedral Priory', *EcHR*, 2nd ser. 7 (1954–5), 345–56; R.B. Dobson, *Durham Priory, 1400–1450* (Cambridge, 1973), esp. ch. 8; R.A. Lomas, 'A Priory and its Tenants', in *Daily Life in the Late Middle Ages*, ed. R.H. Britnell (Stroud, 1998), pp. 103–24.

[13] Cf. Dodds's contribution to this volume; see also his 'Durham Priory Tithes and the Black Death between Tyne and Tees', *NH* 39 (2002), and his paper, 'Production, Population and Pestilence: Some Durham Tithe Evidence from the Later Middle Ages', which was given at the 2002 Economic History Conference in Birmingham and which was published in the conference booklet.

[14] T. Lomas, 'South-East Durham: Late Fourteenth and Fifteenth Centuries', in *The Peasant Land Market in Medieval England*, ed. P.D.A. Harvey (Oxford, 1984), pp. 252–327.

[15] R.H. Britnell, 'Agricultural Technology and the Margin of Cultivation in the Fourteenth Century', *EcHR*, new ser. 30 (1977), 53–66; M. Bailey, 'The Concept of the Margin in the Medieval English Economy', *EcHR*, 2nd ser. 42 (1989), 1–17; and C. Dyer, ' "The Retreat from Marginal Land": The Growth and Decline of Medieval Rural Settlement', in idem, *Everyday Life in Medieval England* (London, 2000), pp. 13–26.

[16] See map 13.1.

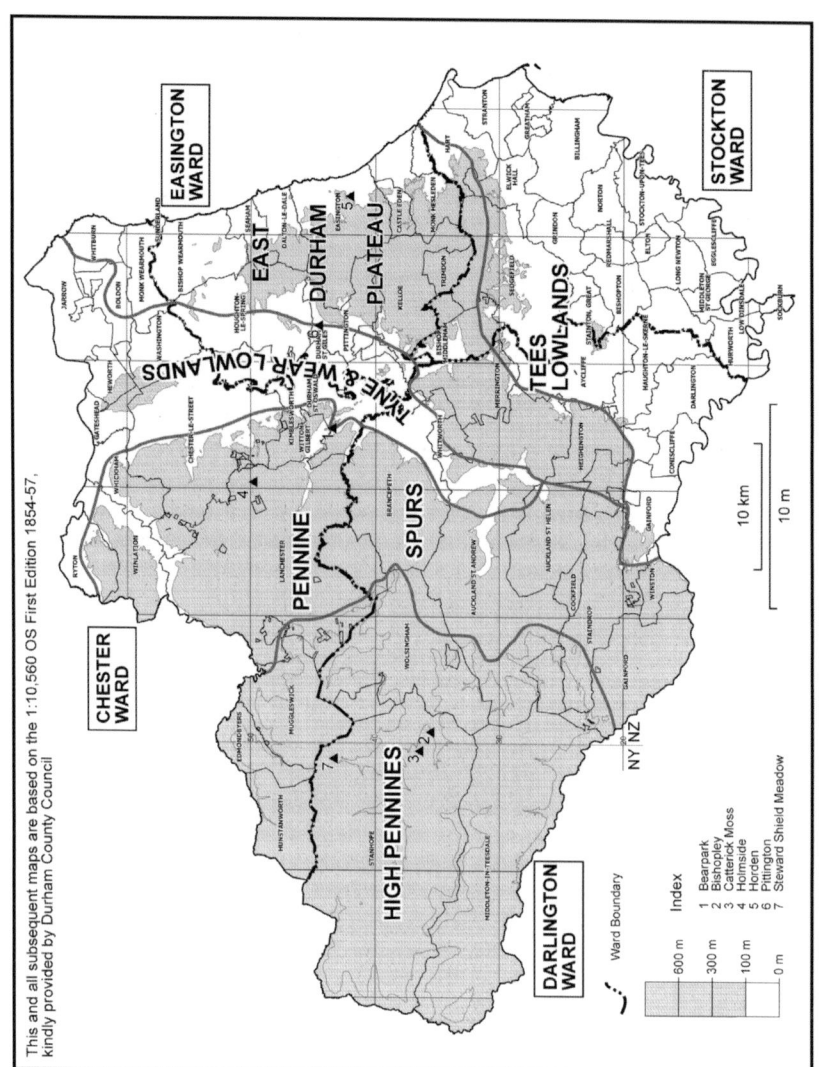

Map 13.1 Parishes, Locations and Physiographic Regions, Co. Durham

Source: R.I. Hodgson, 'Coalmining, Population and Enclosure in the Seasale Colliery Districts of Durham (northern Durham), 1551–1810: A study in Historical Geography' (2 vols, unpublished Ph.D. thesis, University of Durham, 1989), II, 98.

examine the chronology and distribution of any abandonment of land. It will also discuss the distribution of this contraction. More particularly, it will consider whether land abandoned was the more recently colonised land taken from the waste, which may have been less fertile, less accessible, or less attractive for some other reason, and whether its distribution concentrated in the upland zone, which could also be considered marginal by location. Rather than attempt to assess the shifting balance between pasture and arable, which the evidence does not allow, this essay will focus on the extent to which land was tenanted.

The fact of depopulation is very clearly exemplified in plate 13.1 showing a relict field system at Bollihope high up in Weardale (Co. Durham). Bollihope was part of the bishop of Durham's estate associated with Stanhope, and seems to have been colonised after 1183; no evidence for the holdings at Bollihope, which are recorded under the heading of Bishopley in the Hatfield Survey, can be found in Boldon Book.[17] The picture shows the view looking south from Bishopley over Bollihope Burn, and reveals a core of what is now improved pasture in the foreground with clear evidence of arable strips underlying both this improved pasture, and the regenerated moorland further in the distance on the other side of the burn. Although it is impossible to be entirely certain when these strips were originally created, and, indeed, when they were finally abandoned, as such field strips are notoriously difficult to date, it is very likely that some at least belonged to relict fields of medieval creation and abandonment.[18] In the majority of such cases, physical evidence, such as that at Bollihope, can only lead to speculation, and it is impossible to use it for wider assessment. How long was such land in cultivation? Was its abandonment the product of wider patterns of desertion throughout the county and region? Was it symptomatic of a greater amount of desertion in the upland zone? Was the land 'marginal'? If it was, in what way was it marginal? Such images are a powerful reminder of change but can take us little further. In this particular example, however, we are fortunate in having documentary evidence that, though not confirming conclusively the surviving traces of arable fields as medieval, reveals a considerable acreage and a number of what appear to be occupied messuages and tofts at Bishopley and Bollihope in 1381. The entry for Bishopley in the Hatfield Survey indicates a considerably shrunken tenant population. Although there are thirteen separate messuages, two tofts, one bercary and a forge, these several holdings are almost entirely in the hands of three landholders. There are 276 acres recorded as occupied, which seem to be arable. However, there are also 184 acres recorded as waste, amounting to forty per cent of the total acreage in Bishopley, though some of this is recorded as being pasture. Part of this waste acreage at least may account for relict fields of a similar kind to those in the picture found further west along the Bollihope valley below Catterick Moss.[19]

The terms 'waste' or 'wasteland' will be used here to refer to land beyond the boundaries of the settled area with its arable and improved pasture. This land was made up of moorland, woodland and marsh. Such land termed *vastum* was not

---

[17] *HS*, p. 59.
[18] The possibilities and problems are explored in detail by M.M. Beresford, 'Ridge and Furrow and the Open Fields', *EcHR*, new ser. 1 (1948), 34–45, and in an interesting critique in E. Kerridge, 'Ridge and Furrow and Agrarian History', *EcHR*, new ser. 4 (1951), 14–36.
[19] *HS*, p. 59. Cf. B.K. Roberts et al., 'Recent Forest History and Land Use in Weardale, Northern England', in *Quaternary Plant Ecology*, ed. H.J.B. Birks and R.G. West (Oxford, 1973), p. 217.

Ridge and Furrow probably from steam-ploughing underlying regenerated moorland

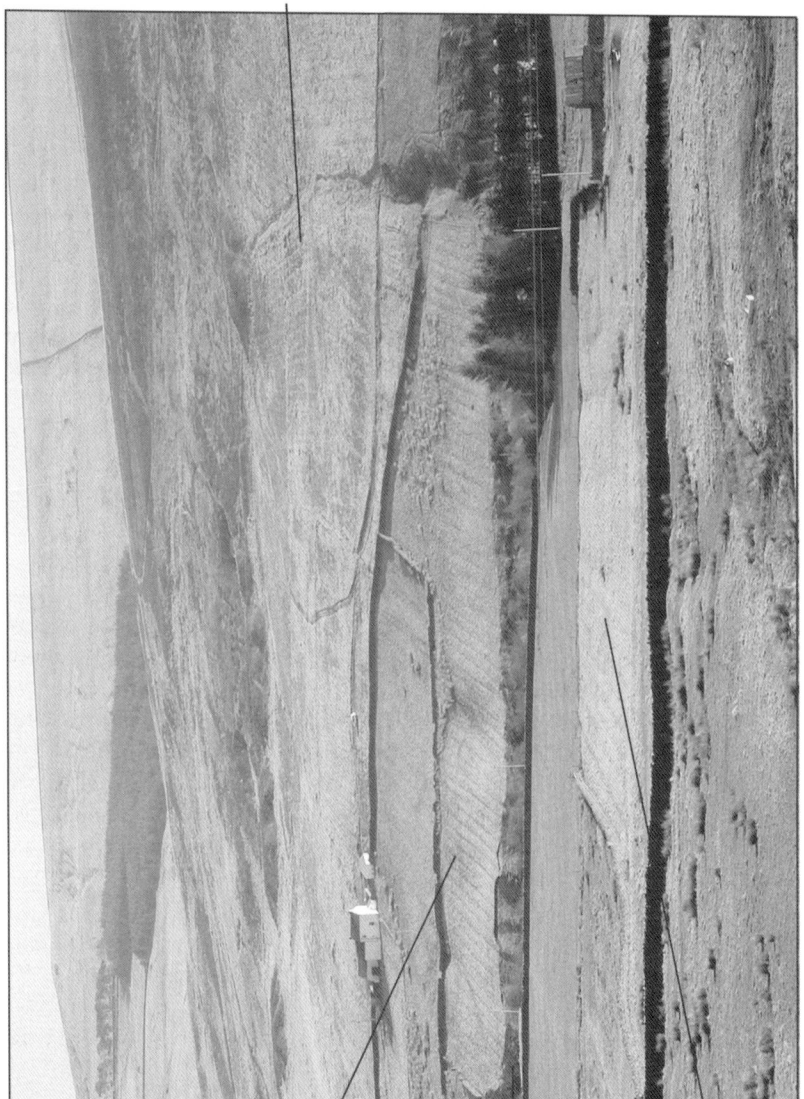

Plate 13.1 Relict Fields at Bishopley and Bollihope in Weardale, Co. Durham

Ridge and Furrow probably from steam-ploughing underlying improved pasture

Bollihope Burn

Early ridge and furrow underlying improved pasture

necessarily permanently abandoned or uncultivated, but there are numerous references in the Durham coroners' accounts to rents that were not paid because the coroner had no idea where the holdings lay. Land recorded as lying waste in successive accounts over several decades is likely to mean that the holding was untenanted.

This study builds on the detailed findings of the project on Settlement and Waste in the Palatinate of Durham based in Durham between 2000 and 2003, whose main findings have recently been published.[20] The project concentrated on identifying the likely extent of the wasteland in the palatinate of Durham in the twelfth century and on showing the means and extent to which wastelands were drawn into cultivation during the thirteenth and early fourteenth centuries. Because of the vast extent of the northern wastes, the breaking of new ground continued longer in Durham than it did in most parts of southern England, and was only terminated by climatic changes, famine and Scottish raids in the earlier decades of the fourteenth century. These findings suggest that although the inhabitants of Durham undoubtedly shared in the period of colonisation experienced by central and southern England during the twelfth and thirteenth centuries, they could not have exhausted supplies of available arable land by the early fourteenth. The work of the project identified two particular classes of waste enclosure as subjects for study. The first of these, exchequer land, was a category of land so termed in the episcopal records because those who held it were supposed to pay their rents at the bishop's exchequer in Durham, though by the fourteenth century most of these rents were collected by the coroners. This class of land did not exist at the time of Boldon Book, so it consisted almost entirely of waste enclosures made after its compilation. The second class of land was an artificial group of 'moorland farms'. These were holdings, which were carved from the waste, mostly on the bishop's estate, and sometimes authorised by episcopal charters, many of which survive to identify and date such enclosures.[21] Map 13.2 plots the grants of waste and moorland farms known from the two centuries or so before the Black Death against the projected extent of the waste in c.1625. The map is remarkable in two respects. First, it reveals the sheer quantity of waste that survived as late as the early seventeenth century. And secondly, it shows the uneven distribution of the grants of waste. Because the grants were predominantly episcopal they inevitably reflect the distribution of the episcopal estate, but it is also clear that the major zone of colonisation was away from the earlier settled eastern seaboard of the Tees Lowlands and the East Durham Plateau, and concentrated in the Pennine Spurs and along the upper Wear valley around the major episcopal estate centres at Wolsingham and Stanhope. Though the work of the Settlement and Waste project focused on the period up to the early fourteenth century, it also permits investigation of the subsequent fate of the waste colonisation after 1315, affording new insights into the extent and distribution of late medieval contraction and the types of land most affected, changes which are often deduced but rarely demonstrated.

Analysis of these issues will make use of three distinct sources of evidence relating

---

[20] H.M. Dunsford and S.J. Harris, 'Colonization of the Wasteland in County Durham, 1100–1400', *EcHR* 56 (2003), 34–56. This three-year project established at the University of Durham was funded by the ESRC and was supervised by Richard Britnell (Department of History) and Brian Roberts (Department of Geography).

[21] For a more detailed discussion of exchequer land and moorland farms, see Dunsford and Harris, 'Colonization of the Wasteland', 41–6.

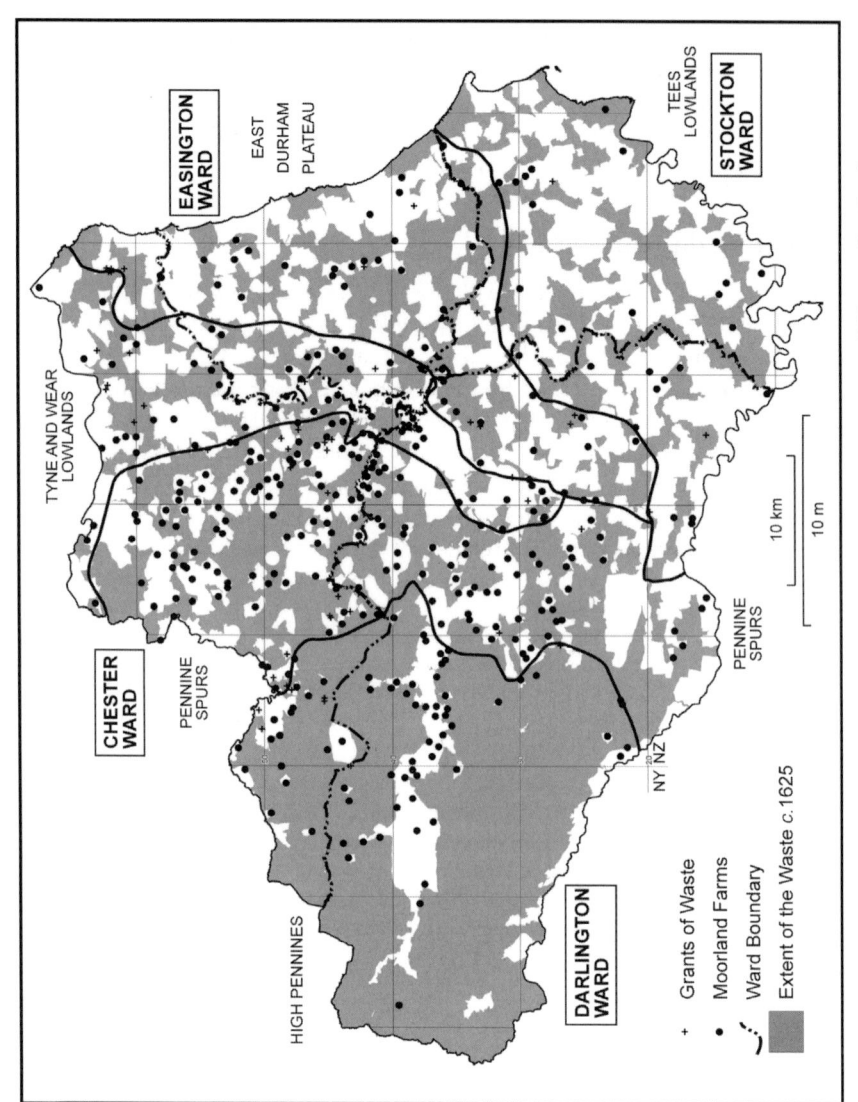

Map 13.2 Reconstructed Limits of Waste (c.1625) and Grants of Waste, Co. Durham

to the estate of the bishop of Durham: the Hatfield Survey, inquisitions *post mortem* and the accounts of the coroners of Durham. These sources are complementary. The evidence from each relates to a slightly different time period, and allows varying degrees of assessment. These sources have major shortcomings, but, taken together, they allow close consideration of the changes in question.

The Evidence of the Hatfield Survey

Statistical analysis of the Hatfield Survey, the great episcopal estate survey made at the end of Bishop Hatfield's pontificate around 1381, allows us to quantify waste over a wide area, covering the four wards of the palatinate (table 13.1). The table records the acreage for exchequer land and for the bishop's demesne land. The total arable acreage includes the totals for both exchequer and demesne land as well as the acreages for cottagers, bondsmen, freemen and drengs. The figures for wasteland record the acreages of those former lands that were out of tenure, and therefore waste at the time of the survey. While the figures are not complete,[22] they still allow broad comparisons to be made between the four wards.

Table 13.1 Comparison of acreages in the Hatfield Survey[23]

Ward	Exchequer Land	Demesne Land	Total Arable Acreage	Wasteland	Total with Wasteland	% of Waste of Total
Darlington	4577.4	2195	14944.93	806.88	15751.81	5.12
Chester	4046.74	1346	10103.54	731.32	10834.86	6.75
Stockton	534.75	1453	6776.2	58	6834.2	0.85
Easington	856.5	1781	9790.15	28.5	9818.65	0.29
Totals	10015.39	6775	41614.82	1624.7	43239.52	3.76

The greatest acreage of the bishop's estate was found in the two larger wards of the palatinate. Darlington and Chester wards were the two inland wards and encompassed the areas of the densest twelfth- and thirteenth-century colonisation in the area of the Pennine Spurs; this is revealed by the large quantities of exchequer land in those wards and the distribution of waste grants in map 13.2. The bishop held more land in these two wards than in the smaller eastern wards of Easington and Stockton, but the ratio of tenanted land to demesne was much larger in the western wards. The differences result from the method by which the pre-Conquest estates of St Cuthbert were acquired, and the manner by which they were eventually divided between the bishop and priory of Durham. As can be seen from map 13.3 the bishop kept some prime

---

[22] Spaces were left in the manuscript of the survey for some figures, which were subsequently never filled in. In other instances, holdings are simply referred to as messuages or tenements, and it is evident that they had appurtenant lands, but we are not told of their extent. Additionally, many of the demesnes have no extent recorded for them because they no longer remained directly in the bishop's hands.

[23] The figures are drawn from P. Dickinson, *The Historical Geography of County Durham during the Middle Ages* (3 vols., unpublished Ph.D. thesis, University of Durham, 1957), II, 1–18, but have been extensively revised from the original Hatfield Survey text (PRO, SC 12/21/28). The figures are based on those estates (predominantly townships) within each parish where figures appear to be directly comparable. The acreage is assumed to be that of the bishop's acre, which was 1½ times the size of a statute acre.

206   SIMON J. HARRIS

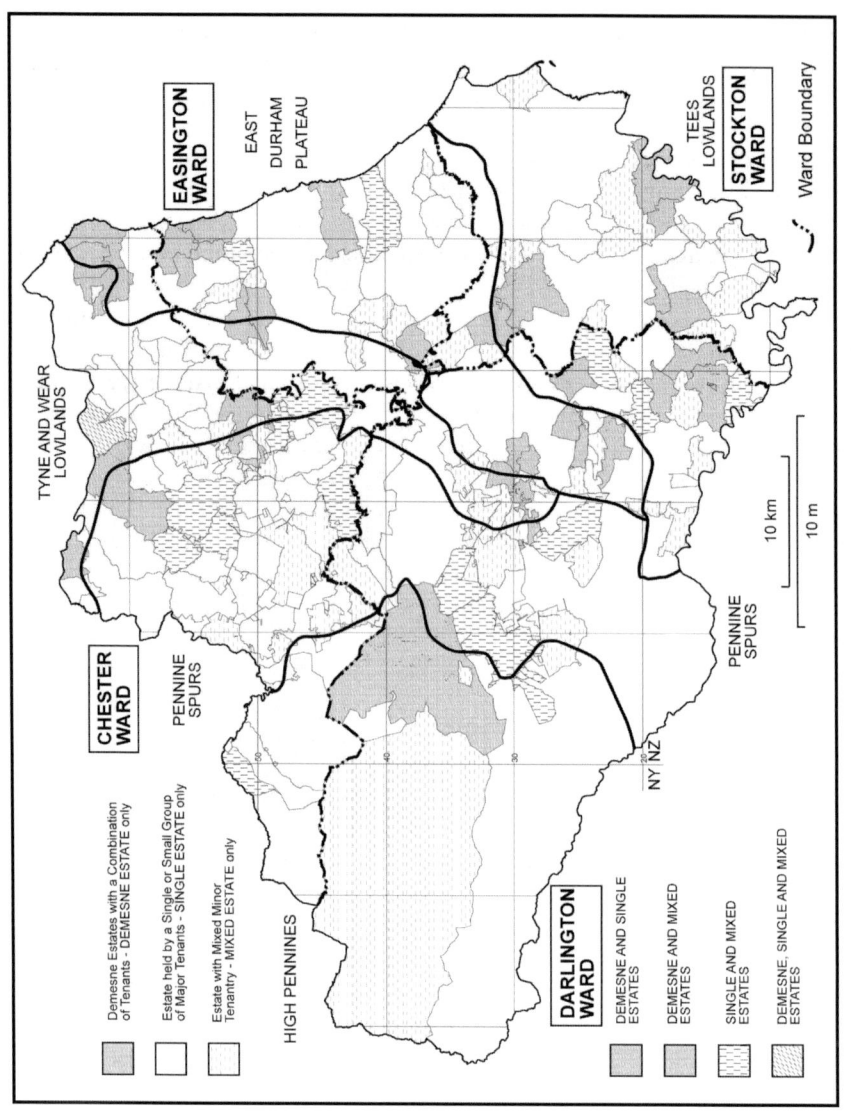

Map 13.3 Episcopal Estates and Ward Boundaries, Co. Durham

demesne-centred estates in the east of the county, but by accident or design also retained estates in the centre and west of the county which contained substantial wastes available for exploitation and colonisation from the twelfth century onwards.[24]

While there was this clear distinction between the wards, the quantity of land recorded as waste throughout the palatinate was not substantial. In the two smaller wards this amounted to less than one per cent. In Stockton ward it was 0.85 per cent of the total acreage, and in Easington it was insignificant, amounting to only 0.29 per cent. In the two larger wards it was substantially more, but still accounted for only a small percentage: in Darlington 5.12 per cent; in Chester 6.75 per cent. In these two wards the waste was relatively localised. In Darlington it was concentrated in the three large multi-township Wear valley parishes of Auckland St Andrew, Stanhope, and Wolsingham, the latter two being predominantly upland parishes, and all three having high concentrations of exchequer land and documented late enclosure.[25] In this one ward there is a striking example of abandoned land that we know was of thirteenth-century colonisation. The moorland farm of Steward Shield (map 13.4), lying a few miles north of Stanhope, seems to have originated in a farm of the Charron family who served as stewards of the bishops of Durham in the later thirteenth century, though it may have had an earlier existence as a seasonal shieling site as the name itself suggests. In the Hatfield Survey the farm lands there are recorded as 'now waste and untenanted' (*modo vaste et extra tenuram*).[26] How long it had been in this condition is unclear, but it would seem that as the survey itself was being drawn up, and as Hatfield's pontificate drew to a close, a new tenant was found to hold the farm for life. Steward Shield was a large tract of eighty acres, but there were still tenants prepared to take on such holdings in 1381.[27] Certainly, the higher percentages of waste can be found in the two wards where we know the bulk of earlier colonisation of the waste had occurred, and, indeed, in the parishes where we know there were numerous moorland farms and high acreages of exchequer land.[28] Yet perhaps more significantly, only 3.76 per cent of the total acreage in the palatinate between Tyne and Tees was recorded as waste in 1381.

Though the Hatfield Survey does not provide sufficiently detailed evidence of the kind of land that was being abandoned, it does give an important indicator of the level of contraction in the first three decades that followed the arrival of the plague. It would seem to indicate that the extent of the retreat was not particularly marked. In part, this is likely to reflect the feudal reaction noted by Britnell, in that the episcopal administration had at that time effectively managed to keep the vast majority of the

---

[24] Dunsford and Harris, 'Colonization of the Wasteland', 50–2.

[25] In Darlington ward the concentrations could be found in the parishes of Auckland St Andrew (where the waste amounted to 8.82 per cent of the total acreage), Stanhope (13.45 per cent) and Wolsingham (11.3 per cent). In Wolsingham the land was recorded as 'old waste' (*antiqua vasta*). In Chester ward the concentrations could be found in the parishes of Durham St Oswald (11.09 per cent), Lanchester (20.87 per cent) and Whitburn (12.11 per cent).

[26] *HS*, p. 73. Map 13.4 shows the current seventeenth- and eighteenth-century bounds of this farm overlaying earlier bounds, which are probably those of the medieval farm.

[27] DCM, Misc. Ch. 6394. The document is a confirmation by Prior Walworth of a life lease made by Bishop Hatfield to Hugh de Westwick, the confirmation being dated 26 April 1381.

[28] In some cases the wasteland acreages are particularly high for places that consisted predominantly of exchequer land, as at Bishopley: *HS*, p. 59.

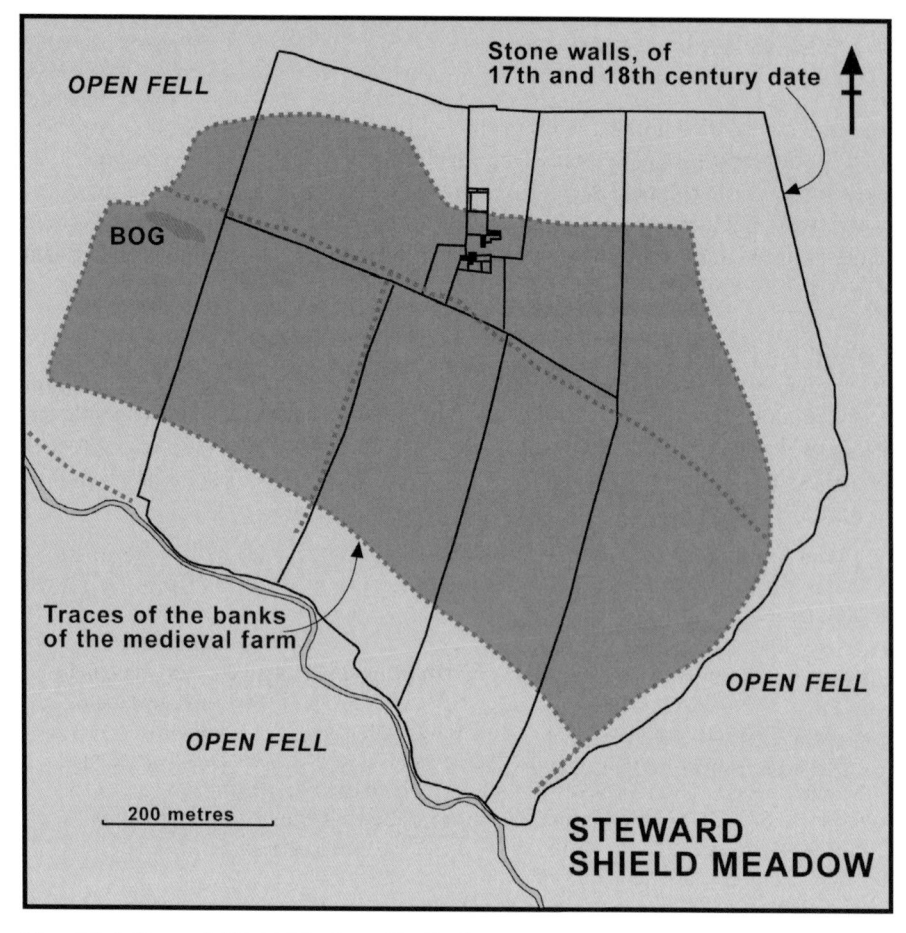

Map 13.4 Steward Shield Meadow, Co. Durham

bishop's estate tenanted, despite a more dramatic demographic decline. But it would also suggest that in total the retreat was minimal. The bishop's administration could only do so much, so that the low level of retreat must be indicative of the limited nature of the impact of economic and demographic change upon the extent of the tenanted acreage of the episcopal estate. It would seem that the lands in the two larger wards, which were the main zone of colonisation and which contained the lands of the Pennine Spurs and the High Pennines, were more likely to be abandoned, whilst the decline in the two smaller wards is of such a small percentage that it seems unlikely that the older core estates of the bishop and his tenants were abandoned to any significant extent. Unfortunately, the evidence does not allow us to know how much land which had once been arable had been converted to pasture, a conversion that was certainly occurring in south-east Durham.[29]

[29] T. Lomas, 'South-East Durham'.

The Evidence of Inquisitions

In Durham IPMs were produced by the bishop's escheators for the estates of those freeholders who died holding lands in chief of the bishop. In this way, they recorded some lands that were held directly from the bishop's estate for which rent was paid and services rendered, but they also included estates which did not form part of the direct estate of the bishop, but which were held of the bishop as other chief lords held of the king. As such, these records allow us a wider view of conditions in Durham over a much longer period, and give information of sorts about a wide variety of lay estates.

Inquisitions, though they are an inherently problematic source because of the strong interests of local people in misrepresenting the truth,[30] present some useful evidence for the abandonment of land throughout the county. Take for example the manor of Horden lying on the coast in the parish of Easington. This manor was part of the extensive Claxton estate and was recorded in the IPM of 1431 of Sir William Claxton.[31] According to the inquisition, Claxton died seised of:

> ... the manor of Horden with appurtenances in which manor is the site of the same manor which is worth nothing beyond reprises... And there are in the same manor 400 acres of demesne land which are valued per annum beyond reprises 6s., twenty-four acres of meadow which are valued per annum beyond reprises 6s., 200 acres of pasture which are valued per annum beyond reprises 12d. And there is in the same manor a wasted vill called the vill of Horden parcel of the aforesaid manor, in which vill are eight messuages and eight cottages wasted, which are valued nothing per annum beyond reprises, 200 acres of land which are valued per annum beyond reprises 16s., six acres of meadow which are valued per annum beyond reprises 18d., 200 acres of pasture which are valued per annum beyond reprises 2s. and not more because all the aforesaid manor with appurtenances are charged to Thomas de Lees, William Tart, William Chaunceller and John White, chaplain, for an annual rent of £20, to be paid to them and their assigns for the term of their lives at the feast of Pentecost and St Martin in Winter by equal portions.

Here we have a manorial seat with its demesne lands still intact including meadow and pasture. However, the tenant settlement of the vill is wasted and presumably entirely abandoned, though the former tenant lands still have value, and the whole valuable manor is in the hands of a group of feoffees along with the receipt of a rent of £20. Clearly there has been a considerable amount of estate restructuring at Horden, which has seen it depopulated, but still to some extent exploited, though we cannot know whether the land was still being used for crops or had been converted to pasture. At Horden, then, we have depopulation and the abandonment of settlement, though the land still made a return.

Horden was an older core estate of the east coast, representing land under ancient cultivation. Evidence for the abandonment of the newer waste enclosures of the twelfth, thirteenth and early fourteenth centuries is slight. There is plenty of waste recorded in the various inquisitions, but nothing to indicate that this was anything

---

[30] C.D. Ross and T.B. Pugh, 'Materials for the Study of Baronial Incomes in Fifteenth-Century England', *EcHR*, new ser. 6 (1953), 186–7.
[31] PRO, DURH 3/2, fols. 256v–258v.

other than rough pasture pertaining to a manor and or commoned by various communities rather than land abandoned during the late Middle Ages. This kind of waste can be found throughout the county, and reinforces the reconstructed limit of the waste revealed in map 13.2.

The few examples that we have demonstrating decay and abandonment suggest that, like the example of Horden, lords used inclusive leases to manage abandoned properties. The 1432 inquisition *ad melius inquirendum* of the estate of Ralph Neville, earl of Westmorland details the decay of two moorland farms. The first of these, Cokside House in the parish of Lanchester, is recorded as largely ruinous, with it would seem, only one barn left of value on the site. The second, Helmeland in the parish of Wolsingham, reveals a wasted manor house. However, neither site seems to have been abandoned; Helmeland possessed fourteen other messuages, 200 acres of arable worth £11, twenty acres of meadow worth £2, a modest amount of woodland, and forty acres of moor.[32] The Nevilles seem to have acquired a considerable number of moorland farms in the later fourteenth century as they set about expanding their landed base, continuing to exploit these waste enclosures by tenanting them, whilst allowing the chief messuage to go to waste.

Perhaps the only real example of what would appear to be total abandonment in the inquisitions is that of Holmside, another moorland farm lying in the parish of Lanchester. This Umfraville manor or vill, the terminology varies, was a 100-acre moorland enclosure. It paid a rent of a silver mark as well as rendering forest service. However, in the IPM of Gilbert Umfraville of 1423–4 it was recorded as being worth nothing because it is *non includitur* ('not enclosed').[33] But even here the abandonment had been of no great time, for it was still apparently occupied in 1421 when it was recorded in the IPM of Agnes, Gilbert's mother.[34] Nor does the farm appear in the 'allowances' or 'respites' of the later surviving Chester coroners' accounts, so that it would seem that rent was being received from it by the 1440s.

Clearly inquisitions can only act as a guide, an indication of what might have been going on. They are of particular use, however, because they record a wider sample of land than just the immediate episcopal estate. They suggest that the reshaping of tenures meant that there was little untenanted land and perhaps little total desertion. All the examples are comparatively late and close together, dating from the second and third decades of the fifteenth century, though this in part reflects the increasing detail found in the IPMs of the later fourteenth and early fifteenth centuries.

The Evidence of the Coroners' Accounts

Coroners' accounts, recording the receipt of rents from manors and townships, can be used as an indicator of the difficulties of rent collection on the bishop's estate. The episcopal lands produced two sets of accounts for the collection of rents and services, those of the coroners, and those of the collectors, which in turn fed into the accounts of the chief episcopal accounting official, the receiver general. Whereas the collectors' accounts were produced from each ward for smaller sums and unfree rents and

[32] PRO, DURH 3/2, fols. 264r–265r.
[33] PRO, DURH 3/2, fols. 211v–212r.
[34] PRO, DURH 3/2, fo. 197v.

were collected by individuals selected from the local communities, the coroners' accounts were compiled by formal officials of the episcopal administration in each ward.[35] Moreover, unlike the collectors' accounts, all of the individual rents at every stage in the coroners' accounts are listed, usually with an explanation of the reason for their inclusion in the 'decays', 'allowances' and 'respites' sections, and this makes the accounts an ideal source for analysis and tabulation. The accounts are not unusual in their format and conform to that described by Christopher Dyer for the bishopric of Worcester. Their structure is illustrated in figure 13.2.[36]

Fig. 13.1 Structure of coroners' accounts

ARREARS Sum total of arrears from previous account.
RENTS Individual rents listed under manor or township, generally stating the tenant and the acreage of the holding. Sum total of arrears and rents.
DECAYS Individual decays and decreases of rent listed. These represent longer-term modifications of the rent received from individual holdings. Eventually, items included here could be included in the 'respites' section.
DELIVERY OF MONEY Sum total of decays and deliveries.
SUM TOTAL OF AMOUNT OWED
ALLOWANCES Individual allowances listed. These were allowances allowed for that particular year, and could include sums for fees for estate officials, liveries to other estate officials, and changes in rents collected. Entries frequently moved to the 'decays' section in subsequent accounts.
SUM TOTAL OF AMOUNT OWED
RESPITES Individual respited rents listed under manor or township. These rents were not expected to be collected, though they were still included in the debt of individual coroners.
IPSUM COMPUTATEM Listing of sums owed and paid by previous coroners.

---

[35] For a detailed description of the role of the coroners and the records they produced, see the website of DUL. In addition, a full listing of the surviving accounts is given under the heading for each ward and a summary of a representative sample account is provided under each ward section.

[36] Dyer, *Lords and Peasants*, p. 162. Note that the section entitled 'respites' stands outside the formal framework of the accounting system as a list of long-term debts, which were considered hopeless cases. Although the 'respites' section was separately titled and individually recorded, it was never formally totalled. The surviving accounts show that 'respites' accumulated from year to year so long as a coroner was in office, but were periodically reset to nought with the appointment of a new coroner. Although

The most obvious deduction from the tabulation of the coroners' accounts in tables 13.2–5 is that the episcopal estate had considerable problems with one particular kind of land – that held by free tenants.[37] This conclusion supports the findings of Arvanigian.[38] In all the wards, substantial quantities of free land were either held at reduced rents or were entirely waste because the land was untenanted. By contrast, in Easington and Stockton wards problems with exchequer land, which we might expect to be more 'marginal' than the free lands, were negligible or non-existent in the 'decays' and 'allowances' categories and were substantially dwarfed in the 'respites' category. In Darlington ward losses of rent from exchequer land are noticeably higher but still dwarfed by the figures for free land. The problems with free land are most pronounced in Stockton ward where the bulk of the nine per cent of the total rent recorded in the 'decays' section in 1413–14 was accounted for by free land. Though this percentage had declined by two-thirds in 1421–2, it remained at a much higher level than in any of the other wards amounting to six per cent in all three remaining accounts. We lack such early accounts for the other wards, but the higher percentage found in the 'decays' in Stockton over all of the accounts suggests that its free rents were hit far harder than in the other wards.

Only in Chester ward were there significant problems with exchequer land, equalling the levels experienced by lands held by free tenants under the 'decays' and 'allowances' sections, and significantly higher in the 'respites' category. In part, this disparity between the wards can be explained by the comparatively small quantities of exchequer land found in the wards of Easington and Stockton. The inclusion of Darlington ward is, perhaps, more surprising, for the ward included substantial acreages of exchequer land, and, as we have seen, had a very similar topography to Chester ward, reaching up into the High Pennines. But here the inclusion of much of the rich and fertile Tees valley may have influenced the results, the figures from older estates in the valley counteracting those from the newer lands along the upper Wear valley from Auckland to Stanhope. It is also noticeable from the individual entries that in Darlington ward, in particular, the bishop's administration had a specific problem with its corn mills (generally included under the freehold section, though

not totalled they were included in the rents of assize totals at the beginning of the account, even though the auditors had accepted that they would never be collected. Each individual coroner remained theoretically responsible for these sums, and some accounts do have additional details after the 'respites' section revealing that some of these sums were collected, but generally speaking a former coroner's liabilities must have remained limited for these arrears. I am grateful to Christopher Dyer for discussing these matters with me and for clarifying my views of the structure of the accounts.

[37] Since there are virtually no years where a whole set of accounts survives for each ward, each ward is examined separately in an attempt to analyse one account from every ward over each decade where it is available. In Darlington, Easington and Chester wards, although the accounts from each are not available from exactly the same accounting years, it is possible to compare years in the middle of each decade. The tables are divided into three categories. Of these, two categories require further explanation. The 'Other Land' category includes lands which are problematic or which do not fit into the 'Exchequer Land' or 'Free Land' categories. It also includes any urban property, which though technically free land would obviously skew the rent totals. The 'Admin.' category includes sums that are entered for reasons unconnected with land tenure. It includes liveries of sums of money, and sums paid to officials for their expenses and wages. The 'Other' category under all three classifications of land includes such items as rent which had been duplicated in other entries, rents allowed for errors in the records, and rents which came from lands that were subject to reorganisation, perhaps being let as part of a larger package of lands for a new rent.

[38] Arvanigian, 'Free Rents in the Palatinate of Durham'.

Table 13.2 Coroners' accounts for Darlington ward

	Accounting Year	Exchequer Land			Free Land			Other Land			Admin.	Totals
		Reduced Rent	Unten.	Other	Reduced Rent	Unten.	Other	Reduced Rent	Unten.	Other		
Decays	1444–5	0	0	0	0	686	238	0	0	0	0	924
	1459–60	0	0	0	0	610	602	720	0	0	0	1932
	1466–7	0	0	0	0	610	602	400	0	0	0	1612
	1476–7	0	0	0	0	610	602	400	0	0	0	1612
	1488–9	0	0	0	0	610	602	400	0	0	0	1612
Allowances	1444–5	160	0	0	2480	0	0	440	0	1231.5	800	51115
	1459–60	0	0	0	0	0	0	0	0	0	3698	3698
	1466–7	0	0	0	0	0	0	0	0	0	3698	3698
	1476–7	0	0	0	0	0	40	346	0	875	2377	3638
	1488–9	0	0	0	0	0	40	506	0	1958	4292	6796
Respites	1444–5	0	0	3685	2110	480	1183.6	0	0	2444	600	10502.6
	1459–60	576	1260	0	5050	2136	252	1625.5	48	0	360	11307.5
	1466–7	1440	4200	0	15508	7120	120	6572	160	1440	600	37160
	1476–7	144	420	0	1450	712	12	621.5	87.5	144	60	3651
	1488–9	720	2112	0	7250	3917.5	60	3133	80	6720	300	24292.5

Accounting Year	Total Rent	Decays Total: percentage of Total Rent	Allowances Total: percentage of Total Rent
1444–5	65250	1.42	7.83
1459–60	64822.125	2.98	5.59
1466–7	66109.5	2.44	5.59
1476–7	67851.75	2.38	5.36
1488–9	70193	2.30	p.68

Note: all figures are given in pence.

Source: the tables are derived from the following accounts: DUL, CCB B/48/1 (190212); 1444–5; CCB B/48/2 (188788): 1459–60; CCB B/48/4 (188790): 1466–7; CCB B/48/5 (190199); 1476–7; CCB B/48/6 (188791): 1488–9.

Table 13.3 Coroners' accounts for Easington ward

Section of Account	Accounting Year	Exchequer Land Reduced Rent	Exchequer Land Unten.	Exchequer Land Other	Reduced Rent	Free Land Unten.	Free Land Other	Other Land Reduced Rent	Other Land Unten.	Other Land Other	Admin.	Totals
Decays	1443–4	0	0	0	80	26	240	0	0	0	0	346
	1455–6	0	0	0	142	26	240	0	0	0	0	408
	1465–6	0	0	0	178	30	240	0	0	0	0	448
	1477–8	0	0	0	178	30	240	0	0	0	0	448
Allowances	1443–4	0	0	0	1024	0	0	0	0	0	0	1024
	1455–6	0	0	0	0	0	0	0	0	3285.75	2880.5	6166.25
	1465–6	0	0	0	0	0	60	0	0	996.75	320	1346.75
	1477–8	0	0	0	20	30	769	0	0	0	0	819
Respites	1443–4	0	330	0	432	6930	420	0	0	0	0	8112
	1455–6	560	224	0	966	824	9380	0	0	0	0	11954
	1465–6	320	120	0	5040	1032	560	0	160	0	0	7232
	1477–8	80	30	0	1830	198	200	0	40	0	0	2378

Accounting Year	Total Rent	Decays Total: percentage of Total Rent	Allowances Total: percentage of Total Rent
1443–4	16505.5	0.28	6.20
1455–6	29663.75	1.38	20.79
1465–6	31105.75	1.44	4.33
1477–8	30856	1.45	2.65

Note: all figures are given in pence.

Source: the tables are derived from the following accounts: DUL, CCB B/49/1 (188725): 1443–4; CCB B/49/2 (188726): 1455–6; CCB B/49/4 (189697): (188725): 1443–4; CCB B/49/9 (188731): 1477–8.

Table 13.4 Coroners' accounts for Stockton ward

Section of Account	Accounting Year	Exchequer Land				Free Land				Other Land				Admin.	Totals
		Reduced Rent	Unten.	Other	Reduced Rent	Unten.	Other	Reduced Rent	Unten.	Other				
Decays	1413–14	0	80	0	0	40	402	80	0	160			0	762
	1421–2	0	0	0	40	0	199	0	0	0			0	239
	1459–60	0	0	0	0	0	371	0	0	0			0	371
	1468–9	0	0	0	0	0	371	0	0	0			0	371
	1479–80	0	0	0	0	0	371	0	0	0			0	371
Allowances	1413–14	0	0	0	0	0	0	0	0	0			200	200
	1421–2	0	0	0	0	0	0	0	0	0			0	0*
	1459–60	0	0	0	48	0	0	0	0	0			0	48
	1468–9	0	0	0	48	0	0	0	0	0			0	48
	1479–80	0	0	0	48	0	0	0	0	0			136	184
Respites	1413–14	0	0	0	0	0	0	0	0	0			0	0*
	1421–2	0	0	0	0	0	0	0	0	0			0	0*
	1459–60	0	0	0	0	624	81	0	0	0			0	705
	1468–9	0	0	0	0	2976	328	2880	0	0			0	6184
	1479–80	0	0	0	0	832	112	960	0	0			0	1904

Accounting Year	Total Rent	Decays Total: percentage of Total Rent	Allowances Total: percentage of Total Rent
1413–14	8402	9.07	2.38
1421–2	6166	3.88	0*
1459–60	6166.25	6.07	0.78
1468–9	6177	6.02	0.78
1479–80	6166	6.02	2.98

Note: all figures are given in pence.
* It is not clear whether the 'respites' in 1413–14 and 1421–2, and the 'allowances' in 1421–2, were for some reason omitted, or did not occur in those years.

Source: the tables are derived from the following accounts: DUL, CCB B/50/1 (188879); 1413–14; CCB B/50/4 (188882): 1421–2; CCB B/50/5 (188883): 1459–60; CCB B/50/10 (188888): 1468–9; CCB B/50/18 (188995): 1479–80.

Table 13.5 Coroners' accounts for Chester ward

Section of Account	Accounting Year	Exchequer Land			Free Land				Other Land				Totals
		Reduced Rent	Unten.	Other	Unten.	Other	Reduced Rent	Unten.	Other	Reduced Rent	Admin	
Decays	1447–8	354	641	140	812	0	0	832	0	0	0	2791
	1457–8	729	653	0	818	0	0	832	0	0	0	3164
	1467–8	701	653	0	824	0	0	832	0	0	0	3262
	1476–7	500	772	0	834	0	0	832	0	0	0	3070
Allowances	1447–8	409	0	8	90	4880	35	80	0	0	1280	7259
	1457–8	51	0	8	0	80	408	1680	0	0	0	2450
	1467–8	16	20	8	0	80	408	0	2973.5	0	0	3644.5
	1476–7	16	124	8	278	80	2368	208	147	0	5955	9318
Respites	1447–8	6658	164060	17445	11955	13640	1492	6135	5620	0	4394.5	23589.55
	1457–8	555	1305	1496	1041	1232	332	563	444	0	264	7516
	1467–8	6069	12496	13594	10650	12320	3200	5678	5120	0	2640	74607
	1476–7	582	1385	1496	1065	1232	332	819	500	0	162	7857

Accounting Year	Total Rent	Decays Total: percentage of Total Rent	Allowances Total: percentage of Total Rent
1447–8	75235	3.71	9.65
1457–8	76926	4.11	3.18
1467–8	Incomplete*	/	/
1476–7	77464	3.96	12.03

Note: all figures are given in pence.

* Three rents are obscured because of damage to the 1467–8 account, so that a figure for the total rent is unavailable. However, although the individual rents did vary from account to account, the surviving figures give no reason to believe that it would be anything other than comparable with the preceding and succeeding accounts.

Source: the tables are derived from the following accounts: DUL, CCB B/44/2 (188651): 1447–8; CCB B/44/3 (188657): 1457–58; CCB B/44/8 (190297): 1467–8; CCB B/45/14 (190176): 1476–7.

some mills did render exchequer rents). Over all of the accounts sums were allowed the coroner for necessary repairs on the mill, for periods when the mills were vacant, or when they could only be let for a drastically reduced rent. Indeed, in the selected accounts, the considerable sums allowed for mills dramatically skewed the figures for 'decays' and 'allowances' in this ward.[39] Problems with mills are of particular interest, for although by their very nature they are very capital-intensive tenancies to hold, mills have traditionally been seen as a significant element both in seigniorial power and in the rental income of the seigniorial economy. If the bishop was facing problems with corn mills, this suggests that they had become comparatively unattractive tenancies, which in turn suggest either a failure in seigniorial authority forcing tenants to mill at designated mills or a more dramatic move away from cultivation, greatly reducing the part played by grain production in the rural economy of this part of Durham.

But it is with Chester ward that our attention should lie. The figures tabulated in table 13.5 indicate that, in that ward alone, there had been a far more dramatic contraction of the tenanted acreage than in any of the other wards. In the 'decays' category the exchequer rents account for a higher amount in every year, and within the exchequer rents there appear both rents that had been reduced and those that were untenanted. Curiously, in the 'allowances' category the free lands and the other lands categories account for the majority of the sums, and exchequer land plays a small part. However, it is in the respited rents that the major difference occurs. Here, in every account, the figures for exchequer land are larger than those from free lands. Within the figures for exchequer land, the sums for the 'untenanted' section are greater than those for 'reduced' rent, whilst an even larger sum can be found in the 'other' section where sums that were included for administrative alterations and mistakes are included. The episcopal estate in Chester ward did not conform to the pattern found in the other three wards. Table 13.1 shows that Chester ward had far greater proportion of exchequer land than any of the other wards, amounting to forty per cent of the total acreage, whilst the next highest concentration was in Darlington ward where it amounted to only thirty per cent, but it would seem that in Chester ward the exchequer land was disproportionately affected by the changes that the palatinate experienced in the later fourteenth and fifteenth centuries.

These differences in the figures found in tables 13.2–5 are not easy to explain. Although, as has already been observed, there were clear differences in the topography and the concentrations of different kinds of lands between the wards, the distinction between the two larger western wards suggest that wards that in other ways seem similar fared differently to the changed circumstances that they faced. That being said, even in Chester ward, where exchequer land was disproportionately affected and was more likely to be tenanted for a reduced rent or to be recorded as waste, problems with free land still remained prominent. For much of the palatinate of Durham, then, it is not the case that the later colonised exchequer land was significantly more likely to be let for reduced rents (because there were problems finding

---

[39] This is particularly evident in the 'allowances' section of the account of 1444–5 in Darlington ward where Wolsingham mill could only be let at £4, when its old rent stood at £5 16s. 8d.; Stanhope mill was let for £4 13s. 4d., a decline of £2; and the two mills of Bishop Auckland were charged for only £8 of their £16 rent because the mill was vacant for sixteen weeks due to want of repair.

tenants) or to remain entirely untenanted. Instead, rather than a wholesale retreat from the later colonised and less accessible uplands, the bishop's administration faced a refusal by its free tenants to pay their full rents. Many of these free tenants were powerful members of the nobility or gentry of the palatinate who simply refused to co-operate, but many were lesser individuals who could still resist the power and authority of the bishop's administration with apparent impunity.

The coroners' accounts do reveal a noticeable degree of contraction. Entries refer to untenanted and wasteland, and statements that 'it is not known where the land lies' or 'it is not known where to charge the rent', are far too numerous for us to doubt this process of retreat. Yet, it was not so much a problem of keeping the land tenanted, but rather making existing tenants pay the full rent for their holdings. To a certain degree, this may well be the truculence of the tenancy that Dyer and Britnell and others have noticed in this period, but as Hatcher has stated, for many tenants, the collapse in the prices that could be obtained for agricultural products must have severely limited the ability of smaller tenants to pay their rents. The shift in power away from landlords to the tenantry may have been rather illusory by the mid-fifteenth century.[40]

The evidence presented here, though at times difficult to interpret, does provide some findings that are able to take us substantially beyond the limitations of images of relict field systems. There was a noticeable level of contraction over the whole period from the later fourteenth to the later fifteenth centuries. In the evidence from the Hatfield Survey the acreage of the land recorded as waste was low, though it varied markedly between the four wards of the palatinate. The IPMs do not allow such an assessment to be made, but do not reveal substantial acreages of abandoned land. The coroners' accounts indicate much more substantial long-term contraction, which became a regular feature of the 'respites' section of the accounts. Nonetheless, at no time is there a suggestion of large-scale abandonment. In certain places such as Bishopley and Bollihope forty per cent of the recorded acreage was abandoned, but we do not see the evidence for entire vills being recorded as waste as Dodds has revealed from his analysis of the tithe accounts of Durham Priory.[41]

The sources used here do not permit any definite conclusion as to the chronology of this contraction beyond the fact that the process had begun by 1381, when it was recorded in the Hatfield Survey, and that there is evidence of ongoing retreat after this time which was largely complete by the 1440s when the coroners' accounts survive in any quantity. These record further lands which were lying waste or in the hand of the lord and which appear to have been in that state for a considerable time stretching back at least to the 1430s.[42] This evidence is not at odds with general trends according to which, following the first outbreak of plague, there was some recovery followed by long-term decline from the late fourteenth century.

---

[40] Dyer, *Lords and Peasants*, p. 184; Britnell, 'Feudal Reaction', 46–7; and Hatcher, 'Great Slump', pp. 259–60.

[41] Dodds, 'Production, Population and Pestilence', pp. 9–10. It is not entirely clear why there should be this apparent difference between the two great estates in Durham. It is possible that the differences were not so great, but that the surviving records magnify more minor differences, though it is of course possible that the priory estate faired far less well in the fifteenth century than did that of the bishop.

[42] Take, for example, the account of the coroner of Chester ward for 1447–8, where the 'respites' section lists respites that run for that year and the preceding ten.

The distribution and type of land abandoned is also of interest for it reveals that overall the land that was more recently colonised, particularly the exchequer land, was only marginally more likely to be abandoned than other classes of land. Although the extent of the abandonment is possibly underassessed, since some of the land that was classified as free was also of more recent colonisation, including the bulk of the moorland farms, it does suggest that land more recently colonised was not necessarily valued less than lands that were settled and exploited earlier. The distribution of the abandoned lands shows, however, that there was considerable variation throughout the county. Certainly, the large parishes of the Pennine Spurs and the High Pennines – Stanhope, Wolsingham and Lanchester – were more heavily affected by the abandonment of land, and it was in Chester ward that the most significant problems with exchequer land were found in the coroners' accounts. Moreover, while the higher percentage of untenanted land here may have simply reflected the increasing shift to pastoral enterprises in an upland area already heavily reliant on pastoral farming, lands that could be considered more marginal because of their location, lying in the more difficult terrain of the Pennines, appear to have proved less attractive than lands in the Tees Lowlands further to the east.

But the impression of contraction of the tenanted land is by no means the whole picture, for at least on the episcopal estate there was a far larger problem with land which was tenanted, but from which the estate was unsuccessful in extracting all or part of its rents. Although the findings here merely emphasise those of Arvanigian, it is clear that this was far more of a problem than that of untenanted land. This particularly affected lands held freely. In part, this must have reflected the growing truculence of tenants, but this can only be part of the picture. It is quite probable that the free tenants, in particular, were also deeply affected by the prevailing conditions in the fifteenth century, and were unable to pay their rents because of the fall in the price that could be obtained for agricultural produce and their own inability to collect rents from their own tenants. As R.L. Storey has shown, the bishops of Durham in the fifteenth century remained very wealthy individuals able to make substantial loans to the king and to monastic houses in difficulty.[43] However, whilst their declining estate income seems to have had very little impact on the bishops themselves, it suggests that their estates were undergoing considerable change. These estates were both contracting in size and facing changes to the relationship they had with their tenants who, though continuing to occupy their lands, found it increasingly difficult to meet their obligations. Any suggestion that there was a general retreat from the margins in Durham seems somewhat premature.

---

[43] Storey, *Thomas Langley*, pp. 91–2.

14

Framing Medieval Landscapes: Region and Place in County Durham

BRIAN K. ROBERTS, HELEN DUNSFORD and SIMON J. HARRIS

All history involves the creation of viable balances between detail, seen for instance in the minutiae of an individual land charter – the legitimate subject of a single learned paper by a historian –[1] and the broader sweeps of regional and national contexts. To create the latter, broad brush representations necessarily replace the finely grained textures. This contrast is to be seen in the antithesis between the Spanish fighting bull, all rush and testosterone, found in a few strokes from Picasso, and the meticulous and bejewelled detail of an artist such as van Eyck. In art, and history, there is a place for both. This essay uses work by the three authors in order to sketch some broad brush lines concerning the medieval landscapes of County Durham.[2]

The land itself and its adjacent sea, a complex of geology, relief, soils, vegetation and water, locked together within frames defined by latitude and longitude, have always been the setting for local human affairs. Clearance and farming, building and destruction, management and usage have all played a part, with each generation maintaining, altering and sometimes destroying the cultural landscapes inherited from previous generations: an endless succession, paradoxically involving both stability and change. One indicator of the problems involved when dealing with historic landscapes is to be seen in field observations of portions of the boundary banks of Steward Shield Meadow (map 14.4). On the eastern side of the site these have actually been cut away by valley-side retreat, itself the result of increased run-off occasioned by woodland clearance and the grazing of many beasts. We know that the site was deserted by the later fourteenth century and the banks can be seen as 'medieval'. They probably were, and the interpretation of the site as an eighty-acre moorland farm (see below and map 14.4) is reasonable.[3] However, the fact that the pollen diagram shows that the major clearance took place long before this date leaves other options open amid a mere sixty-two centimetres of muddy peat: we cannot, without extensive excavation, prove that the banks are not Romano-British or prehistoric. The problem is one of

---

[1] H.S. Offler, 'A Northumberland Charter of King Henry I', in idem, *North of the Tees: Studies in Medieval British History*, ed. A.J. Piper and A.I. Doyle (Aldershot, 1996), ch. 8.
[2] This essay reports some of the major findings of an ESRC-funded research project, supervised by Richard Britnell (Department of History) and Brian Roberts (Department of Geography).
[3] *HS*, pp. 73, 108. In fact, these were almost certainly 'Durham acres', measured with a twenty-one foot land rod.

correlating evidence that can disappear through the fingers like dry sand. Nevertheless, whatever the precise interpretation, the pollen record still provides some information about this dramatic and still visible farmstead and fields set at 380 metres above sea level and a kilometre or so above the main head-dyke in Weardale. In the autumn the steading appears as a patch of rich green set within a sea of brown. It has a story to tell of human endeavour and, as context for such detail, we need broad brush images.

Commons and Terrains

Maps 14.1 and 14.2 complement each other: map 14.1, created by Helen Dunsford, is a map of the common wastes in about 1600. It is shown in this first map in a wholly 'pure' and stark form, without imposed and obfuscating data. Formal enclosure awards with maps are few in Durham.[4] Many enclosures took place in the seventeenth century, broadly between 1580 and 1680, many by agreement, while the Chancery Decree Awards, which record surrender and admittance procedures in the bishop's courts, had no attached maps.[5] However, it is one of the curiosities of the Old Series six inch First Edition Ordnance Survey maps of the county that the commons were systematically named by the officers of the Royal Engineers who did the work. We can only speculate why and how they did this, for most commons had been enclosed long before the 1850s. However, the county is also remarkable because, just before the work of the Ordnance Survey, a series of maps at an approximate scale of 1:25,000 covering the whole northern coalfield, was produced. Published by J.T.W. Bell, between 1843 and 1861, the maps record landownership and must draw upon earlier data – tithe maps, enclosure award maps for some of the commons – as well as a host of private estate documents.[6] The essential accuracy of these surveys is verified by use, and the mainspring of their creation was undoubtedly the royalties that accrued to landowners in the form of rights to sink pits and in the need to create wayleaves for waggonways.[7] This suggestion is hypothesis not proof, but provides a perfectly rational explanation.

Using the Ordnance Survey six inch maps and Bell's maps the former extents of individual township and parish commons could be established, in some cases with absolute precision, in others through a careful 'reading' of the nature of the field

---

[4] W.E. Tate, *A Domesday of English Enclosure Acts and Awards*, ed. M.E. Turner (Reading, 1978), pp. 107–9.

[5] R.I. Hodgson, 'Coalmining, Population and Enclosure in the Sea-sale Colliery Districts of (Northern) Durham, 1551–1810' (unpublished Ph.D. thesis, University of Durham, 1989), pp. 213–49; R.I. Hodgson, 'Agricultural Improvement and Changing Regional Economies in the Eighteenth Century', in *Man Made the Land*, ed. A.R.H. Baker and J.B. Harley (Newton Abbot, 1973), figures 187a and 187b.

[6] J.T.W. Bell, *Plan of the Hartlepool Coal District in the County of Durham, including part of the Wear District, being the First of a Series of Plans of the Great Northern Coalfield* (London, 1843); idem, *Plan of the Tyne and Wear Coal Districts in the County of Durham, being the Second of a Series of Plans of the Great Northern Coalfield* (London, 1843); idem, *Plan of the Auckland Coal District in the County of Durham, being the Fifth of a Series of Plans of the Great Northern Coalfield* (Newcastle-upon-Tyne, 1852); idem, *Plan of the Western Coal District of Durham and Northumberland, being the Sixth of a Series of Plans of the Great Northern Coalfield* (Newcastle-upon-Tyne, 1861). Copies of these are lodged in DUL.

[7] Hodgson, 'Coalmining, Population and Enclosure', pp. 26–59; M.J.T. Lewis, *Early Wooden Railways* (London, 1970), pp. 137–62.

REGION AND PLACE IN COUNTY DURHAM 223

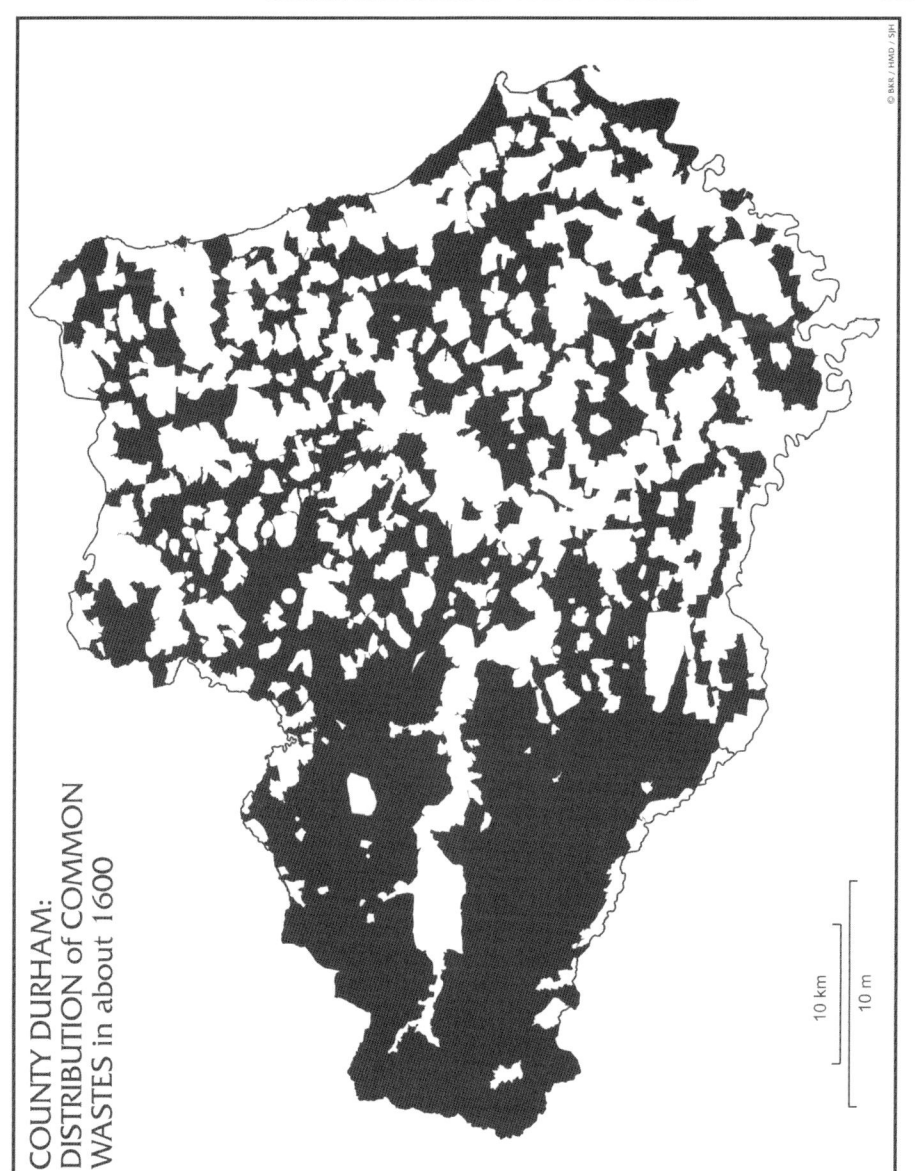

COUNTY DURHAM:
DISTRIBUTION of COMMON
WASTES in about 1600

10 km

10 m

Map 14.1 Commons and Wastes, Co. Durham

boundaries. Straight, geometrically formal field layouts are indicative of enclosures upon commons, but this is only in the most clear-cut of cases, and a great deal of 'professional judgement' – practical experience – was necessary. On many occasions when a near impasse was reached, a combination of the landownership map and place-name evidence for documented farm names, collected by Victor Watts, provided essential support.[8] We regard the resulting map as at least eighty per cent accurate, but will be quite happy when future studies allow corrections to be made. Given that the original map was drawn in an ArcGIS system over the scanned Ordnance Survey six inch (1:10,560) maps of the middle decades of the nineteenth century (kindly provided by Durham County Council), corrections at the scale of an individual field are perfectly possible. These details then merge within the countywide picture. We have been able to map the wastes to about 1600, that is, before the bulk of enclosures by Chancery Decree Award.[9]

The pure distribution shown in map 14.1 is fascinating. What we cannot do is define the nature of the common rights over these tracts of land. Most were subject to common grazing and many must have been stinted. However, as late as the seventeenth century the Teesdale commons were *sans stint*, while in Weardale there are signs that by the earlier fifteenth century the episcopal stockmasters were well aware of the numbers of beasts running upon each pasture.[10] Terms such as 'common waste', 'manorial waste', 'commons', 'rough pasture', 'waste', 'open pasture' and 'wood pasture', 'moorland', 'fell' and the like beg questions we are frankly not able to answer in this broad brush view.[11] All are applicable in measure to the lands within which we are dealing. Further, the boundary between the black (the mapped areas) and the white (unmapped areas) represents a head-dyke, a running boundary between improved and enclosed, generally improved, land, and the open, generally unimproved fells and moors. In this simple observation there lies an important methodological point. The commons were mapped positively: attention was given to assembling data for each township and parish and this in turn allowed a composite county picture to emerge. The white areas also constitute a map, of negative information, of those lands that were *not* common wastes in about 1600, and these lands, like the commons, have their own substance and history of usage. They have been defined at least as tightly as the commons, that is, to a level of eighty per cent accuracy. A later section of this essay will consider these areas. Looking at the distribution of commons several points emerge: first, in the west of Durham the presence of commons and open rough pastures that remain such a feature of upland Durham today is confirmed and vastly extended; secondly, and more surprising, there are large tracts of common in the south and east of the county in about 1600. A rough estimate would suggest that approximately forty per cent of the land surface remained as common waste.

At this juncture map 14.2 must be brought into the argument, a greatly simplified map of terrains. This classifies the land-surface of Durham into three categories –

---

[8] V. Watts, *A Dictionary of County Durham Place-Names* (English Place-Name Society Popular Series 3, 2002).
[9] Hodgson, 'Coalmining, Population and Enclosure', figures 6.1. 6.2, 6.3, 6.4., 6.7.
[10] Cf. the master forester's account of 1438–9: DUL, CCB B/83/1 (190030).
[11] W. Hoskins, 'History of Common Land and Common Rights', and W.I. Jennings, 'Some Legal Problems', in *Royal Commission on Common Land 1955–1958* (London, 1958), pp. 149–66 and 167–184 respectively.

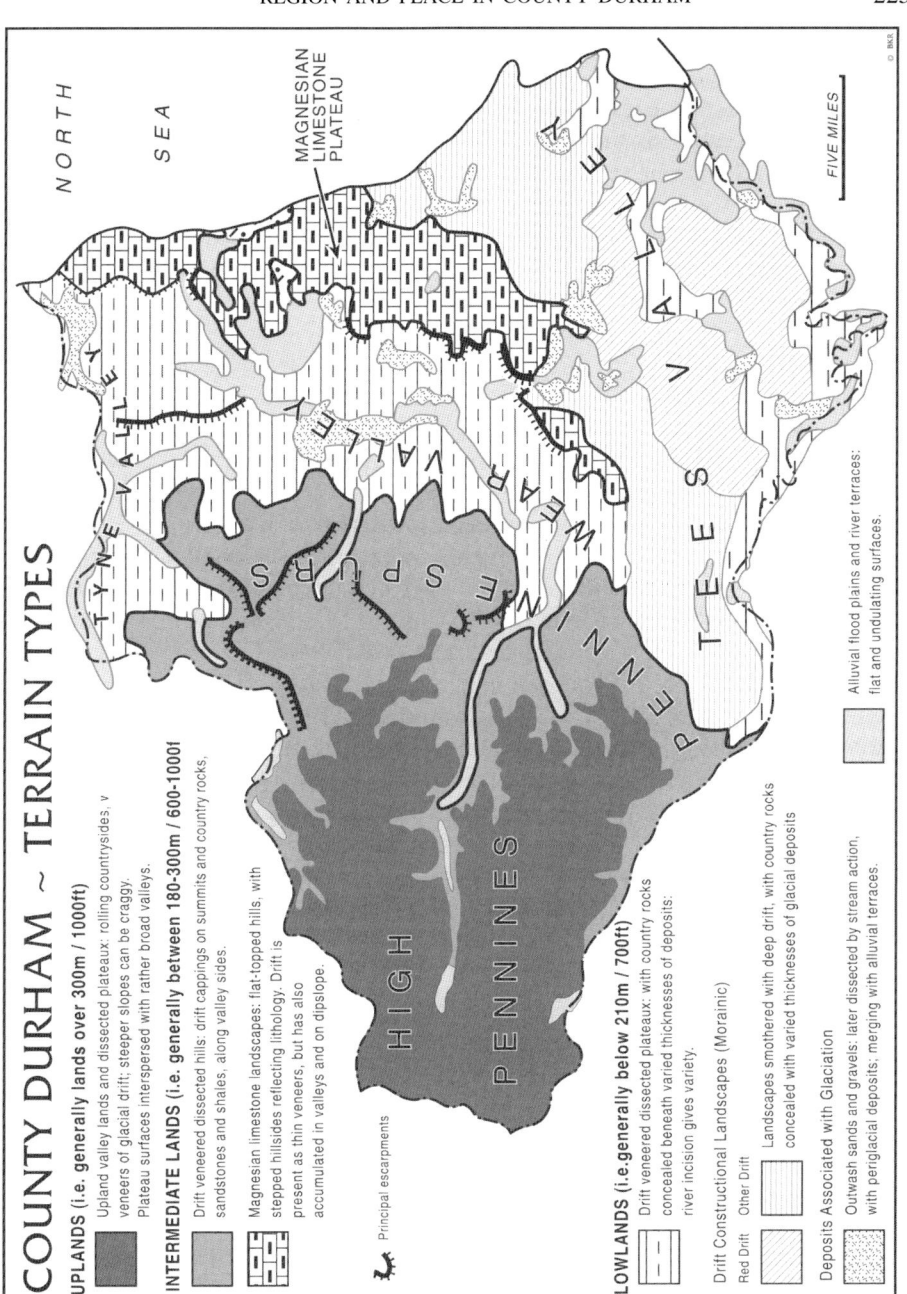

Map 14.2 County Durham Terrains

uplands, intermediate lands and lowlands – and then provides a succinct description of each. The texture inherent in the mapping is designed to reveal to the eye the varied character of the lands involved. However, the lines separating each tract of land from the next are seductive, and in reality each grades into the next, so that subjective decisions must be taken when creating boundaries. Only rarely are sharp breaks visible, seen most clearly in the scarp of the Magnesian limestone, and even this effectively occupies a tract of countryside of the order of two kilometres in width. A comparison between maps 14.1 and 14.2 shows a clear correlation between very extensive areas of common in 1600 and the High Pennines and intermediate lands of the Pennine Spurs on the terrain map. In short, increasing altitude is associated with greater wetness, a later arrival of spring, poorer soils and environments more suitable for grazing than tillage.[12]

For the lowlands in the south and east the same comparison suggests that, in detail, the extensive commons reflect local geology and soils. Commons tend to appear on patches of more difficult soil, itself a highly subjective judgement. They are seen on the Skerne marshes and the coastal marshlands around and north of the Tees estuary. They are also present, upon relatively uniform tracts, such as the thin limestone soils of the top of the Magnesian limestone and the flat drift covered surfaces between Spennymoor, Byers Green and the Gaunless valley. In detail this is a fragmented pattern, a reflection not of dominant environmental controls but of subtle, wholly local circumstances, within each parish and each township. In this detail local land homogeneity may be an important clue to the former presence of commons, because settlements and fields prosper more readily amid landscapes that show heterogeneity, with sharp local variations in relief, drainage and soil characteristics. Such variety offers farmers opportunities in their negotiations with the land.

The Open Pastures and Moorland Farms

Simon Harris's important work on specific grants of waste and moorland farms between about 1150 and 1320 is mapped as map 14.3, with a simple symbol for each farm being superimposed over the common wastes reconstructed in about 1600. With some few exceptions, where a local recession to waste must be assumed, these all lie within the white areas of the distribution and represent successful medieval reclamation. These are discussed elsewhere by Dunsford and Harris and in an essay by Simon Harris in this volume.[13] There is almost certainly a skewing of the distribution away from the lands of the FitzMeldreds in the middle and upper Tees valley, a region distinctive to this day because of the white painted farmsteads of the successor Raby estate, and in the Neville lordship centred on Brancepeth to the south-west of Durham city.[14] The charters for this area appear not to survive, but it is inconceivable that the

---

[12] A. Temple, *The Land of Britain: The Report of the Land Utilisation Survey of Britain: County Durham*, ed. L.D. Stamp (London, 1941), figure 21; P. Beaumont, 'Geomorphology', J. Stevens and K. Atkinson, 'Soils', and K. Smith, 'Climate and Weather', in *County Durham and City with Teesside*, ed. J.C. Dewdney (Durham, 1970), pp. 26–74; R.A. Jarvis et al., 'Soils and their Use in Northern England', *Soil Survey of England and Wales* 10 (1984), figures 2–9.

[13] H.M. Dunsford and S.J. Harris, 'Colonization of the Wasteland in County Durham, 1100–1400', *EcHR* 56 (2003), 34–56.

[14] H.S. Offler, 'Fitz-Meldred, Neville and Hansard', in idem, *North of the Tees: Studies in Medieval British History*, ed. A.J. Piper and A.I. Doyle (Aldershot, 1996), ch. 13.

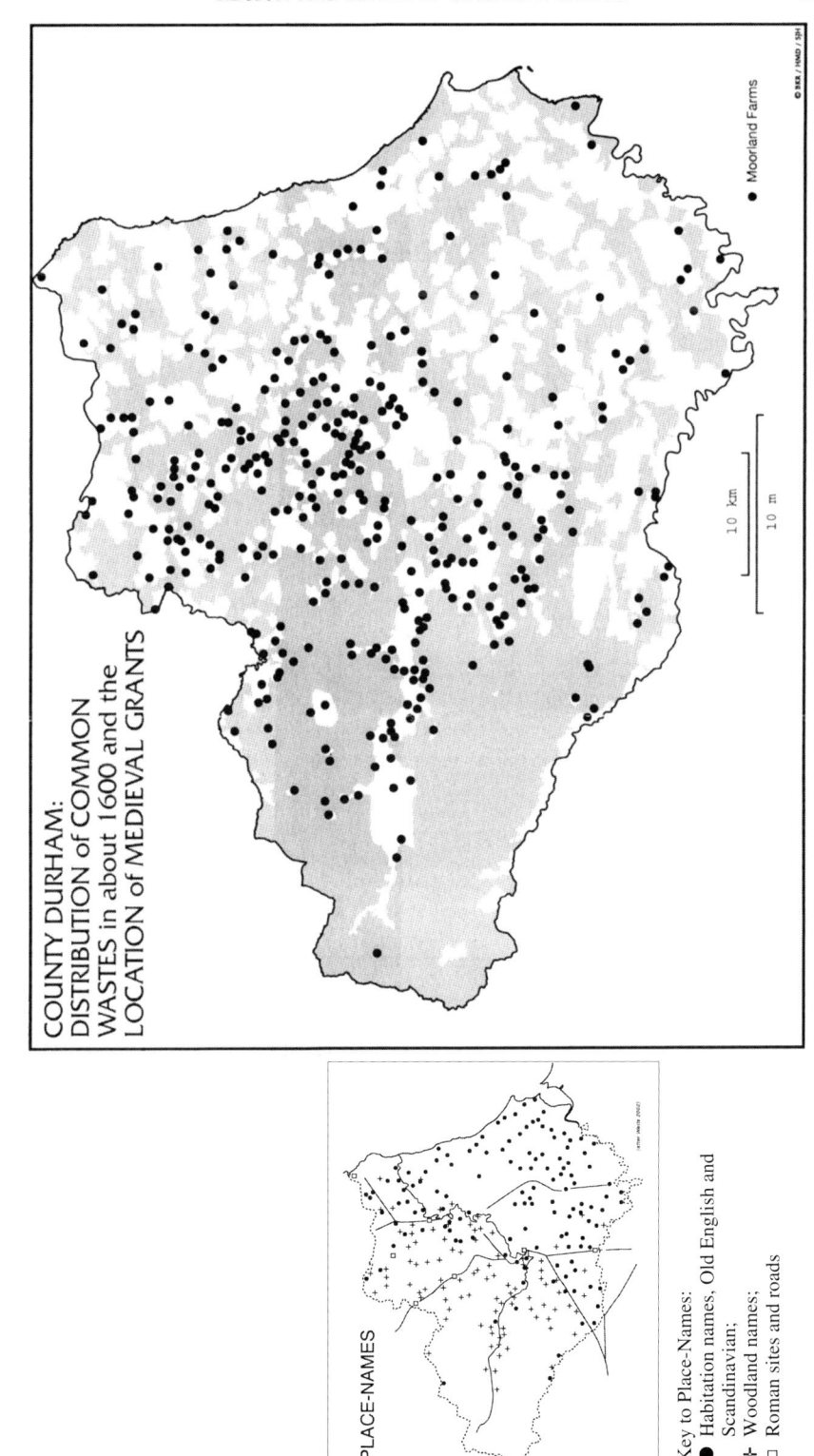

Map 14.3 Commons and Wastes and Moorland Farms, Co. Durham

same processes of colonisation were not equally as active on these estates. Again, and still in broad brush strokes, there is a heavy concentration of farms in the foothills and dales of the west. We have not attempted to give a correct areal extent to each of the symbols. In fact, the real boundaries of each farm are known for about one third of the total, the general extent in terms of acreage of about another third, while the remainder are known as named locations. However, if we abstract from the white areas the land represented by these farms, then we are probing towards a picture of the Durham landscape as it was, let us say, in the middle decades of the twelfth century. Of course, even the remarkable collection of Durham charter material is probably not complete, although Simon Harris has checked his findings against the Hatfield Survey of about 1381 and the Boldon Book of 1183.[15] Like a monitor screen reduced to coarse pixels we can just perceive the shape of an earlier landscape, with the west of Durham dominated by vast tracts of uncultivated land, no doubt a mixture of open pastures and wood pasture. In the middle decades of the twelfth century it is likely that this represented at least eighty per cent of the land surface and can be glimpsed in the reconstruction appearing as the background to map 14.5 of this study. The argument is confirmed by independent but convergent evidence from place-names. Victor Watts has constructed a distribution map of names ending in *-leah, -hyrst, -rydding* and *-wudu*, which shows that in the west of the county, notably in the foothills of the uplands, Old English place-names consistently speak of woodlands and clearings. To the south and east of this lay a zone of habitation names in *-tun, -ham, -worth, -wic, -burh* and *-by*.[16] This defines a zone essentially congruent with limited numbers of fifth-, sixth- and eighth-century burials and chance finds.[17] The boundary line between these two contrasting countrysides runs along the Roman road from Bowes as far as Bishop Auckland, and thence down the Wear to the eastwards turn of the river at Chester-le-Street, and thence northwards up the Birtley ridge to Gateshead.

This retrogressive analysis allows the creation of maps that are more than merely schematic, and touch on the real character of the county nearly one thousand years ago. We would be the first to recognise that much detail needs to be added to our first attempts. To give one instance, the 'bulge' in white – improved land – in central Weardale is fictitious and caused by the presence of the bishop's great park. This we have outlined, but almost certainly, judging by slight earthworks on the valley slopes within the core of the park, it took in lands that had once been reclaimed. We have avoided making judgements at this point, yet the likely pattern, of an attenuating amount of improved land as the dale sides close in, is clear.[18] Map 14.3 provides a necessary framework within which to integrate detailed evidence derived from the

---

[15] *HS*; *BB*; H.S. Offler, 'Re-reading Boldon Book', in idem, *North of the Tees: Studies in Medieval British History*, ed. A.J. Piper and A.I. Doyle (Aldershot, 1996), ch. 12.

[16] Watts, *County Durham Place-Names*, pp. xiv, xvi.

[17] S. Lucy, 'Changing Burial Rites in Northumbria AD 500–750', in *Northumbria's Golden Age*, ed. J. Hawkes and S. Mills (Frome, 1999), figures 2.1, 2.2, 2.3; C. Loveluck, 'The Romano-British to Anglo-Saxon Transition: Social Transformations from the late Roman to Early Medieval Period in Northern England, AD 400–700', in *Past, Present and Future: The Archaeology of Northern England*, ed. C. Brooks et al. (Architectural and Archaeological Society of Durham and Northumberland, Research Report No. 5, 2002), pp. 132–6.

[18] B.K. Roberts, 'Man and land in Upper Teesdale', in *Teesdale*, ed. A.R. Clapham (London, 1978), pp. 141–59; J. Britton, 'Farm, Field and Fell in Upper Teesdale, 1600–1900' (unpublished M.A. thesis, University of Durham, 1974), figure 3.

further study of individual parishes and specific areas of moorland, parklands and ancient woodlands. It represents a framework rather than wholly completed research.

In sharp contrast to this spatial and retrogressive study, map 14.4 allows a glimpse of two pieces of landscape development seen in a 'through time' perspective. The locations of the two pollen diagrams are shown in the inset. Both diagrams are considerably simplified and that for Steward Shield Meadow has been vertically stretched to bring it into chronological accord with that for Hallowell Moss.[19] To move down each diagram is to go backwards in time, through generalised curves of vegetation development based upon a succession of pollen counts from samples. The horizontal axes represent a scale of 100 per cent and show the relative proportions of varied types of plant species, trees, shrubs and herbs and, in the case of Hallowell Moss, bog and aquatic species. Some of the horizons are radio-carbon dated, and the variation in the degrees of error between the two diagrams is a reflection of improving technology. It is helpful to begin analysis at the top of the Steward Shield Meadow diagram created by Pamela Ward. Low tree and shrub pollen counts, less than ten per cent of the total, speak of the moorland landscapes to be seen today, open landscapes with coarse grasses, heather and bracken. The site is exposed to every wind that blows; the tree pollens are brought in the spring across the open landscapes from trees some considerable distance away, probably those in Weardale. The inset diagram shows the problem of interpretation. In a wooded landscape, local pollen is more represented, but as the land is cleared, so the regional component becomes more significant in the overall profile. Whatsoever the problems of interpretation we can say that at Steward Shield the woodland, based upon Scots pine, with mixtures of oak, alder, ash, hazel and willow, was substantively cleared just about the turn of the millennium BC/AD. Given the problems of this extremely small bog, with only sixty-two centimetres of peat, the authors of the report suggested that the climatic deterioration and the Scottish raids of the early decades of the fourteenth century are a likely period when local shrub growth was initiated. This is hardly precise in historical terms, but is sound in terms of the coarser chronologies derived from environmental analysis in the 1960s. The reoccupation of the site, recorded as waste in the Hatfield Survey, had taken place by the later seventeenth century as is indicated by the deeds of the present farm, consulted by kind permission of Mr Arthur Collingwood (now deceased). Steward Shield Meadow is, of course, recorded in map 14.3 as a moorland farm.

The diagram by Alison Donaldson and Judy Turner of Hallowell Moss is much more complex. Sited in the Browney valley, near Witton Gilbert, its local setting is open to influence from a great variety of terrains. Much of the accumulation of peat took place during prehistory and the lower layers reveal mixed oak forest with lime. But between about the turn of the millennium BC/AD and about AD 600 the area was affected by a major clearance phase, which substantively removed both trees – to less than five per cent of the pollen rain – and shrubs, so that herb and bog and aquatic species dominate the diagram. As there is no great increase in shrub pollens we can infer that the landscape was kept open by management and there are high values for those pollen types associated with pastures, although some cereal pollen does appear.

---

[19] B.K. Roberts et al., 'Recent Forest History and Land Use in Weardale, Northern England', in *Quaternary Plant Ecology*, ed. H.J.B. Birks and R.G. West (Oxford, 1973); A.M. Donaldson and J. Turner, 'A Pollen Diagram from Hallowell Moss, near Durham City', *Journal of Biogeography* 4 (1977), 25–33.

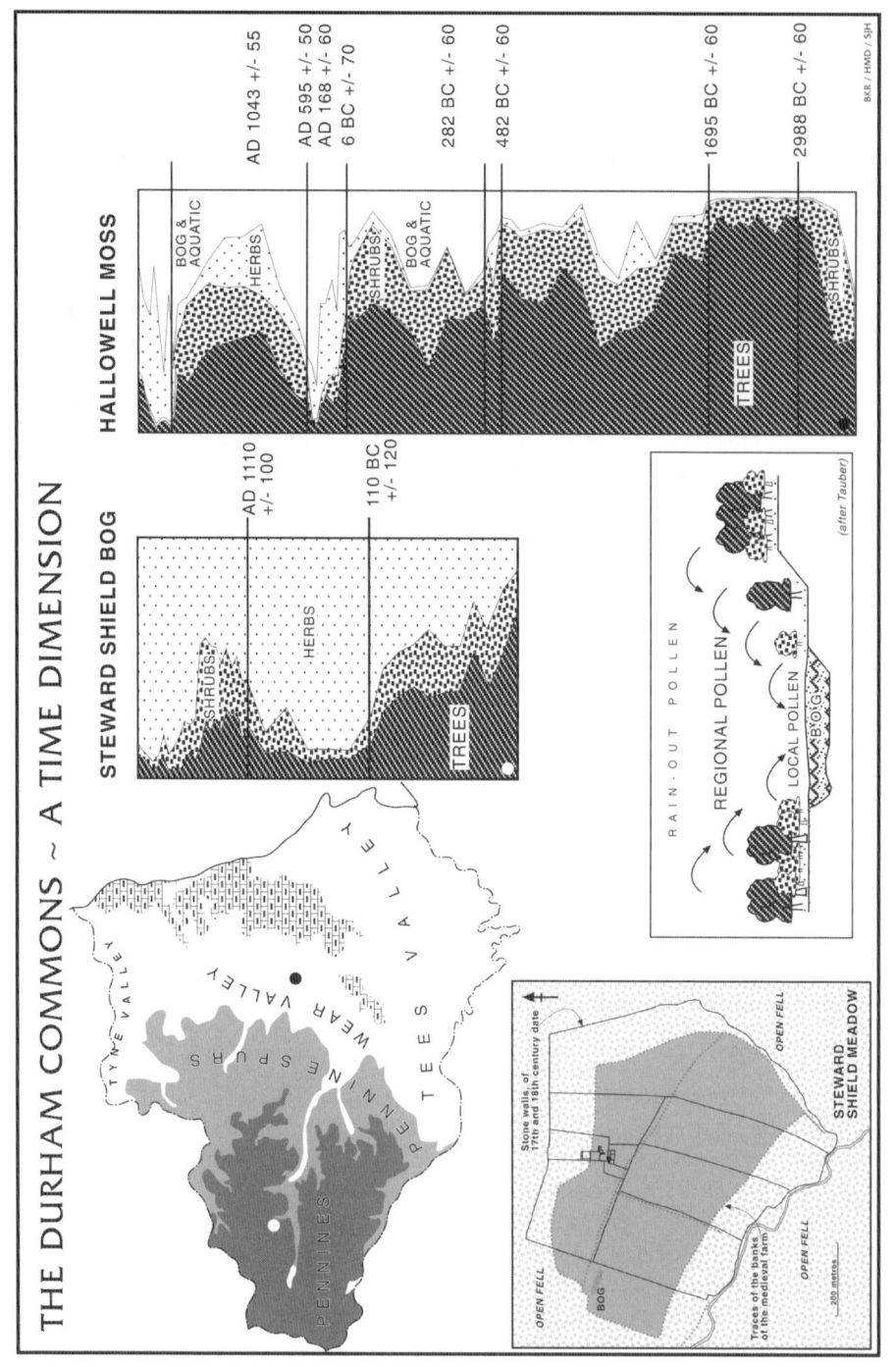

Map 14.4 Hallowell Moss and Steward Shield Meadow, Co. Durham: Summary Diagrams

This picture is likely to reflect regional clearance, namely, the situation extending for several kilometres around the bog. This clearance phase correlates with the Roman and post-Roman occupation. One putative steading site in the Browney valley within a short distance of Hallowell Moss is known from air photographic evidence, and was likely to have been associated with mixed farming, that is, a limited amount of arable coupled with the use of the wastes for extensive grazing. We can only speculate about the extent to which timber removal was part of a system of exploitation for military purposes and fuel (charcoal) supplies, as well as a reflection of the maintenance of open land by increased grazing pressures.[20] The advent of tree and shrub growth – the pastures reverting at first to hazel shrub, then mixed woodland – after about AD 600 is perhaps attributable to a lessening of this intensity of exploitation, but a decline in human population levels is likely to have been an underlying factor. Nevertheless, the pollen frequencies of hazel and birch remain high, and as both are light demanding they suggest that open woodlands were being deliberately maintained, probably simply though grazing. It is reasonable to assume on the basis of map 14.1 that by the twelfth century fuel-cutting, increasing grazing intensity and the extension of improvement were once again encouraging a decline in the quantity of trees and shrubs around Hallowell Moss. This was followed by a gradual spread of improved land represented by the numerous moorland farms along the spurs, while the nearby Bearpark was at first a vaccary in the valley of the Browney and later a country retreat for the priors of Durham. Permission was given in the thirteenth century to enclose and create a hunting preserve or park, hence the name *Beaurepeyr* ('beautiful resort'), an action which in part accounts for the survival of a landscape containing mixtures of trees, shrubs and grasses until comparatively recent centuries.[21] Thus, the picture provided by the time sequence from this fortunately located bog converges neatly with that of map 14.3. The pollen diagram gives a welcome case study for a small area on the boundary between the more extensively cleared tracts and what may be seen as the 'wild west' of the county. This was where cattle, sheep and horses were grazed amid large areas of open pasture with some wood pasture and where improved land occupied only a small proportion of the land surface in particularly favoured locations.

The Inby Lands

The inby, or improved lands, of about 1600, represented in maps 14.1 and 14.3 by the white areas, can be defined as 'negative space', that is, what is left after the outlines of the commons have been mapped. Between the open commons and the inby itself there lies a series of head-dykes, limits of improvement, and we fully recognise the restrictions of our method when dealing with these. The most cursory examination of any six inch to the mile township or parish map raises questions about the detail of the way in which this boundary has advanced, and perhaps retreated, during the last 1,000 years. Our treatment of this evidence, described earlier, has necessarily been rather coarse, although we remain certain that the limits of about 1600 have been reconstructed. However, as Simon Harris has shown, moorland farms can appear as

---

[20] E. Shirley, *Building a Roman Legionary Fortress* (Stroud, 2001), passim.
[21] Watts, *County Durham Place-Names*, p. 6.

enclaves, often defined on the landownership maps of the mid-nineteenth century, and can be clearly separated from the demesne farms and the subdivided townfields of the area's towns, villages and hamlets. Map 14.5 draws together in one map three distributions: Helen Dunsford's map of common wastes is overlaid with the map of Simon Harris's moorland farms (shown only faintly, as 'waste') and a map of villages and hamlets originally created by Brian Roberts in the 1960s, now somewhat revised and redrawn. The correlation is obvious and predictable. Towns, villages and hamlets occupy locations within the white areas. While the areas of townfields cannot yet be mapped positively with any greater precision, namely by mapping each township and parish individually and pursuing this until the complete county picture emerges, the map of commons, together with the distribution of moorland farms, provides a valuable surrogate. Both maps 14.1 and 14.3 build detail into the iconic mapping procedures adopted by Robert Hodgson, using symbols for the varied categories of townfield enclosures.[22] Once again, we do not doubt that detailed work can improve what we present here, but re-emphasise the role of the maps as sustainable archives of accumulated spatial data.

The details of the village forms of Durham and their possible chronology have been discussed elsewhere.[23] Suffice to say that the county is dominated by regular settlement plans in which compartments, rows of tofts or house plots, form the building blocks for a variety of settlement layouts. They range from the constituent boroughs of Durham and the 'Bondgate and borough' plans seen at Bishop Auckland and Darlington, to numerous village and hamlet plans. The vicissitudes of local history have mellowed many of the layouts, concealing and destroying their initial regularity amid later accretions or annihilations. There are good grounds for suggesting that some at least of these plans were present by the twelfth century. Nevertheless, Victor Watts's work is a reminder that, whatever re-developments have occurred, these 'settled places' – to adopt a neutral term – bear Old English and Anglo-Scandinavian names. In the most simple of terms, this shows that the picture provided by maps 14.1, 14.3 and 14.4 must carry our view of County Durham back to pre-Conquest times. It is our current assumption that the pre-Conquest place-names represent a layer earlier than, and chronologically distinct from, the imposition of the regular plans. The framework of the county's settlement system is likely to be pre-Conquest; the visible morphology of plans, while the problem is not yet completely solved, is likely to be immediately post-Conquest. A reassessment of these complex issues by Brian Roberts is currently in progress.

The Boundary and its Meaning?

This discussion has so far neatly circumvented a key question. We argue that County Durham can be divided into two broad landscape categories. To the east and south lay former champion landscapes, dominated by nucleated settlements and open, subdivided townfields; to the west and north-west lay wood pasture and open pasture

---

[22] Hodgson, 'Coalmining, Population and Enclosure', figures 6.1–6.3.
[23] B.K. Roberts, 'Back Lanes and Tofts, Distribution Maps and Time: Medieval Nucleated Settlement in the North of England', in *Medieval Rural Settlement in North-East England*, ed. B.E. Vyner (Architectural and Archaeological Society of Durham and Northumberland, Research Report No. 2, 1990), pp. 107–25.

REGION AND PLACE IN COUNTY DURHAM 233

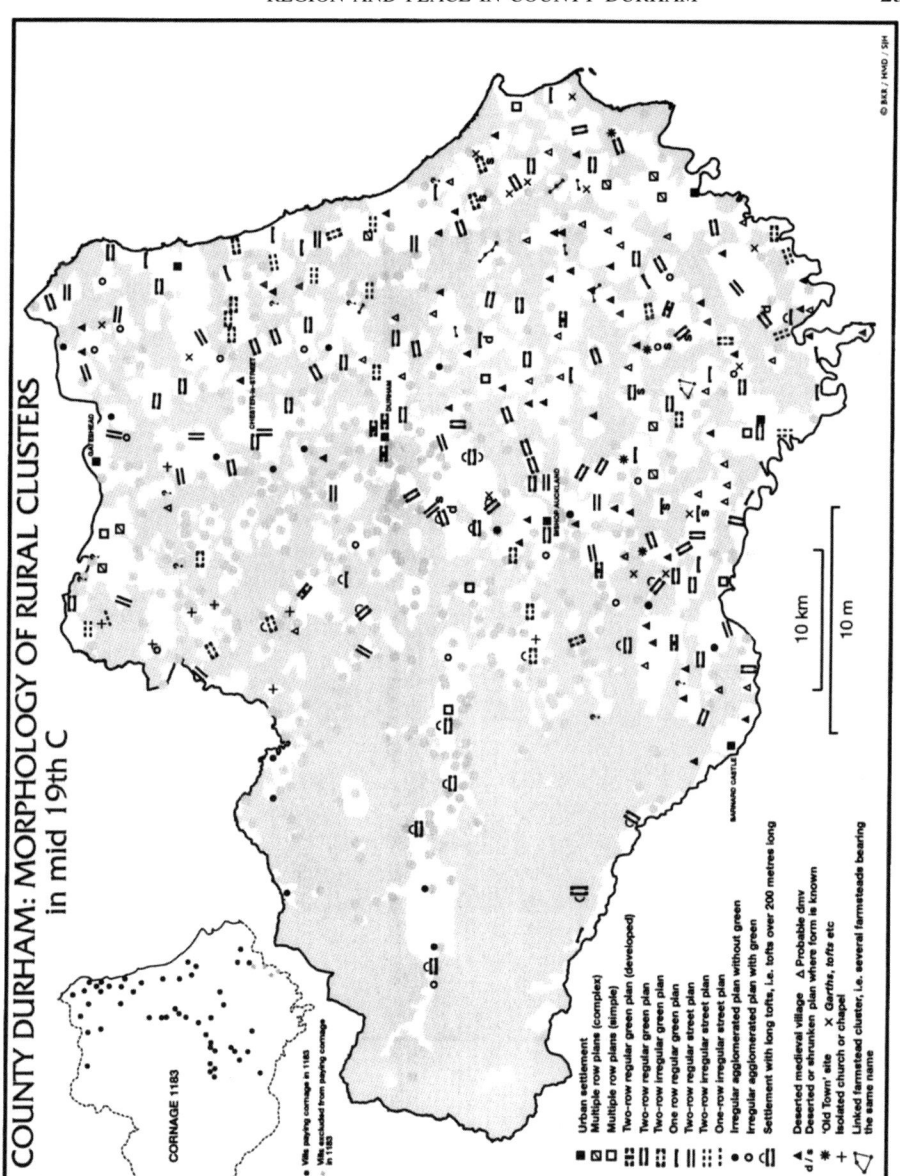

Map 14.5 Commons and Wastes and Village Forms, Co. Durham

landscapes, eventually dominated by scattered farmsteads, hamlets, and some village-sized and/or quasi-urban settlements supported by some townfield land. Where, then, is the boundary between the two, and what does this boundary mean? The consciously charter-like definition of the boundary between pre-Conquest 'woodland' names and habitation names given above ('along the Roman road from Bowes as far as Bishop Auckland, and thence down the Wear to the eastwards turn of the river at Chester-le-Street, and thence northwards up the Birtley ridge to Gateshead') represents only part of the story. Comparison with the map of terrains (map 14.2) suggests that the line follows no physical boundary and is thus cultural in character, and yet it cannot be denied that the configuration of the land does seems to play a subtle part. Furthermore, it can hardly be accidental that Barnard Castle, Bishop Auckland, Durham, Chester-le-Street and Gateshead occupy essentially the same line. This is in no way to suggest that these urban settlements developed because of the line we can now observe. What it does suggest is that putative town sites, as meeting places, defensive and religious sites and trading points, reflect underlying cultural land patterns which may be considerably older than their ostensible foundation dates during and after the eleventh and twelfth centuries.[24] The simple fact that Roman roads can be used as boundary markers may hint at a substantive antiquity for the origin of the landscape contrasts, but it has to be admitted that the distributions earlier than those of the place-names recorded by Watts remain as no more than insubstantial shadows.

The drawing of lines on maps, a long-established geographical practice, is now seen, quite wrongly, as rather dated. Nevertheless, the contents of the areas so defined – regions – remain essential for the understanding and interpretation of cultural landscapes. Basically, the land patterns that result from the accreted superimposed layers of centuries of land-taking, clearance and farming, advances and retreats, are embedded within the subtleties of local regions.[25] Returning to a comparison of two maps, map 14.5 and map 14.2, it can be seen that the lands to the east and south of the Barnard Castle – Bishop Auckland – Durham – Chester-le-Street – Gateshead boundary line – as we will now succinctly define it – fall into two categories. First, villages and their townfields concentrate most densely on the varied drifts of the Tees valley, rather better soils, with a high agricultural potential. It will be observed that an enclave of depopulation sweeps in a great arc to the south and east of Sedgefield, and Hodgson has shown that population numbers in this zone were declining between the sixteenth and the nineteenth centuries.[26] One may speculate that engrossment is an underlying cause of these depopulations, possibly linked by land use changes to local soil qualities. In broad terms, and subject to local terrain variations, this dissected drift plain carries a rather even scatter of villages and larger hamlets. Second, further north, between the Wear valley and the North Sea, the Magnesian limestone plateau intrudes. Its sloping upper surface is characterised by thin soils becoming very clayey to the east where the limestone is overlain by boulder clay. Here, the village

[24] R. Daniels, 'Medieval Boroughs of Northern England', in *Past, Present and Future: The Archaeology of Northern England*, ed. C. Brooks et al. (Architectural and Archaeological Society of Durham and Northumberland, Research Report No. 5, 2002), pp. 184–96.
[25] B.K. Roberts and S. Wrathmell, *Region and Place: A Study of English Rural Settlement* (London, 2002), passim.
[26] Hodgson, 'Coalmining, Population and Enclosure', pp. 168–213, figures 5.1–5.4.

settlements occur in two zones. One lies on the seaward side, where a line of villages is set inland from the coast. Lying on heavy boulder clay many of these are now depopulated, but neither were they, in general, the demesne or tenant vills of the great ecclesiastical estates. They were estates in the hands of the 'knights of St Cuthbert'. The other is to the west, where a line of villages occupies the preferred settlement zone of the scarp slope and where downwash from the limestone intermingles with the drifts of the Wear valley, to give very varied soils attractive to settlement. Near the coast and north of the Wear a dissected drift plateau appears, lying between the Birtley-Gateshead ridge and the much narrowed and much lowered limestone ridge to the east. It is around this latter, again a landscape of more varied soils, that the villages concentrate, villages often in the hands of the Cathedral Priory.

Let us be quite clear what is implied by these arguments. Whatever the ultimate antecedents throughout eastern and south-eastern Durham, pre-Conquest farmers established settlements whose synoptic pattern has just been sketched. Proof of this is to be found in Old English place-names. Twelfth-century evidence in the form of Boldon Book suggests that the most successful of these settlements in agricultural terms lay in the Tees valley and around, rather than on, the East Durham Plateau. The variety of soils and local climates, coupled with contexts in which both north to south and seaward movements were possible, successfully supported grain-producing agricultural communities in these areas.[27] The extension of the arable fields of the communities occupying the scarp slopes of the Magnesian limestone carried cultivation and some village settlement westwards, into the pastures and wastes of the central Wear valley. The Wear itself, sullen and untamed, formed a natural western boundary to this zone. It is the amalgamation of the two settlement patterns and sub-regions, one based on the Tees valley, the other based upon the scarp foot and scarp tail of the Magnesian limestone, that generated the basic Durham pattern of villages. To the west of the Barnard Castle – Bishop Auckland – Durham – Chester-le-Street – Gateshead boundary line lay a third zone, of more scattered ancient *foci*. Here, villages were actively growing in the twelfth and early thirteenth centuries, as at Cockfield, where what was essentially a moorland farm established in the early thirteenth century upon an earlier site rapidly acquired a larger population and tenant strips.[28]

Questions and Conclusions

This essay is a summary of three areas of work: Helen Dunsford's mapping of the commons and wastes; Simon Harris's charter analysis of the medieval farms; together with a general structure and some detail provided by Brian Roberts's longstanding interest in the settlement of the county. We have no doubt that this framework is exceptionally sound and will provide, along with a map of townships and parishes, also created by Helen Dunsford, a geographical foundation for future work, by us and

---

[27] Jarvis et al., 'Soils and their Use in Northern England', figures 10 and 11; Hodgson, 'Coalmining, Population and Enclosure', figure 6.7.

[28] B.K. Roberts, 'Of Landscapes and Words', in *Villages, Fields and Frontiers: Studies in European Rural Settlement in the Medieval and Early Modern Periods*, ed. B.K. Roberts and R.E. Glasscock (Oxford, 1983), pp. 21–42.

by others. The distribution maps, with their potential for use at many scales, provide powerful research tools, but the historical data embodied within them, to the best standards we can currently achieve, possess an archival quality. We are close to grasping the real extent of the wolf-ridden woodlands and mountain pastures of west Durham and precise definition of the very different landscapes of the south and east.[29] If this had long been obvious, it is now given spatial substance and locale. The boundary between these two tracts, far from distinct and never clear-cut, emerges as a historical question in its own right.

The implications of these distributions are worthy of sustained exploration, for many questions remain. Previous generations of scholars have provided a rich harvest of materials from which to build further analyses and to ask new questions. To give but one example: maps 14.1, 14.3 and 14.5 constitute frameworks within which much of the detail of the Boldon Book and the Hatfield Survey can be assessed and reassessed. As an inset to map 14.5 we have included a distribution map of the payment of cornage, usually linked to the enigmatic milch-cow, probably a cow with her follower. It is possible, even likely, that these are forms of archaic rent payment with putative British antecedents.[30] If anywhere near complete – and this has yet to be verified – this distribution raises questions about the pattern of settlements owing these renders based upon cattle. Have we here a pointer towards an even earlier generation of waste-rich vills, peripheral to earlier small settlement nodes, or is the distribution as we now see it merely a fiction created by the documentary record that emphasises the ecclesiastical estates?

Additional geographical questions struggle to the surface. There are hints from Victor Watts's maps that some woodland place-names appear to the east of the Birtley to Gateshead ridge in the north of the county. These, and names such as Hedworth, define one end of the great wedge of thinly settled open and wood pasture land extending from the high Pennine ridges, swinging north of Chester-le-Street, to the sea between the mouth of the Wear and the mouth of the Tyne. This places Jarrow and Monk Wearmouth in most interesting focal locations and must raise questions about the boundary between Bernicia to the north and a possible political entity based upon Catterick (Catraeth?) to the south.[31] It is significant that Simon Harris has found evidence for the destruction and reconstruction of early townships in this zone. In fact, the historical geography of the small region extending east of the Birtley ridge to the sea and between the Wear and the Tyne would repay close study. Furthermore, to the south, the well-settled lands of the Tees valley are no more than an extension of a region embracing the plains of northern Yorkshire. There are grounds for seeing the Barnard Castle – Bishop Auckland – Durham – Chester-le-Street – Gateshead line as significant on a national scale.[32] We must remember that the county boundary of Durham, long established as it is, remains an artificial unit and the territorial unit it replaced, the land of the 'Haliwerfolc', was itself an entity superimposed over more ancient cultural land patterns extending back into Roman and prehistoric times.

---

[29] G.V. Scammell, *Hugh du Puiset, Bishop of Durham* (Cambridge, 1956), p. 212.
[30] R.R. Reid, 'Barony and Thanage', *EHR* 35 (1920), 185 ff.; J.E.A. Jolliffe, 'Northumbrian Institutions', *EHR* 41 (1926), 10 ff.
[31] N. Higham, *The Northern Counties to AD 1000* (London, 1986), pp. 252–3.
[32] Roberts and Wrathmell, *Region and Place*, figures 1.4, 1.13., 1.14.

Ultimately, the grain production of the Tees Lowlands may be rooted in Iron Age traditions enhanced and re-emphasised by the episodic needs of the Roman army of north-east England.[33]

In conclusion, we must journey with St Cuthbert. 'When coming from the south to a river which is called the Wear, on reaching a place called Chester-le-Street, he crossed it and turned aside on account of the rain and tempest to some dwellings used only in spring and summer. But it was then winter time, and the dwellings were deserted. So he unsaddled his horse and led it into the dwelling place, and fastening it to the wall, he waited for the storm to cease.'[34] For St Cuthbert, there was the miracle of half-warm bread concealed in the thatch; for us, there is a near miraculous glimpse of a shieling site *in the middle valley of the Wear* (our italics), set amid the woods and open pastures of Durham.

In memoriam: Sadly, Victor Watts died during the preparation of this essay. We would like to acknowledge here how much we valued his input to our work. In practical terms, pre-publication access to his 2002 study of Durham place-names, and all this implied in terms of source searching and verification, was an essential component in making our maps of the common wastes more reliable. In short, the capacity to provide a documented reference to a particular farmstead often resolved pragmatic problems of the interpretation of patterns seen on the maps. He had much left he wished to do and, as this essay shows, we had reached the point of exciting collaborative possibilities. Vic will be greatly missed.

---

[33] M. Van der Veen, *Crop Husbandry Regimes: An Archaeobotanical Study of Farming in Northern England 1000 BC–AD 500* (Sheffield, 1992), pp. 151–2, 154–5.

[34] *Two Lives of Saint Cuthbert: A Life by an Anonymous Monk of Lindisfarne and Bede's Prose Life*, ed. and transl. B. Colgrave (Cambridge, 1984), p. 71.

Index

Acle, John de, of Stockton, 138
acres, size of, 81
Agincourt, battle of, 72
ale, *see* brewing
Alexander I, king of Scots, 19
Alexander II, king of Scots, 44, 45, 46, 47, 48
Alexander III, king of Scots, 43, 47n, 48
Allerdean, 14, 15
Allertonshire, 5, 128, 132, 133, 135, 136, 139
Alnwick, 62, 137n, 198; abbey, 62; barony, 61, 64; castle, 69
Ancroft, 14, 15, 17
Angus, earls of, *see* Umfraville
Appleby, William, 160n
arable, *see* grain
archidiaconal jurisdiction, 119–26
Armestrong, Thomas, 123
Arundel, Edmund earl of (d. 1326), *see* Fitz Alan
Arundel, Richard, 70
Ask, Conan de, 80
Atholl, David earl of (d. 1335), *see* Strathbogie
Aton, Gilbert, 61
Auchencrow, 18, 20
Auckland, 212; North, *see* Bishop Auckland; park, 81, 84, 89, 91, 92, 94; St Andrew, 79, 80, 81, 82, 85, 86, 88, 89, 207; St Helen, 80, 91; West, 139
Auckland, John, prior of Durham, 163
Aucklandshire, 108
Audley, Hugh de, 58, 60
Augustinian order, 23n
Auldhame, 23
Aycliffe, 27, 179, 190, 193
Ayer, Thomas, of London, 144
Ayre, Richard, 112
Ayton, 19, 20; Nether, 18; Upper, 18; West, 95

Babyngton, John, 121
Bakester, Hugh, of Wolviston, 114
ballads, 31
Balliol, Edward, puppet king of Scots, 33, 41, 51, 59, 65; family, 7; John, puppet king of Scots, 48

Bamburgh, 16, 23; castle, 38, 61, 70
Bamburgh, Thomas of, monk, 158
Bannockburn, battle of, 18, 58, 64, 67, 72, 159
Barmoor, 14, 16, 21
Barnard Castle, 137n, 139, 234, 235, 236; borough, 128n; lordship, 7, 8, 128n
Barne, Joan wife of Richard, 122–3
Barrington, Shute, bishop of Durham, 84
Barry, William, prior of Finchale, 193, 195
Basset, Sir William, 79
Baugé, battle of, 34, 72
Bayles, Agnes de, 68
Beal, 14, 15–16
Beanley, William de, 67
Bearpark, 120, 199, 231
Beauchamp, family, 7; Richard, earl of Warwick (d. 1439), 7; Thomas, earl of Warwick (d. 1401), 7
Beaulieu, 100
Beaumont, Henry de, earl of Buchan (d. 1340), 58, 59, 61, 62, 63, 64, 66; Isabella, sister of, *see* Vesci; Louis de, bishop of Durham, 59, 61, 62, 80, 116, 165n, 166
Beaumont, Roger de, bishop of St Andrews, 25
'Beaurepeyr', 231
Bedale, 135, 139
Bek, Antony, bishop of Durham, 47, 61–2, 66, 80, 111, 153, 157, 159, 165
Belasis of Henknowle, family, 89. See *also* Bellasis
Belford chapelry, 14, 16
Bell, Joan, 120
Bell, Richard, prior of Durham, 162
Bellasis, John of, 114
Benedict XII, pope, 165
Benwell, 65, 146
Berehalgh, family, 80n
Bermeton, Walter de, 80
Bernard, Sir Roger, 79
Bernham, Robert de, 46n
Bernicia, 236
Bernwood Forest, 90, 93
Berrington, 14, 15

Berwick, 13, 20, 24, 36, 39, 65, 67, 138, 159; church, 19, 22, 25; constables, 60, 65, 70; garrison, 67; massacre at (1296), 33; mayor, 58; sheriff, 46n; trade, 65; warden, 63
Berwickshire, 15, 18, 20, 23
Betts, William, 133
Bickerton, Walter de, of Kincraig, 63
Billingham, 27, 116, 184–6, 193, 194
Billymire, 54
Binchester, 81, 85
Birtley, Richard of, bursar of Durham, prior of Finchale, 167n, 176n
Birtley ridge, 228, 234, 235, 236
Bishop Auckland, 8, 75, 77, 79, 80, 81, 82, 83, 85, 86, 89, 91, 92, 122, 138, 228, 234, 235, 236; bailiff; 80; Bondgate, 75, 81, 92, 94, 232; borough and burgages, 81, 82, 83, 128; halmote, 100; mills, 217n; palace, 81n, 84, 94; townfields, 84. See *also* Pollard
Bishop Middleham, 100
Bishopley, 201, 202, 207n, 218
Bisshop, Alan, 114
Blackadder, 19
Black Death, 9, 11, 82, 83, 127, 135, 156–7, 159–60, 161, 162, 164, 167, 168, 170, 173, 175–9, 181, 182, 184, 187, 190, 196, 197, 203, 218
Blackwell, 135n
Blackwell, Richard, monk, 158n
Blakeston, family, 88
Bland, Stephen, 133
Boarstall, cartulary, 93; horn, 91, 93
Bodi, William, of Westoe, 113
Bolbec, Hugh de, sheriff of Northumberland, 44–5
Boldon, Ughtred of, monk, 160n
Boldon Book, 15, 78, 83n, 91, 131, 134, 139, 201, 203, 228, 235, 236
Bolingbroke, Henry, *see* Henry IV
Bollihope, 201, 202, 218; Burn, 201
Bolton, Robert of, 160n
bondmen and bondland, 17, 18, 83, 168n, 205
Bonkill, Ralph de, 46n
Booth, Lawrence, bishop of Durham, 8
border of England and Scotland, definitions, 44–5
borders, *see* Marches
Boroughbridge, 138; battle of, 62
boroughs and burgesses: Bishop Auckland, 81, 82, 83, 128; Darlington, 128, 131; Durham, 111, 128; Elvet, 128n; Gateshead, 128; Hartlepool, 128n; Northallerton, 128; Richmond, 127; St Giles, 128n; Stockton, 128; Sunderland, 128
Boston, 143
Boston, Geoffrey of, 158n

Bosworth, battle of, 39
bovaters, 18
Bowes, 228, 234
Bowes, family, 88
Bowsden, 14, 16, 17, 21
Brack's Farm, 83, 84
Brafferton, 116, 179. See *also* Tours
Brancepeth, 88, 89, 226
Branxton, 22
breach of the peace, 104–5, 114
brewing, 102, 106n, 115
bridges: Winston, 5; Darlington, 139; Elvet, 117
Brinkburn, prior of, 138
Brompton, 95
Browney valley, 229, 231
Broxmouth, 23
Bruce, family, 58; Robert, 58
Brusselton, 80, 91
Buchan, Henry earl of (d. 1340), *see* Beaumont
Buckton, 14, 15
Budle Bay, 13, 21
Burdale, Thomas, 124
Burdon, near Haughton-le-Skerne, 132n
Burdon, Geoffrey, prior of Durham, 159, 164, 166
Burnaby, John, prior of Durham, 158n, 162
Bury, Richard de, bishop of Durham, 80, 81, 112n
Busby, Roland, 137n
Byers Green, 226

Caerphilly Castle, 62
Calverton Darras, 67
Cambridge, Richard earl of (d. 1415), *see* York
Camden, William, 76, 88, 137
Carham, 22, 23, 45; honour, 22; prior and priory, 44, 45, 47
Carlisle, 21, 162; eyre at, 48–9, 51
Carlisle, Andrew earl of (d. 1323), *see* Harclay
Carnaby, William de, 70
Carr, Elizabeth, 125
carts, 115
Casson, family, 132n; Thomas, 132
Castell, Thomas, prior of Durham, 163
Castile, 184
Castle Eden, 121
Catterick, 138, 236; Moss, 201
cattle trade, *see* livestock
Chandy, Simon, of Berwick, 54n
chapelries, 16–17, 19
Charron, family, 207
Chaucer, family, 58
Chaunceller, William, 209

INDEX

Chester, county palatine, 93
Chester-le-Street, 89, 100, 228, 234, 235, 236, 237
Chester ward, 204–7, 210, 212, 216, 217, 218n, 219
Cheswick, 14, 16
Cheviot hills, 21, 22
Chillingham, castle, 68; church, 57n, 72
chivalry, 32, 38–9
Clarence, Thomas duke of (d. 1421), *see* Lancaster
Clarewood, 15n
Claxton, family, 88, 209; Sir Robert, 87; Sir William, 209
Claxton, Richard, prior of Durham, 79n
Claxton, Robert of, 160n
Clervaux cartulary, 136
Clifford, family, 8; Sir John de, 65
cloth industry and trade, 127, 131, 134–5, 136, 139, 142, 143–5, 146–7, 148, 149, 152
coal-working and trade, 115–16, 117, 139
Coatham, family, 196; William, of Pittington, 189–90
Coatham Mundeville, 132n
Cockfield, 235
Cok, Thomas, of Durham, 124
Coke, family, 151
Cokyn, Robert, 122
Cokside House, 210
Colchester, 144
Coldingham, 6, 9, 19, 20, 23, 24, 25; monastic cell, 18, 19, 25–6, 27, 155, 159, 166; monastic church, 26
Coldinghamshire, 18, 20
Colman, Thomas, 124
common land, 224, 226, 227, 232–3, 235
Comyn, family, 58
Convenit, le, 7, 111–12, 114, 116
Conyers of Sockburn, falchion, 8, 76, 90–1, 92, 93, 94; family, 76–7, 88, 90–1, 92, 93, 94, 95; Sir John, 76; Sir John (d. *c.* 1342), 91; Sir John (d. 1396), 90
Corbridge, 137n
cornage, 236
Cornforth, William, 121, 148
Cornhill, 14, 15, 16, 17, 18
Cornwall, duchy of, 177
coroners, 101, 113, 116
Cosin, John, bishop of Durham, 8, 75, 94
cottars, cotmen and cotland, 17, 18, 83, 131, 205
Coundon, 80, 81, 85; Grange, 83, 85, 89; Moor, 81
Coupland, John de, 54n, 64, 65, 66, 72
Cowpen Bewley, 185, 193
Cowton, William of, prior of Durham, 166
Coxhoe, John, 124

Crail, barony of, 61
credit, 149, 152
crisis of 1438–40, 153, 161–2, 193–5, 198
Croft Bridge, 138
Crowland Chronicle, 193
Croxdale, 121
Cumberland, sheriffs of, 46, 48, 51
Cumbria, 21
Cupar Castle, 58
Currour, Thomas, 113
customs, of the northern marches, 53–4
Cuthbert, Joan, 125
Cuthbert, Saint, 36, 237; banner, 9; *barones et fideles*, 76; community, 6; cult, 93; at Holy Island, 25; knights, 235; patrimony, 6, 9, 13–28, 205; pilgrimages to his shrine, 9–10; shrine, 120, 157n; as a symbol, 1. See *also* Darlington, Durham city
Cuxham, 177

Dacre, Sir Hugh, 43
Darcy, Philip, Lord, 68
Darlington, 127–40; administration, 132; archaeology, 130; Bondgate, 129, 131, 232; borough, 128, 131, 132; borough court, 132; borough farm, 132; bridge, 139; church of St Cuthbert, 130; communications and location of, 5, 130, 138–40; fire of 1585, 129, 138; granary, 136; Greenbank estate, 130; halmote, 100; Houndgate, 136; inn, 138; market and fair, 130, 131, 134, 136, 137; merchants, 135, 143; pillory, 136; population, 129–30; shops, 136–7; Skinnergate, 136; tollhouse, 136–7; trade and industry, 5, 128, 131, 134, 135–7, 139; ward, 81, 132n, 204–7, 212–13, 217
Darlington, Adam of, 167n
Darlington, Hugh of, prior of Durham, 163n
Darreyns, Robert, 67
David I, king of Scots, 19, 24, 26; as earl of Northumberland, 21
David II, king of Scots, 35, 53, 65
Dawson, Alice wife of William, 122
debt, litigation concerning, 103, 107, 113, 119, 136
demesne, leasing of, 176, 187, 197–9
deserted and waste medieval villages and townships, 179, 180–1, 209, 218
Despenser, Hugh the younger, 62, 63
Devil's Causeway, 21
Dicenson, Robert, 114
'Dighton', 120
Disinherited, 59, 61
Dixson, Isabella, 123
Dobson, George, 121
Doncaster, 147

Douglas, Archibald Douglas, earl of (d. 1400), 31; Archibald Douglas, earl of (d. 1424), 34; family, 32; James Douglas, earl of (d. 1388), 35; Sir James, 35, 59; William Douglas, earl of (d. 1384), 43
Drax, William, 160n
drengage tenure, 16, 205
Duddo, 14, 16
Dugdale, Sir William, 76
Duket, family, 151
Dumbarton, 37
Dunbar, castle, 36, 59n; family, 58; George de, earl of March (d. 1420), 31–2, 35; Patrick de, earl of March (d. 1308), 58; Patrick de, earl of March (d. 1368), 59, 60–1, 67
Duncan II, king of Scots, 23–4
Dunfermline, 64n
Dupplin Moor, battle of, 59, 72
Durham bishopric and bishops, 5, 8, 13, 21, 47, 60, 61–2, 66, 68, 75, 82, 89, 94, 100, 111; *acta*, 82; boroughs of, 128; coalpits, 139; collectors' accounts, 211; council, 81, 116; courts, 65, 98–109, 111–12, 113; estate and income, 11, 15, 81, 83, 98–9, 131, 198, 205–8, 210–18; exchequer land, 83, 182, 203, 205, 207, 212–17; grants of waste land, 203; household, 79, 80, 81; liberties, *see* Allertonshire, Islandshire, Norhamshire; palace, 131; relations with tenants, 101; servants, 80, 81, 83, 92, 116; stewards, 207. See *also* Boldon Book, Hatfield Survey, *and the names of individual bishops*
Durham city, 8, 55, 112, 119–26, 232, 234, 235, 236; benefactors, 22–4, 36, 130; borough, 128n; borough courts, 111; bridge, 117; castle, 80; cathedral church, 25, 76, 89n, 120; chantries, 117, 155; church discipline, 119–26; communications, 147; county court, 107, 111; Crossgate, 122, 124; Elvet, 124, 178; Framwellgate, 123; gaol, 80; merchants, 143, 144, 145; North and South Bailey, 125, 178; St Giles's borough, 128n; St Margaret's church, 120, 121, 122–3, 124; St Nicholas's church, 116; St Oswald's church, 8, 119, 121, 123, 124, 125, 207n; site, 237; trade, 127, 134, 138, 143, 144
Durham palatinate, 3, 6, 7–9, 80–1, 82, 94, 98, 103n, 111–12; coroners and coroners' accounts, 203, 205, 210–18; four wards, 108, 204, 205, 206–7; law courts, 111; sheriff, 113; taxation, 81. See *also* Durham bishopric and bishops
Durham priory, 4, 8, 10, 13, 141–71; auditors, 179; cells, 17–18, 19, 25–6, 27, 155–6, 159, 167n, 168; charters, 78; control of admission of novices, 163–9; courts, 7, 98–109; 111–17; crisis of 1438, 153, 161–2; elections, 155, 156, 157, 166; estates and income, 11, 13–28, 98, 153, 155, 160, 165, 168, 171, 173–96, 235; funerals, 156; leasing of manors, 176, 187; *Liber Vitae*, 9, 150–1, 152, 155, 157, 160; monks of, 9, 16, 150, 153–71; mortality in, 156–7, 159–61, 162, 163, 169–70; novices and their preparation, 157–8, 164, 168; number of monks, 154–63; obedientiaries, 101, 120, 134, 143–5, 156, 167, 168, 176, 187, 199; purchases, 134, 137, 141–52; relations with tenants, 142, 149, 152; servants and employees, 80, 124, 149; steward, 113; suppliers, 142, 148–51; tithe income, 11, 18, 25, 116, 153, 173–96; tonsuring, 157–8, 160; treasury, 116; visitations, 155, 159, 160, 164–9, 171. See *also* Convenit, le, Oxford, *and the names of individual priors*
Durham, John and William de, of Darlington, 135
Durham, Robert de, 46n

Earl's House, *see* Hogson
Earlston, 19, 20, 25
Easington, 100; ward, 204–7, 212, 214
East Durham Plateau, 203–4, 225, 226, 234, 235
Easter communion, 124
Eastrington, 27
Ebba, Saint, 23, 26
Ebchester, Robert, prior of Durham, 163
Ebchester, William, prior of Durham, 146, 157n, 162
Ebranke, 38
Edgar, king of Scots, 19, 23, 24, 25
Edinburgh, 33, 49; castle, 57, 72
Edlingham, 120
Ednam, 19, 20, 24
Edrom, 18, 19, 20, 24, 25
Edward, monk of Durham, 25
Edward I, king of England, 6–7, 37, 38, 40, 44, 47, 48, 49–50, 51, 55, 61, 66, 80, 90, 92, 97, 99, 108
Edward II, king of England, 51, 52, 58, 61, 62, 63, 66, 67, 90, 159
Edward III, king of England, 33, 38, 41, 50, 51, 52, 53, 59, 60, 65, 68, 135
Edward IV, king of England, 11
Edward the Confessor, king of England, 91, 93
Eilaf, priest, 22
Eleanor of Castile, queen of England, 61
Elison, Antony, 146
Ellingham, 27
Elvet, family, 80n

Elwick, 14, 17, 88
enclosures, *see* waste land and tenements
England, crown of, 8, 127, 133; customs duties, 135; legendary history of, 40–1; northern loyalty to, 39–42; parliament of, 8, 69, 101, 129; and St George, 40; taxation, 81. See *also* statute law, Scotland, *and the names of individual kings*
entry fines, 177
epidemic disease, 122, 127, 136, 138, 169, 187, 189, 193–4, 196. See *also* Black Death
Escomb, 80, 81, 85, 89
Eslington, Isabel de, 65
Espec, Walter, lord of Helmsley, 22
Esyngton, John, of Newcastle, 151
Eugenius III, pope, 17
Eure, family, 88, 89; John de, 67, 68; Sir Ralph, 101
exchequer land, *see* Durham bishopric and bishops
excommunication, 120
Eyemouth, 18, 20

Fabian, William, chaplain, 122–3
falchions, 8, 9, 76, 77, 87, 89–94; representations of, 87, 91
Falkirk, battle of, 19
famuli, 189–90
Farne, master of, 166n
Farne, John, 148; Robert, 122
Farwell, John, of Durham, 121–2
Featherstone of Stanhope, Alexander de, 89n; family, 89; William de, 89n
Felkington, 14, 15
Felton, Sir John de, 62; William de, 68
Fenham, 14, 17, 18
Fenwick, 14, 15
Ferryhill, Isabel of, 114. See *also* Gaugi
ferry service, 51
feudal tenures, 15, 18, 92–3
fields, 201, 202, 221–2, 232, 234, 235; name elements, 84
Finchale, 155, 176, 177–9, 193, 194, 195
firmarii, 18
fish, 142, 146, 149, 151
Fishwick, 18, 19, 20, 22, 24
Fitz Alan, Edmund, earl of Arundel (d. 1326), 59, 61
Fitz Geoffrey, Sir Marmaduke, 79
Fitz Meldred, family, 226
Fitz Nigel, John, 90
Fitz Ralph, Roger, 46n
Flambard, Ranulph, bishop of Durham, 15, 19, 21, 76
Flanders, cloth from, 144, 148; count of, 135; war in, 59

Flemington, 20
Flothad, bishop of St Andrews, 21
football, 104–5
Ford Castle, 68
Fordun, John, chronicler, 73
Fordyce, William, 93
Forest, family, 151
fornication, 119, 120, 124
Fossor, John, prior of Durham, 115n, 160, 162, 164, 167–8, 170
Fox, Richard, bishop of Durham, 133n
France, 184, 193; wars with, 32–4, 37, 38, 52, 53, 60, 65, 71–2
frankpledge, view of, 97, 133
Fraser, Alexander, 63; Andrew, 63
free tenants and land, 7, 18, 94, 103–4, 105–6, 107n, 111–17, 205, 212–19
Freman, Thomas, of Middridge, 114
Froissart, Jean, chronicler, 31, 50
fruit cultivation, 131
Fulwell, 100

gambling, 104
Gateshead, 128, 228, 234, 235, 236; Pipewell in, 148
Gaugi, William, of Ferryhill, 114
Gaunless valley, 226
Gentill, Ingelram, 132; John, 132n
gentry, 77, 80, 81, 86, 89, 91, 94–5, 101
Gervase, John, 125
Gervaux, John, 125
Geryng, Stephen, 104
Gisburn, William de, 78n
Glanvill, 107
Glasgow, 21
Gloucester, Statute of, 103
Glover, Richard, Somerset herald, 86
Goldsburgh, William de, prior of Finchale, 178
Gordon, 25
Gosforth, North, 65
Gospatrick II, earl, 24
Goswick, 14, 15
Graham, John de, 134
grain, production, 173–96; trade, 142, 149, 152
Gray, John, a Scot, 65
Gray of Heaton, Agnes, 73; Elizabeth, 68; family, 12, 57–73, 101; John, 66, 70, 71–2; Juliana, 66n; Sir Ralph, 57n, 72; Sir Robert, 66; Thomas I (d. 1344), 57–64, 66–7, 68, 72; Thomas II, chronicler (d. 1369), 10, 32, 33, 35, 41, 54n, 57, 59–60, 64–6, 67–8, 72, 73; Thomas son of Thomas II, 73; Thomas III (d. 1400), 60, 68–9, 72, 73; Thomas IV (d. 1415), 60, 69–71; Thomas V (d. 1421), 70, 71; William, 73
Gray of Horton, Thomas, 67n; David, 67n

244 INDEX

Greystoke, William, Lord, 65n
Grindon, 14, 15, 16, 179
Grosvenor, family, 39
Guisborough, 139
Guisborough, William of, prior of Durham, 159
Gynour, William, 115

Haggerston, 14, 16
Haldwell, John, 125
Halesowen, 187
Halifax, 127, 144
Haliwerfolk, 9, 236. See *also* Cuthbert
Hall, John, 121, 124
Hallington, Robert of, 156n
Hallowell Moss, 229–31
halmotes, 7, 99–106, 112, 113, 132; character, 108–9; juries, 101, 105, 107; officers, 107; ordinances, 114; procedures, 106–7; records, 99, 102, 107; scope of jurisdiction, 103–6; speed of operations, 107
Halton, 15n
Halyday, Thomas, 120
Hansell, Joan, 124–5
Harcarse, 20
Harclay, Andrew de, earl of Carlisle (d. 1323), 38, 51, 52, 72
Hardyng, John, chronicler, 10–11, 29–42
Hart, 8, 88; lordship of 128n
Hartlepool, 139; borough, 128n; merchants, 143; port, 135, 139; trade, 129, 135
Haswell, 182
Hatfield, Thomas, bishop of Durham, 65, 82, 103n, 115n, 116, 156, 157, 167, 198, 205, 207n
Hatfield Survey, 83, 91, 198, 201, 205, 207, 218, 228, 229, 236
Heaton, 14, 15, 58, 66, 72; castle, 68. See *also* Gray of Heaton
Hebburn, Edward, monk, 150
Hedderwick, 23
Hede, Robert, of Northallerton, 133n
Hedworth, 236
Heighington, 27
Helmeland, 210
Helmington Hall, 79
Helmsley, honour of, 22
Hemingburgh, church, 159
Hemingburgh, John, prior of Durham, 146, 161
Henknowle, 89
Henry I, king of England, 15, 19, 23, 26
Henry II, king of England, 132
Henry III, king of England, 44, 45, 46, 47
Henry IV, king of England, 31, 41, 60, 69, 71
Henry V, king of England, 32, 60, 69–71
Henry VI, king of England, 30, 37, 41
Henry VII, king of England, 53

Henry of Scotland, earl of Northumberland, 26
Herbert, prior of Coldingham, 26
heresy, 124
Heron, family, 65; William, 68
Heselrigg, William, sheriff of Lanark, 57
Heworth, 179
Hexham, 22, 137n
Hexhamshire, 21
Heysham, Roger de, 93n
Higden, Ranulph, chronicler, 57
highway (*via regia*), 115
Hilton, Robert de, 64
Hinderclay, 184
Hogson, William, of Earl's House, 123
Holburn, 14, 16, 21
Holland, Sir Robert, 61, 63
Holmside, 210
Holy Island (Lindisfarne), 14, 15, 16, 17, 21, 22, 23, 24, 27, 28, 65; monastic cell, 17–18, 19, 25–6, 27, 155, 159; monastic church, 25–6; Robert of, *see* Insula
Horden, 209
Horncliffe, 14, 15
horses, for coal-hauling, 139; lost in war, 59; as mortuary, 123; named, 59; overworked, 114; sold, 114, 139
Hoton, Richard de, prior of Durham, 159, 165
Hoton, William, priest, of St Nicholas, Durham, 116
Houghton-le-Spring, 100
Howden, Bernard of, 44, 45, 46, 47
Howdenshire, 165n
Howick, near Alnwick, 66–7
Hugtoun, Thomas, 58
Hull, merchants, 143; port, 135, 139; trade, 145
Humphrey the smith, 83n
hundred, courts, 97–8, 103, 104, 108, 116
Hunter, Geoffrey, 115n
Hurworth, 116
Hutchinson, William, 77
Hylton, family, 88; William, Lord, 68–9
Hyndley, John de, 146
Hyne, Alice, 122

Ilderton, 22
Ilderton, Henry de, 64
inby lands, 231–2
Innocent III, pope, 23
inquisitions *post mortem*, 81–2, 88, 89, 90, 92, 94, 99, 112, 205, 209–10, 218
Insula, Robert de, bishop of Durham, 80, 157
iron, 149, 151
Islandshire, 6, 15, 21

James I, king of Scots, 39
Jarrow, 27, 100, 155, 165n, 179, 236

INDEX

Jedburgh, abbey and abbot of, 27, 47, 49
John, king of England, 9, 134
John son of Emma, 114
Johnson, Agnes, 124
Johnson, William, 122
Joy, Richard, 117

Kellawe, Richard, bishop of Durham, 66, 116, 165, 182
Kelloe, 19, 80
Kelsoe Abbey, 19, 24–5, 27
Kerneth, Ralph, prior of Durham, 111
Kimmerghame, 19
Kingston, Robert of, 166n
Kirk, William del, of Billingham, 114
Kirkham, priory, 22–3
Kirkham, Walter de, bishop of Durham, 78, 79, 182
Kirknewton, 22, 23
knight service, *see* feudal tenures
Knout, Richard, sheriff of Northumberland, 47
Knowes, 23
Kyloe, 14, 15, 16, 17
Kyrkeman, Robert, 104

Labourers, Ordinance of, 104n; Statute of, 103n, 104
Lamberton, 19, 20
Lanark, skirmish at, 57, 58; sheriff, 49, 57
Lancaster, priory, 71
Lancaster, Thomas of Lancaster, earl of (d. 1322), 38, 61, 63
Lancaster, Thomas of, duke of Clarence (d. 1421), 34
Lanchester, 89, 100, 207n, 210, 219
land market, 83
landscape, 4, 11–12, 88, 203, 212, 221–37
Lanercost, king at, 63; priory, 34
Langley, Thomas, bishop of Durham, 9, 116, 165
Lascy, William, 125
law: borough courts, 82, 132, 133; county court, 107; ecclesiastical, 8, 12, 106, 109, 119–26; English royal courts, lawyers and common law, 97–8, 106, 107, 111; eyres, 48–9, 51; free courts of the priors of Durham, 7, 111–17; gaol delivery, 51, 113; liberties, 7–8, 128–9; local courts, 7, 82, 88, 97–109; of the March, 6, 43–55, 71; marshalsea courts, 102, 111; 'ward courts', 108n. See *also* debt, Durham palatinate, halmotes, hundred, manors, statute law
Lawe, Agnes, 150; Thomas, 150; William, monk, 150
Lawson, family, 151
Lawson, Thomas, 193

leather industry, 136
Leeds, 127, 144
Leek, William, 138n
Lees, Thomas de, 209
leet jurisdiction, *see* hundred
Legge, John, of Durham, 123
Leland, John 127, 128, 139
Lemmington, 120
lesio fidei (breach of trust), 119, 122–4
Levesham, Thomas de, 78
Levynston, Agnes, 124
Lilleburn, Sir John de, 67
Lindisfarne, *see* Holy Island
Lintalee, 58n, 59
livestock, output, 175, 190–2, 194, 196, 219; trade, 137, 142, 149. See *also* horses
London, 70, 138, 142, 143, 144–5, 146, 147, 148
Lowick, 14, 16, 17, 21
Low Lynn, 14, 15
Luceby, Nicholas de, prior of Finchale, 179
Lucy, Anthony de, 52
Ludworth, William of, 113
Lumley, castle, 68; family, 69, 88; Ralph, Lord, 68–9
Lumsdaine, 20, 24
Lynton, John de, 178n
Lytham, 155

Magnesian Limestone Plateau, *see* East Durham Plateau
Malcolm III, king of Scots, 22
Malenfant, Robert, 46n
Malise, earl of Strathearn, 49
Malvoisin, William, bishop of St Andrews, 25
Manners, family, 65; Robert de, 59, 62, 63
manors, characteristics of, 88–9, 108; courts, 88, 97–8, 100, 102–3
maps of Co. Durham, 222, 224
March, Roger earl of (d. 1330), *see* Mortimer
March, Scottish earls of, *see* Dunbar
'marchers', 39–40, 41, 65
Marches, East, 43, 64, 69, 71; wardens, 39–40, 41, 65; West, 11, 38, 52, 72
Margaret, St, queen of Scots, 36
Margaret of England, queen of Scots, 43
Margaret of Scotland, 'the Maid of Norway', 48
markets and fairs, 127–8, 136, 142; Bishop Auckland, 82; Boston, 143; Darlington, 131, 136–7, 143; Durham, 134, 143; Norham, 134; Northallerton, 133, 136, 137, 140
Marleys of Unthank, family, 89
marriage, 124–5
Marsh, Richard, bishop of Durham, 78
Matilda of Scotland, queen of England, 22

Mautalent, John, 67
Melrose Abbey, 22, 24, 27, 58, 72
Merrington, 27, 100; church, 100n; vicar, 115; West, 181
Merrington, John of, 114
Merrington, John son of Alan of, 115
Merrington, Thomas son of John son of Robert, 115
Middleham, 137
Middleham, John de, 60
Middlemast Middleton, 67
Middleton, 76
Middleton, Sir Gilbert de, 40, 41, 61, 63, 66–7; William, 67
Middley, William, of Durham, 144
Middridge, *see* Freman
mills, 16, 82, 115, 135n, 159, 193, 217; fulling, 135; suit of, 16
Minot, Lawrence, chronicler, 34
Mitford Castle, 63
Monk the cook, 78n
Monkton, 179
Monk Wearmouth, 100, 165n, 236; cell at, 155, 167n
Montague, William de, earl of Salisbury (d. 1344), 59, 64
moorland farms, 203, 207, 210, 221, 227, 231, 232. See *also* waste land and tenements
Moray, earl of, 68
Morpeth, 137n
Mortimer, Roger de, earl of March (d. 1330), 62–3, 90
Mortmain, Statute of, 103
mortuaries, 121–4
Mowbray, Joan, sister of Thomas de, 68; John de (d. 1322), 59, 61; Robert de, earl of Northumberland, 22; Thomas de, duke of Norfolk (d. 1399), 68, 69
Muggleswick, 191
multura, 81
Murton, 14, 17, 63n
Muschamp, family, 22; Robert de, 21

Neasham ford, 138
neifs (*nativi*), 101, 105–6
Nenthorn, 25
Nesbit, 59, 67, 73
Neville, Alice, daughter of Ralph de, 69; family, 11, 38, 58, 72, 88, 226; Ralph de (d. 1367), 61, 63, 66; Ralph, earl of Westmorland (d. 1425), 5, 38, 69, 210; Richard, earl of Warwick (d. 1471), 137; Robert, bishop of Durham, 157n
Neville's Cross, battle of, 35, 39, 53, 59, 65, 72
Newbiggin, 14, 16
Newburn, manor of, 63

Newcastle-upon-Tyne, 141–52; burgage at, 67; communications, 147; Edward I at, 38; economy, 152; eyre, 48–9, 51; gaol delivery, 51; location, 5; mayor and bailiff, 135; merchants, 143, 148, 151; military encounter, 31; port, 135, 139; St Nicholas's church, 124; town, 127; trade, 4–5, 65, 135, 137n, 141–52
Newhouse, 179
Newton, 25
Newton Bewley, 186, 193
Newton Cap, 81, 85, 89
Newton Ketton, 179
Nigel the huntsman, 91, 93
Nisbet, East, 19
Norfolk, Thomas duke of (d. 1399), *see* Mowbray
Norham, 14, 15, 16, 17, 18, 22, 27, 28, 59; castle, 22, 58n, 59, 60, 61, 62, 63, 70; constable, 62n; market, 134
Norhamshire, 6, 16, 21, 47, 58, 116
Northallerton, 5, 27, 127–40; administration, 133, 139; archaeology, 131; borough and burgesses, 128–9, 133; borough bailiff, 133n; borough court, 133, 139–40; borough farm, 133, 137; castle, 132; church, 132; communications and location, 138, 139–40, 147; first mention, 132; manor, 132; market and fair, 133–4, 136, 137, 140; parliamentary representation, 129; population, 129; trade and industry, 134–7, 139
Northampton, constitutions of, 168n
North-East, as a region, 1–12, 38; and external trade, 147–8, 151
Northumberland, county of, 2, 7–8, 10; Durham bishopric and priory estates in, 13–28; earls of, 60, 69, 70, 103, 164n. See *also* David I, Henry of Scotland, Mowbray, Percy; knights of the shire, 68, 69; loyalty of, 41–2; sheriff, 46n, 47, 48, 70
Northumbria, kingdom of, 1–2; name and its significance, 10; local jurisdiction in, 108
Norton, John de, 178n
Nostell Priory, 22
Nunstainton, 179

Ogle, family, 72; Robert de, 65n
Old Cambus, 18, 20, 24, 25
Oll, John, 168n
Ord, 14, 16
Ordainer, lords, 66
Otterburn, battle of, 31, 35, 60, 72
Ovingham, 146
Owain Glyn Dwr, 71
Oxen-le-Fields, 5

INDEX

Oxford, Durham College, 151, 156, 161, 167n; Merton College, 147

Palatinate of Durham, *see* Durham palatinate
Papedy, sheriff of Norham, 15
Paris, Matthew, map of, 147
pasture, *see* livestock
Paxton, 20, 24
Pease Bay, 13
Pease Dean, 36
Peirson, Joan, 124
Pennines, 203–4, 205, 208, 212, 219, 225, 226, 230, 236
Percy, estates, 197–8; family, 11, 31–2, 37–8, 41–2, 43, 58, 60, 64, 69, 71, 72; Henry (d. 1352), 61, 62, 63; Henry (d. 1368), 64, 66; Henry, earl of Northumberland (d. 1408), 43; Henry son of 'Hotspur' (d. 1455), 71n; rebellion, 41, 70; Sir Henry ('Hotspur') (d. 1403), 31, 34n, 35, 37; standard, 31
Perth, 36, 61; sheriff of, 49
Pickering Lythe, wapentake, 95
Piercebridge, 130, 139
Pilgrimage of Grace, 5, 138
Pittington, 27, 100, 102, 187, 188, 189–90, 191, 193, 196, 199
place-name elements, 84, 227, 228, 232
plague, *see* Black Death, epidemic disease
poaching, 120
Pocklington, William, monk, 169n
Poitou, Philip of, bishop of Durham, 15, 78
Pole, de la, family, 58
Pollard, family: armorial bearings, 86, 87, 92; boar, 93; Dionisia, wife of John II, 81–2, 89, 94; falchion, 9, 77, 87, 89, 91–3; family and lands, 9, 12, 77–95; Hall, 77, 79, 84, 86; Isabel, wife of William III, 79, 83; John II, 79, 81–2, 86, 89, 94; John III, 79, 83, 86, 91; Leonard, 84, 87, 92; Nicholas, 79, 80, 91; John IV, 79, 83; seal, 86, 92; *Pollardus* (John I), 78–9; Ralph, 87, 95; William I, 78–9; William II, 79–80, 82, 91; William III, 79; William IV, 86, 87, 89, 94
Pollards Lands, township, 84–5
pollen analysis, 221, 229–31
Poore, Richard le, bishop of Durham, 7, 111
population, *see* Black Death, Durham priory, epidemic disease
Portchester, 71
Porter, John, 124–5
pottery, Tees, 5
Prenderguest, 19, 20
Presfen, William de, 68; Margaret, daughter of William, 68
Preston, Michael, 122
Preston-le-Skerne, 116, 179

Puiset, Hugh du, bishop of Durham, 15, 78, 130, 131, 132
prices, 189–90; grain, 142, 174, 183, 184, 193; transport, 147–8
purchasing, through agents, 145–7; from tenants, 142

quo warranto proceedings, 90, 97, 98, 108

Raby estate, 226. See *also* Neville
Railey, 139
Rainton, mine at, 115–16; East, 101; West, 101, 105
Rakett, family, 151
Ralph, prior of Holy Island, 26
Rames, Robert de, 58
Ramsey Abbey, 198
Reddenburn, 22, 45
Rede, Edmund, 93
Renton, 18, 20
rents, 16, 136, 177–8, 187, 189, 193–4, 196, 198–9, 211–19, 236; paid in kind, 142, 191n; paid in labour, 198
Reston, 20; East, 18; West, 18
Rhodes, Robert, 8, 146–7
Richard the chaplain, 78n
Richard II, king of England, 60, 68, 69
Richard III, king of England, 39
Richard son of Gilbert, 23
Richardson, family, 151
Richmond, 127, 135, 139; archdeaconry of, 21; burgesses, 127
Richmond, Thomas de, 80
Richmondshire, knights of, 80
Ricknall Grange, 179
Ridel, William, 61
Ripon, 10, 127, 139
Ripon, Robert, prior of Finchale, 187
Robert the reeve, 78n
Robert I, king of Scots, 33, 35, 37, 41, 52
Robert fitz Roger, lord of Warkworth, 58, 60
Robinson, family, 151
Robinson, John, of Elvet, 124
Robinson, John, of Newcastle, and his wife Maiona, 150
Roger son of Scholastica, 113
Roslin, battle of, 58
Ross, 14, 15, 16, 21
Rothbury, 123
Rothbury, Simon of, 166n
Roxburgh, 39; forest of, 48
Ryslaw, 20
Ryton, 146
Ryton, William, of Willington, 114

Sadberge, 100; wapentake, 7, 108

248 INDEX

St Albans Abbey, 22
St Andrews, 21, 24, 25
St Calais, William of, bishop of Durham, 19, 22, 132
Salisbury, William earl of (d. 1344), *see* Montague
Saltholme, near Billingham, 191–2, 194–5
Salvayn, Gerard, 68
Sancroft, William, 75
Scaccario, William de, 166n
Scalacronica of Sir Thomas Gray, 10, 57, 58, 62, 63, 64, 73
Schapp, Simon de, 81
'Schatteby', 24
Scota, daughter of Pharoah, 36
Scotland: border with England, 6–7, 43–55; coinage of, 35; the Great Cause, 48; kings of, 9, 19, 22, 23–4, 30, 35, 45–6, 48, 53; law of, 46–7, 55; legendary origins of, 36; England's wars with, 2, 11, 13, 18, 28, 31–7, 39, 41, 42, 44, 49, 50, 58–61, 63, 65, 67, 68, 71, 72, 80, 134, 153, 159, 181, 203; and St Cuthbert's patrimony, 9, 13–28. See *also* Scots
Scots, English attitudes to and perceptions of, 11, 34–7, 39, 40; itinerant, 138; pirates, 52
Scougall, 23
Scremerston, 14, 16
Scrope, family, 39, 58, 70; Henry, Lord, 70; rebellion, 38, 40; Richard, archbishop of York, 38, 40
Seaton, John of, 166n
Seaton, Jordan of, 156n
Sedgefield, 181, 234
Segefeld, Robert, chaplain, 120
Segefeld, Robert, proctor, 121
Selby, Walter de, 67
Selkirk, abbey, 27; forest, 58
serpents, slaying of, 76, 77
Seton, Christiana de, 64
settlement layouts, 232–3
sheep farming, 191, 194
Sherburn, South, 184, 187
Shields, South, 120, 143
ships, le Cuthbert, 135
shires (small), 109, 130
shops, 136–7
Shoreswood, 14, 17, 18
Shotton, William, 148
Shrewsbury, battle of, 34, 42
Simpson, Richard, 145
Sireston, Robert de, 160
Sixhills, convent, 64
Skarlett, Edmund, 133; Thomas, 133
Skemerston, William de, 46n
Skerne, marshes, 226; river, 139

Skinner, William, of Darlington, 136
Skirlaw, Walter, bishop of Durham, 68, 103, 168n
Slaver, John, of Darlington, 135
Sluys, expedition to, 59, 67
Smailholme, 25
Smyrk, John, 121
Smyrke, Richard, 123, 124
socage tenure, 16
Sockburn, 76, 90–1, 94, 95; church, 76. See *also* Conyers
Solway, river, 44; Firth, 51
Somerton Castle, 63
songs, abusive, 33
Soppeth, Robert, 62
Soules, Nicholas de, 45, 46
Southampton plot, 69–71
Spennymoor, 177, 226
spices, 145, 146, 149
Spink, Robert, monk, 150
Staindropshire, 108
Stamford, 155, 167n
Stanes, Richard, of Osmotherley, 139
Stanhope, 78, 80, 88, 89, 104, 201, 203, 207, 212, 217n, 219
Staplay, Thomas, 160n
Stapleton, Miles, 75
statute law, in the palatinate of Durham, 103–4, 111
Steward Shield Meadow, 207–8, 221, 229–30
Stichill, 20; Robert de, bishop of Durham, 78, 79n, 80
Stirling Castle, 58, 61
Stockton, 100, 128, 139; ward, 204–7, 212, 215
Stockton, John de, monk, 138
Stokesley, 137n, 139
Strathbogie, David of, earl of Atholl (d. 1335), 51, 59, 63,
Strivelyn, John de, 72
Styr son of Ulf, 130
Suffolk, earl of (d. 1369), 64
Sunday observance, 124
Sunderland, 128
Sunderland Bridge, 121
Surtees, family, 88
Surrey, earl of, *see* Warenne
Sutherland, William Sutherland, earl of (d. 1371), 59
Swinburnes of Edlingham, family, 39; Sir William, 60
Swineshead, John, monk, 158n
Swinewood, 18, 20
Swinton, 18, 19, 20, 22, 24, 25
symbols of conveyance, 89–90. See *also* falchions

INDEX

Tadcaster, William, 122
Talkan, Hugh, of Westoe, 113
Tancarville, county of, 72
Tang, family, 80n
Tart, William, 209
Tees and Tees valley, 5, 6n, 7, 8, 11, 75–6, 88, 91, 130, 138, 139, 199, 212, 224, 225, 226, 230, 234, 235, 236, 237
Tempest, Richard, 66
Teviot, river and valley, 20, 21
thanage, 15
Thomas, Stephen, 122
Thomlynson, Thomas, priest, 120
Thomson, Anthony, 137n
Thomson, John, of Witton Gilbert, 120
Thor Longus, 24
Thornton, 14, 15
Thropton, John de, 81
Thurstan, archbishop of York, 22
Tickhill, John de, prior of Finchale, 178, 187n
Tickhill, Roger de, 83
Till, river, 14
Tillmouth, 14, 15
tithes, 11, 18, 25, 116, 120, 121, 153, 173–96, 199
Tours, John de, of Brafferton, 116
townships (vills), 15–18, 21, 23, 84–5, 99, 100, 105n, 116, 179, 209, 224, 232, 236
transport and transport costs, 138–9, 147–9
Trent, escheater north of, 66
Trollope, John de, 67
Trollopp, William, 168n
Turgot, prior of Durham, 17, 19, 21
Tursdale, 117
Tweed, river and valley, 6, 7, 13, 14, 19, 20, 22, 44, 45, 51, 59
Tweedmouth, 14, 16, 17, 21
Twizell, 14, 16
Tyne, river and valley, 5, 10, 11, 12, 225, 230, 236
Tynedale, 41
Tynemouth, 22
Tyningham 23; abbey, 23–4

'Ughrotherestrother', 64
Ulster, Robert de, 46n
Umfraville, Agnes, 210; family, 11, 38, 58, 210; Gilbert, earl of Angus (d. 1307), 39; Robert, earl of Angus (d. 1325), 39; Sir Gilbert (d. 1421), 34, 210; Sir Robert (d. 1436), 31–3, 38, 39
Unthank, 89
Upsettlington, 14, 15, 16, 17

Venables of Kinderton, family, 76

Vesci, Isabella, widow of John, 61; John, 61
vill, *see* townships
villani, 196n

Wadley, 87
Wadylove, William, of Northallerton, 139
wager of law, 115
wages, arrears of, 114; changes in, 182, 189–90, 193; in kind, 182, 189
Wallace, William, 35, 57
Walsingham, Thomas, chronicler, 10
Walter the chaplain, 78n
Walworth, Robert, prior of Durham, 160, 161, 162, 164, 168, 207n
war, *see* France, Scotland
Wardlaw, 53
Warenne, John, earl of Surrey (d. 1304), 58, 60, 90, 92
Wark on Tweed, castle, 22, 64, 69, 72
Wark in Tynedale, 70
Warkworth, 58, 64, 155
Warwick, Richard earl of (d. 1439), *see* Beauchamp
Warwick, Richard earl of (d. 1471), *see* Neville
Warwick, Thomas earl of (d. 1401), *see* Beauchamp
Warwickshire, 95; Arden region, 89
waste land and tenements, 80, 82, 83, 177–82, 194, 197–219, 204, 218, 223, 224, 231, 235; colonization and enclosure of, 24, 82, 83–4, 182, 203, 217–18, 219, 221, 226–8
Wear, river, valley and dale, 10, 79, 87, 177, 201, 202, 203, 207, 224, 225, 228, 229, 230, 234, 235, 236, 237
Wearmouth, 131. See *also* Monk Wearmouth
Wearmouth, Reginald of, 167n.
Wensley, 138
Werdale, family, 132n; William de, 132
Wessington, John, prior of Durham, 27, 116, 156, 161, 162, 195
Westminster, 135; abbey, 171n; palace, 90. See *also* England
Westmorland, Ralph earl of (d. 1425), *see* Neville
Westoe, prior's grange, 113
Westwick, Hugh de, 207n
Whitburn, 207n
White, John, 209
Whitehead, Hugh, prior of Durham, 157, 163
Whitehead, Robert, 145
Whitrig, John de, 160n
Whittington, Great, 15n
Wigmore, abbey, 90; castle, 90
William II, king of England, 19, 21, 132
Williamson, Thomas, 121, 123
Willington, 79. See *also* Ryton

Willy, Christopher, monk, 151; Edward, 151; Elizabeth, 151; Henry, monk, 151; Richard, 151; Robert, monk, 151; siblings of Christopher and Henry, 151
wine trade, 139, 143, 145–6, 148, 149, 151, 152, 184
Wingate, 176n
Witton Gilbert, 124, 229. See *also* Thomson
Witton-le-Wear, 80, 88, 89
Wodeham, Reynold son of Simon de, 66n; Walter de, 66
Wolsingham, 78, 88, 100, 203, 207, 210, 217n, 219
Wolviston, 115n, 186, 193. See *also* Bakester
Woodburn, Hugh of, 156n
Woodham, 179
Woodhouses, manor of, 83
wool and wool trade, 5, 65, 135, 139
Wooler, barony, 17, 21, 22; castle, 21

Wren, Richard, 145
Wright, William, 145
Wydouson, Thomas son of John, 105
Wyntoun, Andrew, chronicler, 73

Yarm, 139
Yokefleet, 177
York, appeal to, 123; archbishop, 65; archiepiscopal rights, 10, 21, 22; cloth industry, 127, 135, 144–5; fifteenth-century recession, 127, 135, 143; merchants, 143; Minster, 10; parliament at, 129; saddlers' guild, 136; sheriff, 63, 64, town, 127; trade, 145
York, Edward of York, duke of (d. 1415), 70; Isabel, daughter of Richard, 70; Richard of, earl of Cambridge (d. 1415), 70
Youle, John, 146